British Columbia
RECREATIONAL
Atlas

SCALE 1 : 600 000
(1 cm = 6 km)

INTRODUCTION

There is magic in maps. From the comfort of your armchair they will take you back in memory down byways long forgotten, or lead you on to unknown places on trails you have yet to tread. This atlas spreads the broad horizons of British Columbia conveniently before you in a single volume, inviting you to explore, and providing the basic knowledge of location and access that will help you translate imagined journeys into reality.

For the ever-increasing throngs of outdoor enthusiasts, the atlas offers a ready means to orient themselves in the field, to find new places to pursue their interests, or to retrace past trips. Hunters particularly, and fishers and others using the outdoor environment will find it an almost indispensable aid to compliance with provincial regulations. The maps show the definitive boundaries of the wildlife management units, the bases of British Columbia's wildlife management program and regulations, revised and up-to-date to the time of publication.

But there is much more here than boundaries: topography, place names, roads, trails, elevations, streams, lakes, parks, sanctuaries and places of special interest are all catalogued and mapped. Whatever your interest in the outdoors, whether you hunt, fish, photograph, run rivers, hike, camp, study wildlife, or enjoy the outdoors in some other way, the atlas can be your guide to safe, more pleasant and adventurous outdoor experiences.

MINISTRY OF ENVIRONMENT

Province of British Columbia
Ministry of Environment

A JOINT PUBLISHING VENTURE OF

®**Informap**
publishing division of
ptc phototype composing ltd.

ACKNOWLEDGEMENTS

The Recreational Atlas, Second Edition, was compiled in cooperation with the BRITISH COLUMBIA MINISTRY OF ENVIRONMENT which supplied the updates of the official Wildlife Management Unit Boundaries. In addition, the Ministry expanded its contribution of data on a variety of recreational and environmental activities.

Gratefully acknowledged is the help of many caring individuals throughout the province who called attention to errors and omissions in the first edition and provided useful material, comments and suggestions.

For this Second Edition, we recognize our indebtedness to the following sources for their generous assistance:

B.C. Forest Service (Ministry of Forests - Regions and Districts)
Ministry of Transportation and Highways - Regions and Districts
Ministry of Tourism and Provincial Secretary
Ministry of Crown Lands
Ministry of Parks
Parks Canada
Royal British Columbia Museum
Beautiful British Columbia Magazine
Canadian Forest Products Ltd.
Crestbrook Forest Industries Ltd.
Enso Forest Products Ltd.
Fletcher Challenge Canada Ltd.
Galloway Lumber Company Ltd.

MacMillan Bloedel Ltd.
Northwood Pulp and Timber Ltd.
Skeena Cellulose Inc.
Slocan Forest Products Ltd.
Tanizul Timber Ltd.
Weldwood of Canada Ltd.
Westar Timber Ltd.
Western Forest Products Ltd.
Weyerhaeuser Canada Ltd.
Whistler Village

Information in this atlas is as factual as possible at date of publication. Readers are invited to present suggestions, corrections and/or updates to:

P.T.C. Phototype Composing Ltd.
2647 Anscomb Place
Victoria, B.C.
V8R 2C7
Fax (604) 592-8138

CANADIAN CATALOGUING IN PUBLICATION DATA
P.T.C. Phototype Composing Ltd.
British Columbia Recreational Atlas

Includes Index
ISBN 0-9693607-1-1

1. Recreational areas - British Columbia -
Maps. 2. Wildlife management areas -
British Columbia - Maps. 3. British Columbia -
Description and travel - Guide-books. I. Title
G1171.E63W55 1989   912'.133378'09711   C88-091478-5

Typesetting by RAPIDRAFT, Larry and Elaine Wells, Victoria, B.C.

Printed in Hong Kong

GENERAL INFORMATION

COLOUR BANDS

Information relating to topics noted to the left of these colour bands can be found in the back of the Atlas on pages marked in corresponding colours.

WILDLIFE VIEWING, WILDLIFE RESERVES, FISH HATCHERIES

PARKS VISITOR INFORMATION & FACILITIES GUIDE

GAZETTEER OF PLACES, LAKES, RIVERS AND MOUNTAINS

B.C. FOREST SERVICE RECREATION SITES

For information regarding specific sites, particulars may be obtained from **District Offices** . . . . **Page 89**

HUNTING AND FISHING INFORMATION

Hunters should refer to the current British Columbia Hunting and Trapping Regulations Synopsis for information detailing no shooting, limited entry and other regulations governing each Management Unit. Particulars may be obtained from **Ministry of Environment and Conservation Officer contacts** . . . . **Page 90**

Fishers should refer to the current British Columbia Freshwater Fishing Regulations Synopsis for information detailing closed areas, class restrictions and other regulations governing each region. Particulars may be obtained from **Ministry of Environment and Conservation Officer contacts** . . . . **Page 90**

CIVIL AVIATION

The B.C. Air Facilities Map is a valuable guide to air facilities and services throughout the province. Showing some popular VFR routes through the Canadian Rockies and over the magnificent west coast, the map will help you to organize your flight. The Air Facilities Map is available from the B.C. Aviation Council, 303-5360 Airport Road South, Richmond, B.C., V7B 1B4. TELEPHONE: (604) 278-9330 FAX: (604) 278-8210

Once you have selected your B.C. destinations, official air navigation charts and publications may be obtained from Transport Canada or from Canadian chart dealers.

KEY MAP AND LEGEND OVERLEAF . . .

ATLAS MAP LEGEND

HIGHWAY/ROAD MARKERS

British Columbia/Alberta

1 Trans-Canada	**3** Crowsnest	**16** Yellowhead
97 BC Prov Hwy	**35** Alta Prov Hwy	**731** Alta Secondary Rd

United States

5 Interstate	**101** US Highway
	20 Primary State Rd

ROADS/SERVICES

Interchange ▭▭	Divided Highway ❶	-----------	Trail ❷
━━━━	Highway	—VIA RAIL—	Passenger Railway
═══	Highway (Gravel)	----FERRY-	Ferry
━━━	Paved Road	Ⓒ	Customs
═══	Gravel Road	Ⓒ	Customs at Airport
=====	Rough Road ❷	○ ●	Hospital ❸

PLEASE NOTE:

❶ May be Toll Highway

❷ May be private or seasonally impassable. Enquire locally

❸ For locations see Gazetteer on Pages 108-130

POPULATION INDICATORS ❹

●	under 250	◎	2 500 – 5 000	◉	25 000 – 50 000
○	250 – 1 000	■	5 000 – 10 000	◉	50 000 – 100 000
◉	1 000 – 2 500	▢	10 000 – 25 000	▣	over 100 000
		▱	Suburban Area		

PLEASE NOTE:

❹ These symbols are used throughout the Atlas except in the Lower Mainland and Greater Victoria

BOUNDARIES

━ ··· ━ International	━ ·· ━ Provincial /Territorial /State

Scale of Atlas Maps 1 : 600 000

10   20   30   40   50

kilometres

If you spot a Forest Fire
dial 0
and ask for Zenith 5555

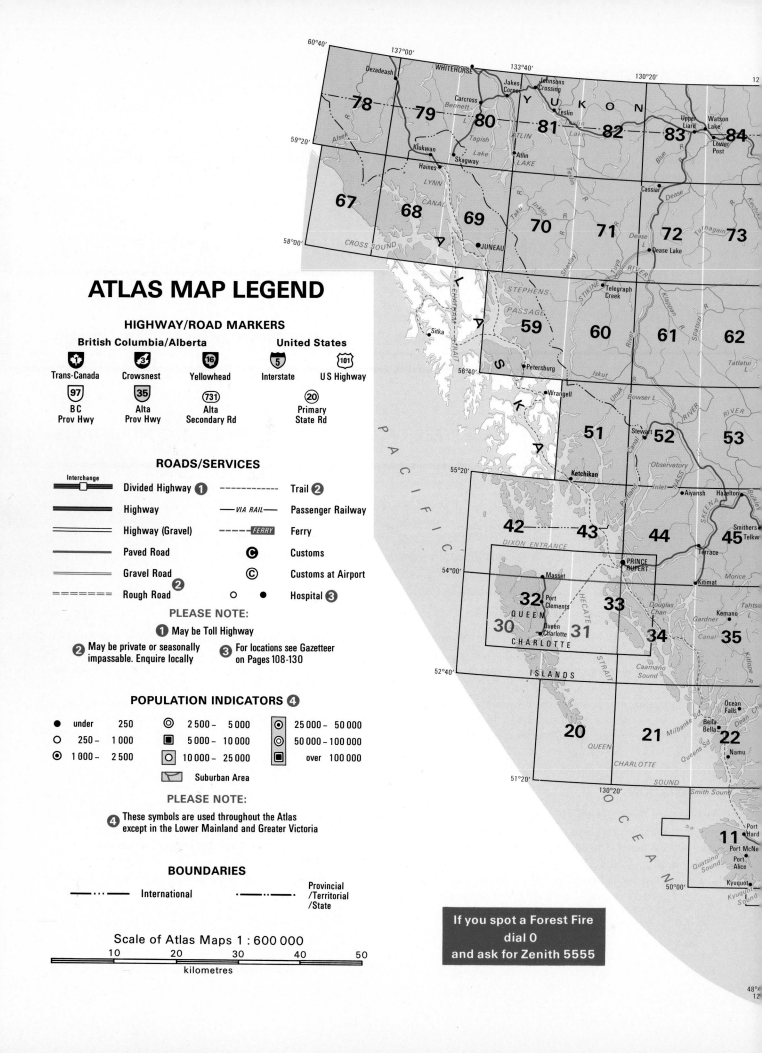

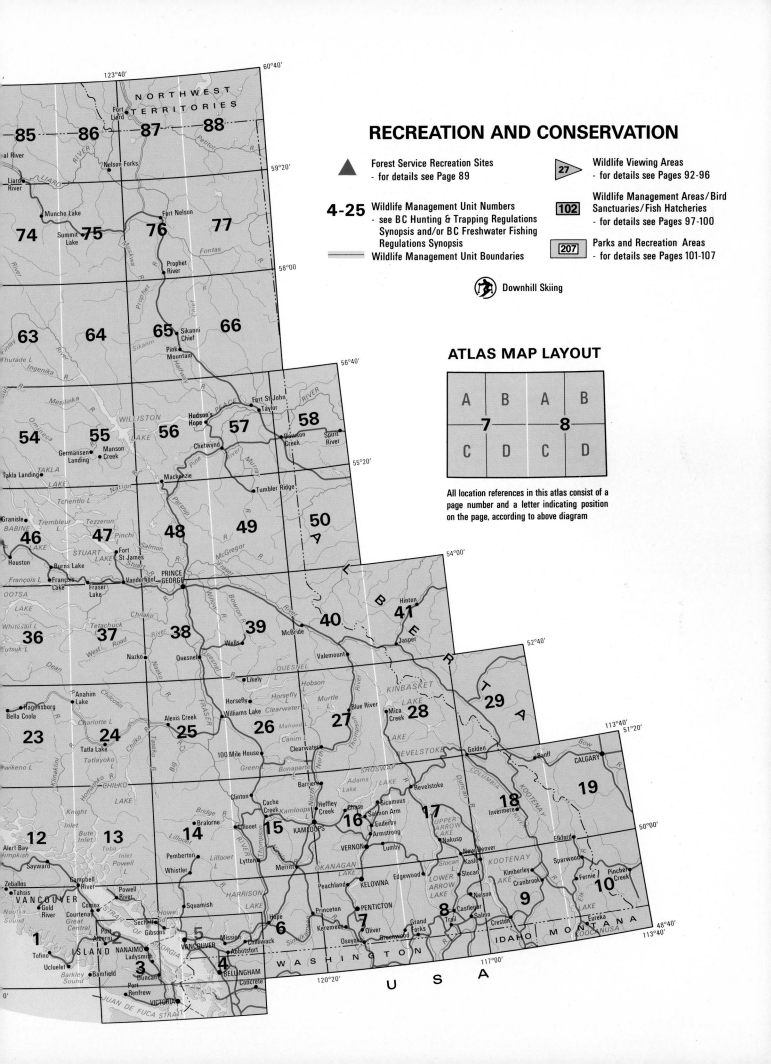

RECREATION AND CONSERVATION

▲ Forest Service Recreation Sites
- for details see Page 89

4-25 Wildlife Management Unit Numbers
- see BC Hunting & Trapping Regulations Synopsis and/or BC Freshwater Fishing Regulations Synopsis

───── Wildlife Management Unit Boundaries

🚶 Downhill Skiing

◁27 Wildlife Viewing Areas
- for details see Pages 92-96

102 Wildlife Management Areas/Bird Sanctuaries/Fish Hatcheries
- for details see Pages 97-100

207 Parks and Recreation Areas
- for details see Pages 101-107

ATLAS MAP LAYOUT

A	B	A	B
	7		**8**
C	D	C	D

All location references in this atlas consist of a page number and a letter indicating position on the page, according to above diagram

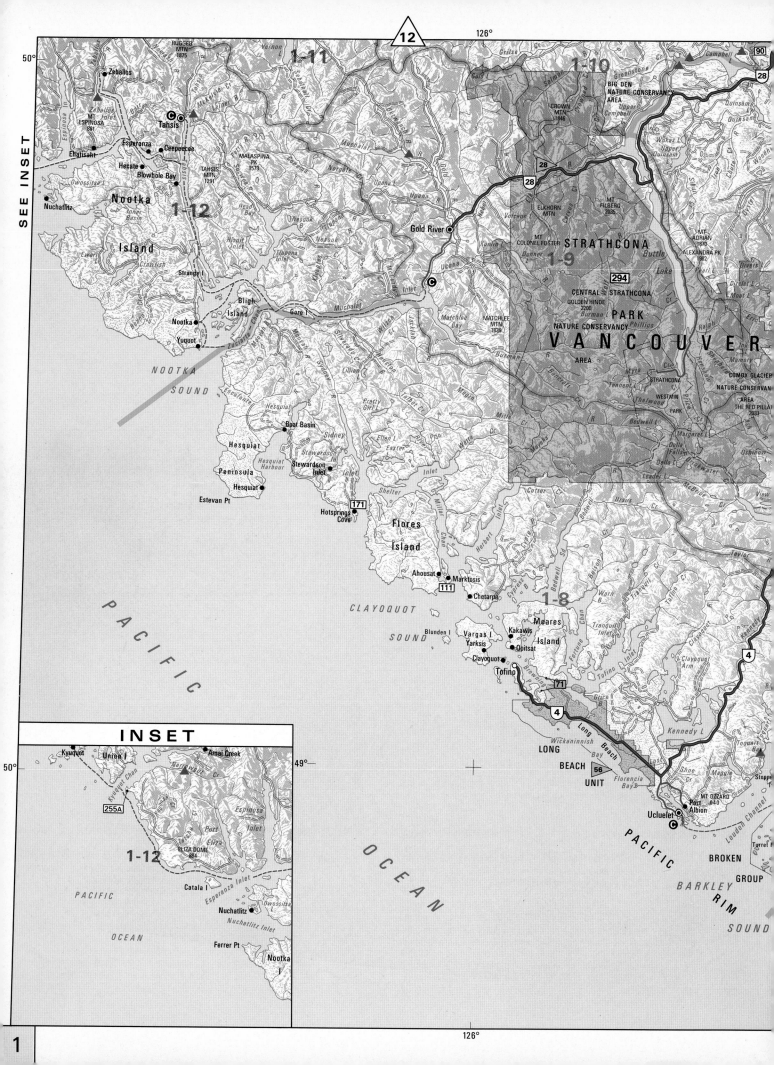

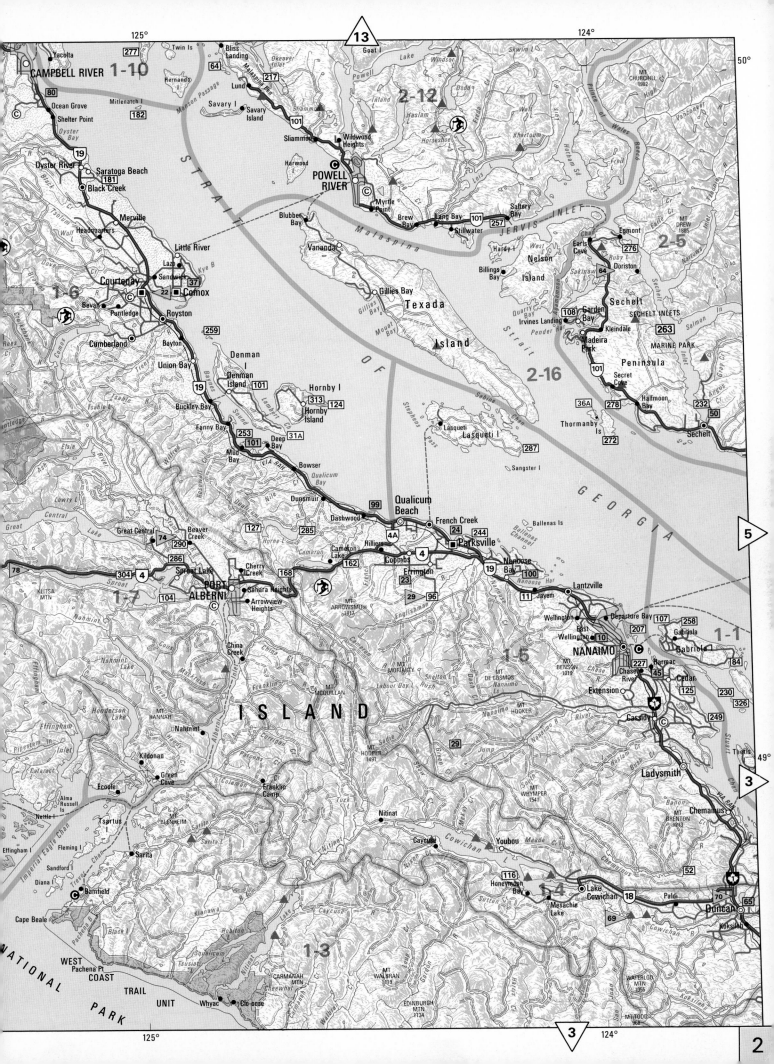

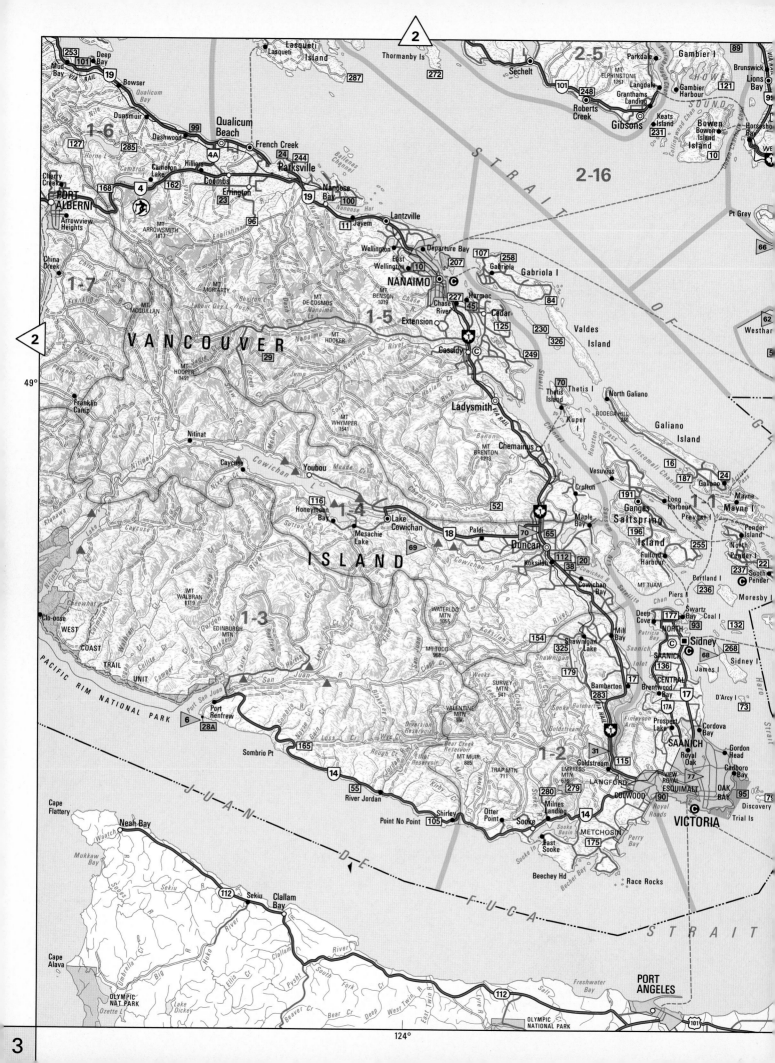

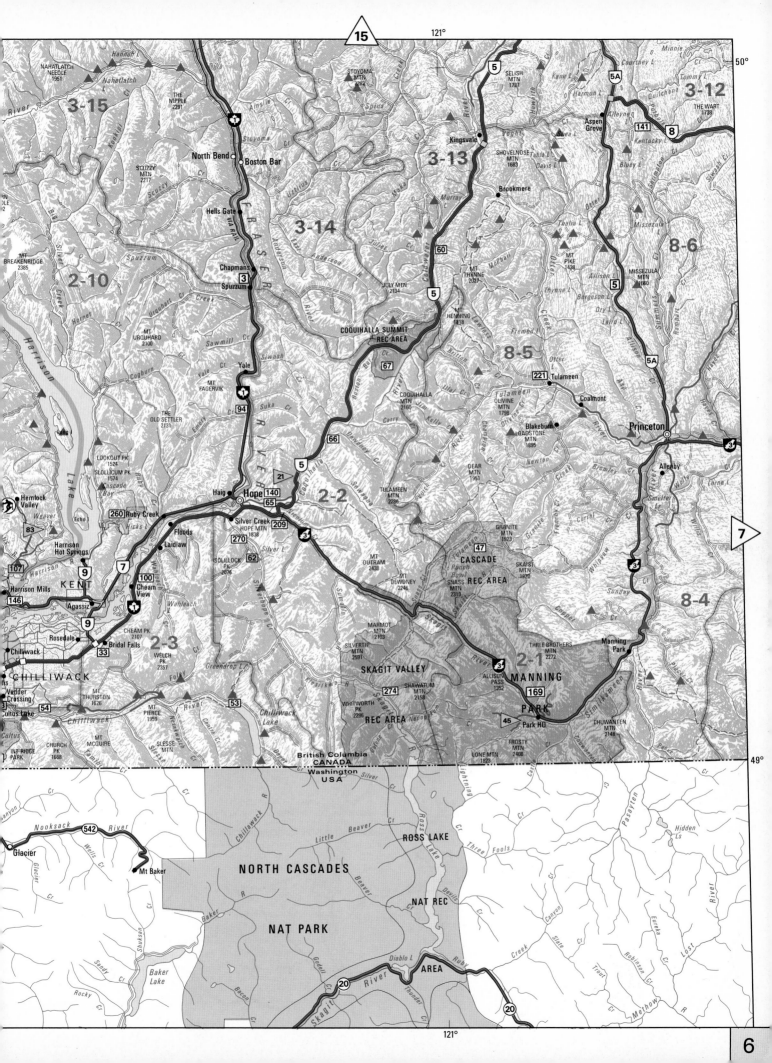

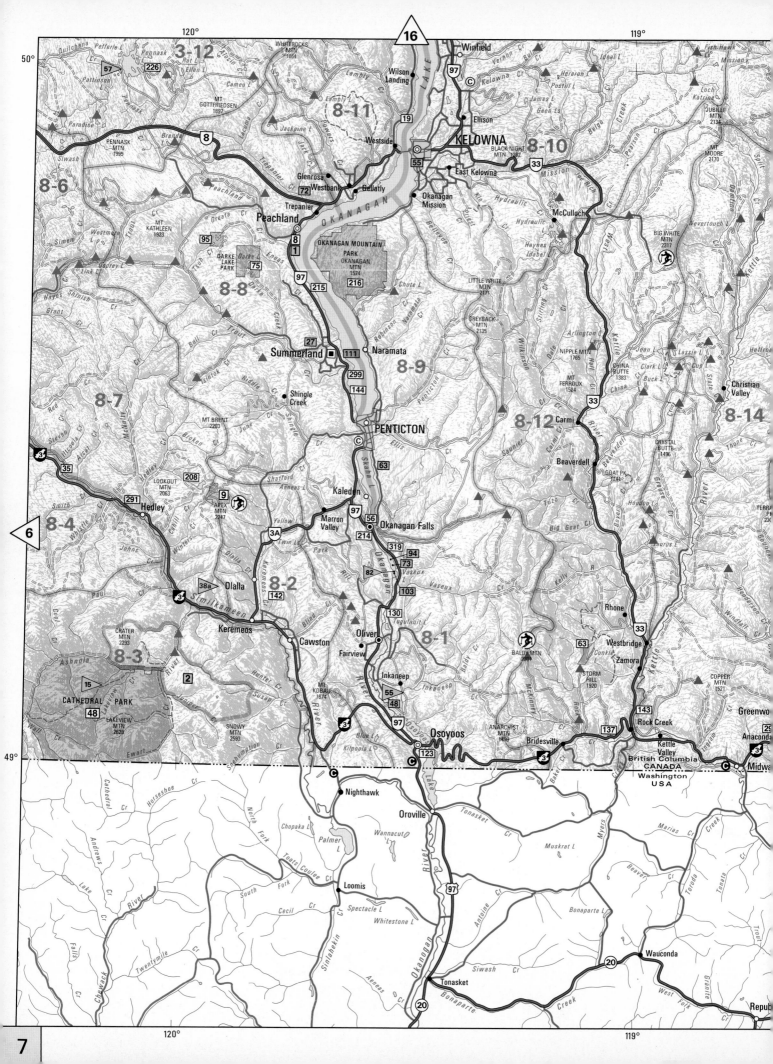

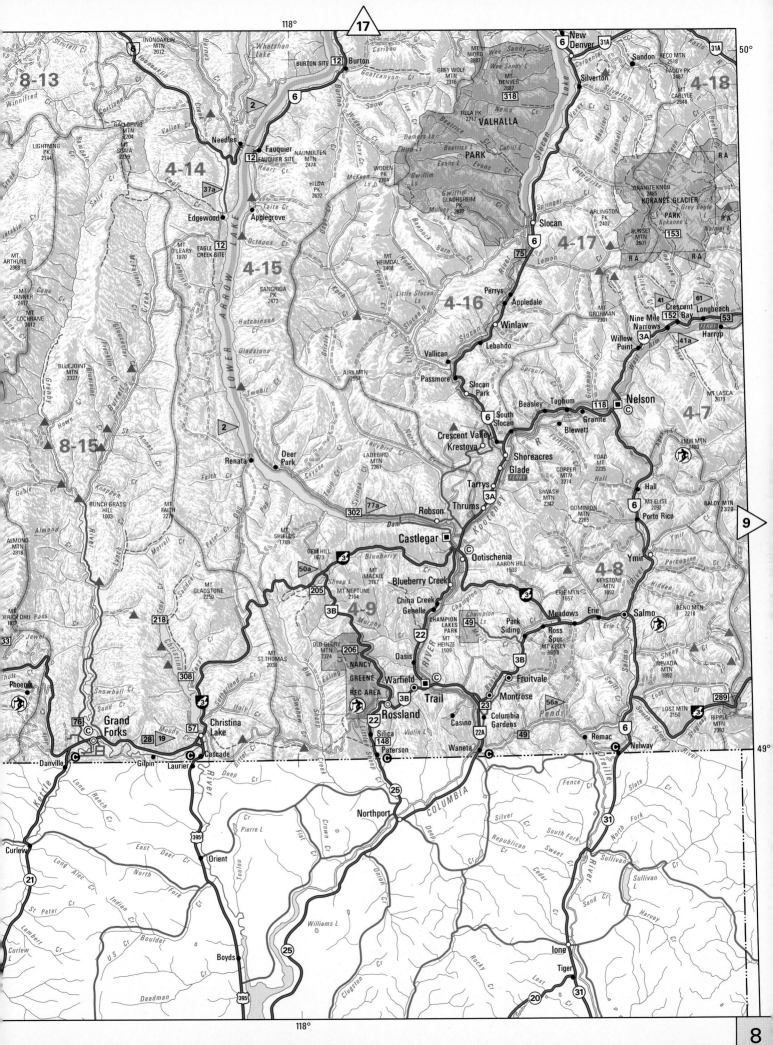

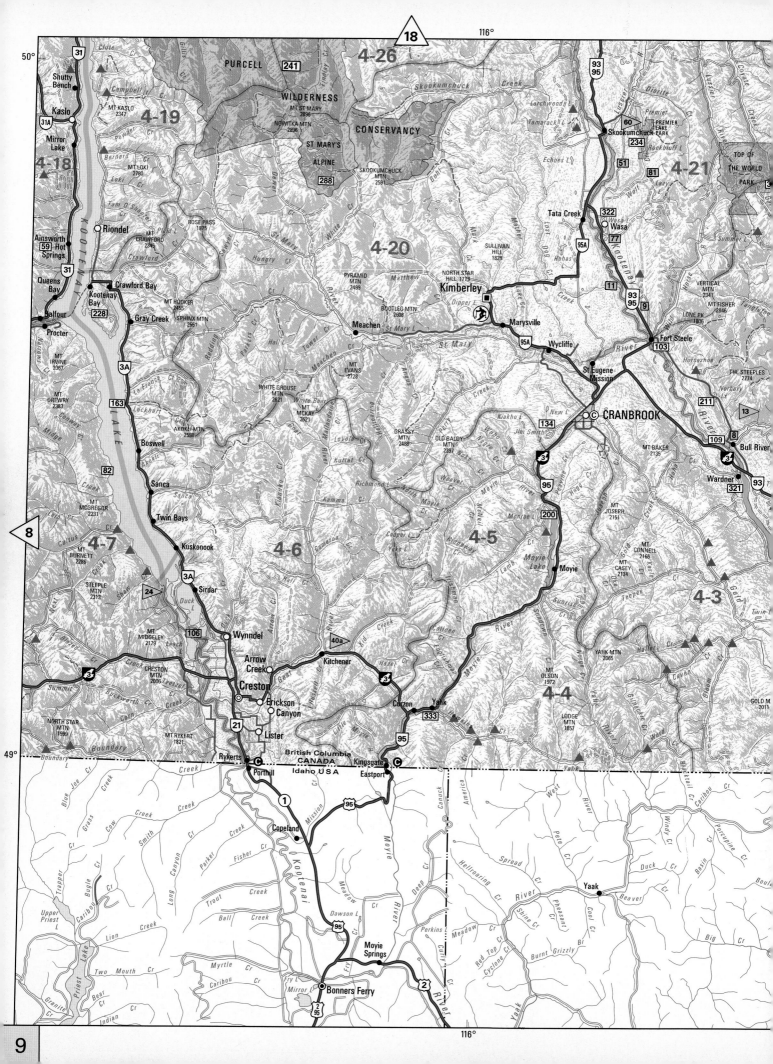

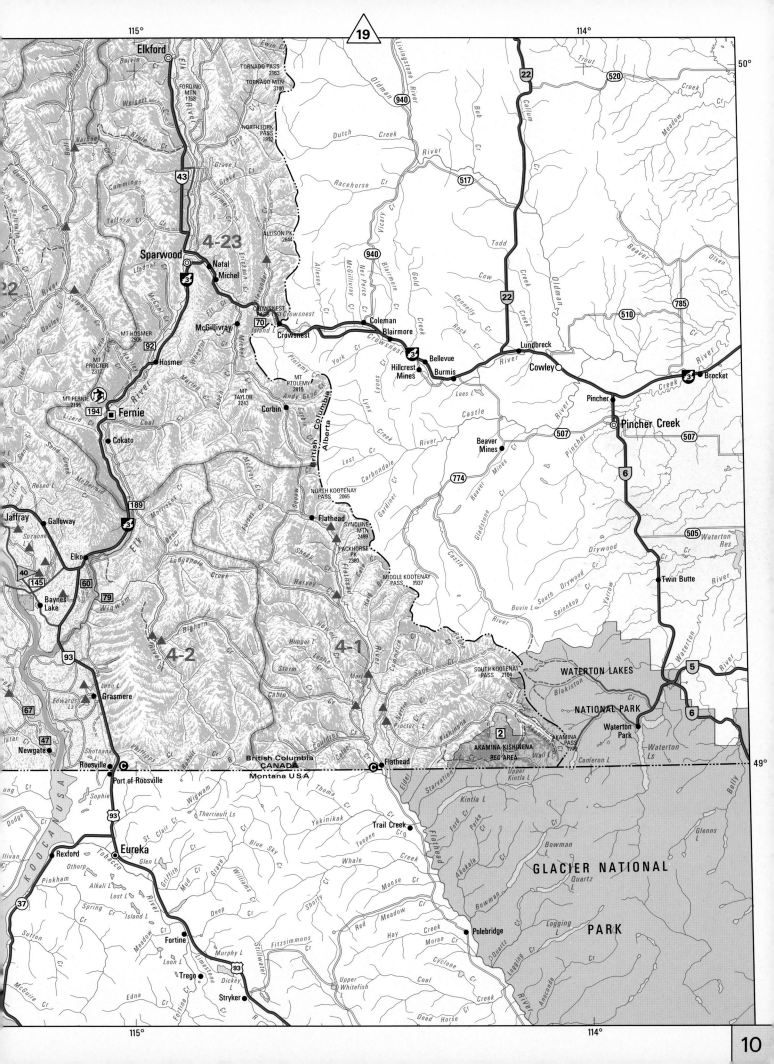

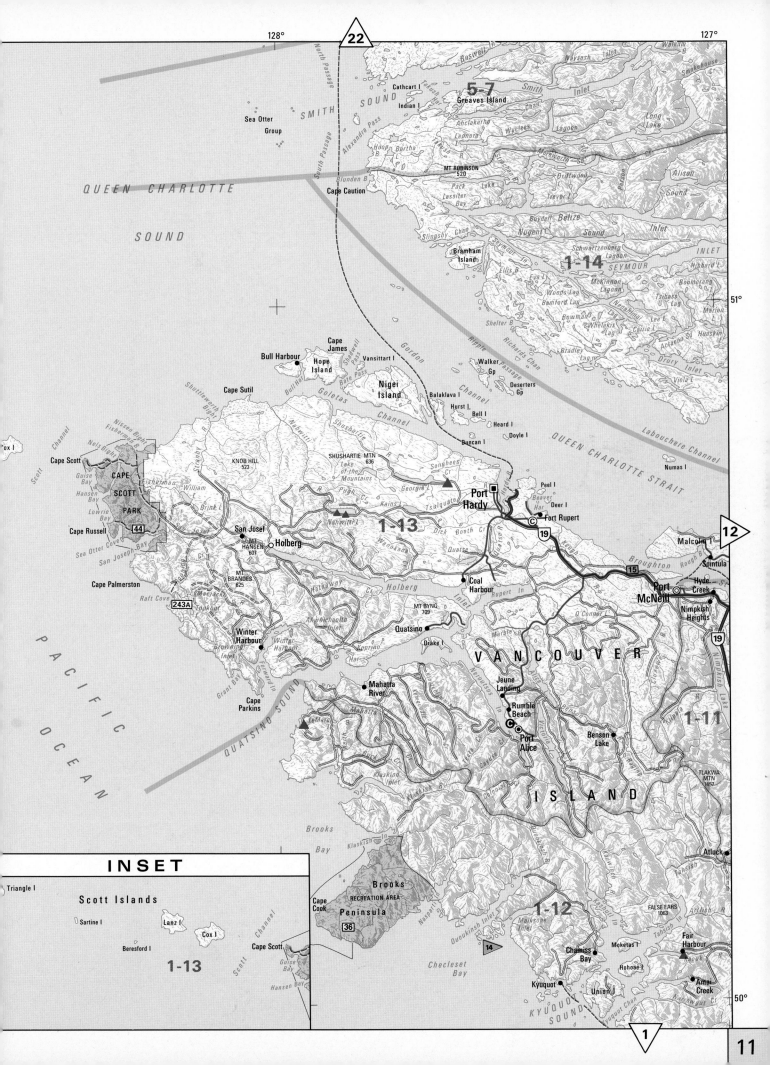

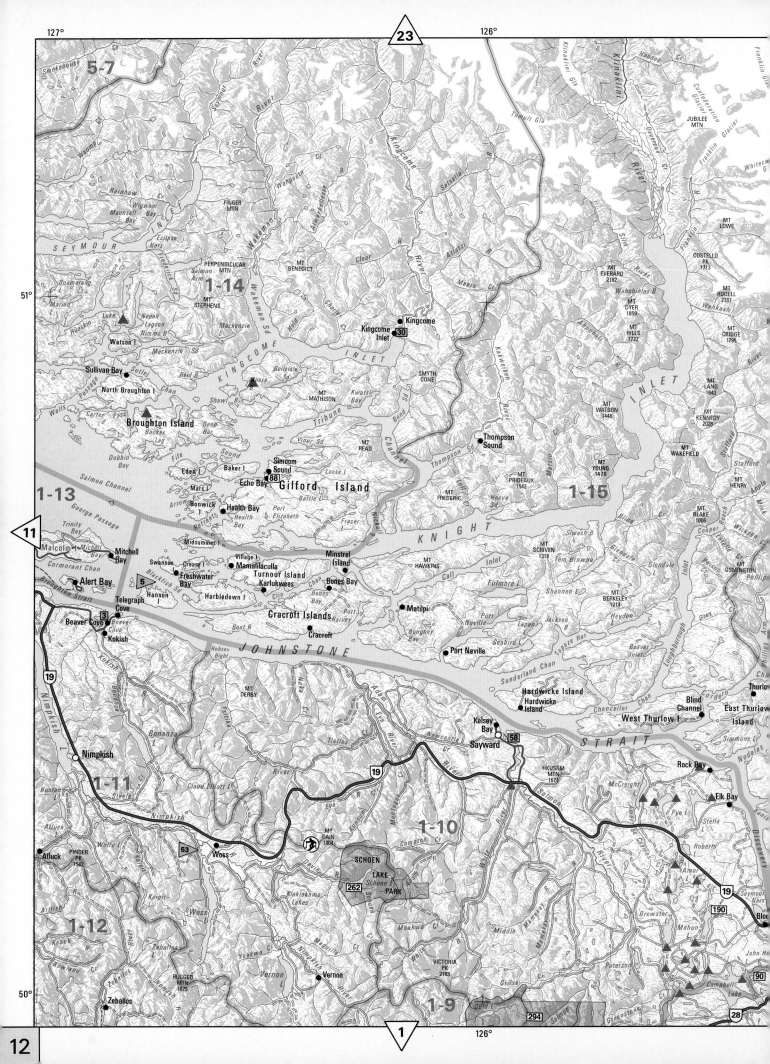

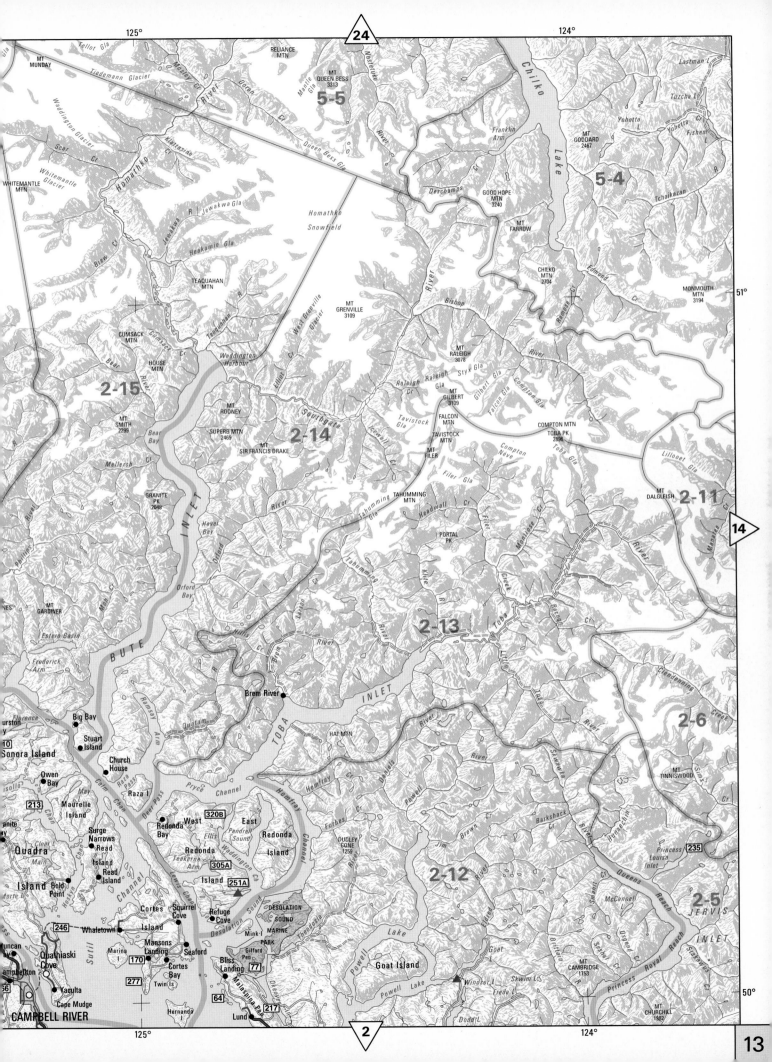

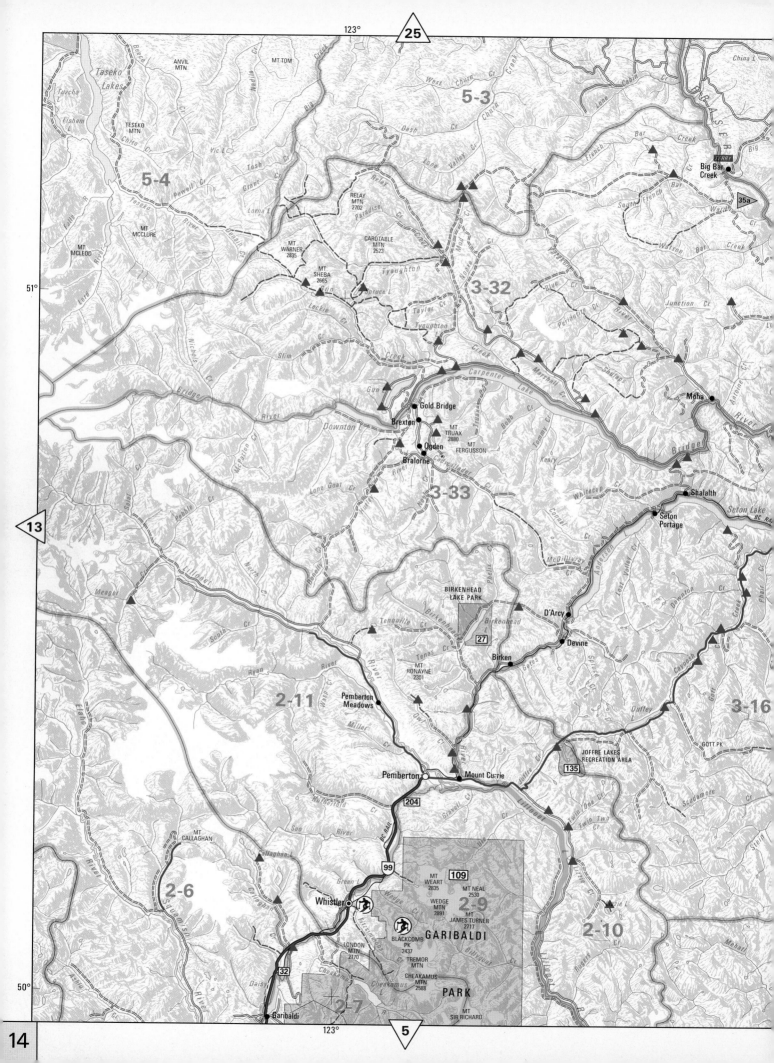

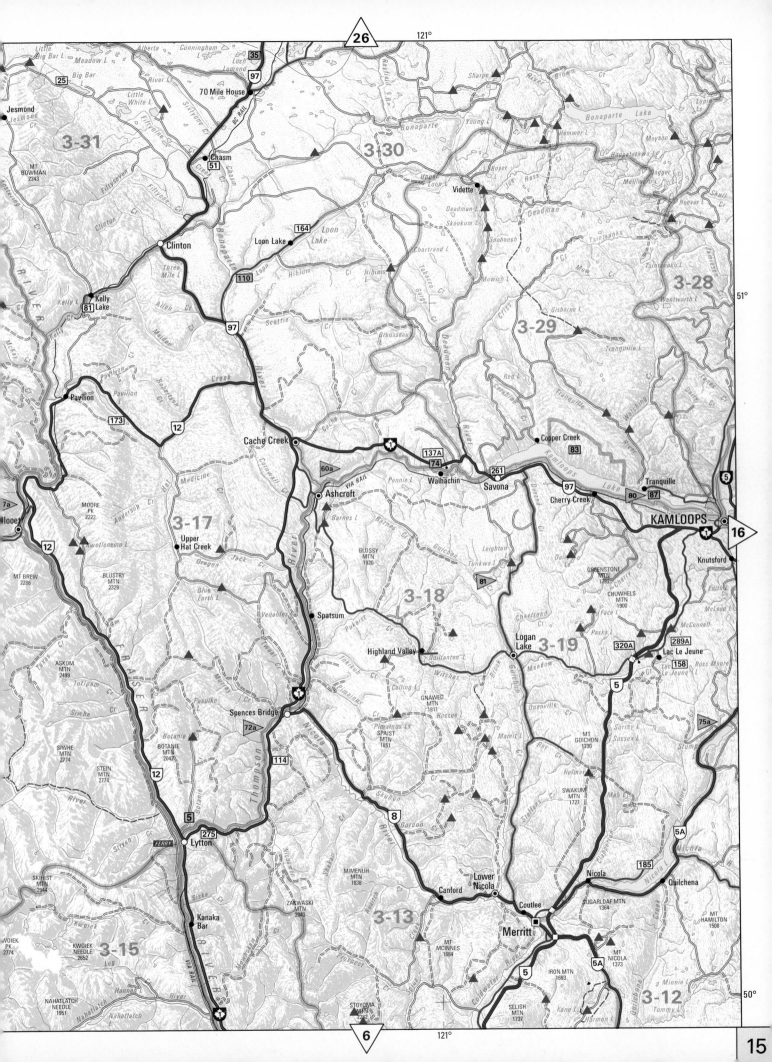

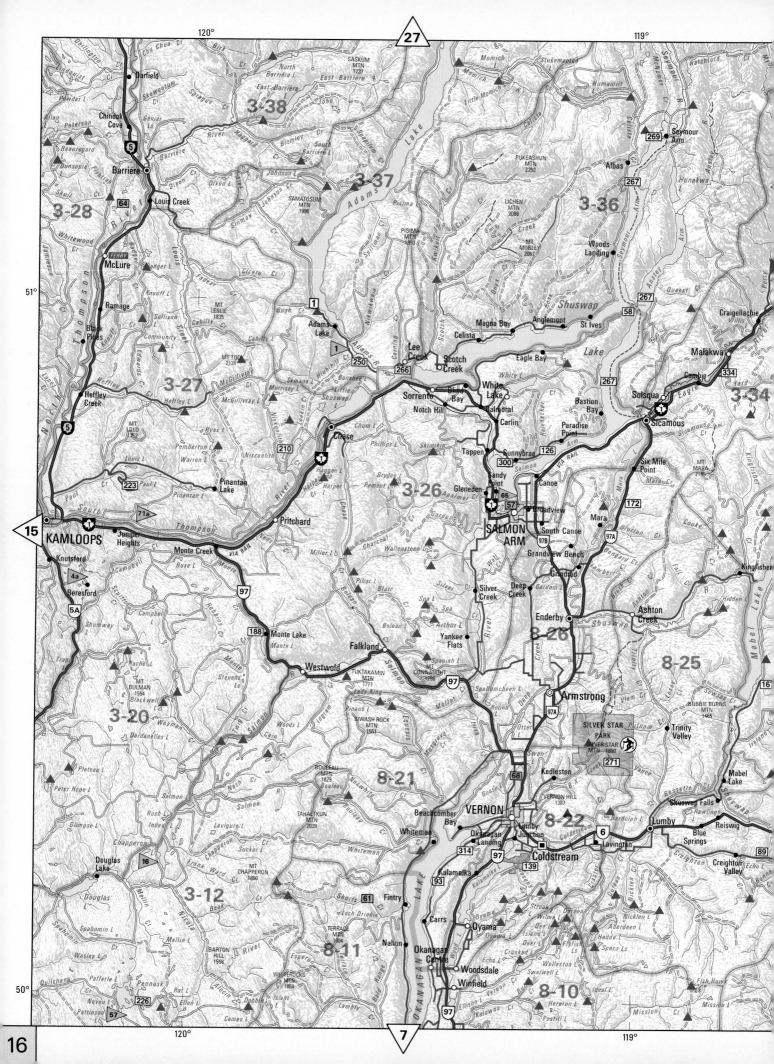

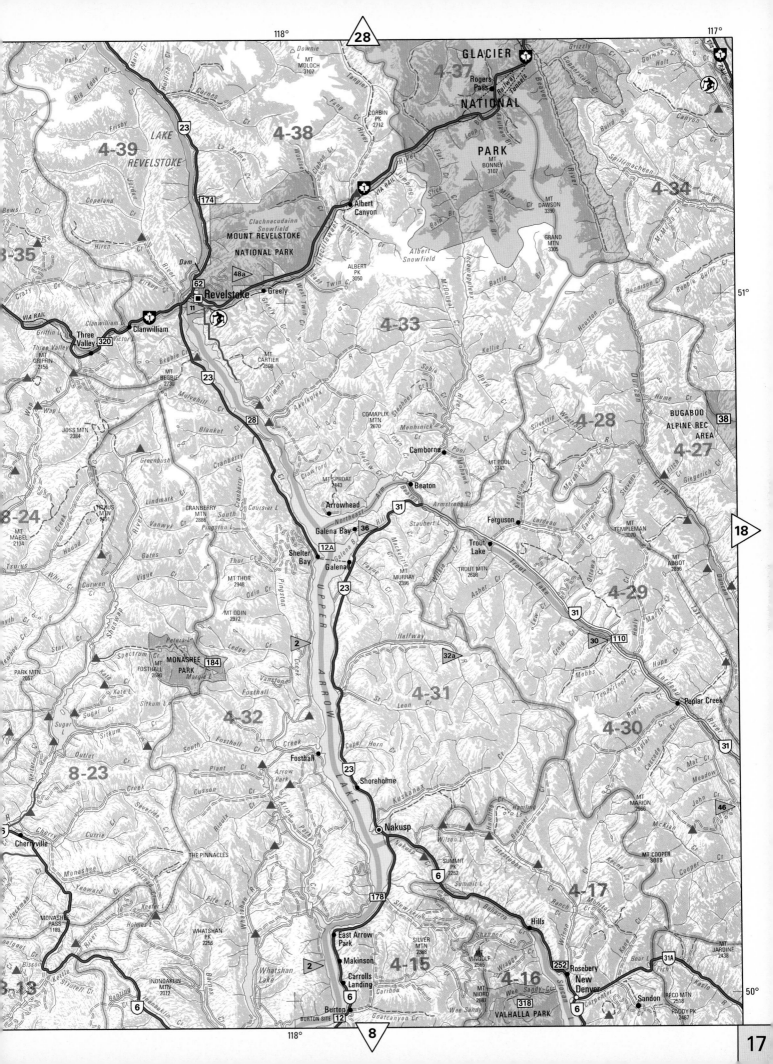

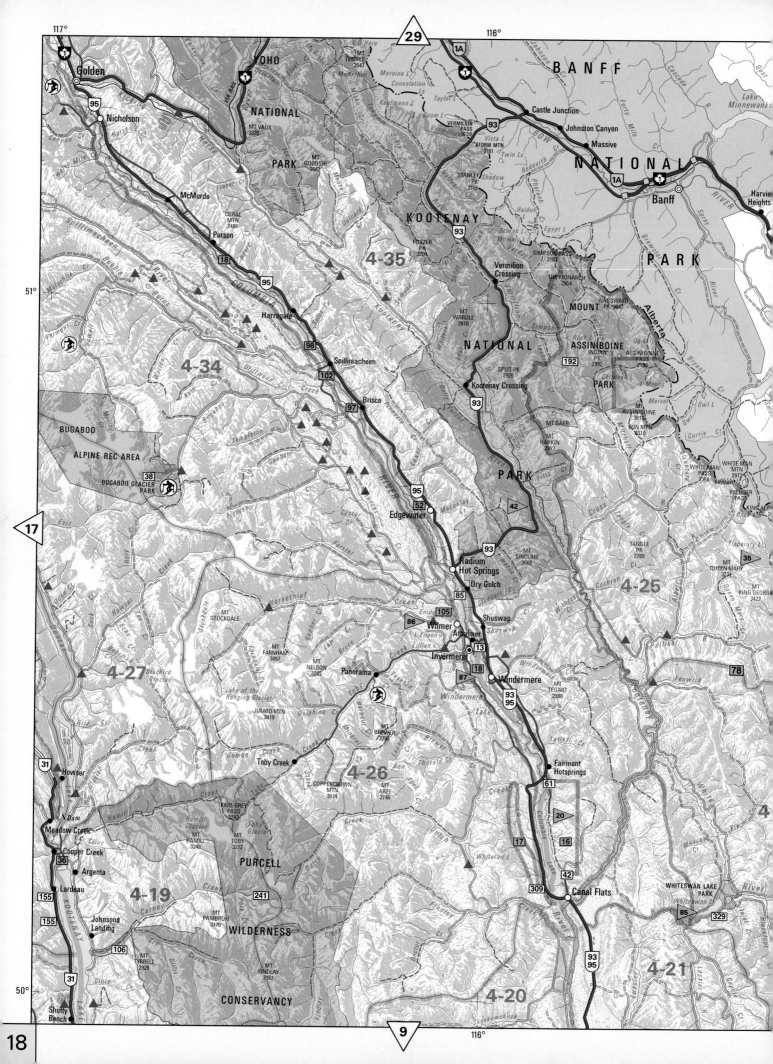

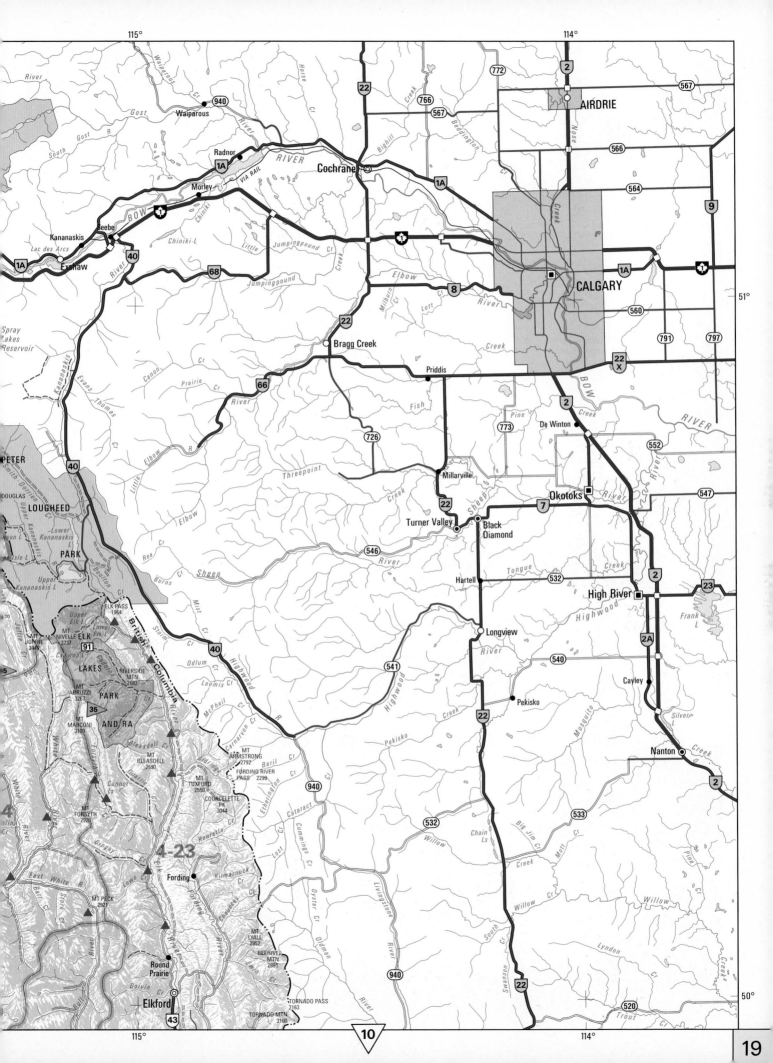

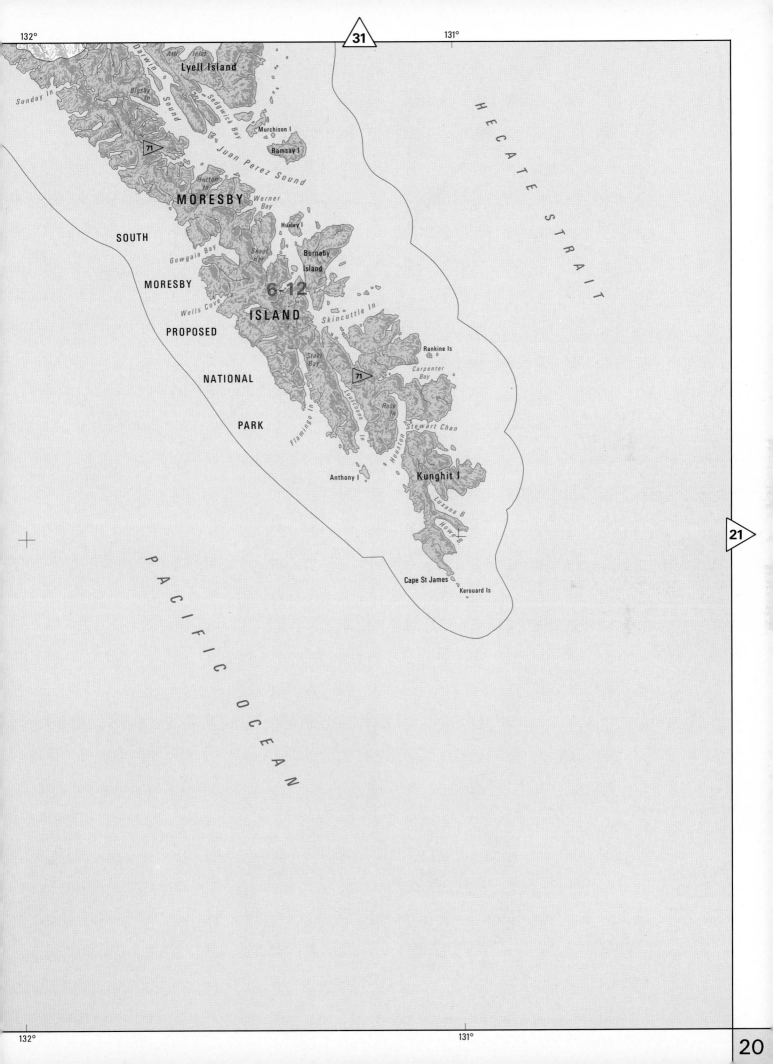

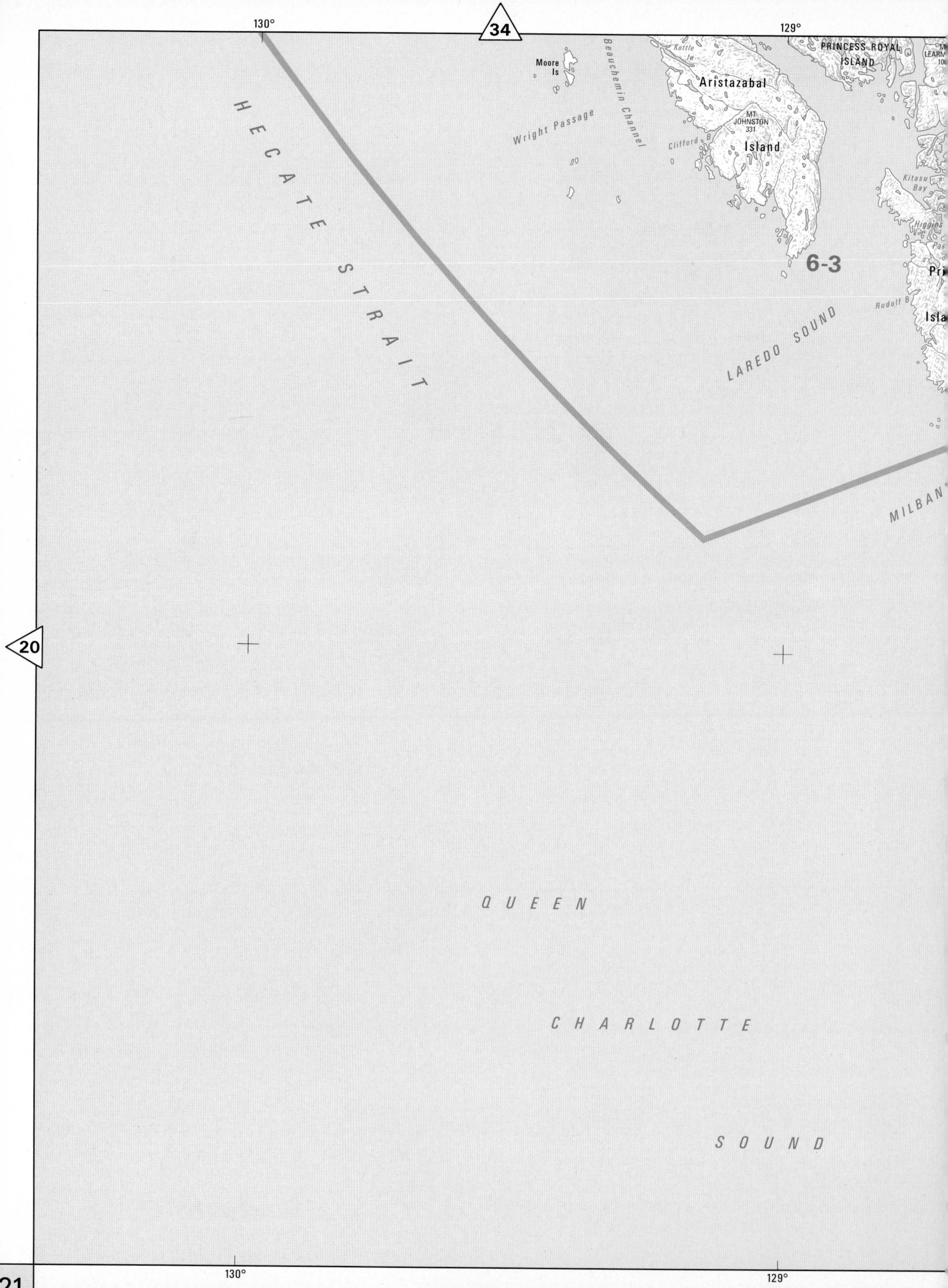

130°   129°

PRINCESS ROYAL
ISLAND

Moore
Is

Beauchemin Channel

Kettle
In

Aristazabal

Wright Passage

MT
JOHNSTON
331

Island

Clifford B.

Kitasu
Bay

Higgins
Pas

6-3

Pr

LAREDO SOUND

Rudolf B.

Isla

H E C A T E   S T R A I T

MILBAN

Q U E E N

C H A R L O T T E

S O U N D

130°   129°

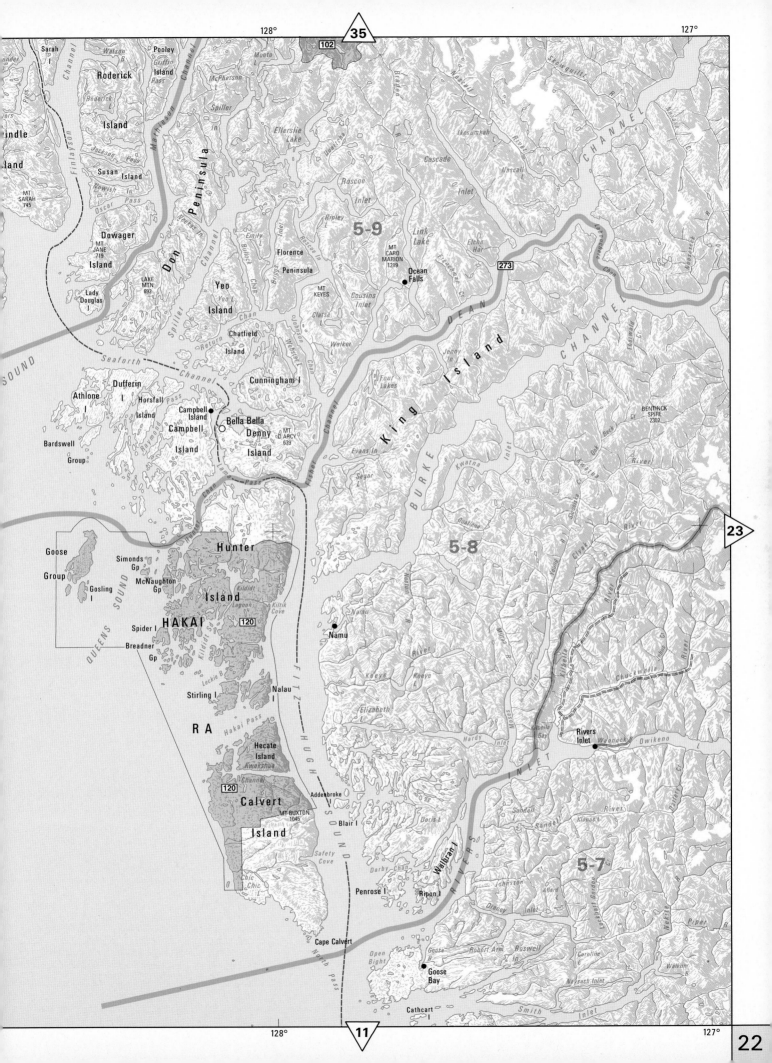

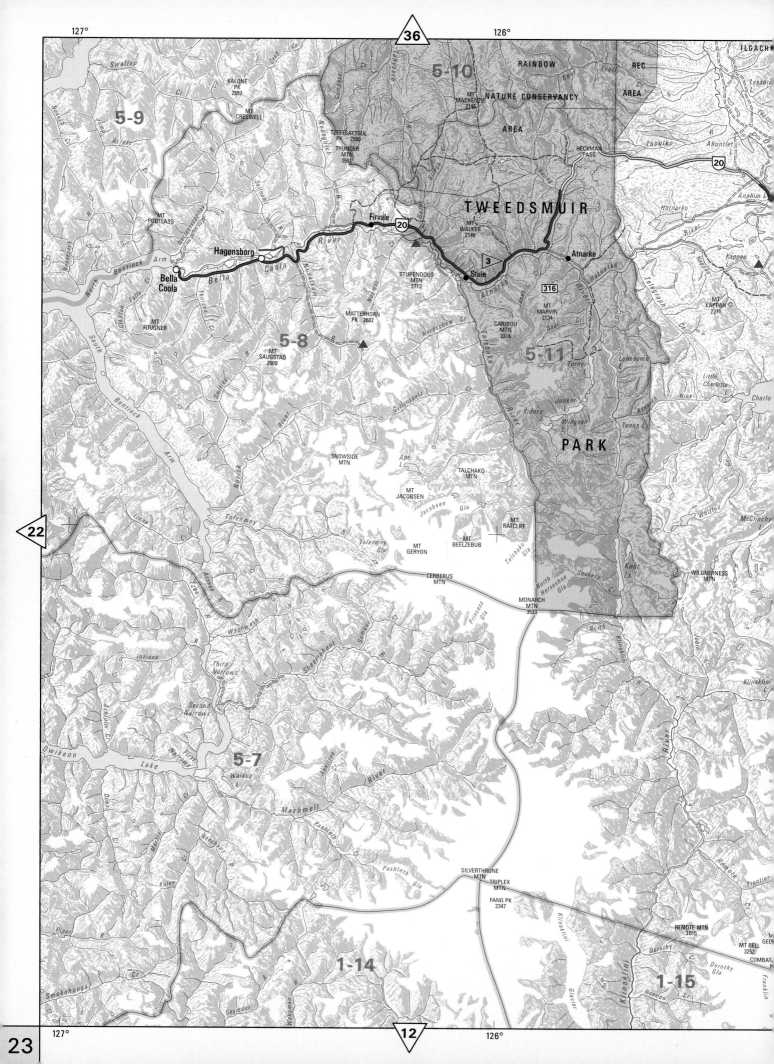

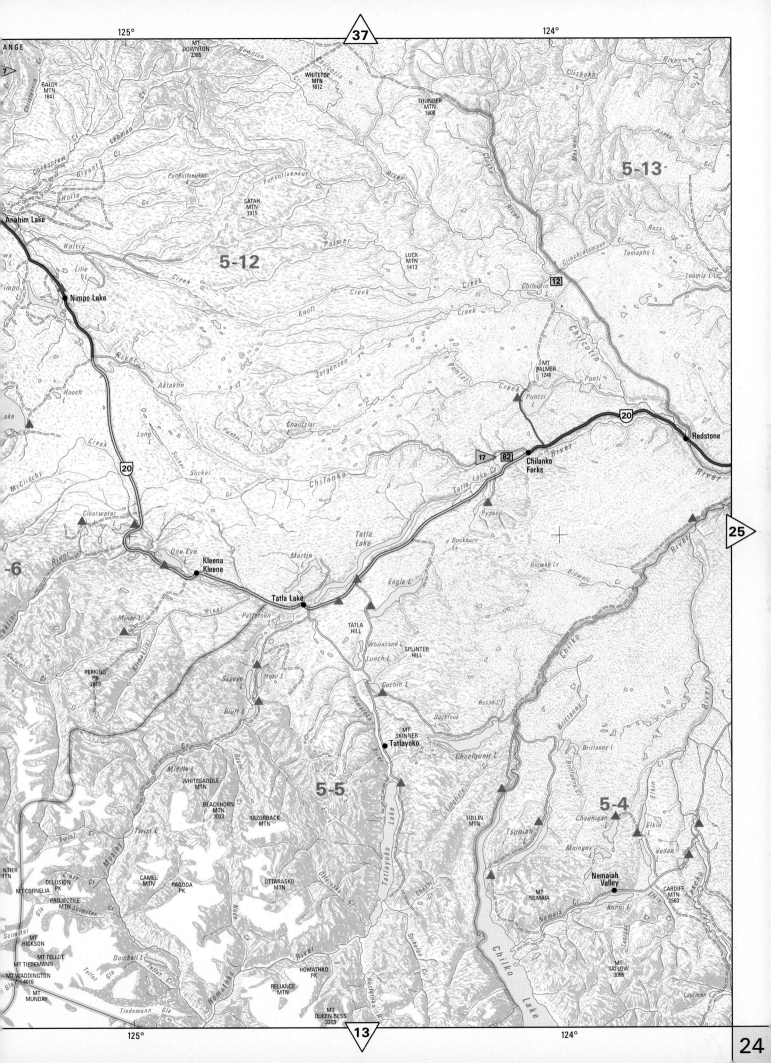

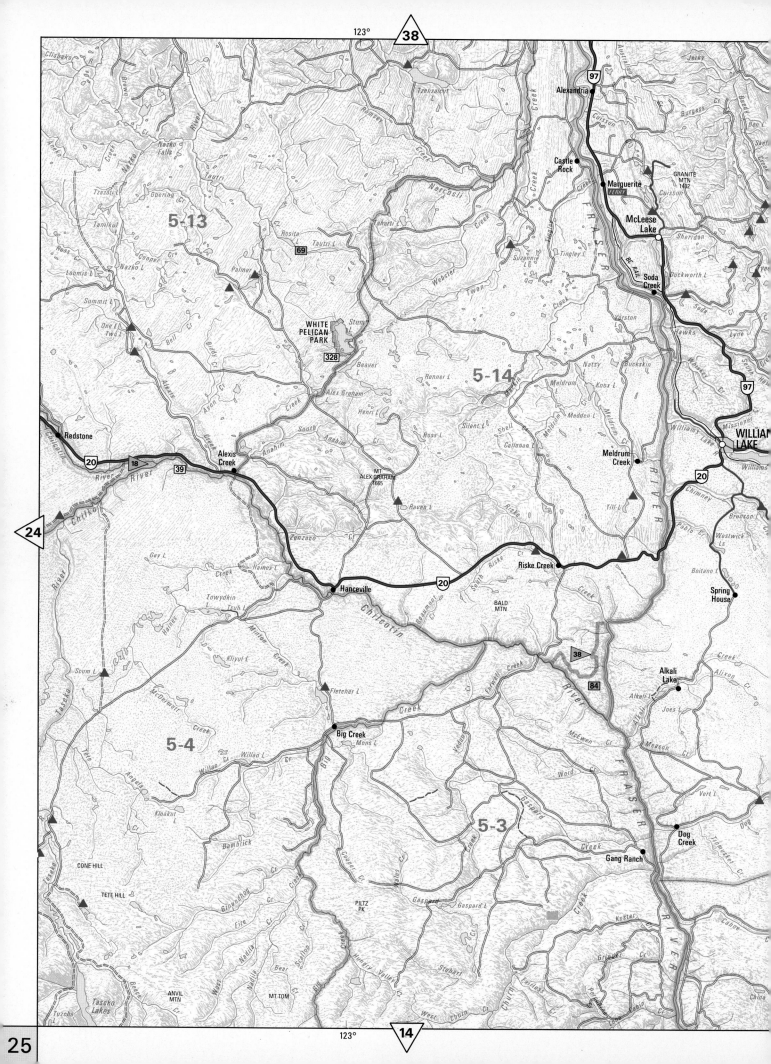

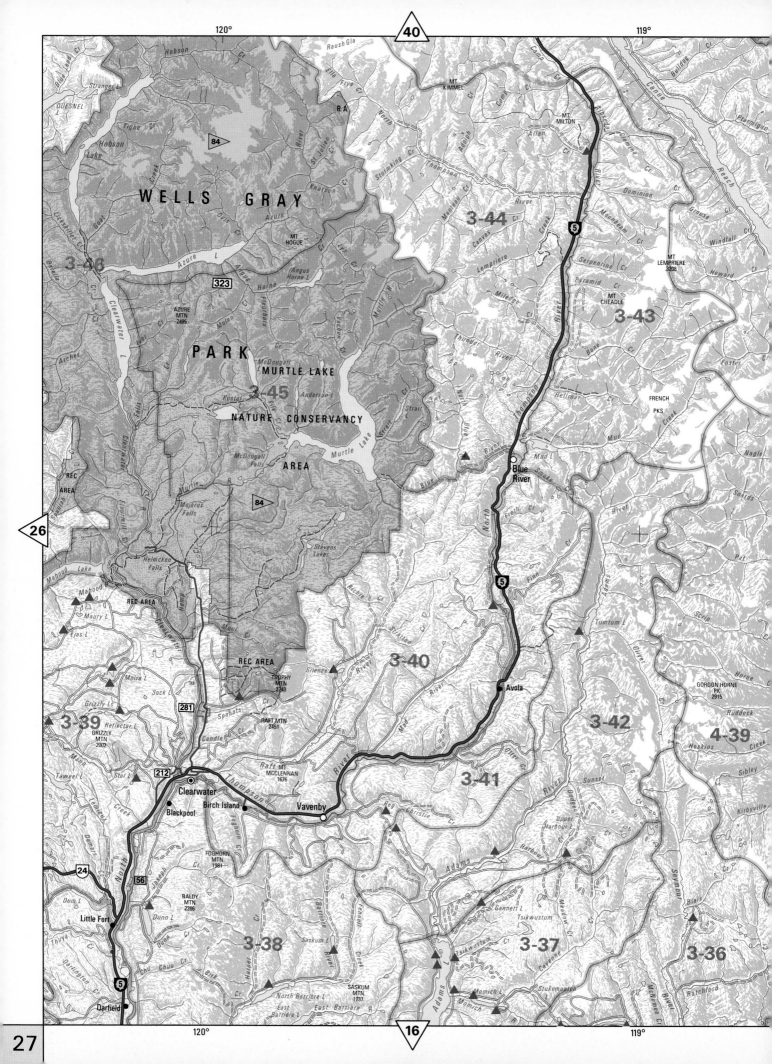

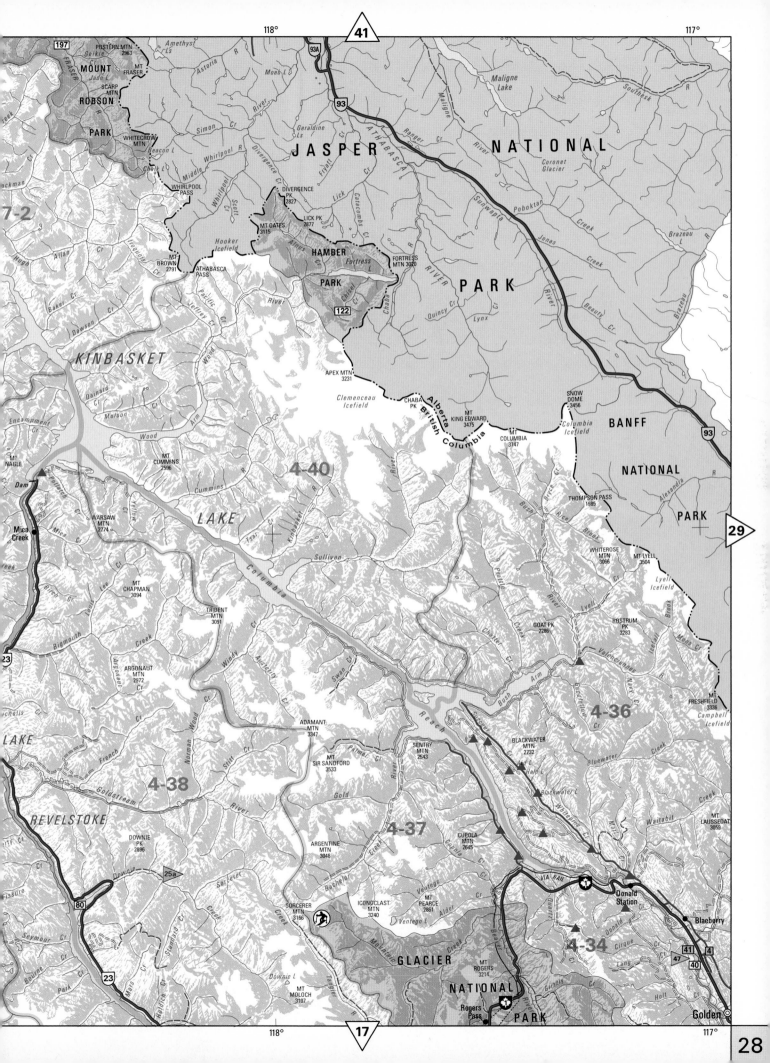

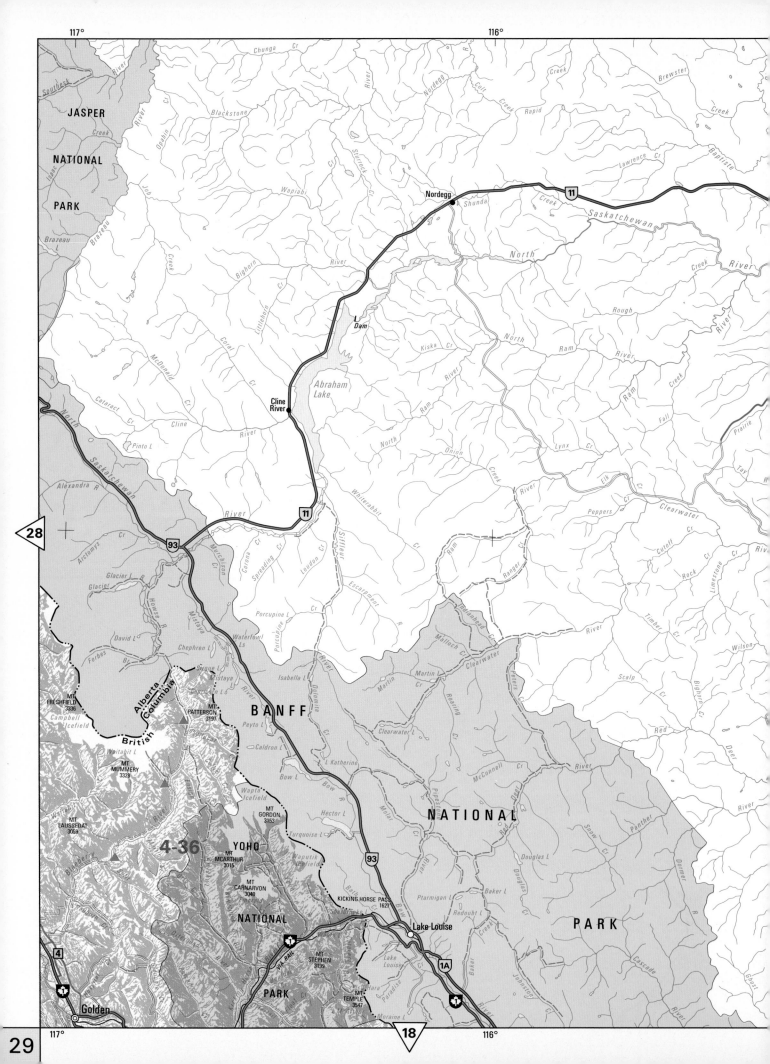

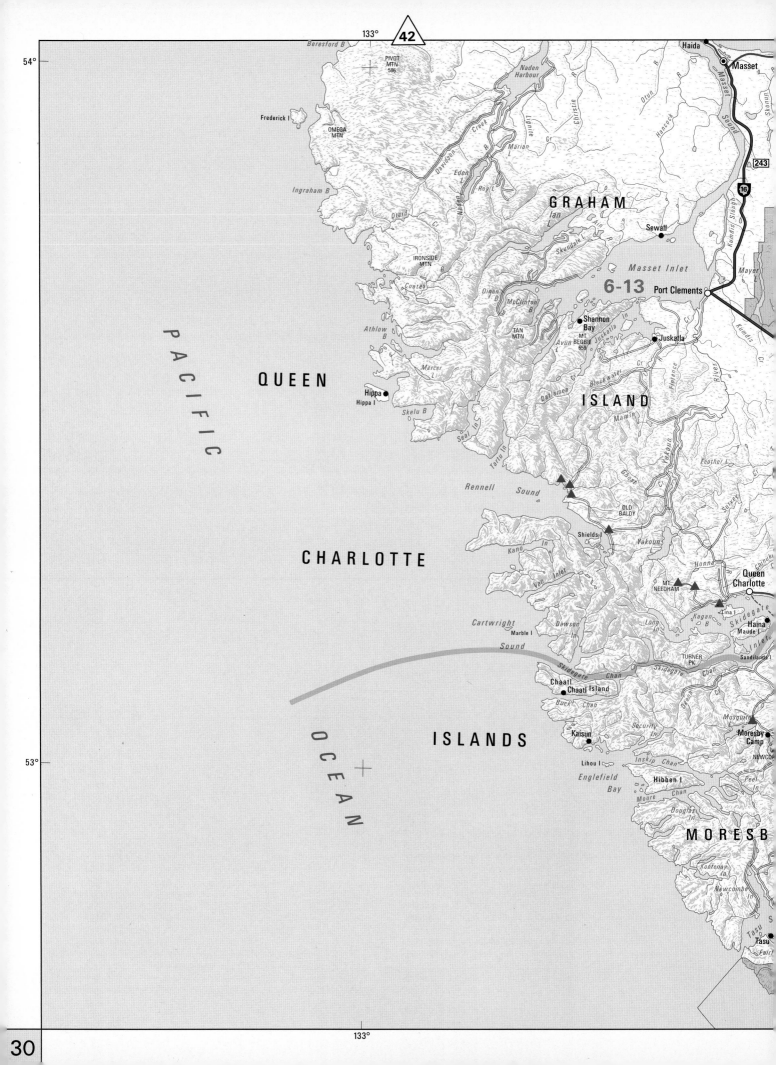

133°

54°

Beresford B

PIVOT
MTN
586

Frederick I

OMEGA
MTN

Naden Harbour

Creek

Naden R

Christie R

Lignite Cr

Marian
L

Eden

Davidson
R

Roy L

Ingraham B

Otard
Cr

Naden R

Skungale R

Ain R

Ian
L

GRAHAM

Sewall

Masset Sound

Masset

Haida

243

16

Otun R

Hancock R

Kumdis Slough

Mayer

IRONSIDE
MTN

Coates R

Dinan
B

McClinton
B

Masset Inlet

6-13 Port Clements

Kumdis Cr

QUEEN

Athlow
B

TAN
MTN

Shannon
Bay

Avun
L

MT
BEGBIE
659

Juskatla In

Juskatla

ISLAND

Mercer
L

Hippa

Hippa I

Skelu B

Seal In

Tartu In

Datlamen Cr

Blackwater Cr

Florence R

Mamin R

Mamin L

Yakoun R

Ghost Cr

Feather L

Soulay R

PACIFIC

CHARLOTTE

Rennell   Sound

Kano In

Van Inlet

OLD
BALDY

Shields I

Yakoun

Honna R

MT
NEEDHAM

Queen
Charlotte

Kagan
B

Tina I

Skidegate

Haina

Maude I

Inlet

Cartwright

Marble I

Sound

Dawson In

Long In

Ohane Cr

Skidegate Chan

TURNER
PK

Skidegate Chan

Chaatl   Chan

Sandilands I

ISLANDS

Chaatl
Chaatl Island

Buck   Chan

Security In

Mosquito

Kaisun

Lihou I

Inskip Chan

Moore Chan

Englefield
Bay

Hibben I

Douglas In

Moresby
Camp

NEWCO

Peel In

MORESB

53°

OCEAN

Koatenay In

Newcombe

Tasu S

Tasu

Faich

133°

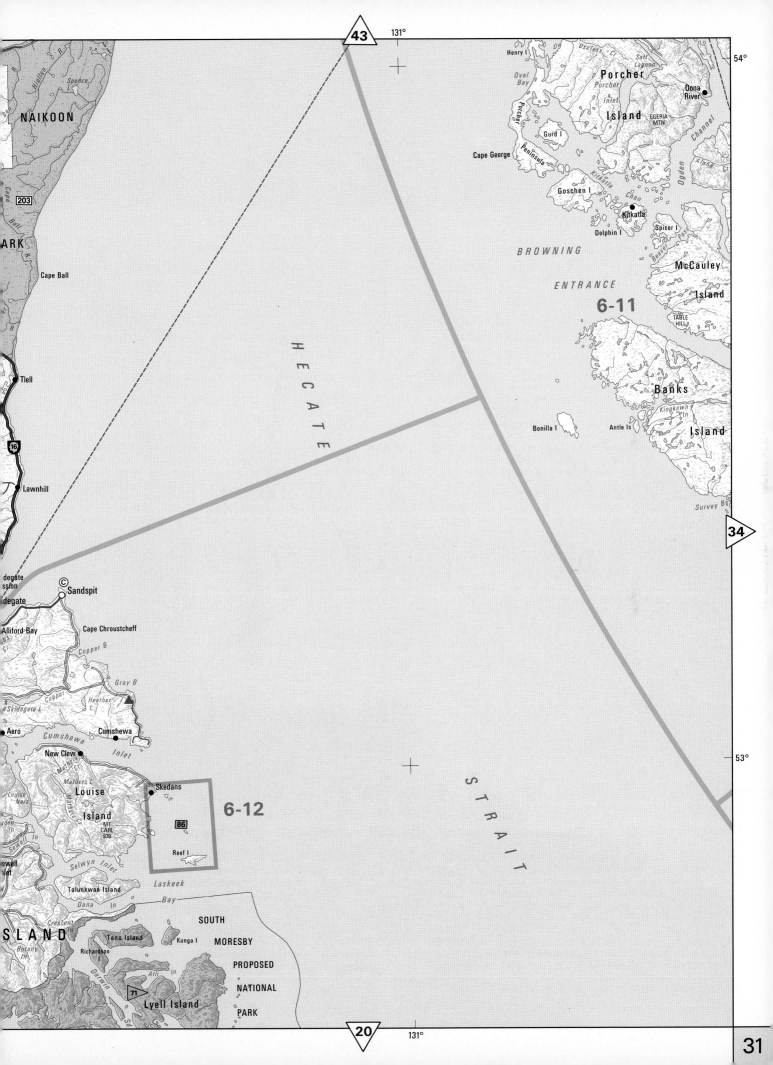

131°
54°

NAIKOON

Henry I
Useless Cr
Salt Lagoon

Porcher
Porcher
Inlet
Island
Oona River
EGERIA MTN

Oval Bay

203

Cape George
Peninsula
Gurd I
Goschen I
Kitkatla Chan
Kitkatla
Spicer I
Beaver Pass

Dolphin I

Ogden Channel
Alpha Cr

Cape Ball

BROWNING

McCauley

ENTRANCE
Island

6-11
TABLE HILL

Tlell

H
E
C
A
T
E

Banks

16

Bonilla I
Antle Is
Kingkown In
Island

Lawnhill

Survey B

degate
ssion
degate

C
Sandspit

Alliford Bay
Cape Chroustcheff

Copper B

Gray B

Heather L

Skidegate I

Aero
Cumshewa
Cumshewa
Inlet

New Clew
Mathers Cr

53°

Mathers L
Louise
Island
MT CARL 938

Skedans

S
T
R
A
I
T

86
6-12

Louise Nart

Reef I

Selwyn Inlet

Sewell In
ewell
nlet

Talunkwan Island
Dana In

Laskeek
Bay

Crescent

SOUTH
MORESBY

Botany In
Tanu Island
Kunga I
Richardson

PROPOSED

Darwin Sd

Atli In

NATIONAL

71
Lyell Island

PARK

SLAND

131°

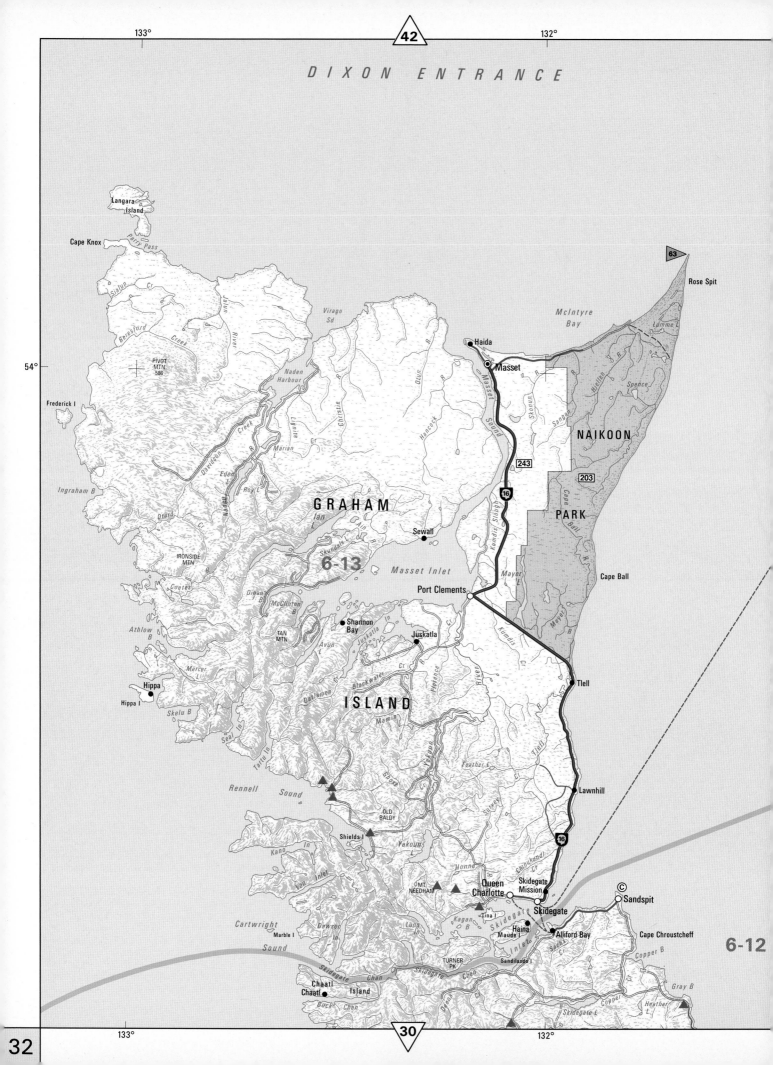

DIXON ENTRANCE

133°

132°

Langara
Island

Cape Knox

Parry Pass

54°

Frederick I

Beresford Creek

Siahin Cr

Jalun River

PIVOT
MTN
586

Virago Sd

Naden
Harbour

Davidson Creek

Lignite Cr

Marian L

Eden L

Roy L

Christie R

 Quun R

Masset Sound

Haida

Masset

McIntyre
Bay

Hellen R

Spence

NAIKOON

63

Rose Spit

Lumme L

Sangan R

Skonun R

243

GRAHAM

Ingraham B

Otard Cr

Ian L

Ain R

Skundale

Sewall

6-13

Masset Inlet

16

PARK

Cape Ball R

Cape Ball

IRONSIDE
MTN

Coates

Dinan B

Mc Clinton B

Port Clements

Mayer

Kumdis Slough

203

Athlow B

TAN
MTN

Shannon
Bay

Juskatla In

Juskatla

Kumdis Cr

Mayer R

Hippa

Hippa I

Skelu B

Mercer L

Seal In

Tartu In

Datlamen Cr

Avun L

Blackwater Cr

Florence R

Yakoun River

Tlell

ISLAND

Mamin R

Feather Cr

Tlell R

Rennell Sound

OLD
BALDY

Shields I

Kano In

Yakoun R

Gold Cr

Survey Cr

Lawnhill

16

Van Inlet

MT
NEEDHAM

Honna R

Chinukundl Cr

Skidegate
Mission

©

Sandspit

Queen
Charlotte

Cartwright

Dawson

Marble I

Long In

Lina I

Kagan B

Skidegate

Haina

Skidegate Inlet

Alliford Bay

Cape Chroustcheff

Sound

Maude I

Sachs Cr

Copper B

6-12

Skidegate Chan

Djana Chan

TURNER
PK

Sandilands I

Copper R

Chaatl

Chaatl Island

Buck Chan

Skidegate L

Gray B

Heather L

133°

132°

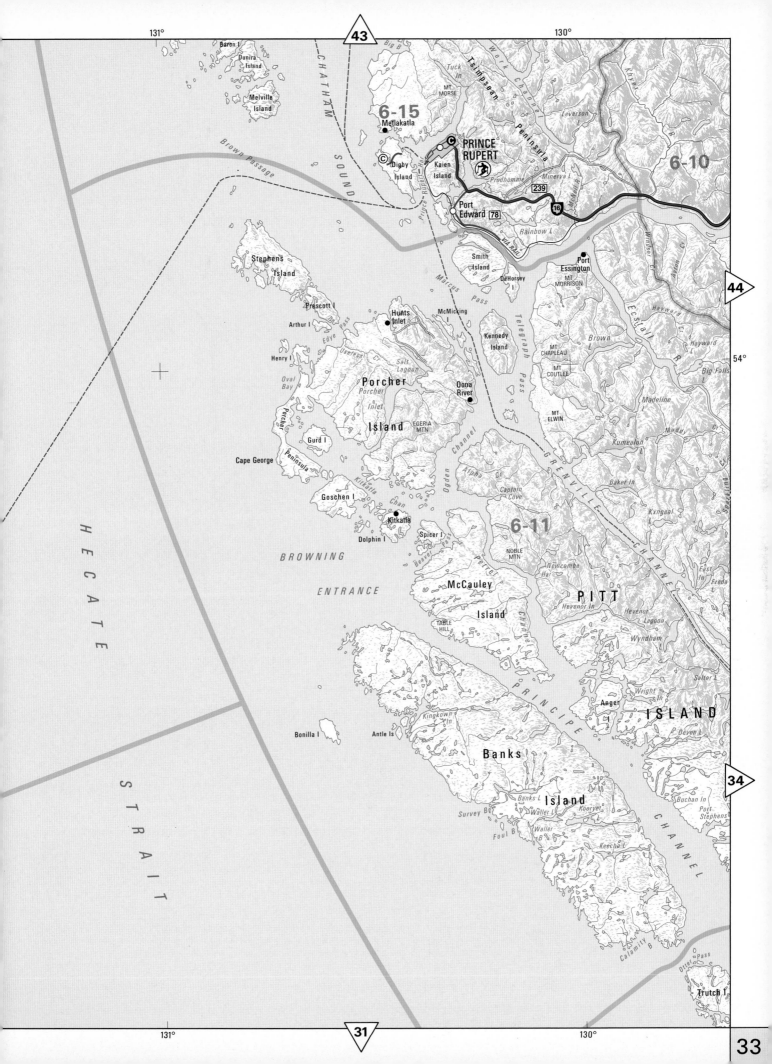

131°

130°

CHATHAM SOUND

Baron I
Dunira Island
Melville Island

Brown Passage

Big B

Tuck In

Work Channel

Tsimpsean

MT MORSE

Peninsula

Leverson L

Khyex R

6-15
• Metlakatla

PRINCE RUPERT

Minerva L

6-10

© Digby Island

Kaien Island

239

16

Prudhomme

McNeill R

Port Edward

78

Rainbow L

Smith Island

DeHorsey

Port Essington

MT MORRISON

Ecstall R

Hayward Cr

Stephens Island

Prescott I

Arthur I

Edye Pass

Henry I

Oval Bay

Porcher

Useless Cr

Salt Lagoon

Porcher Inlet

Island

Gurd I

Porcher Peninsula

Cape George

Goschen I

Kitkatla

Dolphin I

Hunts Inlet

McMicking

Kennedy Island

Oona River

EGERIA MTN

Ogden Channel

Alpha Cr

Chan

Spicer I

Beaver

Marcus Pass

Telegraph Pass

MT CHAPLEAU

MT COUTLEE

MT ELWIN

Brown L

GRENVILLE

Captain Cove

McCauley

Island

TABLE HILL

Perrel Channel

NOBLE MTN

Newcombe Har

Hevenor In

CHANNEL

Madeline L

Mudd L

Kumealon L

Baker In

Kxngeal L

Kingkown In

6-11

PITT

Hevenor Lagoon

Wyndham L

East In

Freda L

HECATE

BROWNING

ENTRANCE

Bonilla I

Antle Is

Banks L

Survey B

Waller L

Foul B

Waller B

Banks

Island

Kooryet

Keecha I

Calamity B

Anger

Wright In

ISLAND

Devon L

PRINCIPE

Salter L

Buchan In

Port Stephens

Ottel Pass

Trutch I

STRAIT

131°

130°

54°

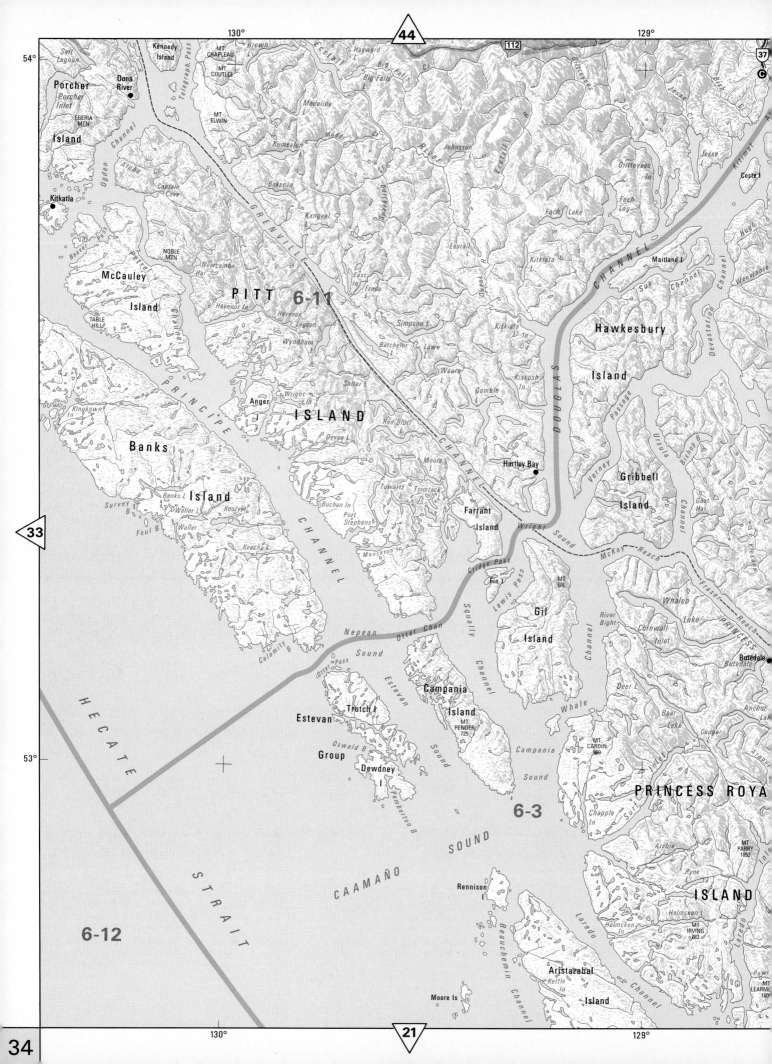

130°

129°

54°

Salt
Lagoon

Kennedy
Island

MT
CHAPLEAU

Brown
L

Hayward
L

Big
Falls
Cr

112

37
C

Porcher

Oona
River

MT
COUTLEE

Big Falls

Porcher
Inlet

EGERIA MTN

Telegraph Pass

MT
ELWIN

Madeline
L

Johnston
L

Gittoyees
In

Jesse
Cr

Jesse
L

Coste I

Island

Ogden

Channel

Muddy
Cr

Kumealon
L

Speelond
Cr

Foch
Lake

Foch
Lag

Kitkatla

Alpha
Cr

Captain
Cove

Baker In

Kxngeal
In

Eestall
R

Eestall
L

Kitkiata
L

Beaver Pass

GRENVILLE

Newcombe
Har

NOBLE
MTN

East
In

Freda
L

Kitkiata
In

Maitland L

McCauley

Pattel

Hevenor In

Hevenor

Simpson L

Sue
Channel

DOUGLAS

Hawkesbury

Island

Kitkiata
In

Devastation Channel

Weewanie

Island

TABLE
HILL

Wyndham

Lagoon

Batchelor
L

Lowe
L

Kiskosh
In

Island

Ursula

Channel

Bishop B

Hugh
L

PRINCIPE

PITT 6-11

Salter L

Wright
In

Weare
L

Gamble
L

Goat
Har

Kelate

Anger
I

Red Bluff

CHANNEL

ISLAND

Devon L

Moore
L

Hartley Bay

Gribbell

Verney Passage

Island

Banks

Banks L

Tuwartz

Tsimtack

Farrant

Whale

Whalen
Lake

River
Bight

Island

Waller L

Kooryet
L

Buchan In

Island

Wright

Sound

Cornwall
Inlet

PRINCESS

Survey
B

Foul B

Waller
B

Keecha L

Port
Stephens

Cridge Pass

McKay

Reach

Fraser

Reach

Butedale

Monckton In

Fin I

Lewis Pass

MT
GIL

Deer
L

Butedale
L

33

Nepean

Otter Chan

Squally

Gil

Bear
L

Anchor
L

Sound

Otter
Pass

Estevan

Sound

Island

Channel

Cougar
L

Archie
L

Calamity
B

Estevan

Trutch I

Campania

Campania
Sound

MT
CARDIN
960

Chapple
In

Surf

PRINCESS ROYA

Oswald B

Island

Pyne
L

Group

Dewdney
I

MT
PENDER
725

Campania

Inlet

MT
PARRY
1052

53°

Pemberton B

Sound

HECATE

CAAMAÑO

SOUND

Rennison
I

Beauchemin Channel

Laredo

Helmcken
In

Helmcken L

MT
IRVING
283

ISLAND

Laredo

Channel

Pow
I

MT
LEARM
100

STRAIT

6-12

6-3

Aristazabal

Kettle
In

Island

Moore Is

130°

129°

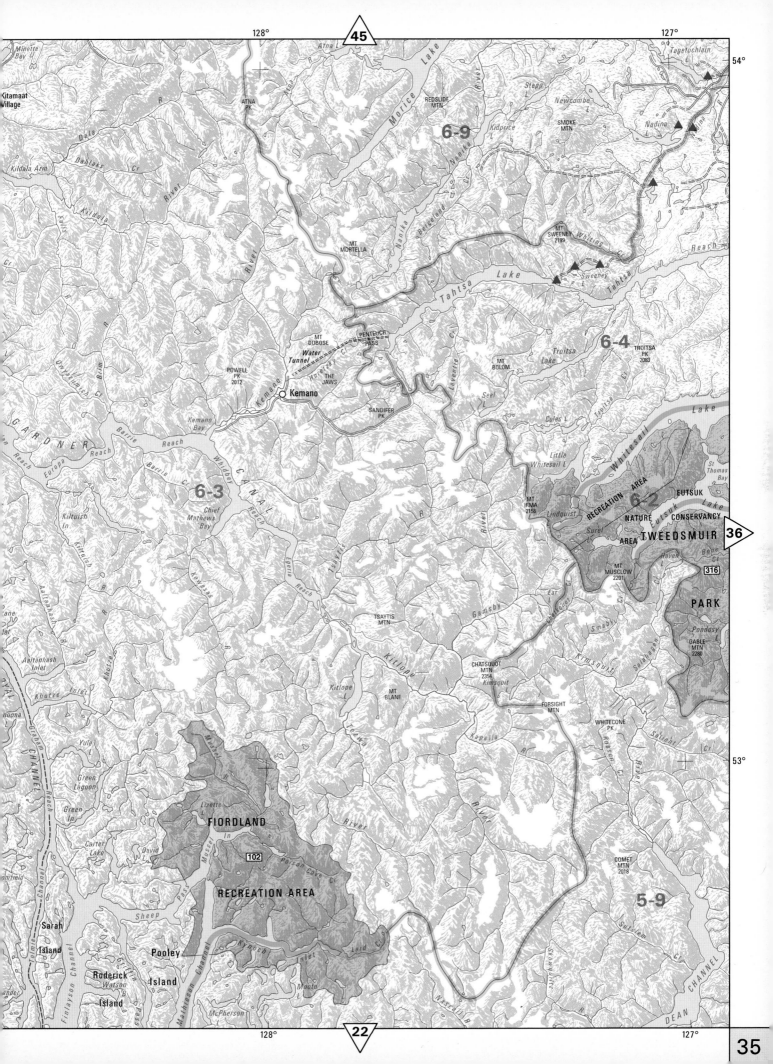

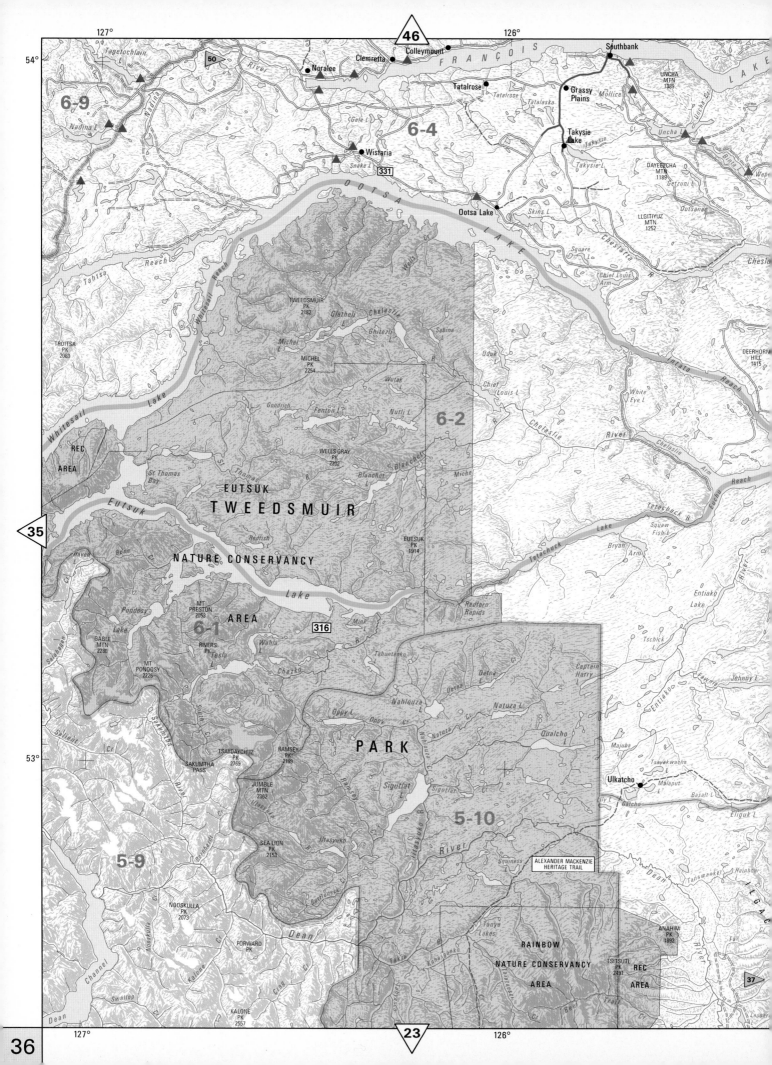

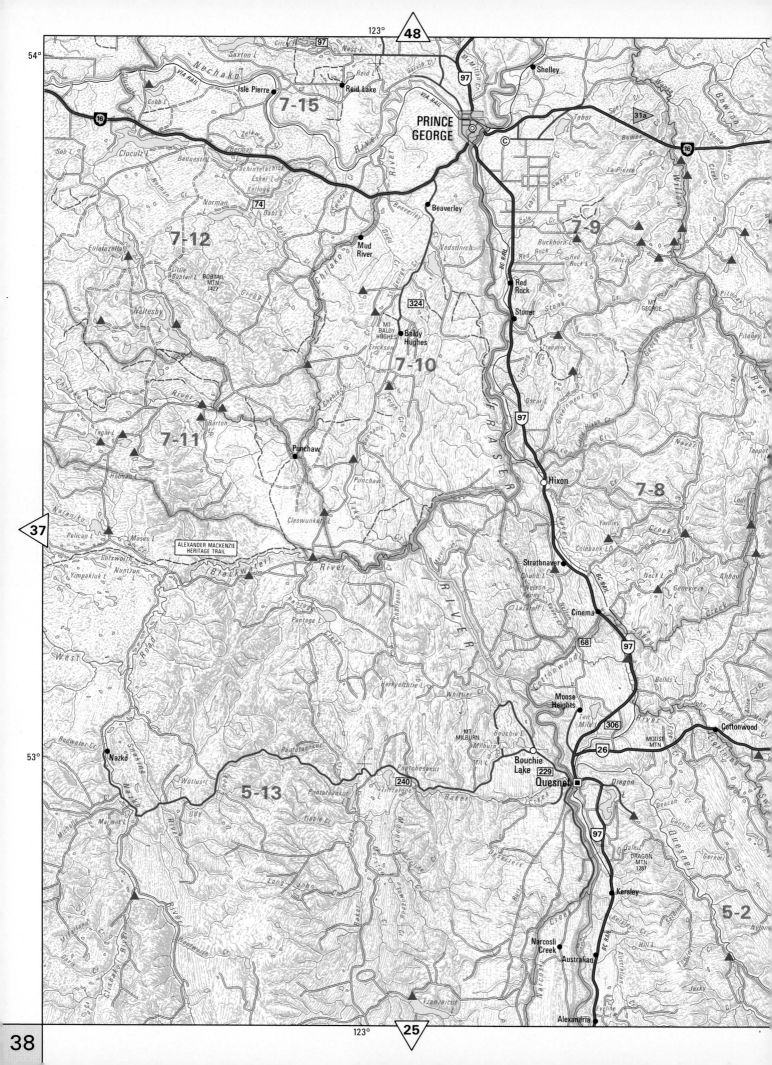

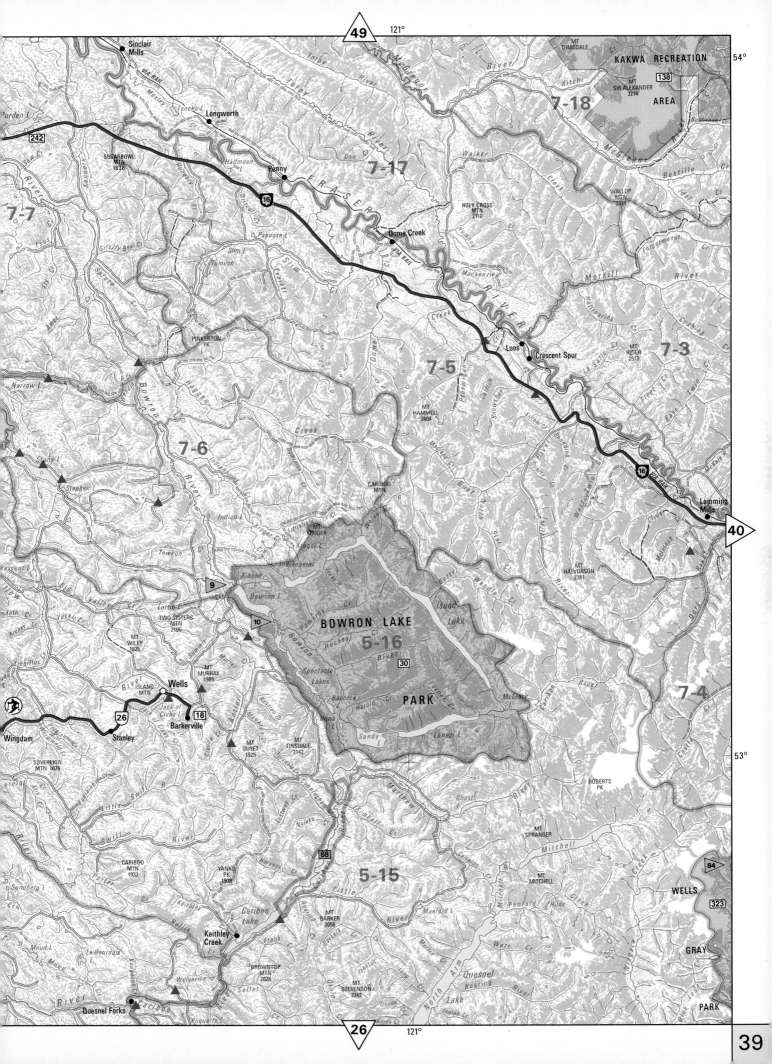

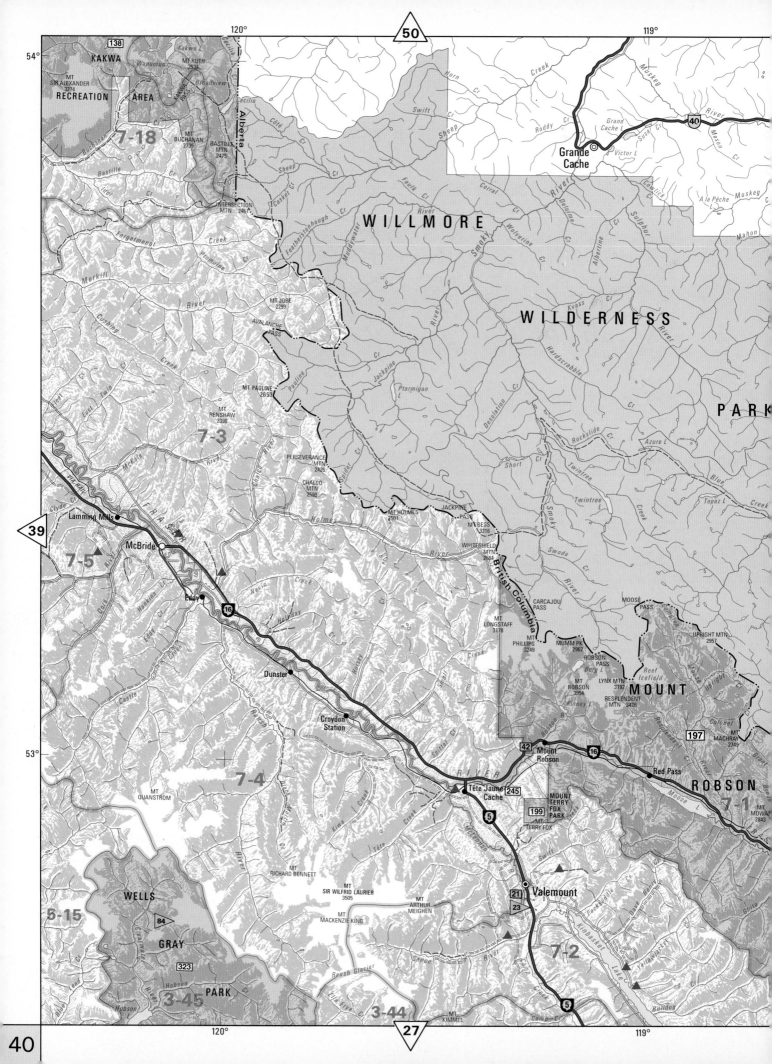

54°

120°

119°

KAKWA

138

MT SIR ALEXANDER 3274

MT RUTH 2534

Kakwa L

Wapunum

Broadview

Cecilia Cr

Kakwa Pass

RECREATION AREA

7-18

Buchanan

Bastille Cr

Igor Cr

MT BUCHANAN 2735

Côté Cr

BASTILLE MTN 2475

INTERSECTION MTN 2461

Alberta

Cecilia Cr

Creek

Sheep Cr

Casket Cr

Featherstonhaugh

Horn Creek

Swift Cr

Sheep Cr

Cr

Grande Cache L

40

Victor L

Muskeg River

Susa Cr

Grand Cache Cr

Roddy Cr

Grande Cache

Cowlick Cr

Mason Cr

A la Pêche Muskeg C

Mahon

Morkill River

Forgetmenot Cr

Promaine Cr

Creek

MT JOBE 2299

AVALANCHE PASS

Muddywater

River

Smoky

WILLMORE

Faulk Cr

Corral Cr

River

Wolverine Cr

Delome Cr

Sulphur Cr

Albertine Cr

W I L D E R N E S S

Kvass Cr

Cushing Creek

MT PAULINE 2653

MT RENSHAW 2398

Pauline Cr

7-3

Chalco River

Jackpine

Cr

Ptarmigan L

Suide Cr

Hardscrabble

River

Desolation Cr

Rockslide Cr

Short Cr

Twintree

Azure L

P A R K

PERSEVERANCE MTN 2426

CHALCO MTN 2598

Holmes

MT HOLMES 2501

JACKPINE PASS

MT BESS 3216

Twintree Creek

Blue Creek

Topaz L

East Twin Cr

Fleet Cr

McKale River

FRASER

Clyde Cr

Lamming Mills

Hankins Cr

39

7-5

McBride

Eddy

16

River

Dore River

Nevin Creek

Holliday Cr

Holmes River

WHITESHEELD MTN 2684

British Columbia

Swoda River

Smoky River

CARCAJOU PASS

MOOSE PASS

UPRIGHT MTN 2957

Reef Icefield

Uright Cr

MT LONGSTAFF 3178

MT PHILLIPS 3249

MUMM PK 2962

ROBSON PASS

Berg L

LYNX MTN 3192

M O U N T

Moose Cr

Dunster

Castle Cr

Raush River

MT QUANSTROM

7-4

Blackwater Cr

Kiwa Creek

Horsey Cr

Small Creek

Spittal Cr

Croydon Station

R I V E R

Robson R

MT ROBSON 3954

Kinney L

RESPLENDENT MTN 3426

Colonel Cr

197

MT MACHRAY 2749

42

Mount Robson

16

Resplendent Cr

Red Pass

R O B S O N

7-1

Moose L

MDWAT 2843

T.R.A.S.

WELLS

5-15

84

GRAY

323

PARK

3-45

Castle Cr

Clearwater R

Blue Lead Cr

Hobson Cr

Hobson L

MT RICHARD BENNETT

MT SIR WILFRID LAURIER 3505

MT ARTHUR MEIGHEN

MT MACKENZIE KING

Raush Glacier

Tête Creek

Kiwa Creek

Ella Frye Cr

Tête Jaune Cache

245

5

Whitman Cr

MOUNT TERRY FOX PARK

199

MT TERRY FOX

21

23

Valemount

Swift Cr

Canoe River

7-2

Kinbasket

Backsaddle Cr

Dave Henry Cr

Yellowjacket Cr

Ghita Cr

Camp Cr

Canoe R

5

MT KIMMEL

3-44

53°

40

120°

119°

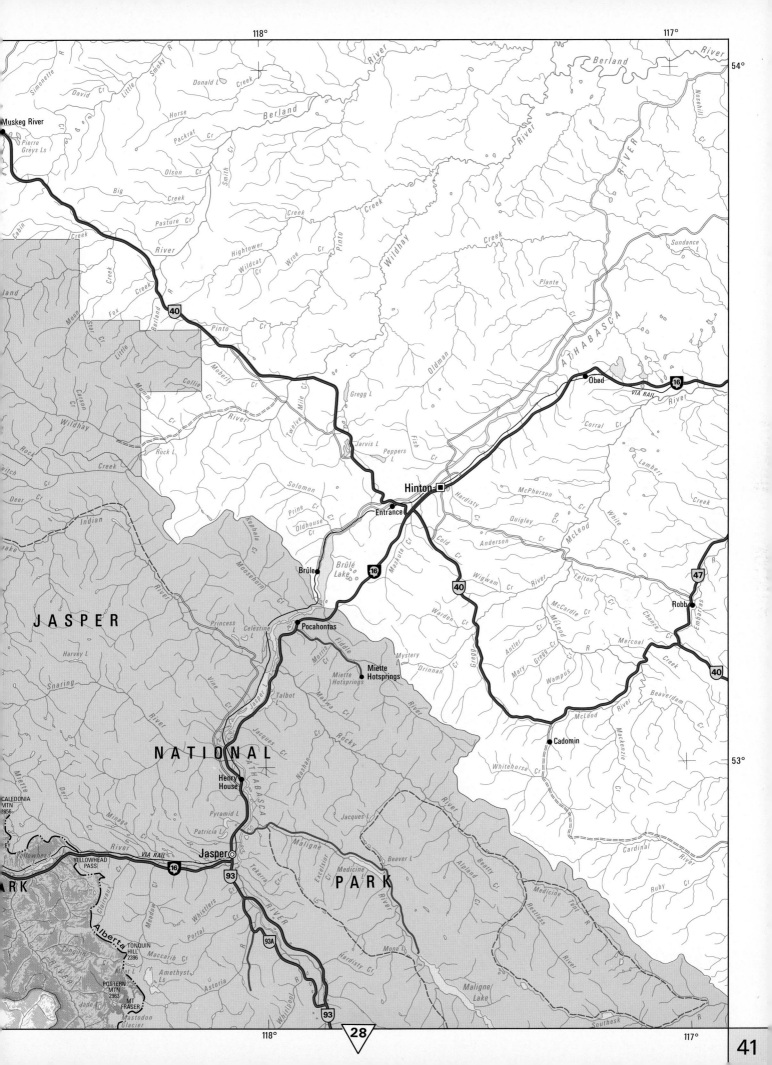

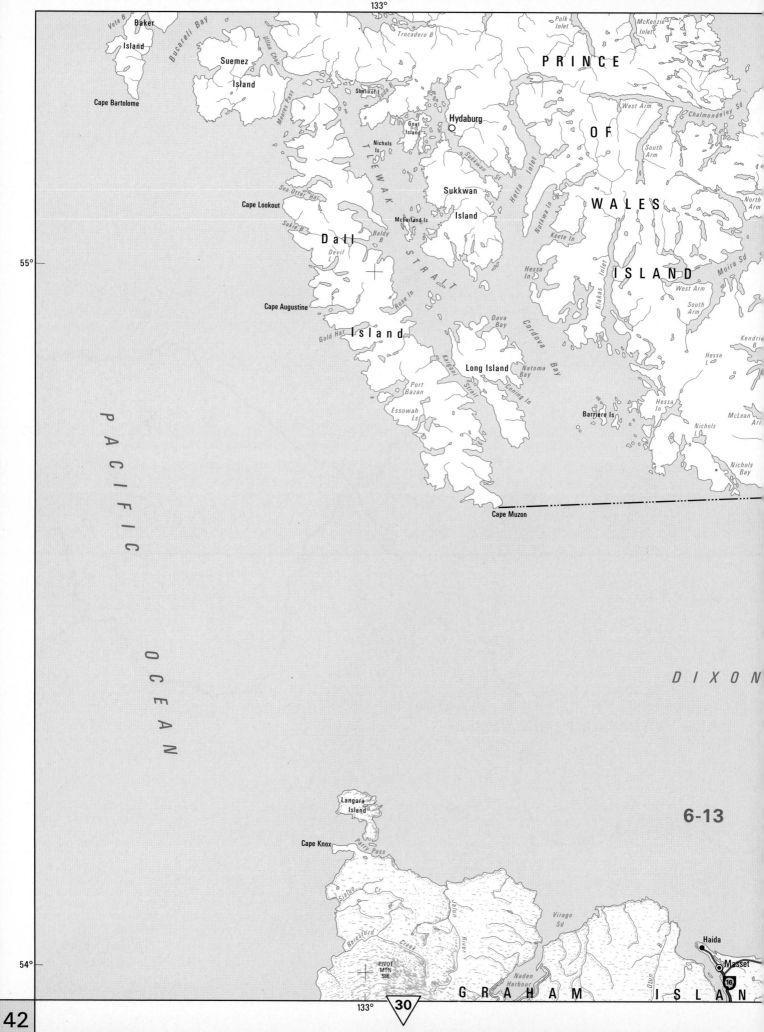

133°

Veta B
Baker
Island
Suemez
Island
Cape Bartolome

Bucareli Bay
Trocadero B
Polk Inlet
McKenzie Inlet

PRINCE

Shelikof I
Soda B

Nichols Is

Goat Island
Hydaburg

OF

WALES

West Arm
Chalmondeley Sd

South Arm

TLEWAK

Sukkwan
Island

Sukkwan St

Hetta Inlet

Nutkwa In

Keete In

Klakas Inlet

ISLAND

Moira Sd

North Arm

55°

Sea Otter Har

Cape Lookout

Sakie B

Dall

Devil L

Baldy B

McFarland Is

STRAIT

Hessa In

West Arm

South Arm

Cape Augustine

Rose In

Gold Har

Island

Dova Bay

Cordova Bay

Hessa L

Kendrie B

Long Island

Natoma Bay

Kaigani Strait

Caning In

Port Bazan

Essowah Is

Barriere Is

Hessa In

McLean Arm

Nichols L

PACIFIC

Cape Muzon

Nichols Bay

DIXON

OCEAN

6-13

Langara
Island

Cape Knox

Parry Pass

Sialun Cr

Beresford

Creek

Jalun River

Jalun R

Virago Sd

Haida

Naden Harbour

GRAHAM

ISLAN

Masset

16

54°

PIVOT MTN 586

30

133°

42

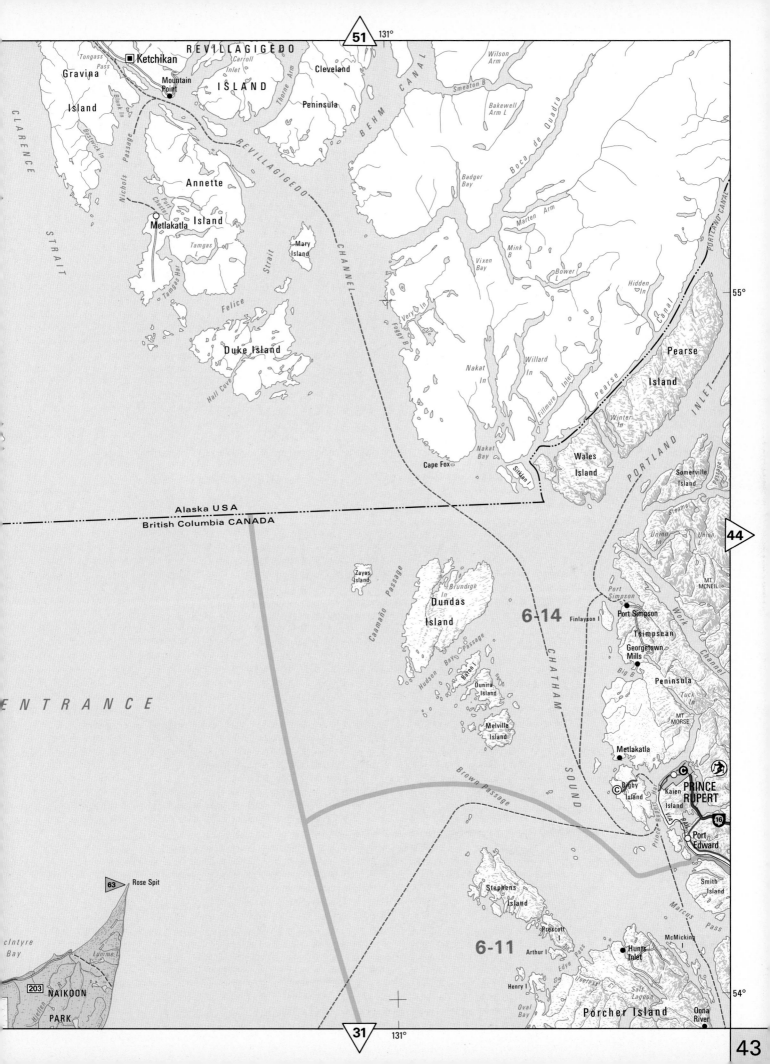

REVILLAGIGEDO
51 131°

Ketchikan
Gravina

Mountain
Point

ISLAND

Cleveland

Peninsula

BEHM CANAL

Wilson
Arm

Smeaton B.

Bakewell
Arm L.

Boca de Quadra

Island

Annette

Tongass
Pass

Blank In.

Nichols Passage

Port Chester

Metlakatla

Island

Tamgas

REVILLAGIGEDO CHANNEL

Mary
Island

Badger
Bay

Marten Arm

Mink
B.

Bower
L.

Hidden
In.

55°

Pearse

Island

PORTLAND CANAL

Tamgas Har.

Felice

Strait

Duke Island

Hall Cove

Vixen
Bay

Nakat
In.

Willard
In.

Fillmore Inlet

Foggy B.

Very In.

Nakat
Bay

Cape Fox

Pearse

Winter
In.

Wales
Island

Canal

Somerville
Island

Passage

Sitklan I.

CLARENCE   STRAIT

Steamer

PORTLAND   INLET

Alaska USA
British Columbia CANADA

44

Union
In.

Union
In.

MT.
McNEIL

Zayas
Island

Caamaño Passage

Brundige
In.

Dundas
Island

6-14

Finlayson I.

Port
Simpson

Port Simpson

Tsimpsean

Work Channel

ENTRANCE

Hudson Bay

Baron I.

Passage

Dunira
Island

Georgetown
Mills

Big B.

Peninsula

Tuck
In.

MT
MORSE

Melville
Island

Metlakatla

CHATHAM   SOUND

Digby
Island

Kaien
Island

PRINCE
RUPERT

Prince Rupert Har.

Brown Passage

Port
Edward

16

Rose Spit
63

Stephens
Island

6-11

Arthur I.

Prescott

Hunts
Inlet

McMicking

Smith
Island

Marcus Pass

Edye Pass

McIntyre Bay

Lumme L.

Hellen R.

203

NAIKOON

PARK

Henry I.

Useless

Oval
Bay

Salt
Lagoon

Porcher Island

Oona
River

54°

31 131°

43

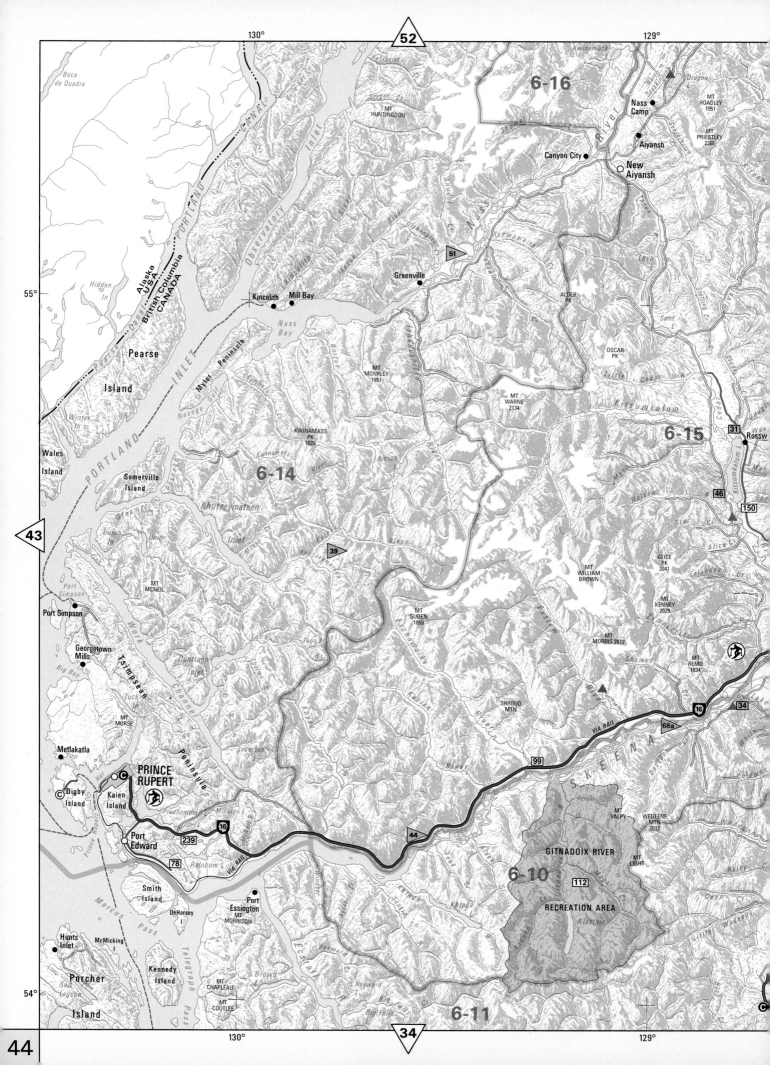

43

6-16

Dragon
MT HOADLEY
1951
Nass
Camp
MT PRIESTLEY
2368
Kwinamuck

Aiyansh

Canyon City

New
Aiyansh

Kelsikst

Stagoo Cr

MT HUNTINGDON

Shumal

51

Greenville

ALDER
PK

6-15

Rossw

31

Kincolith   Mill Bay

55°

Nass Bay

OSCAR
PK

46

150

Boca
de Quadra

Hidden
In

Alaska
U.S.A.
British Columbia
CANADA

Pearse
Island

Winter
In

Mylor Peninsula

MT MONKLEY
1951

MT WARNE
2134

Nasoga Gulf

Columbas Cr

KWINAMASS
PK
1829

Kwinamass River

6-14

MT
WILLIAM
BROWN

ALICE
PK
2041

MT
KENNEY
2029

Wales
Island

Somerville
Island

Khutzeymateen

Khutzemateen River

39

MT SUDEN
1859

MT
MORRIS 2012

MT REMO
1934

MT McNEIL

Union
In

Steamer

Port
Simpson

SHROUD
MTN

68a

16

34

Port Simpson

MT
MORSE

Quattoch Inlet

Leverson

99

Georgetown
Mills

Big Bay

Metlakatla

PRINCE
RUPERT

Kaien
Island

Digby
Island

Prudhomme

16

239

Port
Edward

78

Rainbow I

Smith
Island

DeHorsey

Port
Essington
MT
MORRISON

Hunts
Inlet

McMicking

Kennedy
Island

MT
CHAPLEAU

MT
COUTLEE

Porcher
Island

Marcus Pass

Telegraph Pass

44

MT VALPY

WEDEENE
MTN
2012

MT
LIGHT

GITNADOIX RIVER

6-10

112

RECREATION
AREA

6-11

54°

130°   129°

34

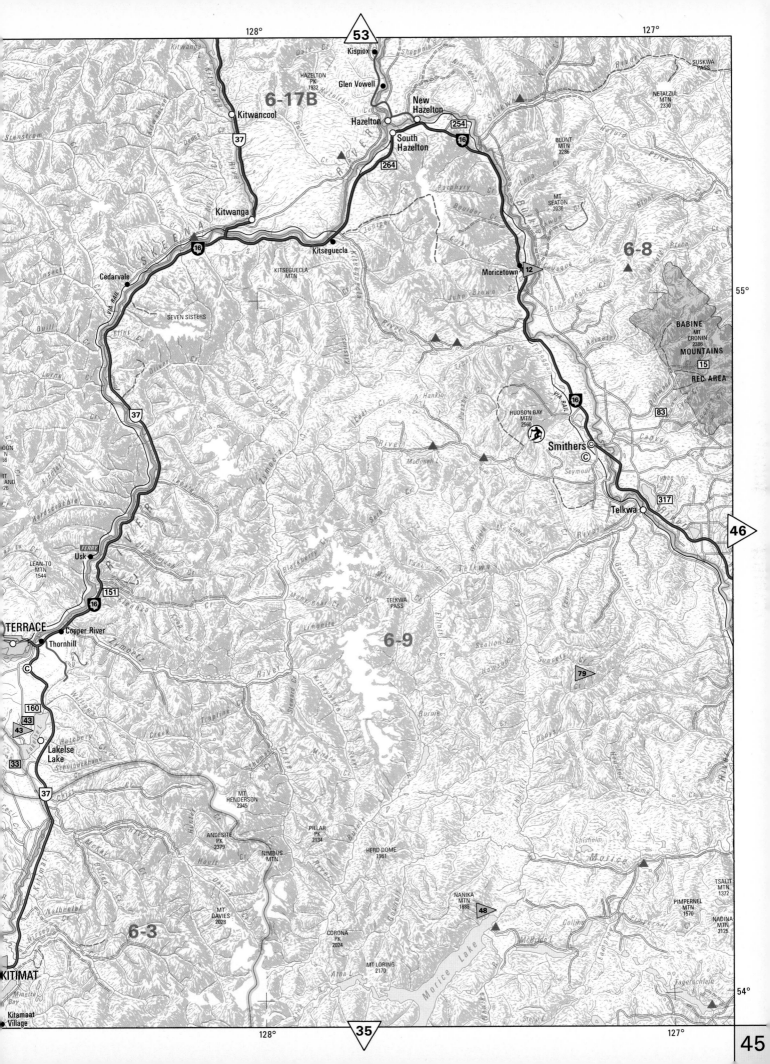

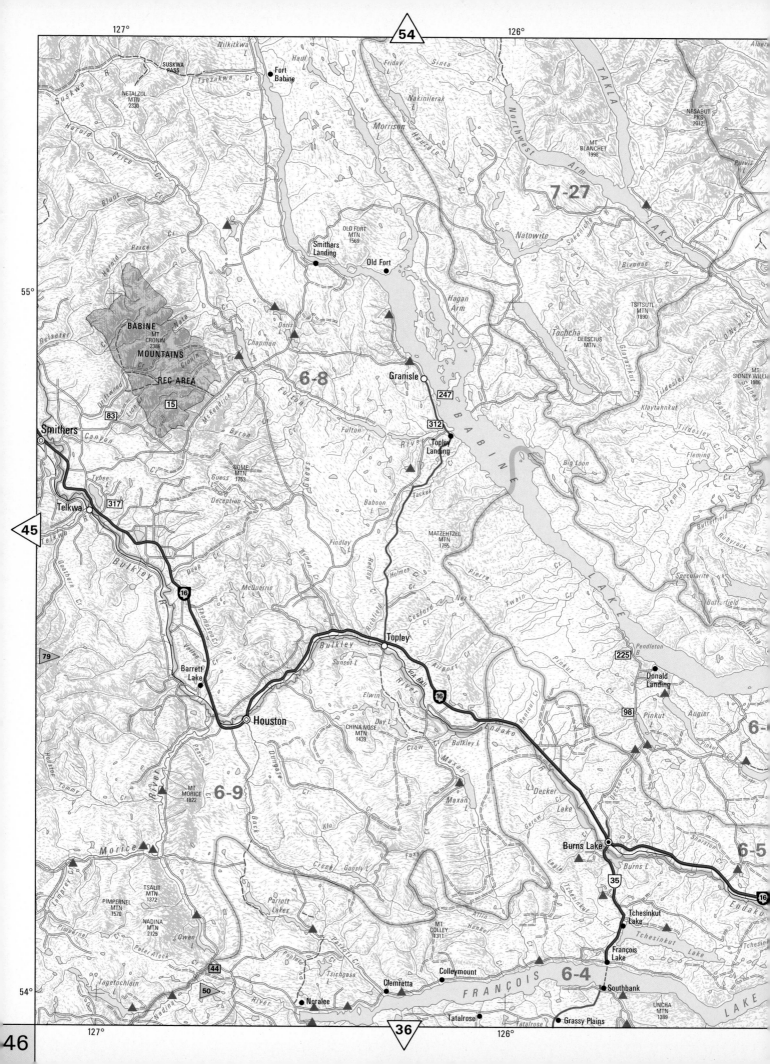

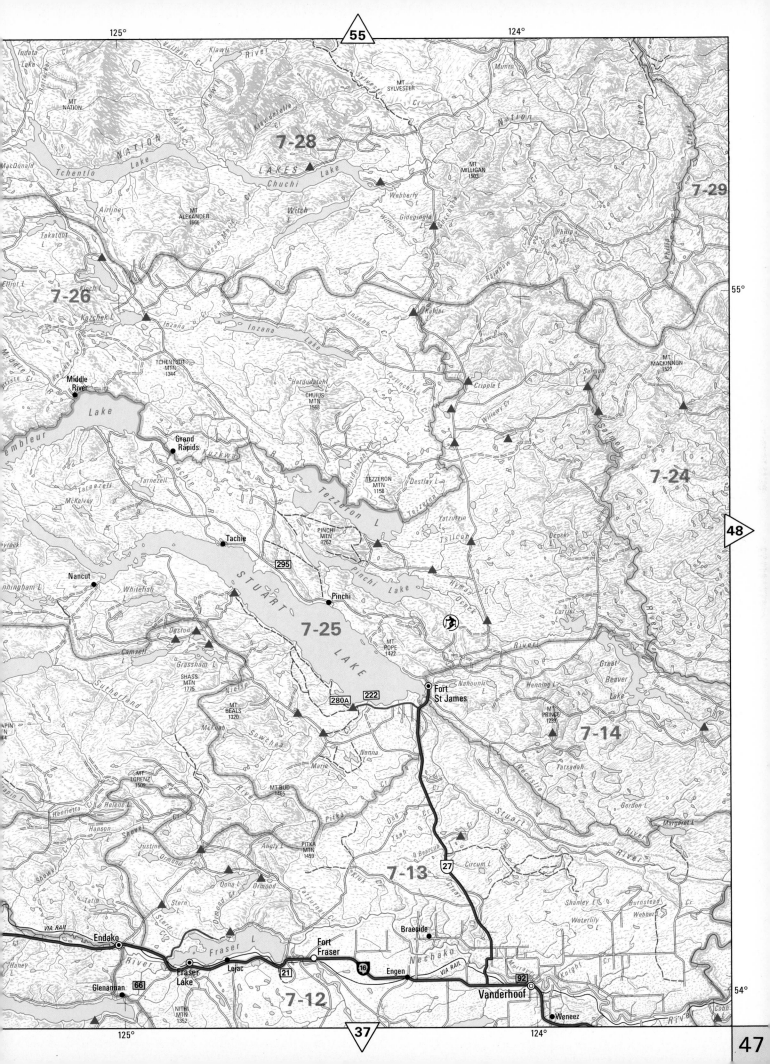

125°
124°

7-28

7-29

MT
SYLVESTER

MT
NATION

MT
MILLIGAN
1503

NATION

Webberly
L

Chuchi Lake

Gidegingla
L

Witch
L

LAKES

MT
ALEXANDER
1666

Airline
L

Rainbow Cr

55°

Takatoot
L

Kalder

7-26

Elliot L

Kloch L

Cripple L

MT
MACKINNON
1527

Kazchek L

Inzana

Inzana Lake

Inzana Cr

Salmon

Middle
River

TCHENTOUT
MTN
1344

Willowy Cr

Hatdudatehl

CHUIUS
MTN
1568

Lake

Grand
Rapids

Kuzkwa

7-24

Destlay L

Tarnezell

Tachie

TEZZERON
MTN
1158

Yatzutzin

McKelvay

Tezzeron L

Tazzeron

Tsilcoh

Oceek

Nancut

PINCHI
MTN
1267

Whitefish

Pinchi Lake

Hymal Cr

295

Pinchi

7-25

Cartier

Ogston

STUART

MT
POPE
1472

Camsell
L

Grassham L

SHASS
MTN
1775

LAKE

Nielsp

Fort
St James

Nahounli
Cr

Great
Beaver
Lake

MT
BEALS
1320

Sowchea

280A

222

MT
PRINCE
1295

7-14

McNab

Nenna

Henning L

MT
LORENZ
1509

Marie

Helene L

Tatsadah

Henrietta L

Stuart

Hanson

MT BUD
1465

Pitka

Gordon L

Shovel Cr

Ormond Cr

River

27

Margaret L

Justine L

Ormond

PITKA
MTN
1459

Tsah Cr

Circum L

Oona L

Skyuk

O Bearcub

Stern

Angly L

Shanley L

Burnstead
Cr

Stern

7-13

Tatsuma

Webber Cr

Waterlily L

VIA RAIL

Endako

Braeside

7-12

Fraser L

Fort
Fraser

Nechako

Fraser
Lake

Lejac

21

16

Engen

VIA RAIL

92

Glenannan

66

NITHI
MTN
1352

Vanderhoof

Weneez

Cobb

125°
124°
54°

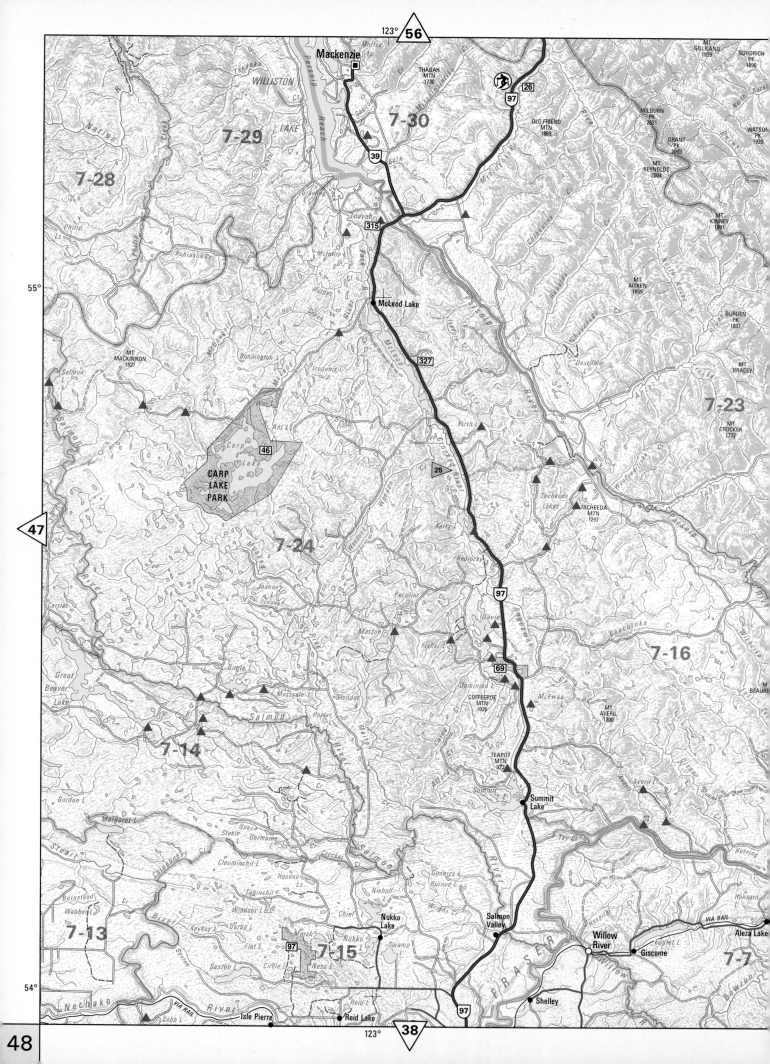

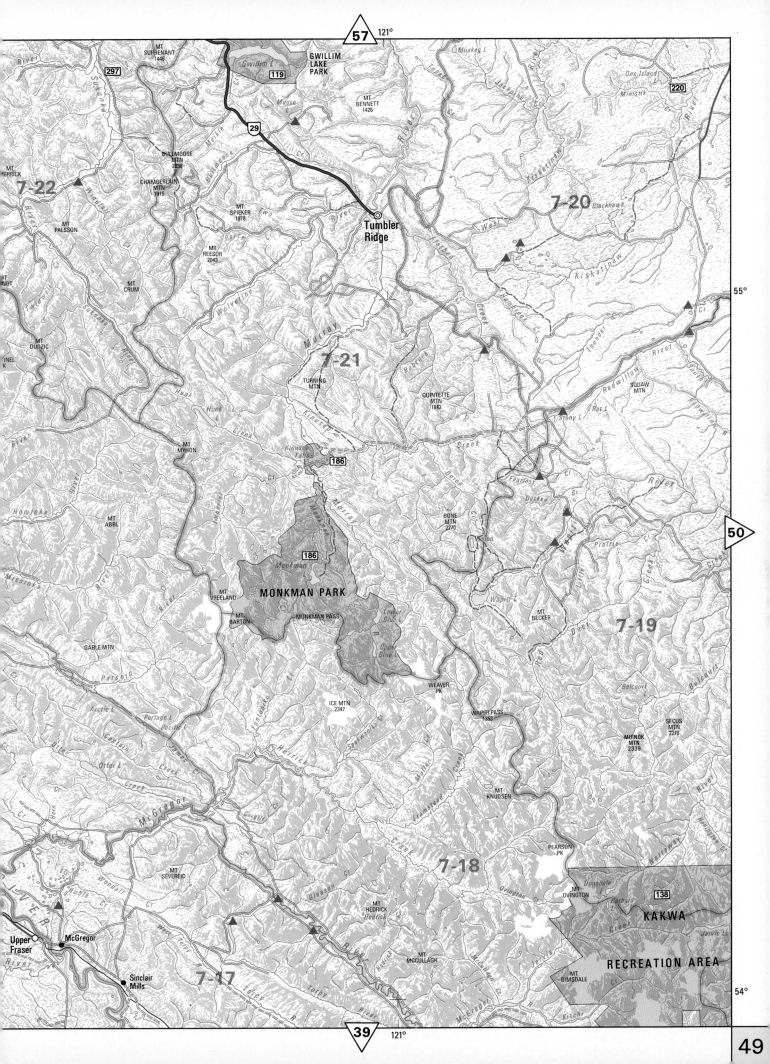

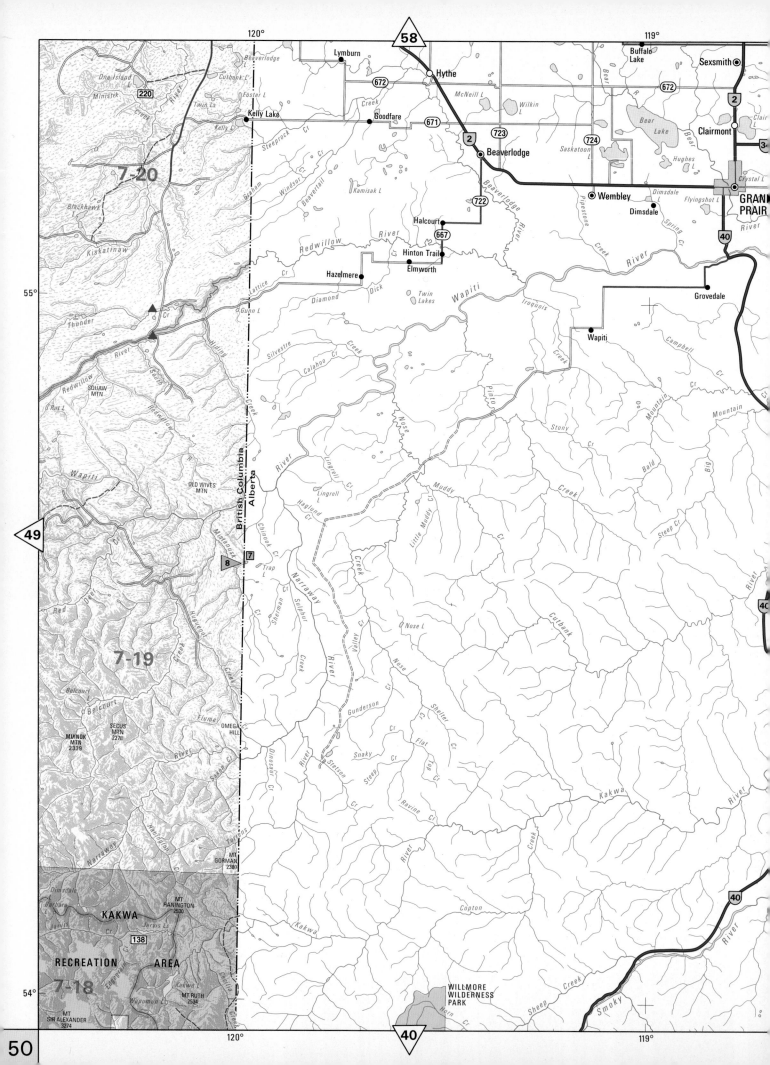

120°

119°

Lymburn

Buffalo
Lake

Sexsmith

Hythe

672

McNeill L

672

Wilkin
L

2

Beaverlodge
L

One Island
L

Ministik

220

Cutbank L

Foster L

Kelly Lake

Goodfare

671

723

724

Clairmont

7-20

Kelly L

Steeprock Cr

Windsor Cr

Cr

Cr

Beavertail Cr

Kamisak L

Beaverlodge

722

Wembley

Saskatoon
L

Bear
Lake

Dimsdale
L

Flyingshot L

Dimsdale

Hughes
L

Crystal L

GRAN
PRAIR

Blackhawk
L

Kiskatinaw

Graham

Redwillow

River

Halcourt

667

Beaverlodge River

Pipestone Creek

Spring Cr

40

55°

Lattice Cr

Hinton Trail

Elmworth

Hazelmere

Dick Cr

Twin
Lakes

Wapiti

Iroquois

River

Wapiti

Grovedale

Thunder

Cr

Redwillow

River

Hiding Creek

Sacht

Diamond

Silvestre

Calahoo Cr

Creek

Nose

River

Pinto

Creek

Stony Cr

Campbell

Cr

Mountain

Squaw
MTN

O Rat L

Redwillow R

Old Wives
MTN

Lingrell Cr

Lingrell
L

Muddy Cr

Little Muddy Cr

Bald

Big

Mountain

Wapiti

British Columbia
Alberta

Misaulusk

49

Creek

7

8

Trap
L

Chinook Cr

Haglund
Cr

Creek

Steep Cr

Red
Deer

Huguenot

Cr

Sherman Cr

Sulphur

Narraway River

Valley Cr

Nose L

Nose Cr

Cutbank Creek

Creek

40

7-19

Belcourt
L

O Belcourt L

SECUS
MTN
2278

Flume

OMEGA
HILL

Saxon Cr

River

River

Gunderson Cr

Snaky Cr

Steep Cr

Shelter Cr

Flat Top Cr

MUINOK
MTN
2339

Dinosaur Cr

River

Stetson

Ravine Cr

Kakwa

River

River

Narraway

Hanington

MT
GORMAN
2380

Steep
Cr

Copton

Creek

Smoky

River

40

Dimsdale

Barbara
L

MT
HANINGTON
2530

KAKWA

Jarvis
Cr

Jarvis Ls

138

Kakwa

Creek

Sheep

Creek

River

RECREATION

AREA

7-18

Eikenpan

Wupumin

Kakwa
L

MT RUTH
2534

WILLMORE
WILDERNESS
PARK

Horn Cr

MT SIR
ALEXANDER
3274

Dokita Cr

119°

54°

120°

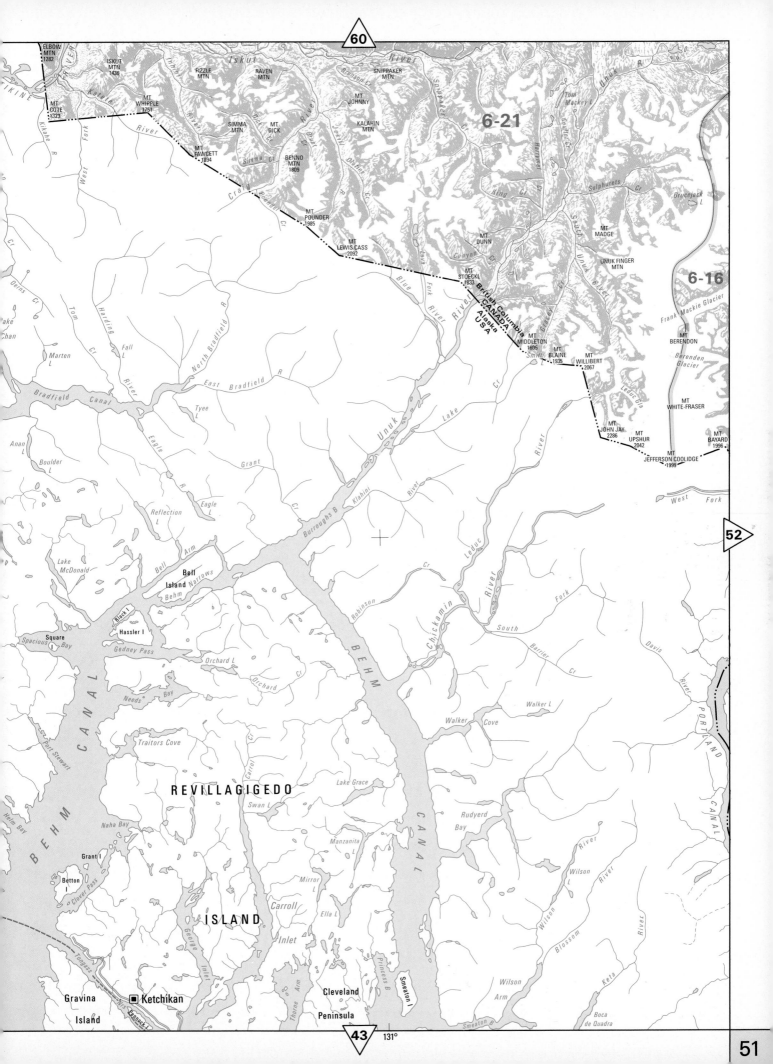

ELBOW
MTN
1282

ISKUT
MTN
1436

FIZZLE
MTN

RAVEN
MTN

Iskut River

SNIPPAKER
MTN

Tom
Mackey L

6-21

MT
COTE
1323

MT
WHIPPLE
1751

SIMMA
MTN

MT
DICK

MT
JOHNNY

KALAHIN
MTN

MT
FAWCETT
1894

BENNO
MTN
1809

Sulphurets Cr

Brucejack
L

MT
POUNDER
1985

MT
LEWIS CASS
2092

MT
DUNN

MT
MADGE

UNUK FINGER
MTN

6-16

MT
STOECKL
1833

British Columbia
CANADA
Alaska
USA

Frank Mackie Glacier

MT
MIDDLETON
1605

Smith L

MT
BLAINE
1935

MT
WILLIBERT
2067

MT
BERENDON

Berenden
Glacier

MT
WHITE-FRASER

MT
JOHN JAY
2286

MT
UPSHUR
2042

MT
JEFFERSON COOLIDGE
1999

MT
BAYARD
1996

West Fork

Oerns Cr

Tom Harding Cr

North Bradfield R

Fall L

Marten L

Bradfield Canal

East Bradfield R

Tyee L

Grant R

Eagle L

Reflection L

Anan L

Boulder L

Eagle R

Bell Arm

Bell Island

Behm Narrows

Lake McDonald

Black I

Hassler I

Burroughs B

Klahini River

Leduc River

Chickamin River

South Fork

Barrier Cr

Davis River

Square Bay

Spacious Bay

Gedney Pass

Orchard L

Robinson Cr

Walker L

Needs Bay

Orchard Cr

Orchard L

Traitors Cove

BEHM CANAL

Walker Cove

Port Stewart

Carroll Cr

Helm Bay

Naha Bay

Carroll Inlet

REVILLAGIGEDO

Lake Grace

Swan L

BEHM CANAL

Rudyerd Bay

PORTLAND CANAL

Grant I

Betton I

Clover Pass

Mirror L

Manzanita L

Wilson River

Wilson River

ISLAND

Carroll Inlet

Ella L

Blossom River

Wilson Arm

Keta River

Gravina Island

Ketchikan

George Inlet

Thorne Arm

Princess B

Smeaton I

Cleveland

Peninsula

Smeaton Bay

Boca de Quadra

Tongass Narrows

131°

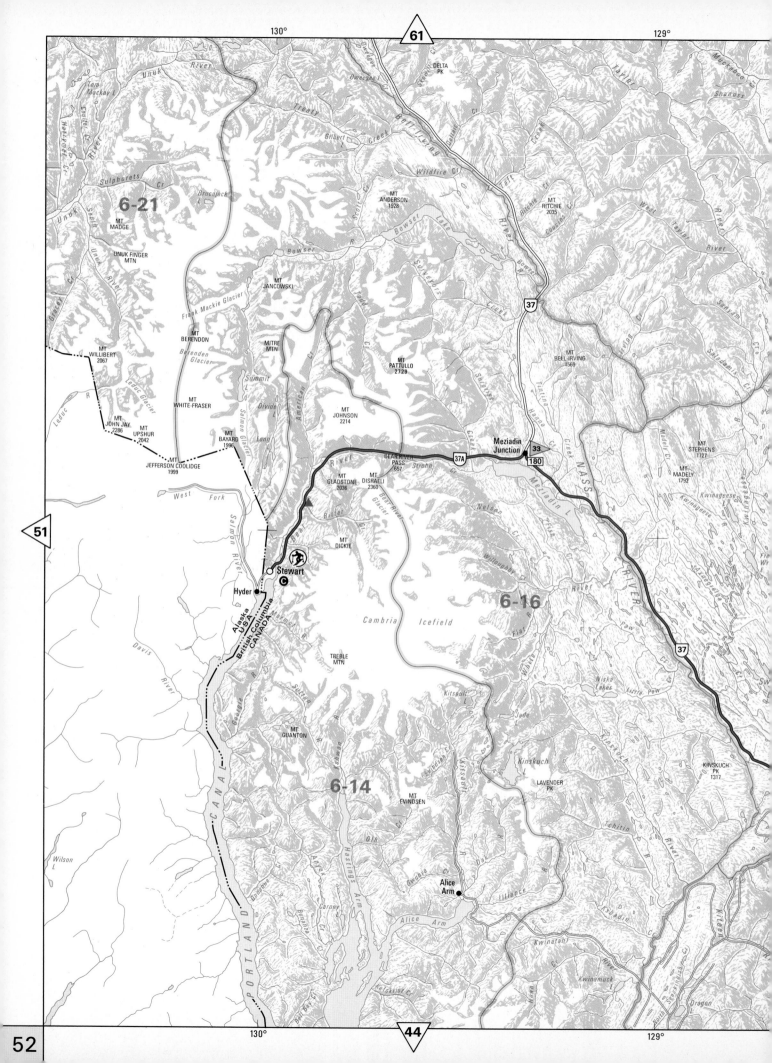

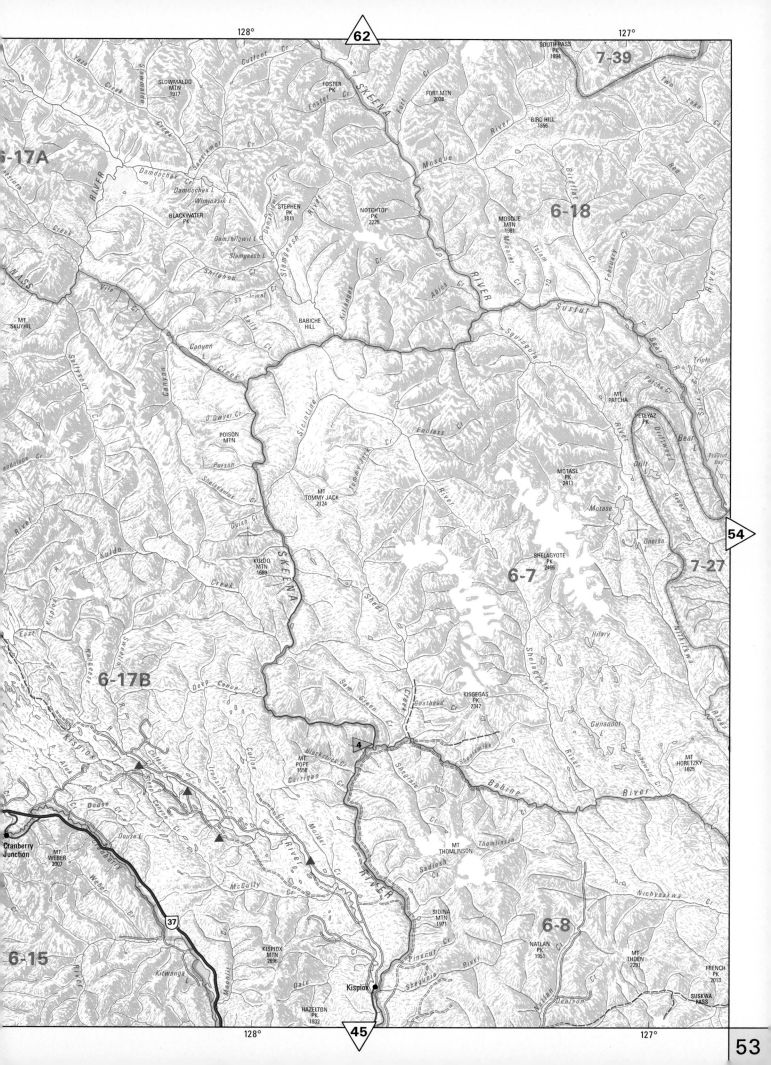

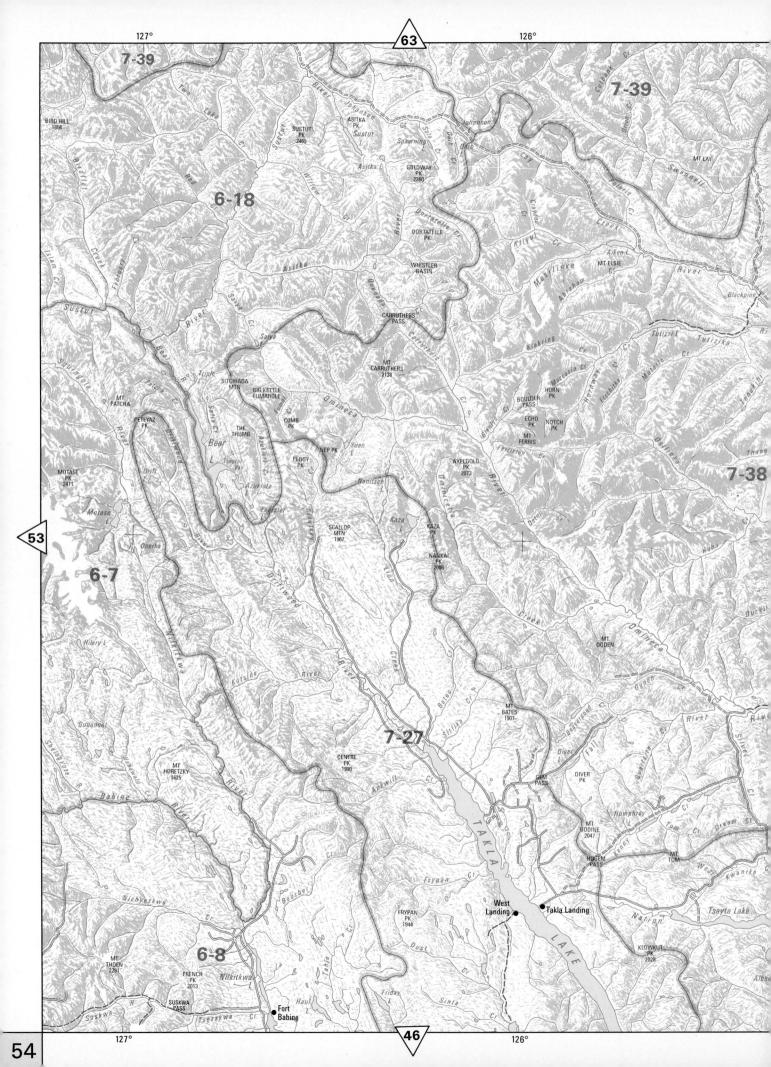

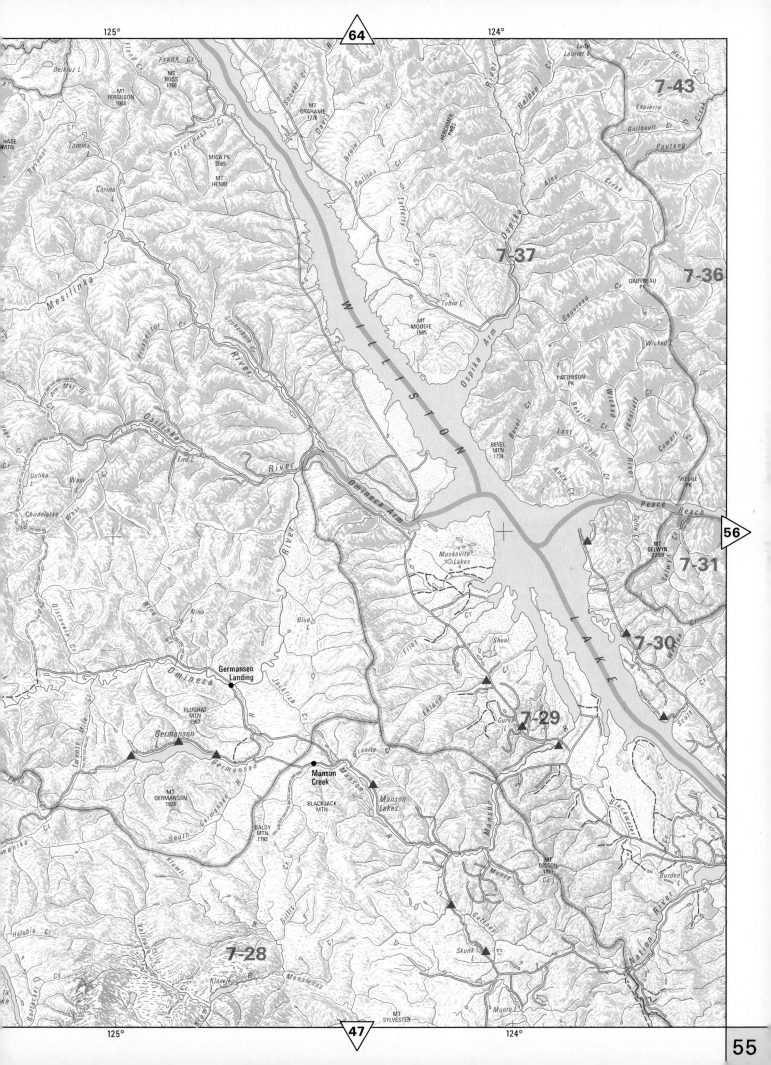

125°

124°

Delkluz L

HASE MTN

Ravenal Cr

Tomias L

MT FERGUSON 1988

Frank Cr

MT ROSS 1766

Flood Cr

Shovel Cr

Davis Cr

MT GRAHAME 1726

Lady Laurier L

Horn Cr

7-43

Balden Cr

Lapierre Cr

Guilbault Cr

Poutang Cr

MICA PK 2065

MT HENRI

Factor Ross Cr

Carina L

Mesilinka

Collins Cr

Tafferty Cr

Brain Cr

HERCIMER PASS

Ospika River

Aley Creek

7-37

GAUVREAU PK

7-36

Prospector Cr

Connachute Cr

Tobin L

MT MOODIE 1565

Gauvreau Cr

Wicked L

PATTINSON PK

Jim May Cr

Osilinka River

End L

River

Bevel Cr

Lost Cabin Cr

Beattie Cr

Ignatieff Cr

Wicked River

Cowart Cr

Tarlatt Cr

Vega Cr

Uslika L

Wasi Cr

Wasi L

Omineca Arm

BEVEL MTN 1734

Andy Cr

WEDGE PK

Chudelatsa L

Peace Reach

MT SELWYN 2299

56

Muskovite Lakes

Gohi Cr

Selwyn Cr

7-31

Discovery Cr

River

Nina L

Blue L

W I L L I S T O N

L A K E

7-30

Cr

Scott Cr

Germansen Landing

Jackfish Cr

Fries Cr

Shoal Cr

Ekland Cr

Curve L

7-29

R

Twenty Mile Cr

Omineca

PLUGHAT MTN 1967

Germansen L

Ripe Cr

Pine Cr

Granite Cr

Manson Creek

Manson Cr

Manson Lakes

Manson R

Blackwater

Germansen R

MT GERMANSEN 1926

BLACKJACK MTN

Klawli Cr

BALDY MTN 1782

South Germansen R

Gullis Cr

MT BISSON 1851

Burden Cr

wanika Cr

Halobia Cr

7-28

Klawli R

Moosmoos Cr

Munro Cr

Gaffney Cr

Nation River

Twin

Rockecker Cr

take

Klawli R

Skunk L

MT SYLVESTER

Munro L

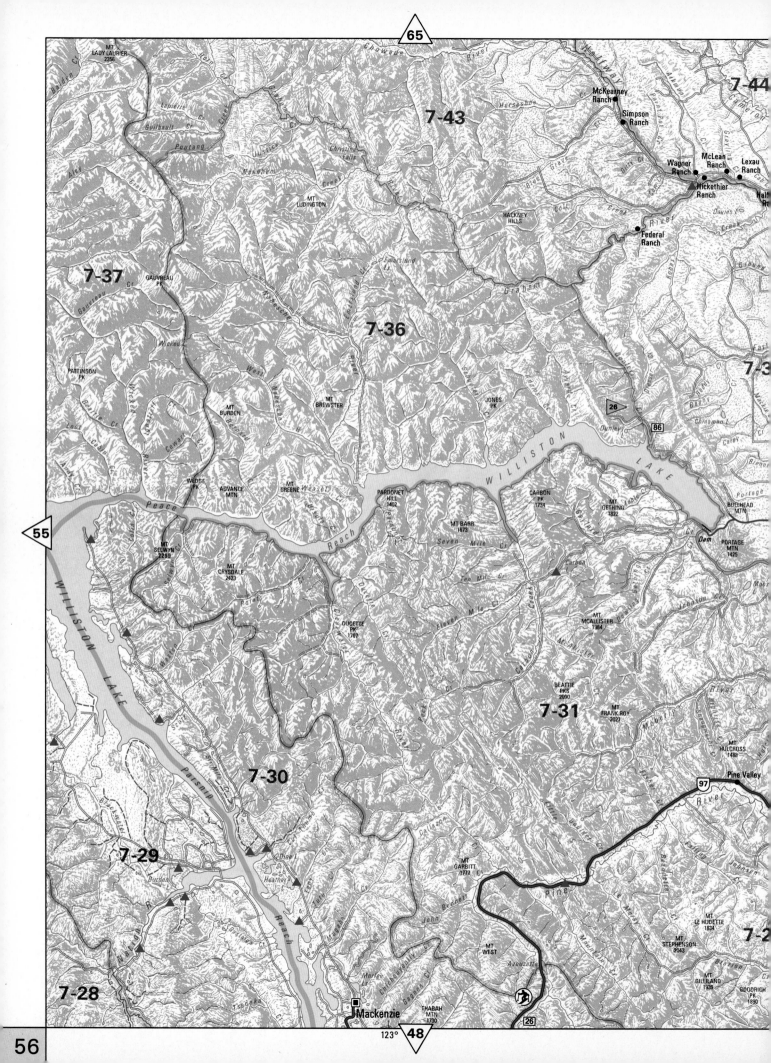

7-44

7-43

McKearney
Ranch

Simpson
Ranch

Wagner
Ranch

McLean
Ranch

Lexau
Ranch

Hickethier
Ranch

Half
Ra

7-3

7-37

GAUVREAU
PK

Federal
Ranch

MT
LADY LAURIER
2356

MT
LUDINGTON

HACKNEY
HILLS

7-36

MT
BREWSTER

MT
BURDEN

JONES
PK

26

86

PATTINSON
PK

WEDGE
PK

ADVANCE
MTN

MT
GREENE

PARDONET
HILL
1402

CARBON
PK
1734

MT
GETHING
1822

BULLHEAD
MTN

WILLISTON   LAKE

MT
SELWYN
2298

MT
CRYSDALE
2423

MT BARR
1673

Dam

PORTAGE
MTN
1425

DUCETTE
PK
1707

MT
MCALLISTER
1984

Carbon

WILLISTON   LAKE

BEATTIE
PKS
2090

MT
FRANK ROY
2027

7-31

MT
HULCROSS
1488

7-30

Pine Valley

97

7-29

MT
GARBITT
1777

MT
LE HUDETTE
1834

7-28

MT
WEST

MT
STEPHENSON
2043

7-2

Mackenzie

THABAH
MTN
1730

26

MT
GILLILAND
1939

GOODRICH
PK
1890

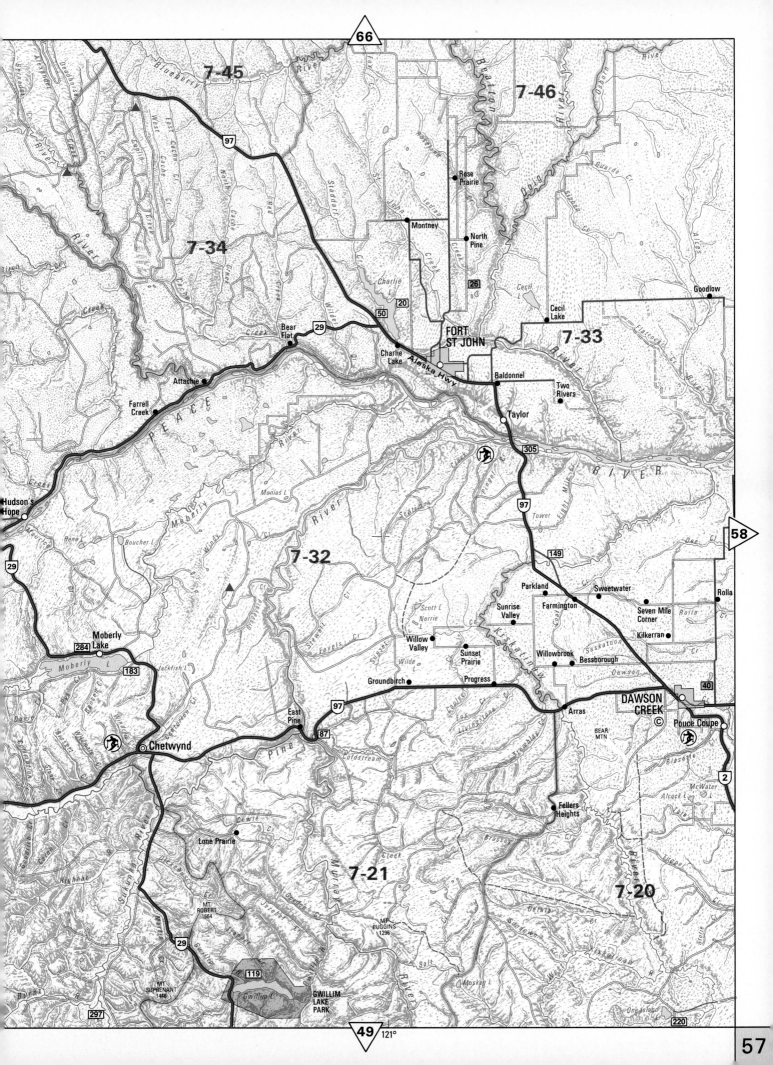

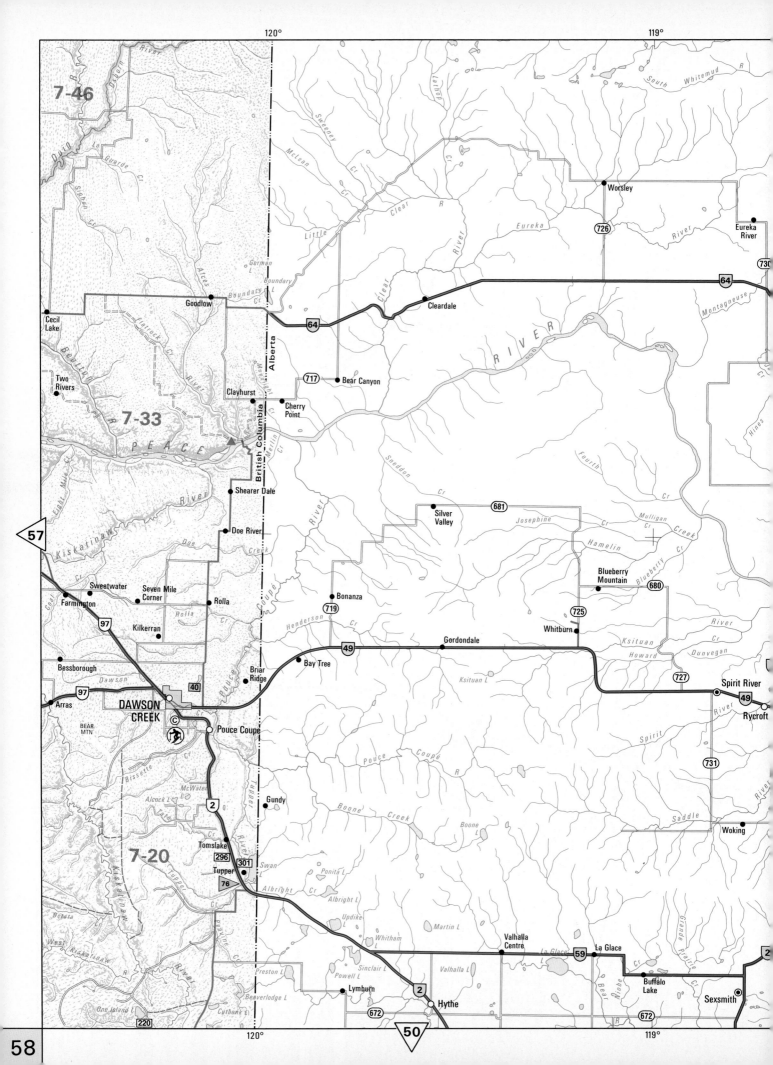

7-46

7-33

7-20

PEACE

RIVER

120°

119°

Worsley

Eureka River

726

730

64

Cecil Lake

Goodlow

Cleardale

64

717

Bear Canyon

Clayhurst

Cherry Point

Two Rivers

Shearer Dale

Silver Valley

681

Josephine

Blueberry Mountain

680

Doe River

57

Bonanza

719

Whitburn

725

Sweetwater

Seven Mile Corner

Rolla

Gordondale

Kilkerran

Bessborough

Bay Tree

49

Briar Ridge

Spirit River

727

97

Farmington

Arras

97

40

DAWSON CREEK

Pouce Coupe

49

Rycroft

731

BEAR MTN

Gundy

Woking

2

Tomslake

296

301

Tupper

76

Valhalla Centre

La Glace

59

220

Lymburn

2

Hythe

672

Buffalo Lake

Sexsmith

672

2

50

58

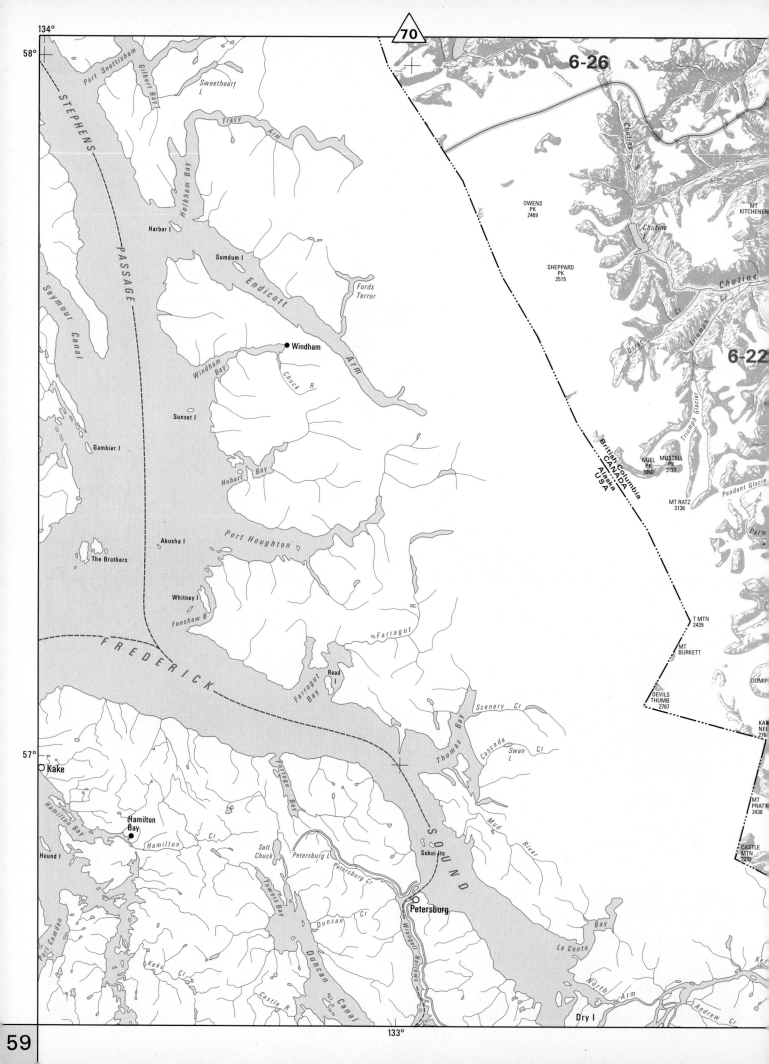

134°

58°

STEPHENS

Port Snettisham

Gilbert Bay

Sweetheart L

Tracy Arm

Holkham Bay

PASSAGE

Harbor I

Sumdum I

Endicott

Fords Terror

• Windham

Seymour Canal

Windham Bay

Chuck R

Arm

Sunset I

Gambier I

Hobart Bay

Akusha I

Port Houghton

The Brothers

Whitney I

Fanshaw B

Farragut R

FREDERICK

Farragut Bay

Read

57°

Kake

Hamilton Bay

Hamilton Bay

Hamilton Cr

Salt Chuck

Petersburg L

Petersburg Cr

Sukoi Its

Hound I

Towers Bay

Duncan Cr

Cr

Petersburg

Port Camden

Keku Cr

Castle R

Duncan Canal

Wrangell Narrows

Dry I

6-26

OWENS PK 2469

SHEPPARD PK 2515

Chutine R

Chutine I

Chutine

MT KITCHENER

Dist Cr

Triumph Cr

6-22

British Columbia
CANADA
Alaska
USA

NOEL PK 3060

MUSSELL PK 3127

Triumph Glacier

Pendant Glacier

MT RATZ 3136

Palm

T MTN 2439

MT BURKETT

DOMIN

DEVILS THUMB 2767

KA NE 276

SOUND

Scenery Cr

Thomas Bay

Cascade

Swan L

Cr

Mud River

MT PRAT 2438

CASTLE MTN 2233

Bay

Le Conte

North Arm

Andrew Cr

133°

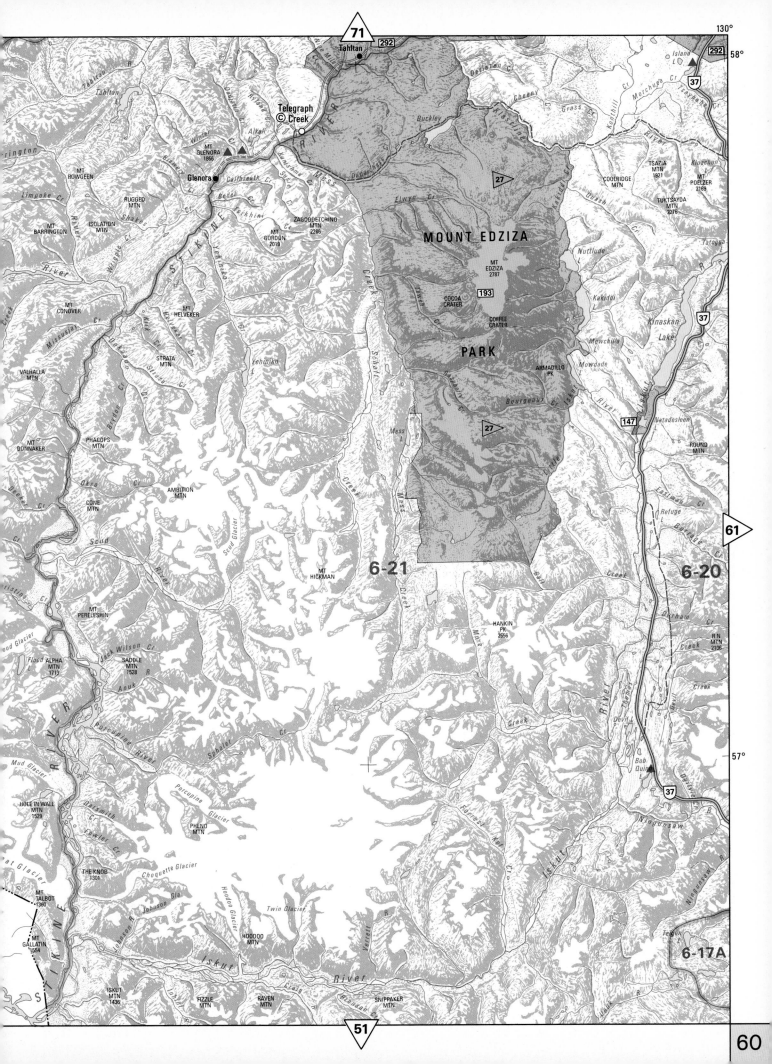

292

130°
58°

Island
L

292

37

Tahltan

Defieten Cr

Cheeny Cr

Grass Cr

Morchuea Cr

Tsorbahehe Cr

Telegraph
© Creek

Buckley

Klastline R

Foothill Cr

Quash L

TSAZIA
MTN
1921

Kluachon
L

COOLRIDGE
MTN

MT
POELZER
2169

MT GLENORA
1866

Glenora

Callbieeth Cr

Winter Cr

Alkali

Susie Cr

Kanashma Cr

Tsikhini

Bodel Cr

Zagoddetchino
MTN
2286

MT
GORDON
2019

Dagan hess

Elwyn Cr

27

MOUNT EDZIZA

MT
EDZIZA
2787

193

Kakidd Cr

Nuttlude
L

TUKTSAYDA
MTN
2276

Kakiddi
L

MT
ROWGEEN

MT
BARRINGTON

Limpoke Cr

ISOLATION
MTN

RUGGED
MTN

Shakes Cr

Wapple Cr

STIKINE RIVER

MESS

River

Kiklban Cr

MT
CONOVER

MT
HELVEKER

STRATA
MTN

Helvekan Cr

Kirk Cr

Dukwan Cr

Strata Cr

Yehiniko
L

Yehiniko

37

Kinaskan
Lake

VALHALLA
MTN

PHACOPS
MTN

Bordon Cr

Oksa Cr

Schielt Creek

Mess
L

COCOA
CRATER

COFFEE
CRATER

PARK

ARMADILLO
PK

Bourgeaux Cr

Iskut

Mowchilla

Mowdade

147

Natadesleen
L

ROUND
MTN

MT
DONNAKER

Queen Cr

Cr

Christina Cr

CONE
MTN

AMBITION
MTN

Scud

River

Scud Glacier

MT
HICKMAN

27

6-21

Mess

Creek

More

Creek

Iskut

River

6-20

61

Wood Glacier

Flood
L

MT
PERELESHIN

ALPHA
MTN
1713

Jack Wilson Cr

SADDLE
MTN
1528

Anuk R

HANKIN
PK
2556

Bixby Cr

Creek

Durham Cr

R N
MTN
2106

Mud Glacier

RIVER

HOLE IN WALL
MTN
1529

Darsmith Cr

Fowler Cr

Porcupine River

Sphaler Cr

Porcupine Glacier

PHENO
MTN

Creek

Forrest Kar Cr

Iskut River

Devil L

Bob
Quin
L

37

Ningunsaw

57°

rat Glacier

STIKINE

MT
TALBOT
1360

THE KNOB
1301

Choquette Glacier

Johnson R

Gla.

Hoodoo Glacier

Twin Glacier

Verrett R

Bronson Cr

Ningunsaw R

Teigen Cr

6-17A

MT
GALLATIN
1554

S

Iskut

River

ISKUT
MTN
1436

Johnt Cr

FIZZLE
MTN

RAVEN
MTN

HOODOO
MTN

Craig R

SNIPPAKER
MTN

Unuk R

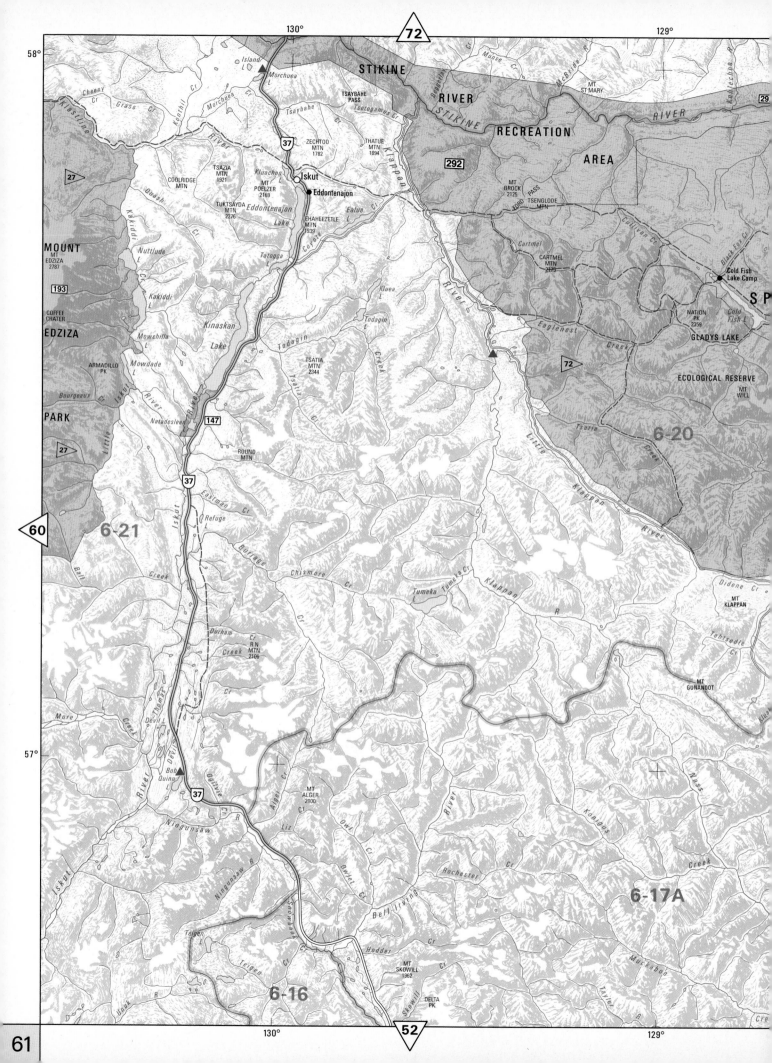

58°

130°

129°

STIKINE

RIVER

RECREATION

29

AREA

Cheeny Cr

Grass Cr

Island L

Morchuea L

Moose Cr

Bagenin R

McBride R

Kalechea R

MT ST MARY

Klastline River

Konthil

Morchuea Cr

Morchuea Cr

TSAYBAHE PASS

Tsaybahe Cr

Tsetogamus Cr

STIKINE

Klappan

292

27

Ouash Cr

COOLRIDGE MTN

TSAZIA MTN 1921

Kluachon L

MT POELZER 2169

ZECHTOO MTN 1782

THATUE MTN 1894

Iskut

MT BROCK 2125

FORD PASS

TSENGLODE MTN

Black Fox Cr

Cold Fish Lake Camp

S P

Kakiddi Cr

Nuttlude L

TUKTSAYDA MTN 2276

Eddontenajon

Eddontenajon Lake

Coyote Cr

EHAHEEZETLE MTN 1939

Ealue L

Cartmel Cr

CARTMEL MTN 2125

Collivan Cr

NATION PK 2359

Cold Fish L

MOUNT

MT EDZIZA 2787

193

Kakiddi L

Tatogga L

Kluea L

Eaglenest

Creek

GLADYS LAKE

COFFEE CRATER

Mowchilla L

Kinaskan Lake

Todagin L

Todagin Creek

ECOLOGICAL RESERVE

MT WILL

EDZIZA

ARMADILLO PK

Mowdade L

Tsatia Cr

TSATIA MTN 2344

72

Tsetia Creek

6-20

Bourgeaux Cr

Iskut River

Natadesleen L

147

Little Klappan River

PARK

27

Little Iskut R

ROUND MTN

60

6-21

37

Eastman Cr

Refuge L

Burrage Creek

Chismore Cr

Tumeka Cr

Tumeka Cr

Klappan R

Didene Cr

MT KLAPPAN

Ball Creek

Durham Creek

DURHAM Cr RN MTN 2106

Tahtsedle Cr

MT GUNANDOT

57°

More Cr

Thomas Cr

Devil L

Bob Quinn L

37

Devil Cr

Ogilvie Cr

Alger Cr

MT ALGER 2100

Owl Cr

River

Kondgus Cr

Klappan

Ningunsaw R

Liz Cr

Owlet Cr

Rochester Cr

Nass

6-17A

Iskut River

Teigen Cr

Teigen Cr

Snowbank Cr

Bell Irving River

Hodder Cr

MT SKOWILL 1962

Skowill Cr

DELTA PK

Muckaboo Creek

Taylor Cr

6-16

Kle

Cre

130°

52

129°

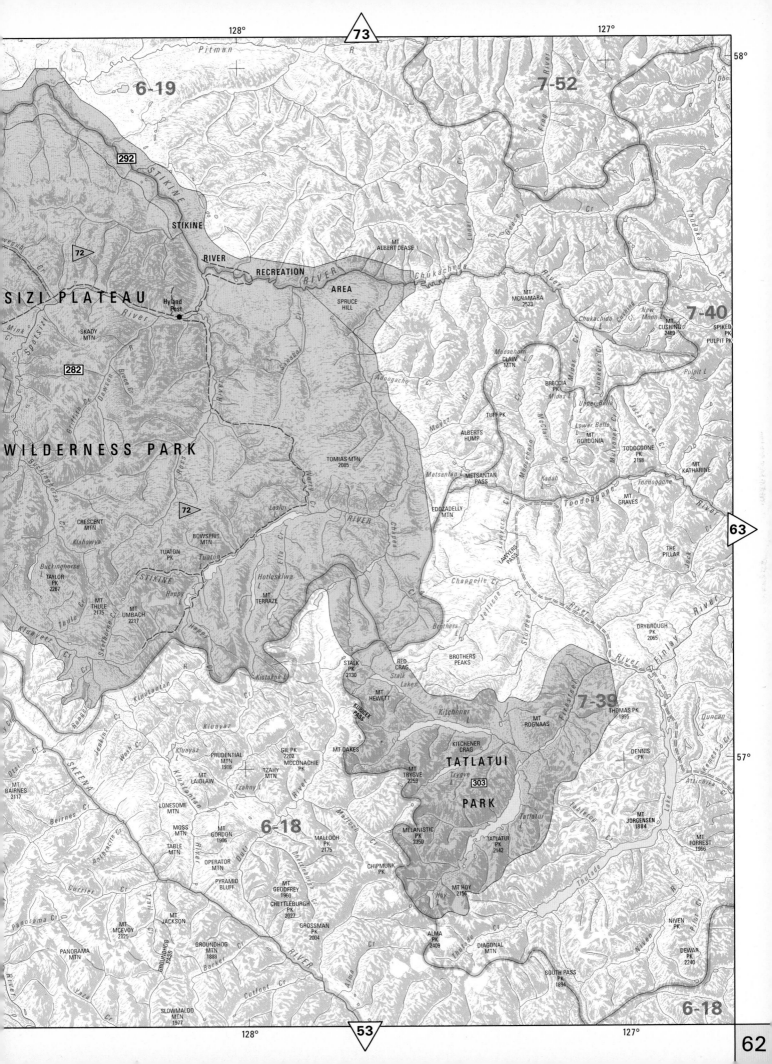

128° 127°
58°

6-19   7-52

7-40

Pitman   R

STIKINE

292

STIKINE

RIVER   RECREATION   RIVER

72

MT ALBERT DEASE

SPRUCE
HILL

Chukachida

River

MT
MCNAMARA
2523

Chukachida   Cushing   New
Cr   Moon   L

MT
CUSHING
2469

SPIKED
PK

PULPIT PK

SIZI PLATEAU

Hyland
Post

SKADY
MTN

282

Spatsizi

River

Sanaha

Adoogacho

Cr

Moosehorn

MOOSEHORN
CLAW
MTN

Midas   Cr

Pulpit L

Upper Belle
L

BRECCIA
PK   Midas L

McGlain   Cr

Lower Belle
L

MT
GORDONIA

Jack Lee   Cr

TODOGGONE
PK
2198

MT
KATHARINE

WILDERNESS PARK

Griffith Cr   Dawson Cr   Ross   R

TOMIAS MTN
2085

Warry Cr

TUFF PK

ALBERTS
HUMP

Moyez   Cr

Metsanten L

METSANTAN
PASS

EDOZADELLY
MTN

Mudserhorn Cr   Kadah   L

Lawyers Cr

Toodoggone

MT
GRAVES

Toodoggone   L

River

63

THE
PILLAR

CRESCENT
MTN

Klahowya
L

72

BOWSPRIT
MTN

Laslui   L

Ella Cr   RIVER   Chapea   Cr

LAWYERS
PASS

Chappelle Cr

Jellicoe   Cr

Sturdee   River

Jack   Cr

Buckinghorse   Stikine   R

Buckinghorse
L   TAYLOR
PK
2267   TUATON
PK   Tuaton
L

HOTLESKLWA
L

MT
TERRAZE

Brothers
L

River

DRYBROUGH
PK
2065

Finlay

River

57°

Kluayerz Cr   Skethorne Cr   Happy   L   Happy   R

MT
THULE
2175   MT
UMBACH
2217

STIKINE

Kistakok L

STALK
PK
2130

MT
HEWETT

RED
CRAG   Stalk

Stalk   Lakes

BROTHERS
PEAKS

Kitchener
L

MT
ROGNAAS

7-39

THOMAS PK
1995

Duncan   L

Ranger Cr   Kluatantan   R

Kluayaz
L   Kluayaz   L

GIL PK
2202

KUBICEK
PASS

MT OAKES

MT
TRYGVE
2259

KITCHENER
CRAG

Trygve
L

303

TATLATUI

DENNIS
PK

Kemess S. Cr

Attichika   Cr

MT
BAIRNES
2117   Otsi Cr   Jenkins Cr   Wash Cr   PRUDENTIAL
MTN
1916   MT
LAIDLAW   Tzahy L   TZAHY
MTN   MCCONACHIE
PK

MELANISTIC
PK
2350

PARK   Tatlatui
L

Tablerop Cr   MT
JORGENSEN
1884

Lake

Beirnes Cr   LONESOME
MTN   Kluatantan   River   6-18   MALLOCH
PK
2175   CHIPMUNK
PK   Mudjatib   Cr   TATLATUI
PK
2142   Tatlatui   L

MT
FORREST
1966

Anthracite Cr   MOSS
MTN   MT
GORDON
1906

MT HOY
2156   Hoy   L   Thutade

NIVEN
PK

Currier   Cr   TABLE
MTN   OPERATOR
MTN   MT
GEODFREY
1960   Chetleburgh Cr   ALMA
PK
2409   DIAGONAL
MTN   Thutade

Niven   Cr

Panorama Cr   PYRAMID
BLUFF   CHETTLEBURGH
PK
2027   GROSSMAN
PK
2004   Alma   Cr   SOUTH PASS
PK
1894   Pilot   Cr

DEWAR
PK
2240

PANORAMA
MTN   MT
MCEVOY
2125   MT
JACKSON   GROUNDHOG
MTN
1888   Barker   Cr   RIVER

GROUNDHOG
PASS   SLOWMALDO
MTN
1977   Cutfoot Cr   6-18

SKEENA   Ou   R   Chetleburgh   R   RIVER

Yala   Cr

128°   127°

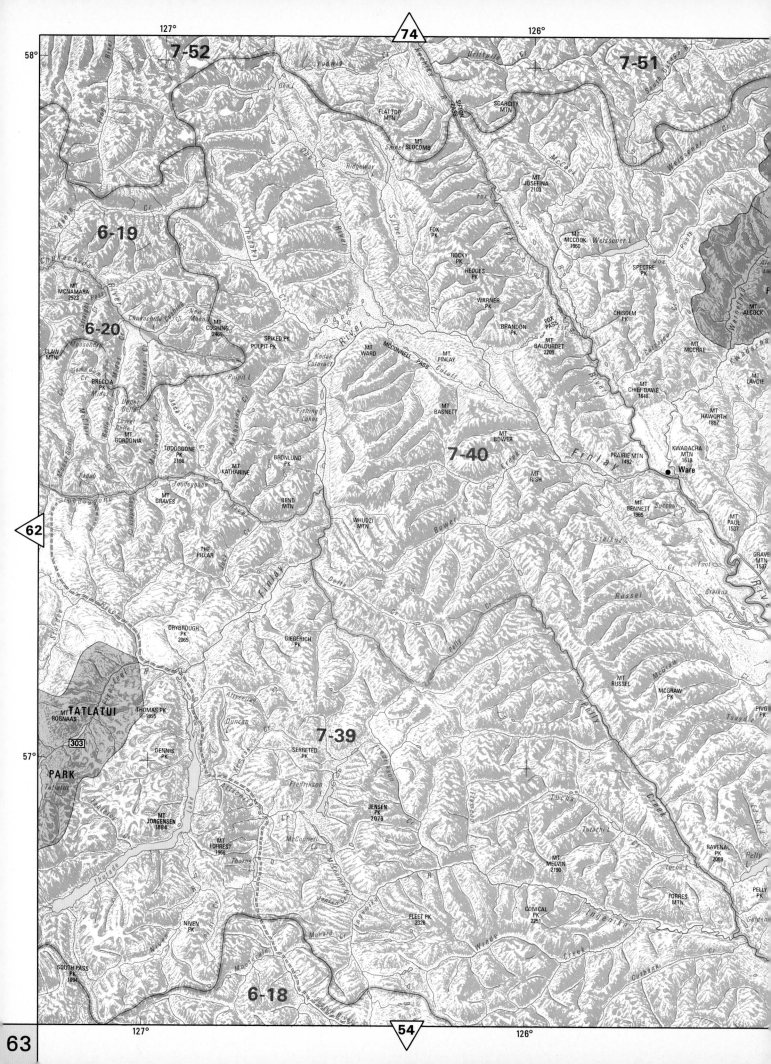

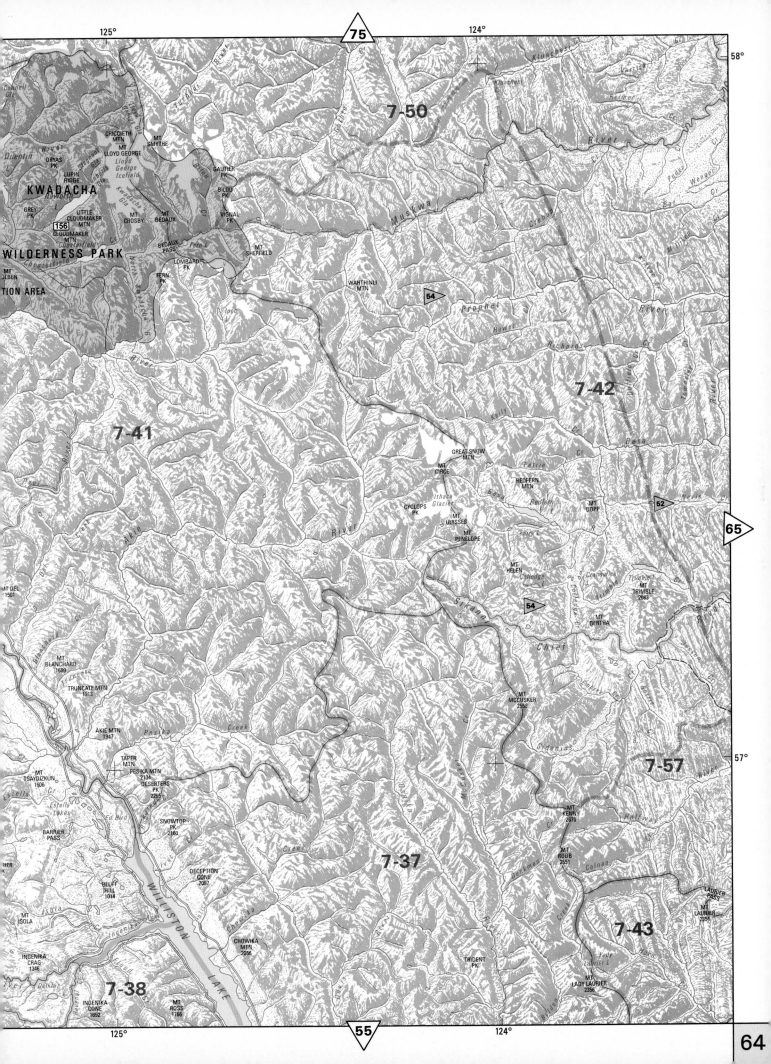

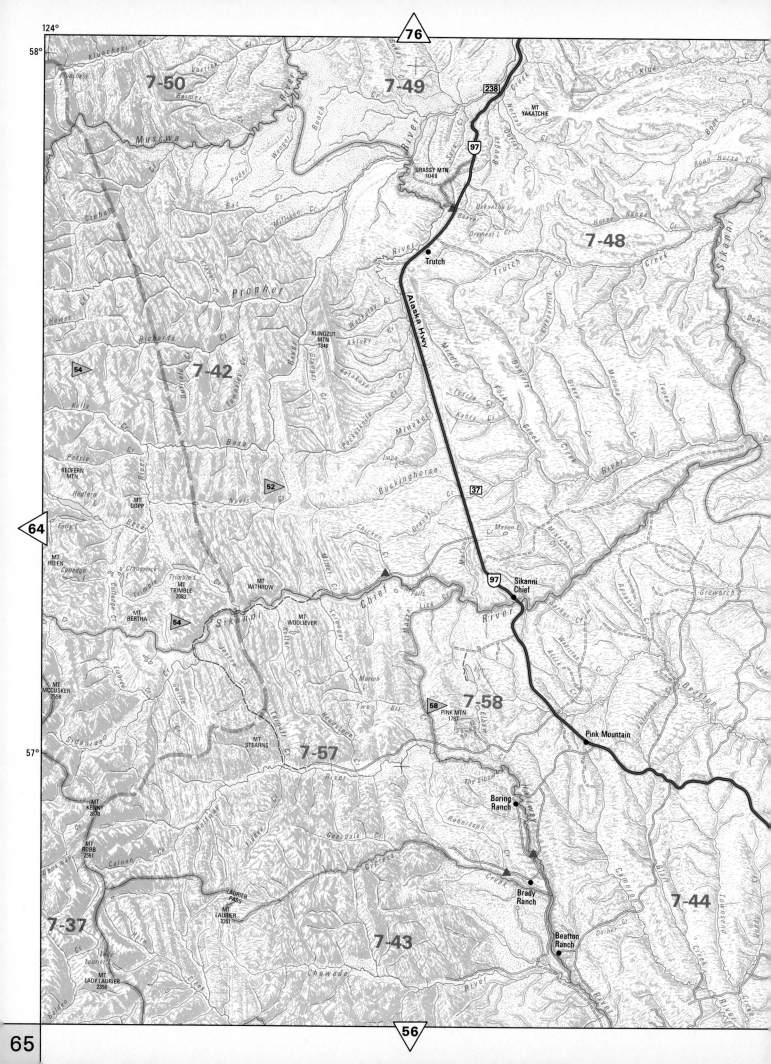

124°
58°

7-50

7-49

238

MT YAKATCHIE

97

Kluachesi Cr.

Kluachesi

Muskwa

Varrick

Bunch

Reimer

Seebe Cr.

Puder Cr.

Wenger Cr.

Milliken Cr.

Bat Cr.

River

GRASSY MTN
1049

Bougie Creek

Dotay Cr.

Klue Cr.

Boot Cr.

Prophet

River

Dekoncho L.

Beaver

Drymeat L. Cr.

Trutch

Horse Range

7-48

Sikanni

Crehan Cr.

Hewer Cr.

Richards Cr.

Dariela Cr.

Townsley Cr.

KLINGZUT
MTN
1846

Washutan Cr.

Akfuky

Katakose Cr.

Alaska Hwy

Matchie

Tescla

Kahta Cr.

Trutch

Daniels

Green Cr.

Medana

Tepee Cr.

Donna Cr.

54

7-42

Kelly Cr.

Besa

Navis Cr.

River

Pockeknife Cr.

Minaker River

Grangel Cr.

52

Impa Cr.

Buckinghorse

Chicken Cr.

Grassy Cr.

Mason Cr.

Mason L.

37

Creek

River

Mistobee Cr.

Grewatch

64

Petrie Cr.

REDFERN
MTN

Redfern L.

Besa

MT DOPP

Fairy L.

River

MT HELEN

Colledge Cr.

Cranswick L.

Colledge Cr.

Trimble Cr.

Trimble L.

MT
TRIMBLE
2083

MT
WITHROW

Millet Cr.

Chief

Falls

Lick Cr.

97

Sikanni
Chief

River

Barker Cr.

Wariston Cr.

Apsessip Cr.

Juniama Cr.

54

Sikanni

MT
WOOLIEVER

Loxengen Cr.

River

Mason Cr.

Alich Cr.

Beatton

MT
BERTHA

Jesson Cr.

Garfie Cr.

Embree Cr.

Rolfin Cr.

Marion L.

Two Bit

Lily Cr.

MT
McCUSKER
2558

Sidenius Cr.

Turnoff Cr.

Headwater Cr.

58

PINK MTN
1787

7-58

Elbow Cr.

57°

7-57

River

MT
STEARNS

Cypress Cr.

Halfway

Cameron Cr.

Blair Cr.

Townsend Cr.

MT
KENNY
2670

MT
ROBB
2551

Onknuk Cr.

Calnan Cr.

Geesdale Cr.

The Elbow

Boring
Ranch

Robertson Cr.

Pink Mountain

Jed Cr.

7-44

7-37

LAURIER
PASS

MT
LAURIER
2351

Hbrn Cr.

Baldon Cr.

7-43

Chowade River

Brady
Ranch

Beatton
Ranch

Darber Cr.

River

Cr.

Lady Laurier L.

MT
LADY LAURIER
2356

56

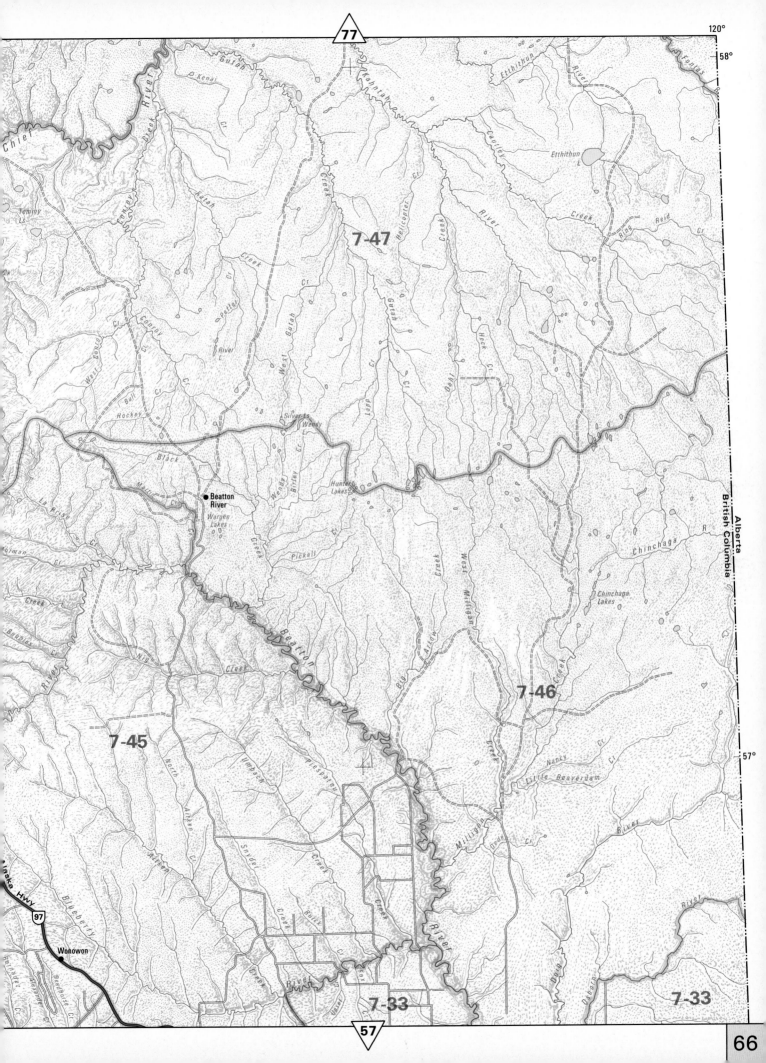

120°
58°

Chief

Gutah

Kenai

Etthithun

River

River

Kahntah

Cautley

Etthithun L.

7-47

Helicopter

Creek

Creek

River

Creek

Ring

Reid

Cr

Conroy Creek

Kotah

Creek

Cr

Tommy Ls.

West Gutah

Gutah

Cr

Cr

Peller

Dahl

Heck Cr.

Creek

River L.

Cr

Conroy Cr.

West Conroy

Bull

deep

Cr

Hockey

Silverts

River

Wendy L.

Alberta

British Columbia

Black

Wendy

Birley Cr.

Hunters Lakes

Beatton River

Creek

Warren Lakes

Pickell

Chinchaga

La Rose

Cr

Cr

Creek

Chinchaga Lakes

Colman

West Milligan

Creek

Creek

R

Big Arrow

Bubbles

Cr.

Nig

Creek

Creek

7-46

River

7-45

North

Umbach

pleasant

Nancy

Cr.

Cr

57°

Little Beaverdam

Aitken Cr.

Snyder

Creek

Creek

Creek

Milligan

Dodd

Cr.

River

laska HWY

Blueberry

Aitken Cr.

Buick

Creek

Creek

River

97

Wonowon

Alexander Cr.

Osborn

River

Creek

River

7-33

7-33

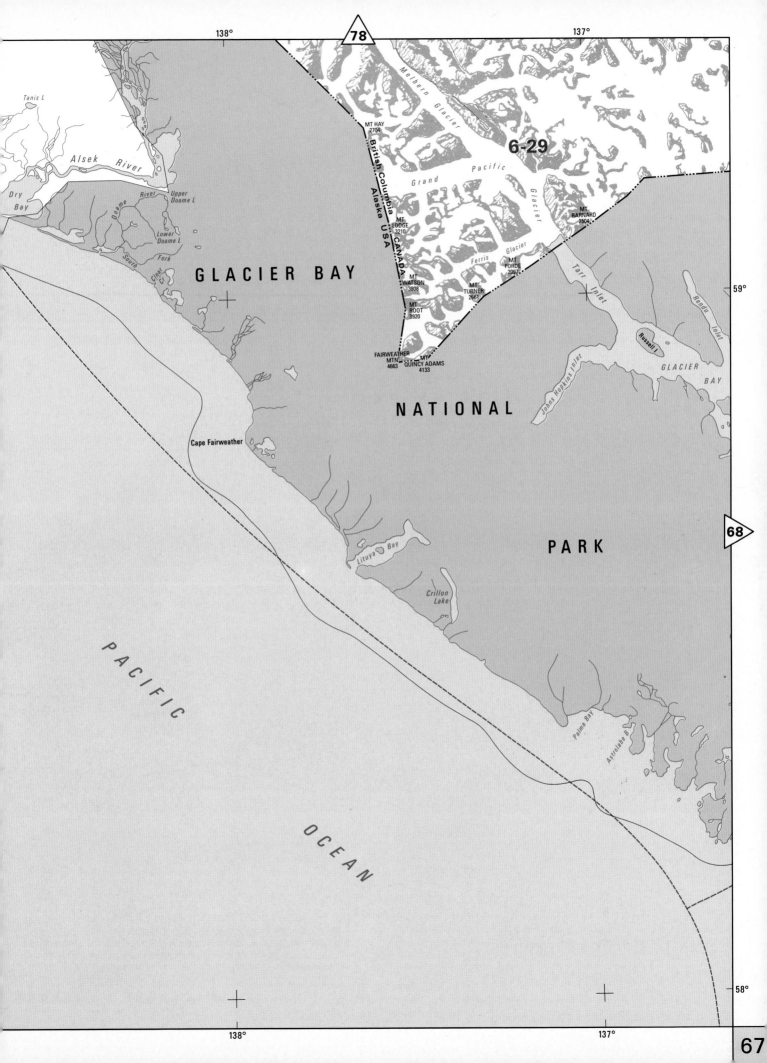

138°

137°

6-29

Tanis L

Alsek River

Dry Bay

Upper Doame L

Doame River

Lower Doame L

South Fork

Clear Cr

MT HAY
2704

Melbern Glacier

Grand

Pacific

Glacier

British Columbia
Alaska USA
CANADA

MT LODGE
3210

MT WATSON
3808

MT ROOT
3920

Ferris Glacier

MT TURNER
2661

MT FORDE
2092

MT BARNARD
2504

GLACIER BAY

FAIRWEATHER MTN
4663

MT QUINCY ADAMS
4133

Tarr Inlet

Russell I

Rendu Inlet

GLACIER BAY

59°

NATIONAL

Johns Hopkins Inlet

Cape Fairweather

PARK

Lituya Bay

Crillon Lake

Palma Bay

Astrolabe B

PACIFIC

OCEAN

58°

138°

137°

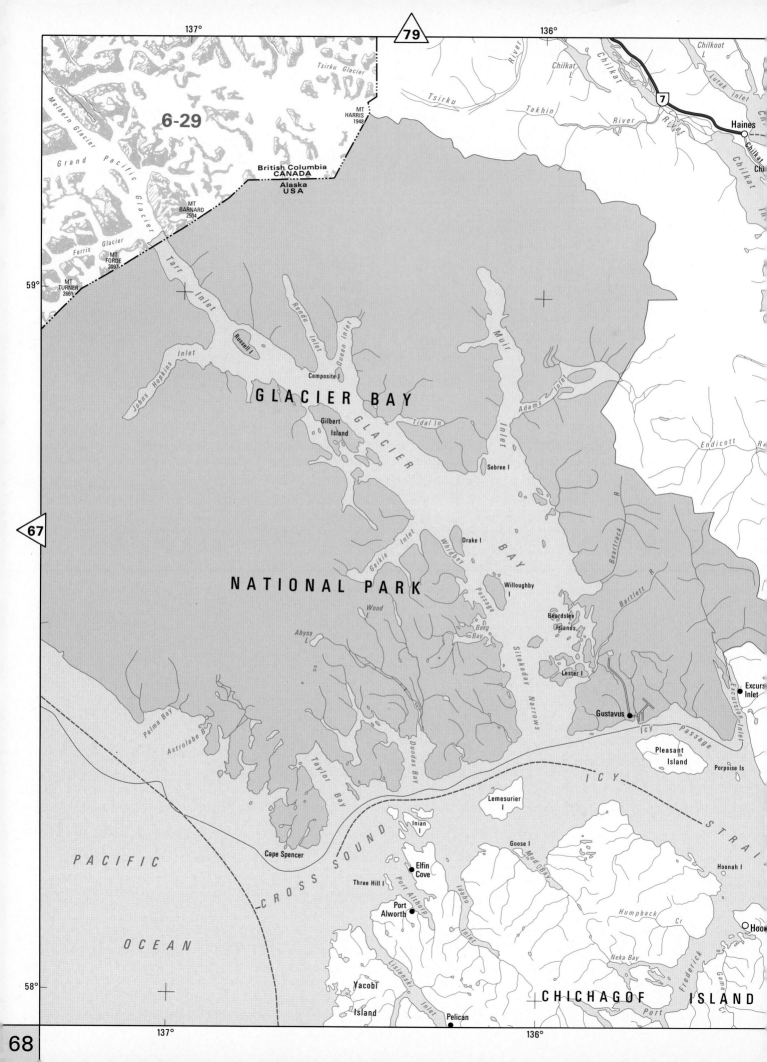

137°

136°

6-29

Chilkoot
L

Chilkat
L

Chilkat

Lutak Inlet

Tsirku Glacier

River

Chilkat

River

7

Haines

MT
HARRIS
1948

Tsirku

Takhin

River

Chilkat

Ch

British Columbia
CANADA
Alaska
USA

Grand Pacific Glacier

Melbern Glacier

MT
BARNARD
2504

Ferris Glacier

MT
FORDE
2097

MT
TURNER
2661

59°

Tarr Inlet

Russell I

Reid Inlet

Rendu Inlet

Queen Inlet

Composite I

Muir Inlet

Adams Inlet

GLACIER   BAY

Tidal In

Endicott

R

Gilbert
Island

GLACIER

Sebree I

Johns Hopkins Inlet

Geikie Inlet

Whidbey Passage

Drake I

BAY

Beartrack R

△ 67

NATIONAL   PARK

Willoughby
I

Bartlett R

Wood
L

Beardslee
Islands

Abyss
L

Berg
Bay

Sitakaday Narrows

Lester I

Excurs
Inlet

Palma Bay

Astrolabe B

Gustavus

Excursion Inlet

Icy   Passage

Taylor Bay

Dundas Bay

Pleasant
Island

Porpoise Is

ICY

Lemesurier
I

Cape Spencer

Inian
I

Goose I

STRAIT

PACIFIC

CROSS   SOUND

Elfin
Cove

Port Althorp

Idaho Inlet

Mud Bay

Hoonah I

Three Hill I

Hoo

OCEAN

Port
Alworth

Humpback   Cr

Neka Bay

Port

Frederick

Game Cr

58°

Yacobi
Island

Lisianski Inlet

CHICHAGOF   ISLAND

Pelican

137°

136°

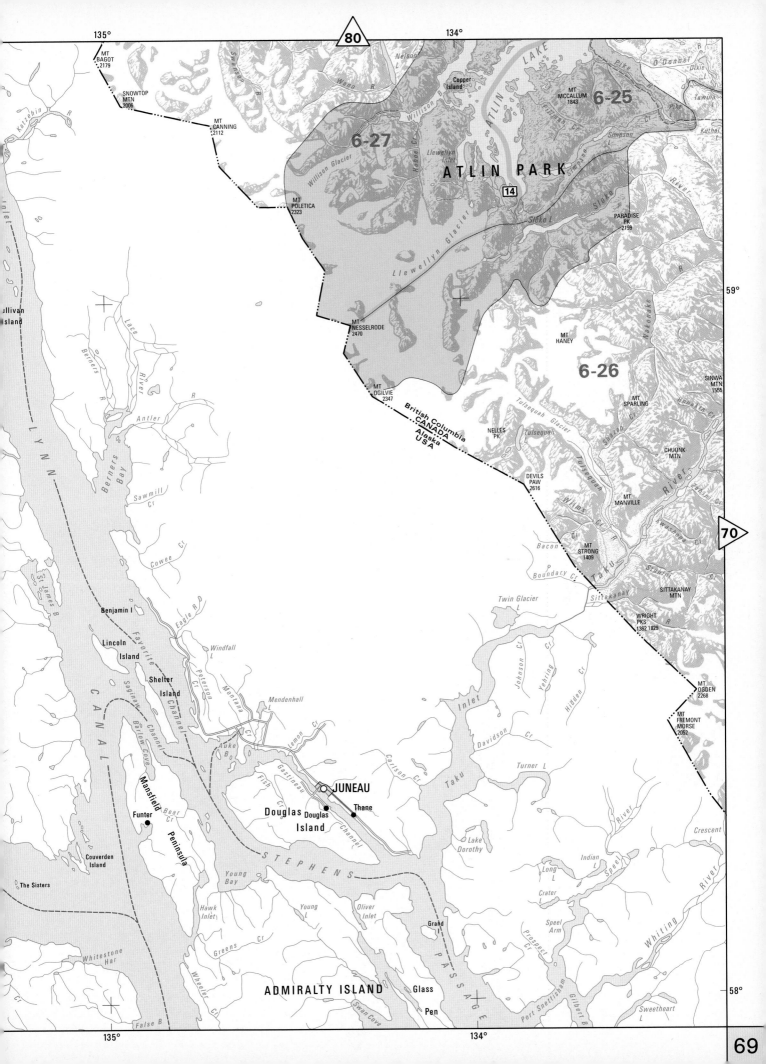

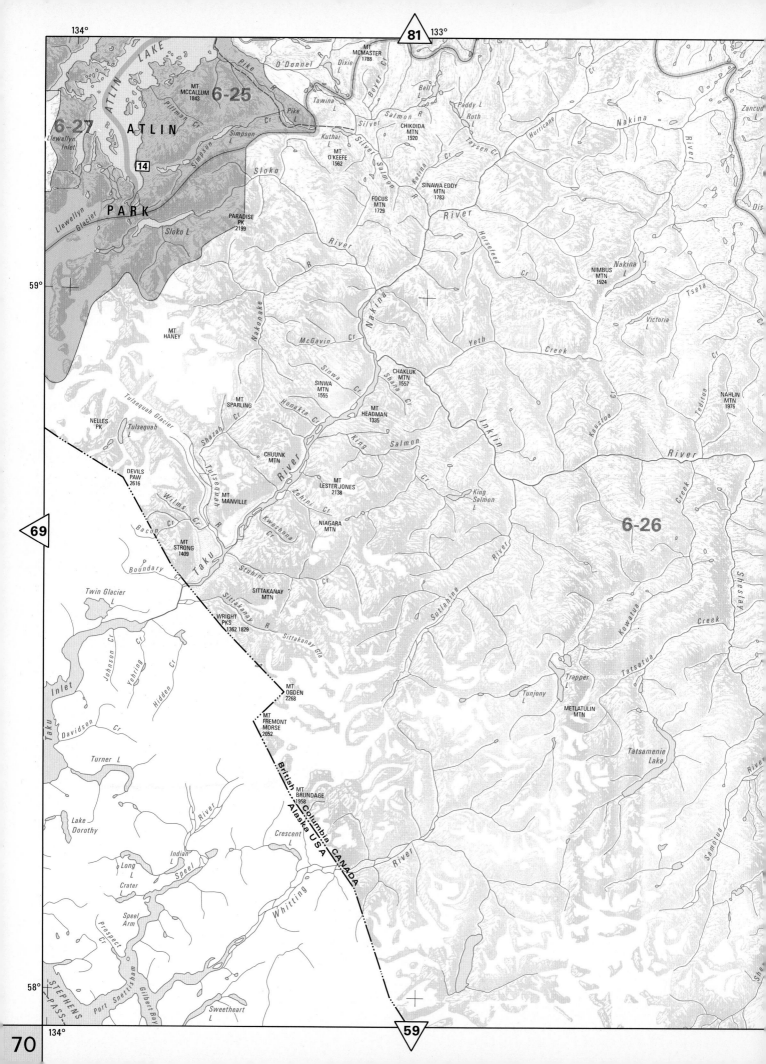

134°   133°

MT
MCMASTER
1788

O'Donnel   Dixie

ATLIN   LAKE

Pike

Bell

Paddy L

Hurricane

Nakina

Cr

Zancud

MT MCCALLUM
1843   6-25

6-27

ATLIN

Llewellyn
Inlet

Llewellyn   Glacier

PARK

14

Pittman   Cr

Tawina

Pike
L

Simpson   Cr

Kuthai
L

Silver

Salmon

Ruth

Taysen Cr

CHIKOIDA
MTN
1920

SINAWA EDDY
MTN
1783

Nakina

River

NIMBUS
MTN
1924

Nakina
L

Victoria
L

Tseta

MT
O'KEEFE
1562

Silver   Salmon

Katina

Cr

Horsefeed

Cr

Simpson
L

Sloka

FOCUS
MTN
1729

River

59°

Sloko L

PARADISE
PK
2199

River

McGavin   Cr

Nakonake

Nakina   R

Yeth

Creek

Tseta   Cr

NAHLIN
MTN
1976

MT
HANEY

Sinwa

Cr

CHAKLUK
MTN
1557

Shana Cr

Inklin

River

Kowatua   Cr

Tedirua   Cr

Tulsequah   Glacier

MT
SPARLING

SINWA
MTN
1555

Honakta Cr

MT
HEADMAN
1335

NELLES
PK

Tulsequah
L

Shazah   Cr

CHUUNK
MTN

King   Salmon

Salmon

King

Cr

King
Salmon
L

6-26

DEVILS
PAW
2616

MT
MANVILLE

River

Zohini   Cr

MT
LESTER JONES
2138

Wilms   Cr

Tulsequah   R

Kwashona   Cr

NIAGARA
MTN

Suttahine

River

Kaustua   Cr

69

Bacon   Cr

MT
STRONG
1409

Stuhini   Cr

Trapper
L

Tatsatua

Creek

Sheslay

Boundary   Cr

Taku

SITTAKANAY
MTN

Tunjony
L

METLATULIN
MTN

Twin Glacier
L

Sittakanay   R

WRIGHT
PKS
1362 1829

Sittakanay Gla

Kowatua

Tatsamenie
Lake

Taku

Inlet

Johnson Cr

Yehring   Cr

Hidden   Cr

MT
OGDEN
2268

MT
FREMONT
MORSE
2052

River

Davidson   Cr

Turner L

British   Columbia   CANADA

Alaska   USA

MT
BRUNDAGE
1958

River

Samolua

Lake
Dorothy

Indian
L

Speel

River

Crescent
L

Long
L

Crater
L

Speel
Arm

Whiting

River

Prospect   Cr

STEPHENS
PASSAGE

Port Snettisham

Gilbert Bay

Sweetheart
L

58°

134°

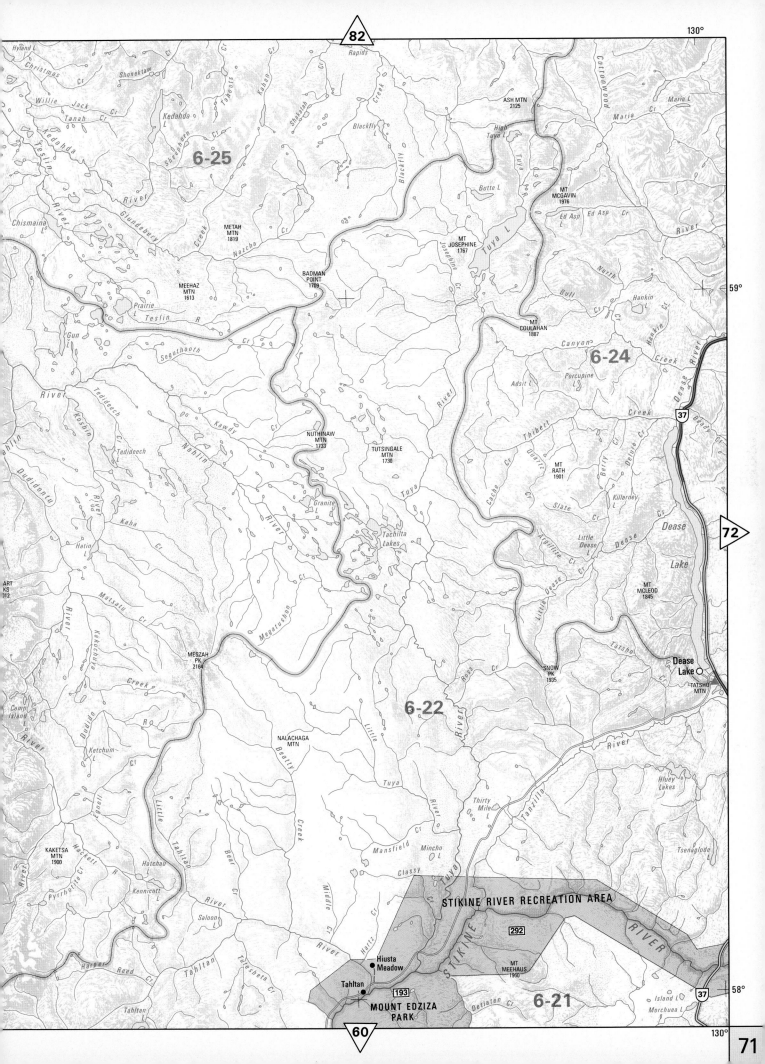

130°

Hyland L
Christmas
Cr
Willie
Jack
Cr
Shonektaw
Cr

Tanah
Cr
Kedahda
L
Kedahda

Teslin
River

Kahan Cr
Tahenis Cr

Rapids

ASH MTN
2125

Cottonwood
Cr
Maria L
Maria L

Shakatah

Blackfly

High
Tuya L

Maria
Cr

6-25

Glundeberry
Creek
Nazcha
Cr

Blackfly
Creek

Tuya L

MT
MCGAVIN
1976

Ed Asp
L
Ed Asp Cr

Chismaina
L

METAH
MTN
1819

MT
JOSEPHINE
1767

Josephine
Cr

North
Bull

Hankin
L
Hankin Cr

59°

Prairie
L
Teslin R

MEEHAZ
MTN
1613

BADMAN
POINT
1709

MT
COULAHAN
1887

Canyon

6-24

Creek

Gun
L

Dease
River

37

Seguthooth
Cr

Adsit L

Porcupine
L

Tedideech

Koshin

Nahlin
River

Kawdy
Cr

NUTHINAW
MTN
1733

TUTSINGALE
MTN
1730

River

Thibert
Cr

MT
RATH
1901

Quartz
Cr
Berry Cr
Deluxe Cr
Killarney
L

Tedideech

Tedideech
Cr

Tuya
Cr

Cache
Cr

Slate
Cr

Little
Dease
L

Dease
Cr

Dease

River

72

Hatin
L

Kaha
Cr

Granite
L

Tachilta
Lakes

Argillite Cr

Little Dease

Lake

ART
KS
012

Matsatu
Cr

Megatushon

MT
MCLEOD
1845

Dudidontu

Kakuchuya
Cr

MESZAH
PK
2164

SNOW
PK
1935

Ross
Cr

Tatsho

**Dease
Lake**

Camp
Island
L

River

Duldido
R

6-22

Little

NALACHAGA
MTN

River

Beatty

TATSHO
MTN

Ketchum
L
Cr

Tuya

River

Tanzilla

Hluey
Lakes

Egnell Cr

Hackett

Little Tahltan River

Bear
Cr

Thirty
Mile
L

Tsenaglode
L

KAKETSA
MTN
1900

Hatchau

Kennicott
L

Mansfield
Cr

Mincho
L

Classy
Cr

Tuya

STIKINE RIVER RECREATION AREA

Pyrrhotite Cr

Saloon
L

Middle Cr

Hartz Cr

292

STIKINE

RIVER

Harper
Reed Cr.

Tahltan

Tuesheta Cr

● Hiusta
Meadow

MT
MEEHAUS
1960

● Tahltan

193

Detiaten Cr

6-21

Island L
Morchuea L

**MOUNT EDZIZA
PARK**

37

58°

130°

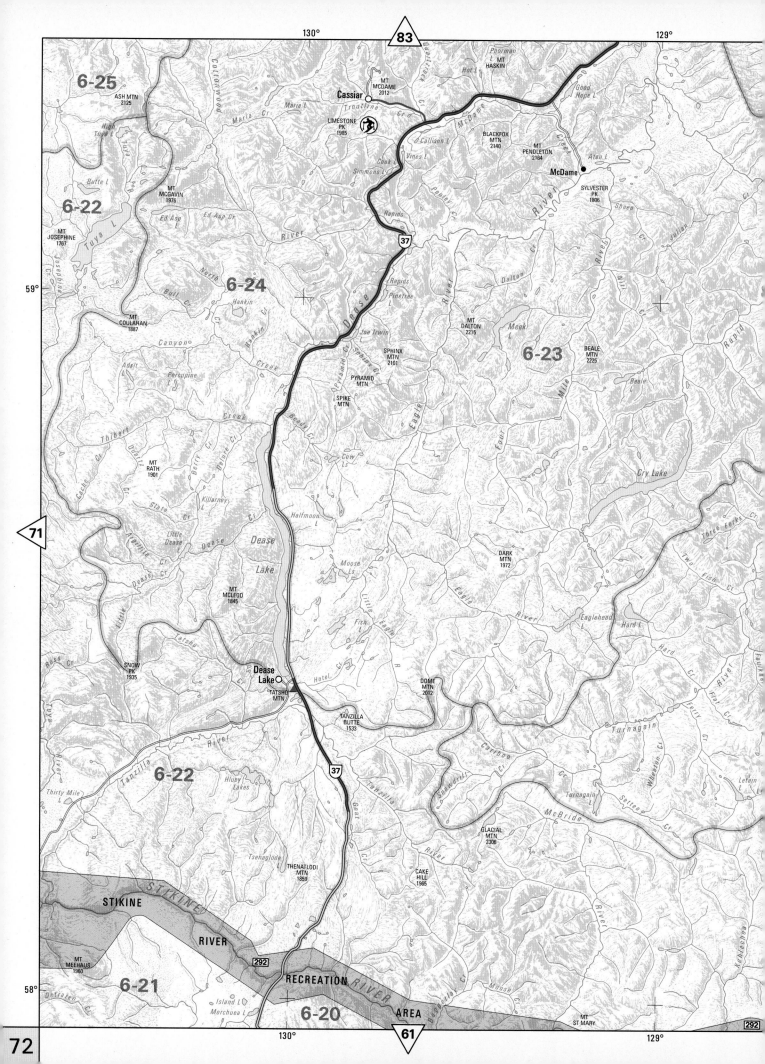

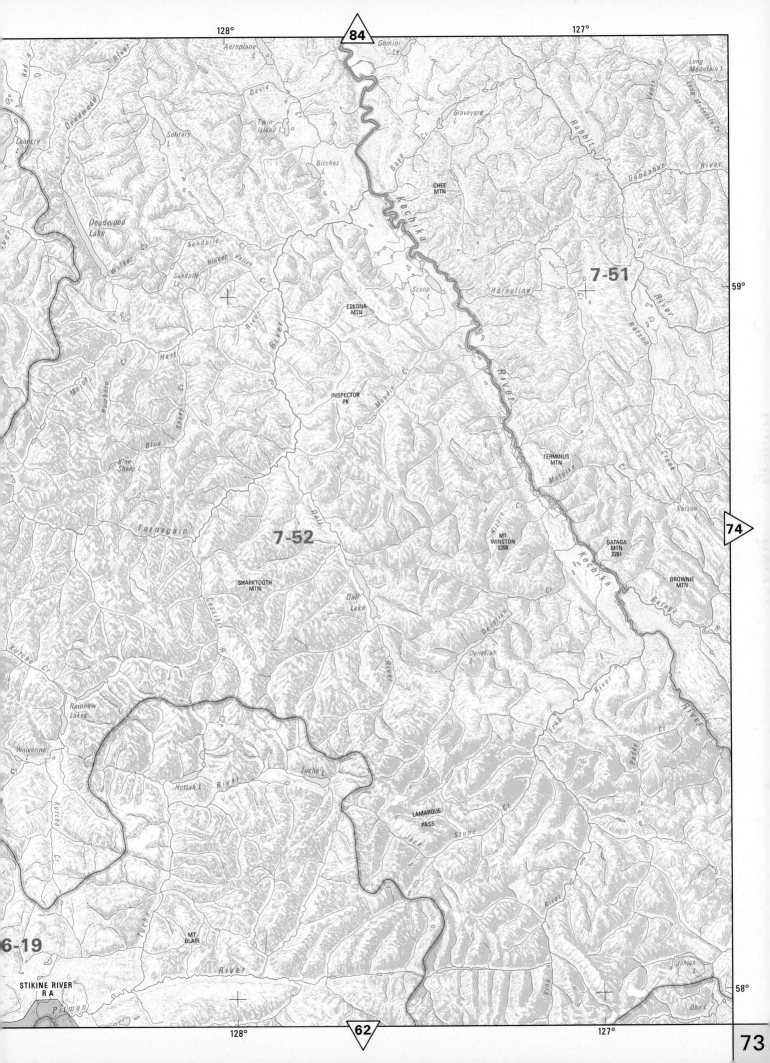

128°

127°

Aeroplane L

Gemini Ls

Red River

Deadwood River

Davie Cr

Looncry L

Solitary L

Twin Island L

Birches L

Boya Cr

Graveyard L

CHEE MTN

Rabbit River

Long Mountain L

Long Mountain Cr

Vants R

Gundahoo River

Kechika

Deadwood Lake

Sandpile Cr

Hidden Valley Cr

Sandpile Ls

Walker Cr

Scoop L

Horveline

59°

ESKONA MTN

River

River

Hart Cr

Major Cr

Rainbow Cr

Sheep Cr

Blue Sheep Cr

Blue Sheep L

INSPECTOR PK

Moodie Cr

River

Nelson River

TERMNUS MTN

Matulka Cr

Nelson Creek

Turnagain

Dall Cr

MT WINSTON 2358

Hyland Cr

Cr

GATAGA MTN 2281

Gataga Cr

SHARKTOOTH MTN

Cassiar R

Dall Lake

River

Denetiah Cr

Denetiah L

BROWNIE MTN

Gataga River

Kechika

Kutcho Cr

Rainbow Lakes

Wolverine Cr

Kutcho Cr

Hottah L

Tucho River

Tucho L

Jack Cr

Frog River

Paddy Cr

LAMARQUE PASS

Stone Cr

Frog River

MT BLAIR

STIKINE RIVER R A

River

Pitman

Johiah Cr

Oho L

128°

127°

58°

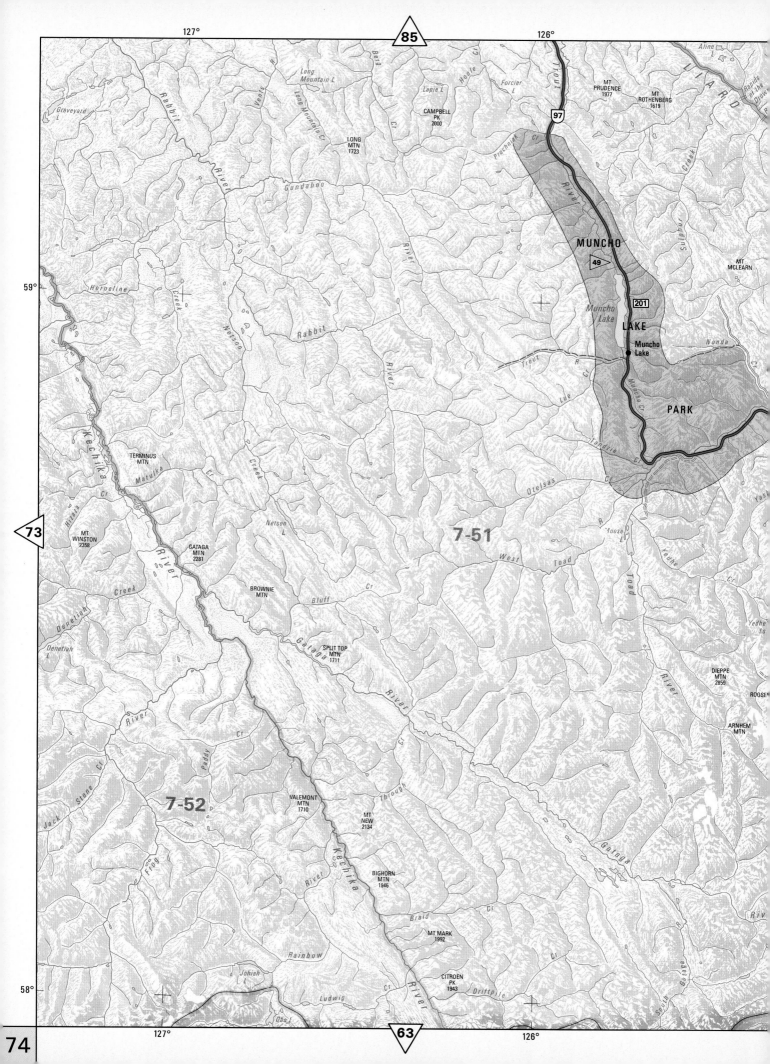

127°   126°

LIARD

Graveyard
L

Long
Mountain L

Berg Cr

Hoole Cr

Forcier
L

Trout

MT
PRUDENCE
1977

MT
ROTHENBERG
1619

Rapids
of the
Drow

Aline L

Rabbit

River

Vents Cr

Long Mountain Cr

Lapie L

97

CAMPBELL
PK
2000

Prochniak Cr

Gundahoo

LONG
MTN
1723

River

MUNCHO

49

River

MT
MCLEARN

Sulphur Cr

Horneline

59°

Netson

Creek

Rabbit

River

Muncho
Lake

201

LAKE

Muncho
Lake

Nonda

Trout

R

Tuc

Cr

Muncho Cr

PARK

73

Kechika

Matulka

Cr

TERMINUS
MTN

MT
WINSTON
2358

Creek

Netson
L

Bluff

Cr

Otelsas

Cr

Tlandrie

Cr

R

Moose
L

West

Toad

Yedhe Cr

7-51

Toad

River

DIEPPE
MTN
2859

Yash

Yedhe
L

ROOSE

Hirara
Cr

GATAGA
MTN
2281

BROWNIE
MTN

Gataga

River

SPLIT TOP
MTN
1711

Denetiah

Creek

Denetiah
L

River

Padoy Cr

7-52

VALEMONT
MTN
1710

MT
NEW
2134

Through

Cr

River

ARNHEM
MTN

Jack

Stone

Cr

Frog

River

Kechika

River

BIGHORN
MTN
1946

Braid

Cr

Gataga

Riv

South Gataga R

Johiah
L

Rainbow

Cr

MT MARK
1992

Ludwig

Oba L

River

CITROEN
PK
1943

Driftpile

Cr

58°

127°   126°   63

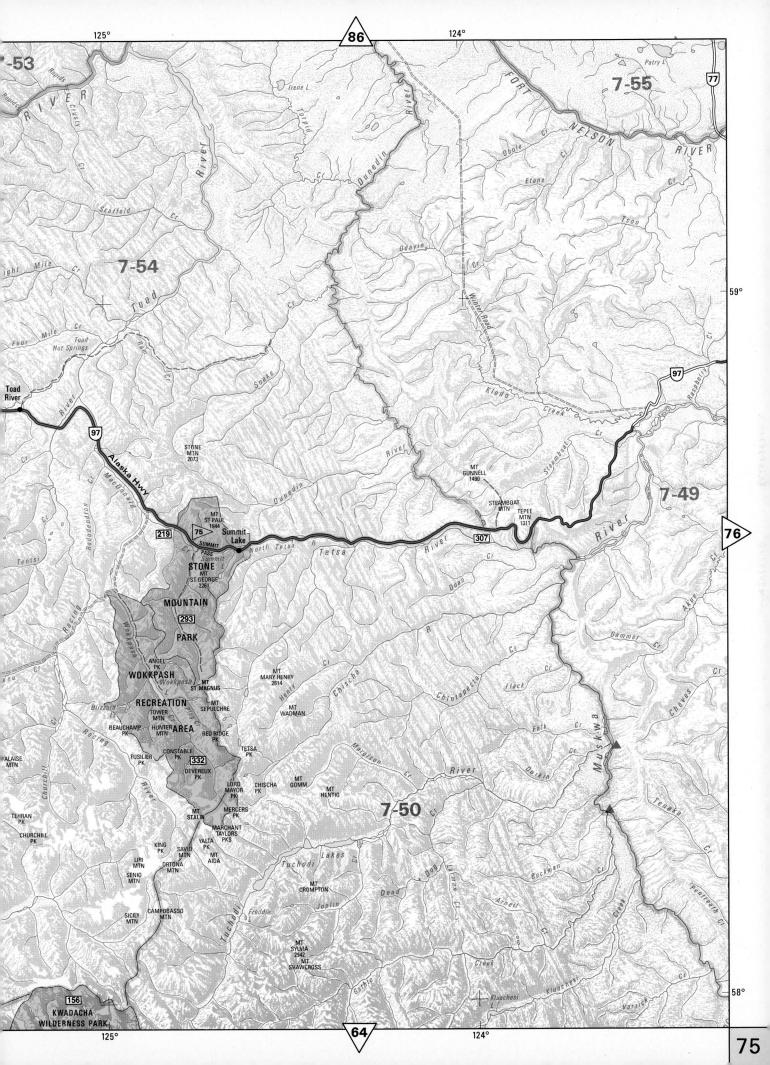

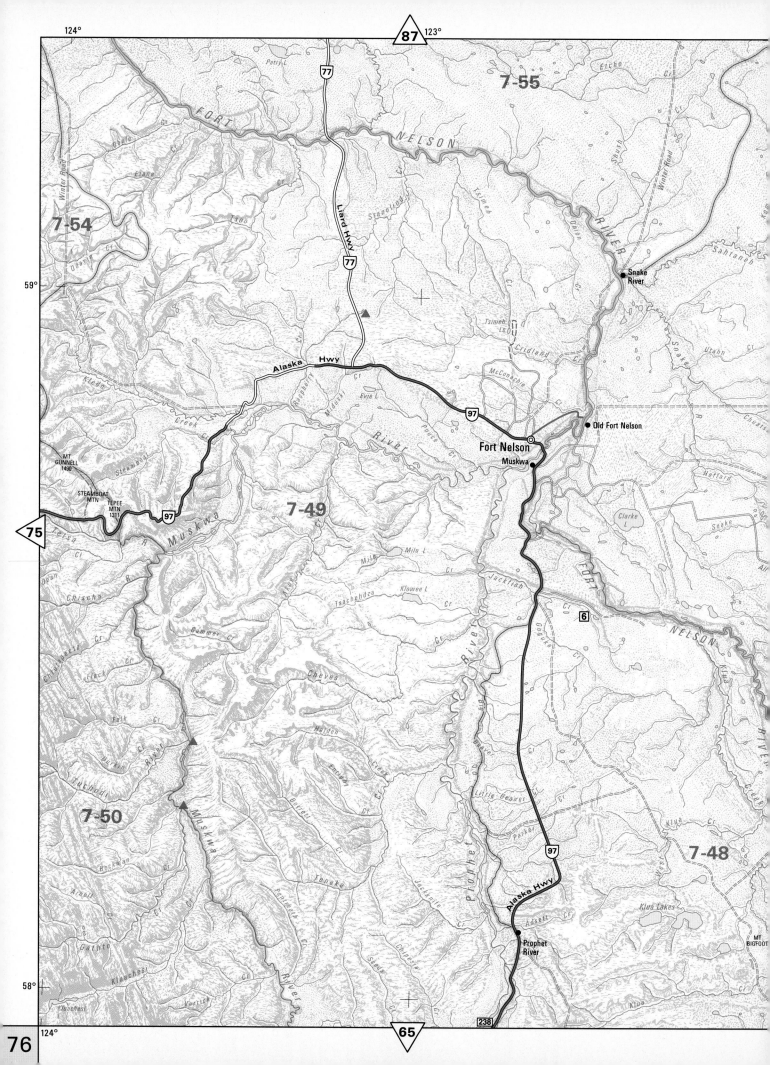

124° 123°

7-55

77

7-54

Liard Hwy

77

59°

Alaska Hwy

97

Fort Nelson

Old Fort Nelson

Muskwa

MT GUNNELL 1490

STEAMBOAT MTN

TEPEE MTN 1311

97

7-49

Snake River

Clarke L

75

6

7-50

7-48

97

Alaska Hwy

MT BIGFOOT

Prophet River

58°

238

124° 65

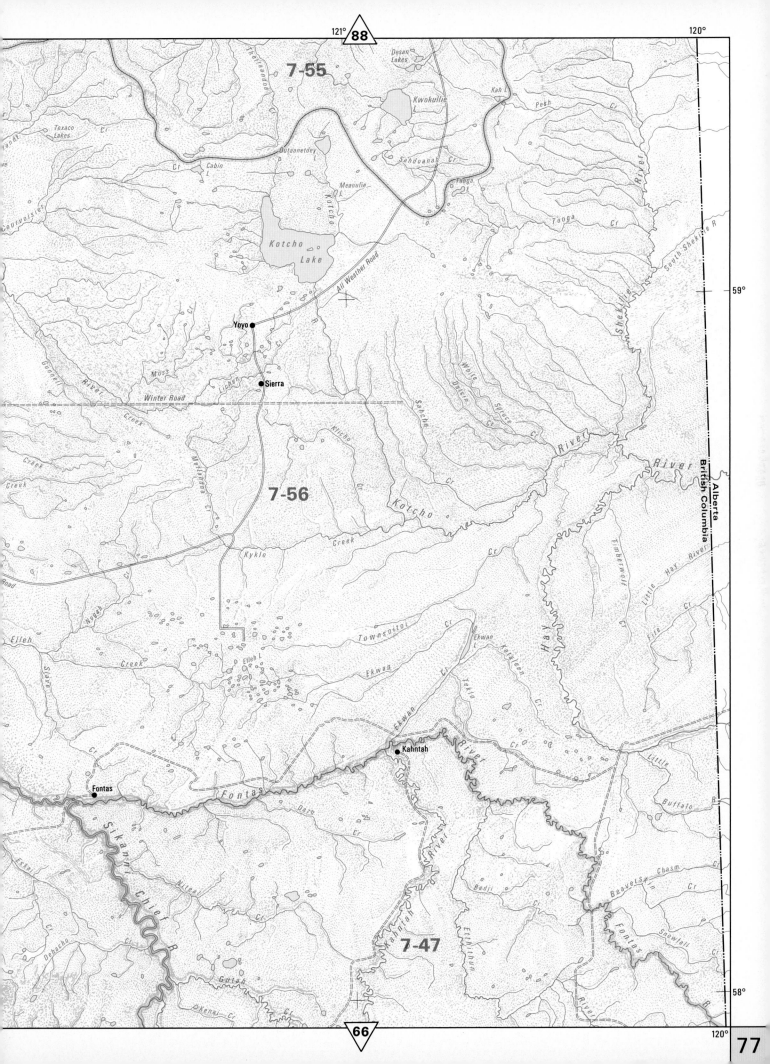

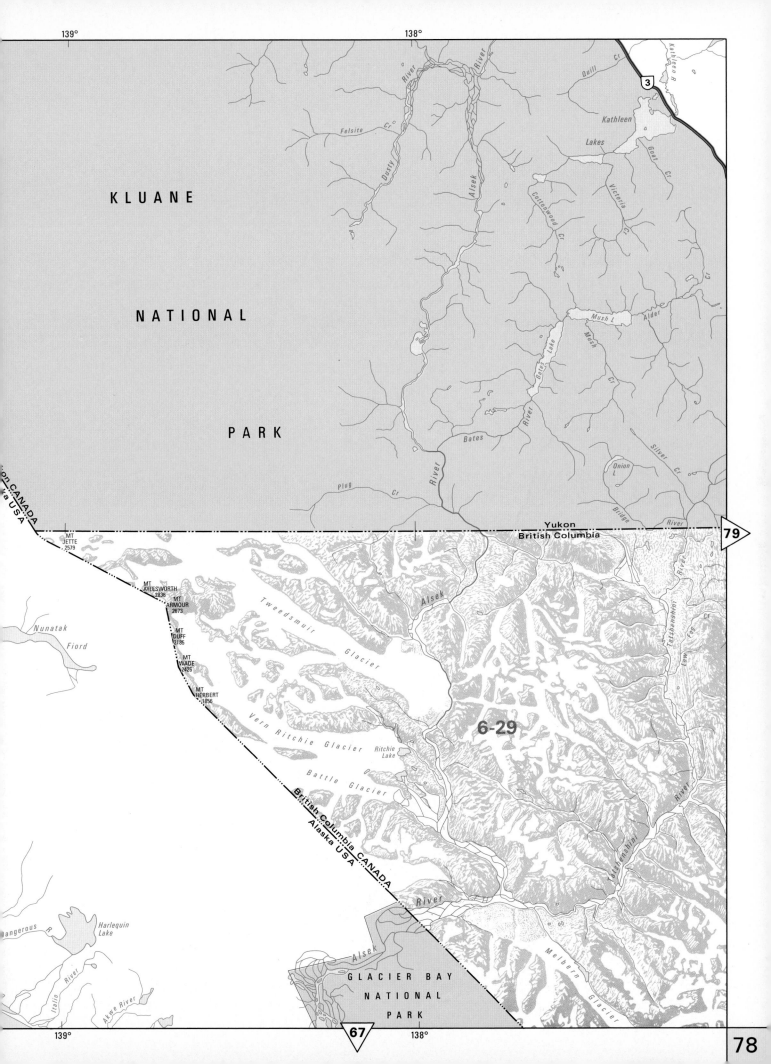

138°

K L U A N E

N A T I O N A L

P A R K

Felsite Cr°

Dusty Cr°

River

Alsek

River

Quill Cr

Kathleen R

3

Kathleen

Lakes

Cottonwood Cr

Victoria Cr

Goat Cr

Mush L

Alder

Bates Lake

Mush

Mush Cr

Silver Cr

Bates

River

Plug

Cr

River

Onion L

Bridge

River

Yukon

British Columbia

79

on CANADA
ka USA

MT
JETTE
2579

MT
AYLESWORTH
2838

MT
ARMOUR
2673

MT
DUFF
2185

MT
WADE
2426

MT
HERBERT
1856

Nunatak

Fiord

Tweedsmuir

Glacier

Alsek

Tatshenshini
River

Taw Cr°

Vern Ritchie Glacier

Ritchie
Lake

Battle Glacier

6-29

Tatshenshini
River

British Columbia CANADA
Alaska USA

angerous R

Harlequin
Lake

River

River

Melbern
Glacier

Alsek

River

GLACIER BAY

NATIONAL

PARK

Italio

Akwe River

67

138°

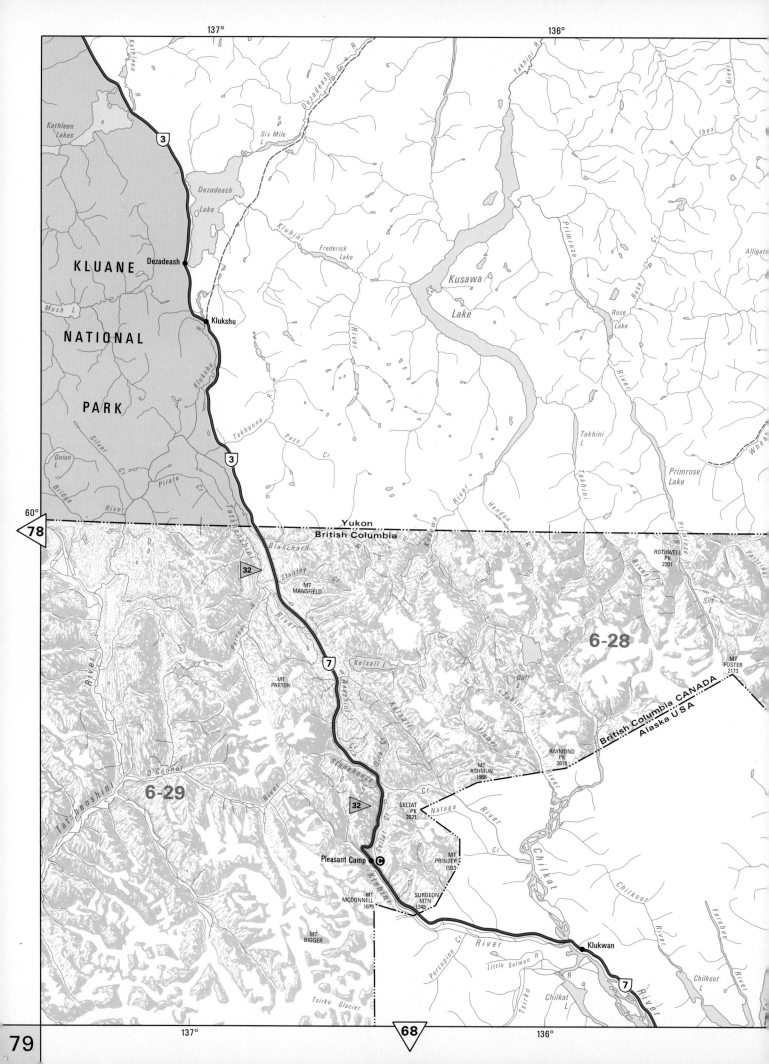

3

Kathleen
Lakes

Kathleen R

KLUANE

Dezadeash

Six Mile
L

Dezadeash
Lake

Kluhini

Frederick
Lake

Kusawa
Lake

Takhini R

Ibex

Rose Cr

Primrose Cr

Alligate

NATIONAL

Mush L

Klukshu

River

Rose
Lake

PARK

Silver Cr

Onion
L

Takhanne

Pass

Cr

Takhini L

Takhini

Primrose
Lake

Bridge River

Pirate Cr

3

Takhanne R

Klukshu R

78

Yukon
British Columbia

Tatshenshini R

32

Blanchard

Stanley Cr

MT
MANSFIELD

Kusawa River

Hendon R

ROTHWELL
PK
2201

Silt
L

6-28

MT
FOSTER
2173

7

Parton R

MT
PARTON

Kelsall L

Kelsall Cr

Takhini

Duff Cr

Flener R

RAYMOND
PK
2018

British Columbia CANADA
Alaska USA

6-29

Tatshenshini River

O'Connor River

Stonehouse Cr

32

Nadahini Cr

Dick Cr

Seltat Cr

SELTAT
PK
2021

MT
ASHMUN
1966

Nataga Cr

River

Chilkat

Pleasant Camp

C

Klehini

R

MT
MCDONNELL
1679

MT
PRINSEP
1933

SURGEON
MTN
1348

River

Chilkat

Chilkoot

MT
BIGGER

Porcupine Cr

Little Salmon R

River

Klukwan

Ferebee River

Tsirku Glacier

Tsirku R

Chilkat L

Chilkat R

7

Chilkoot
L

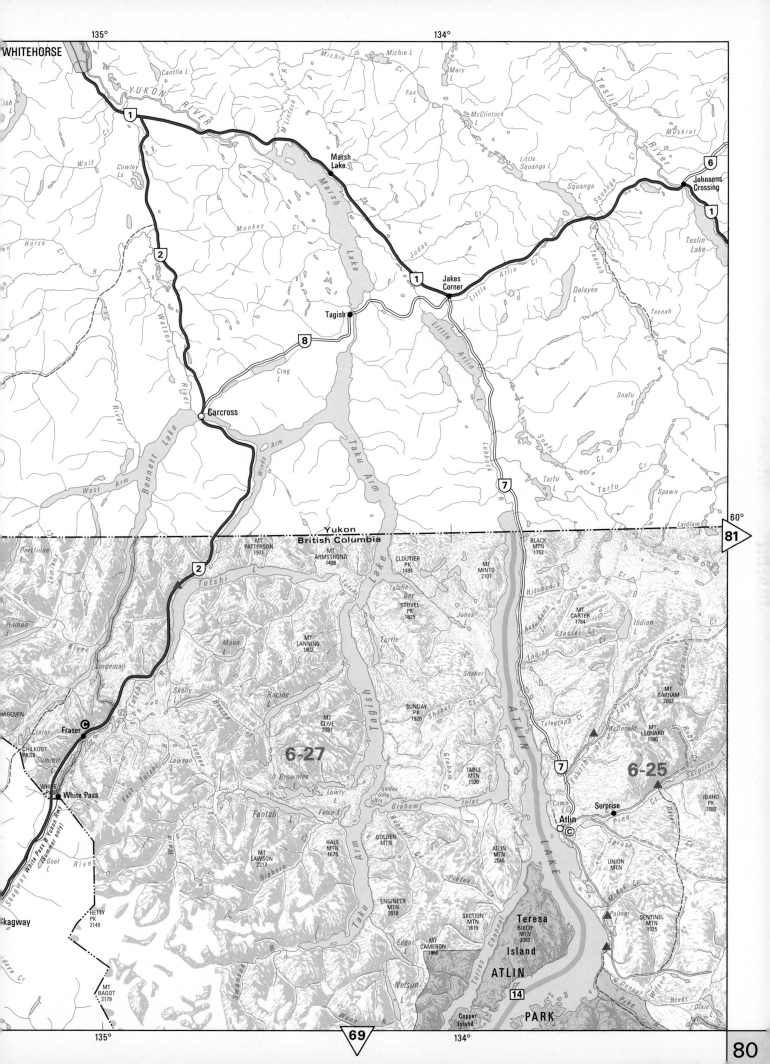

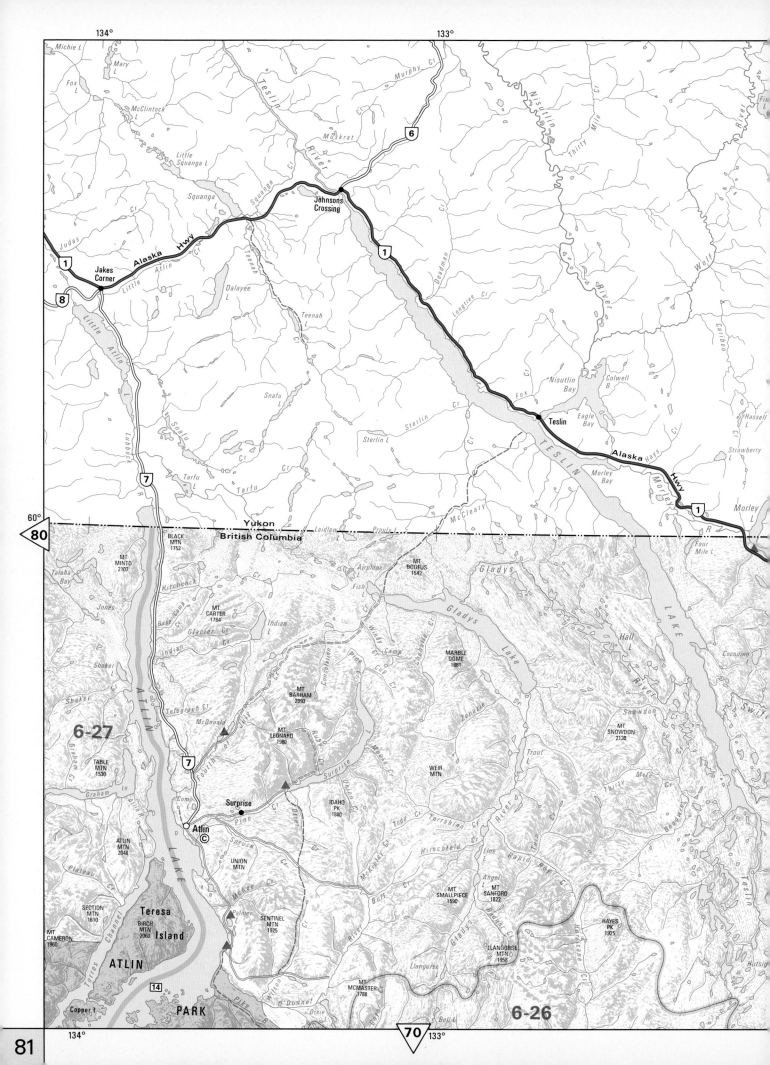

134°   133°

Michie L
Mary L
Fox L
McClintock L
Teslin River
Murphy Cr
Nisutlin River
Thirty Mile Cr
Fish R

Little Squanga L
Muskrat L
6

Squanga Cr
Squanga L
Squanga L
Teenah R
Johnsons Crossing
1
Deadman Cr
Longtree Cr
Nisutlin Bay
Colwell B
Hassell L

Alaska Hwy
Jakes Corner
1
8
Atlin Little
Teenah L
Teenah L
Dalayee L
Fox Cr
Teslin
Eagle Bay
Strawberry L

7
Little Atlin L
Lubbock R
Snafu Cr
Snafu L
Sterlin Cr
Sterlin L
Sterlin L
TESLIN
Alaska
Hays Cr
Morley Bay

Tarfu L
Tarfu Cr
Tarfu Cr
McCleary L
Morley Bay
Morley R
Hwy
1
Morley L

60°
80
Yukon
British Columbia
Laidlaw L
Proulx L
McCleary L
Four Mile L

Black Mtn 1752
MT Minto 2107
Hitchcock Cr
Airplane L
MT Boofus 1542
Gladys
LAKE

Talaha Bay
Jones L
Base Camp
MT Carter 1784
Glacier Cr Cr
Indian Cr
Fish Cr
Gladys Lake
Hall River

Shaker L
Indian
Indian L
Long Shallow Cr
Pine Cr
Cup Cr
Camp
Chahells Cr
MARBLE DOME 1881
Snowdon L
Coconino L

6-27
Shaker Cr
Telegraph Cr
McDonald
MT Barham 2093
Ruby Cr
Moose Cr
Zenalale Cr
MT Snowdon 2130

Graham Cr
TABLE MTN 1530
7
Fourth of July Cr
MT Leonard 1980
Surprise Cr
WEIR MTN
Trout L
Thirty Mile Cr

Graham In
Comp L
Surprise
Atlin
C
Pine Cr
Otter Cr
IDAHO PK 1880
Todd Cr
Torrahina Cr
Rapid Roy Cr
Boulder Cr

Plateau Cr
ATLIN MTN 2046
McKee Cr
UNION MTN
Spruce Cr
Bull Cr
McKinley Cr
Hirschfeld L
Line L
Teslin R

SECTION MTN 1610
BIRCH MTN 2060
Teresa Island
Palmer
SENTINEL MTN 1925
Wilson Cr
MT SMALLPIECE 1590
Ahgel Cr
MT SANFORD 1822
Waddell Cr
HAYES PK 1925
Hutsig L

MT CAMERON 1960
Torres Channel
ATLIN
LAKE
14
Pike R
PARK
O'Donnel R
Dixie Cr
MT MCMASTER 1788
Llangorse L
LLANGORSE MTN 1958
Gladys R
Bell Cr
Hurricane Cr

Copper I
134°
70
133°
6-26

81

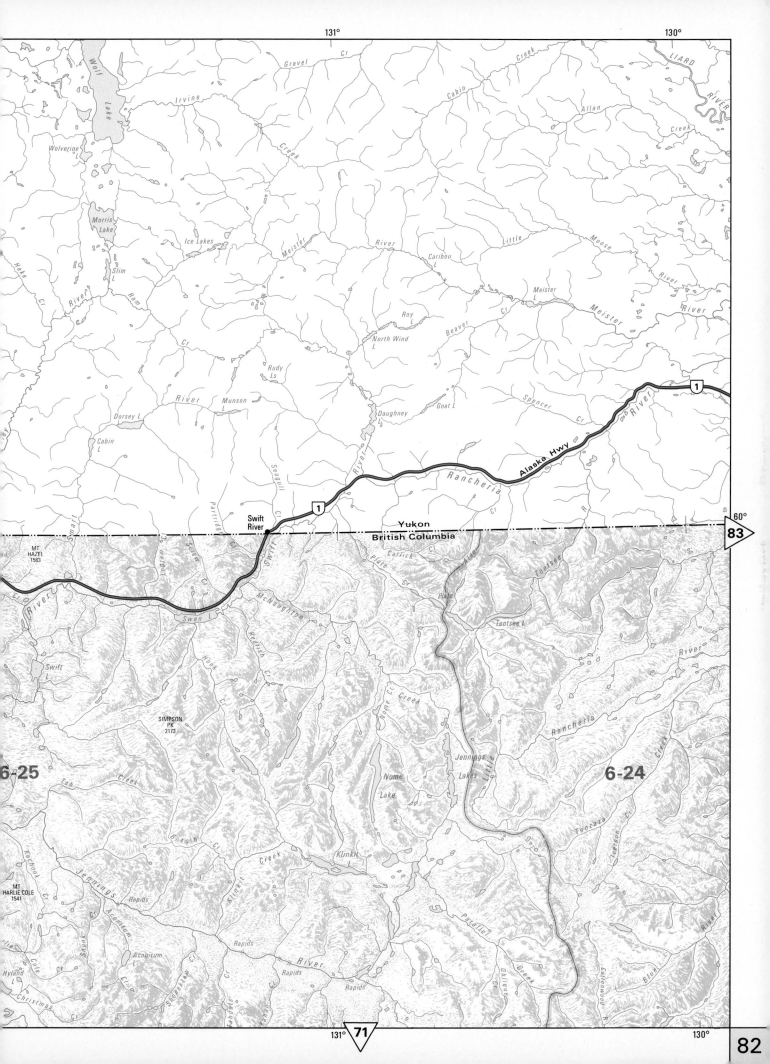

LIARD

RIVER

Wolf
Lake

Irvine

Gravel   Cr

Cabin   Creek

Allan

Creek

Wolverine

Morris
Lake

Ice Lakes

Meister   River

Little   Moose

River

Hake
Cr

Slim
L

Ram

Caribou
L

Meister
L

Meister   River

Dorsey L

River   Munson
L

Roy

North Wind
L

Beaver

Spencer   Cr

Cabin
L

Rudy
Ls

Daughney

Goat L

Alaska Hwy   River

1

Seagull   Cr

River

Rancheria

1

Partridge   Cr

Swift
River

Cr

Smart   Cr

60°

83

MT
HAZEL
1583

Swift   Cr

Carlick   Cr

Plate   Cr

Alan

Tootsee

Cr   River

Cougar   Cr

Screw   Cr

McNaughton

Plate

Swan L

Tootsee L

6-25

SIMPSON
PK
2173

Redfish   Cr

Hook   Cr

Nome Cr   Creek

Jennings   Little   Rancheria

River

6-24

Teh   Creek

Botsin   Cr

Nome
Lake

Jennings
Lakes

Tuozaza   Cr

Trenson   Cr

Cottonwood   Creek

MT
HARLIE COLE
1541

Kechook   Cr

Jennings   Cr

Aconiteum   Cr

Klinkit   Creek

Klinkit   Cr

Patallel   Cr

Bluet   River

Hyland
L

Acontium

Rapids

Rapids

River

Rapids

Oblique   Creek

Christmas   Cr

Shopektaw Cr

Tahdou   Cr

Kahn   Cr

Rapids

Rapids

Yukon
British Columbia

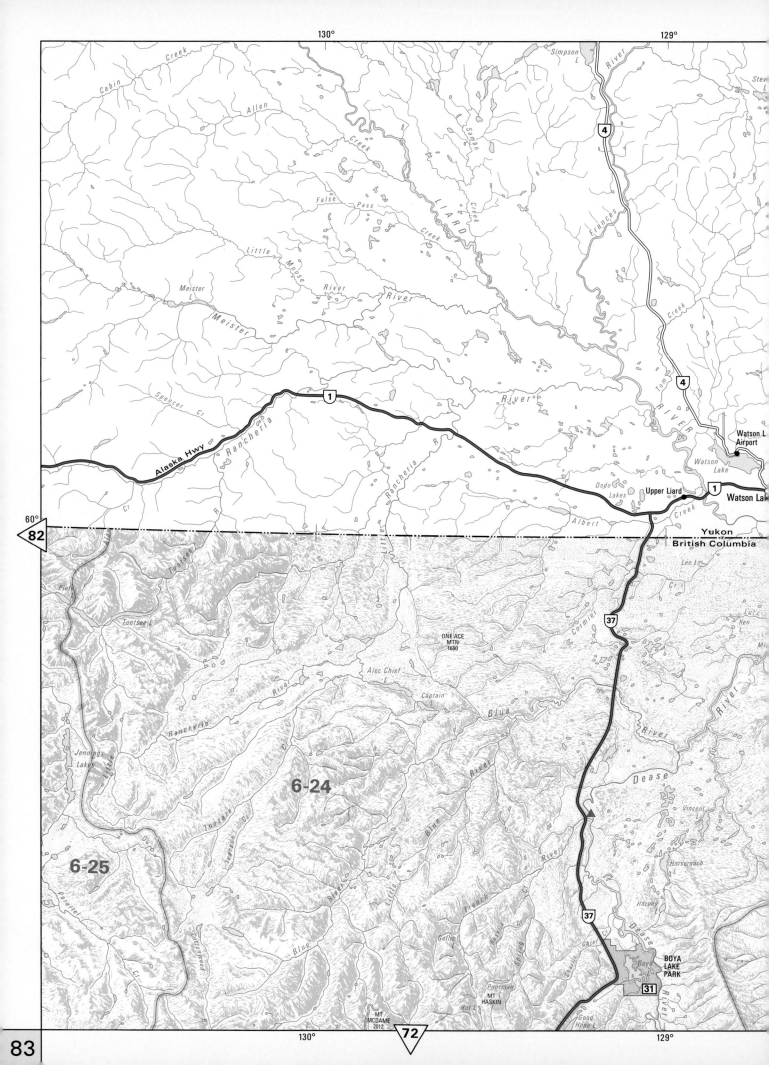

Simpson L

River

4

Frances

4

LIARD

Tom

Sambo Creek

Creek

Cabin

Creek

Allen

Creek

Little

Moose

River

River

False

Pass

Creek

Meister L

Meister

Spencer Cr

Alaska Hwy

1

Rancheria

Rancheria R

River

RIVER

Watson L
Airport

Watson
Lake

Dodo
Lakes

Upper Liard

1

Watson Lak

Albert   Creek

82

60°

Yukon
British Columbia

Plate

Tootsee

Tootsee L

Little

Leo L

Cormier

Cr

Lutz

Ken

Mt

ONE ACE
MTN
1690

Rancheria

River

Alec Chief

Captain
L

Blue

River

37

River

Dease

Jennings
Lakes

Little

6-24

Blue

River

Vincent
L

Hot

Little

Toozaza Cr

Jackson Cr

River

French Cr

Spring Cr

River

Harseranch
L

6-25

Parallel Cr

Cottonwood

Cr

Blue

Cr

Gallic
L

Beatin Cr

Whaleba Cr

Harvey
L

Chief Cr

Dease

River

37

BOYA
LAKE
PARK

Boya
L

31

Peprman
MT
HASKIN

Hot L

72

MT
MCDAME
2012

Good
Hope L

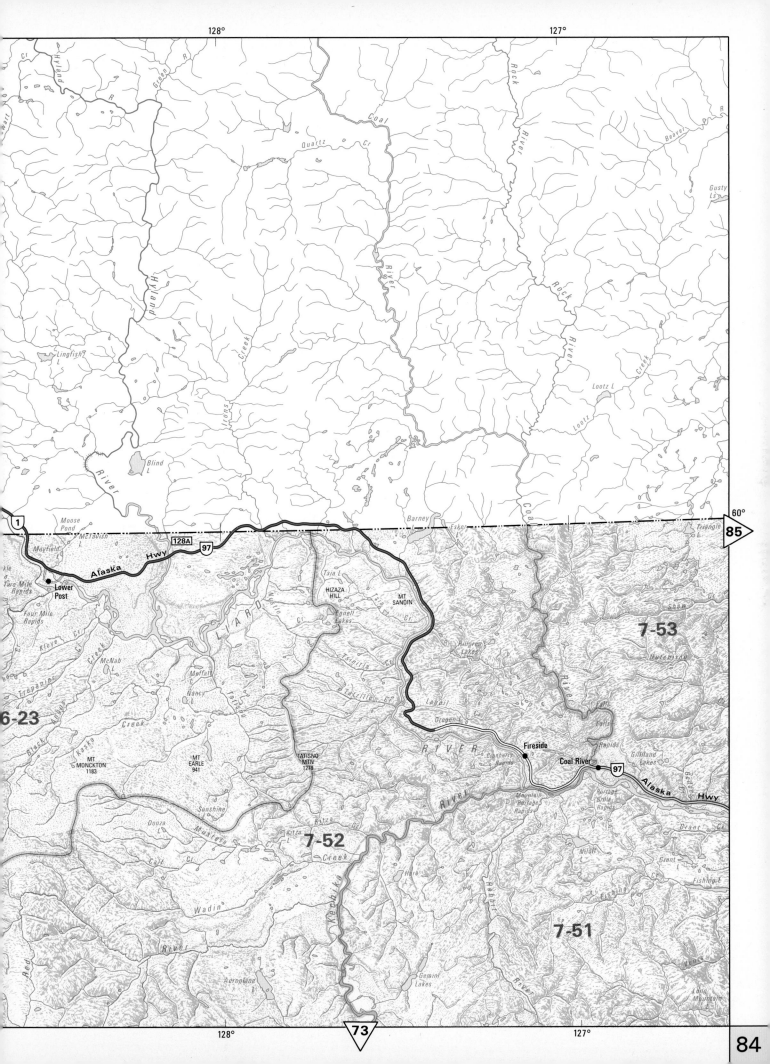

128°

127°

60°

Hyland

Green R

Coal

Quartz Cr

Rock River

Beaver R

Gusty Ls

Lingfish L

Irons Creek

Rock River

Lootz Creek

Lootz L

River

Blind L

Coal

Barney

Esker

Triangle L

1

Moose Pond

McTavish L

Alaska Hwy 128A 97

Shaw

Mayfield

Tsja L

7-53

Two Mile Rapids

Lower Post

HIZAZA HILL

MT SANDIN

Hutchison

Four Mile Rapids

LIARD

Nuttio Cr

Egnell Lakes

Isla Cr

Hilgren Lakes

River

Falls

Kloya Cr

McNab

Tsinijia Cr

Egnell

Falls

Black Angus

Trepanier

Creek

Moffatt L

Nancy L

Tatshao

Taizille Cr

Otegan L

Fireside

Cranberry Rapids

Coal River 97

Rapids

Alaska Hwy

Gilliland Lakes

Kaska Creek

MT MONCKTON 1183

MT EARLE 941

TATISNO MTN 1278

R I V E R

Mountain Portage Rapids

Portage Skila Rapids

Grant Cr

Dooza L

Mustova Cr

Sunshine

Kitza Cr

Kitza

7-52

Creek

River

Niloit

Grant L

Fishing L

Calf Cr

Wadin

Kechika

Herb

Hehan

7-51

Red

River

Aeroplane L

Gemini Lakes

River

Dease

Long Mountain

128°

127°

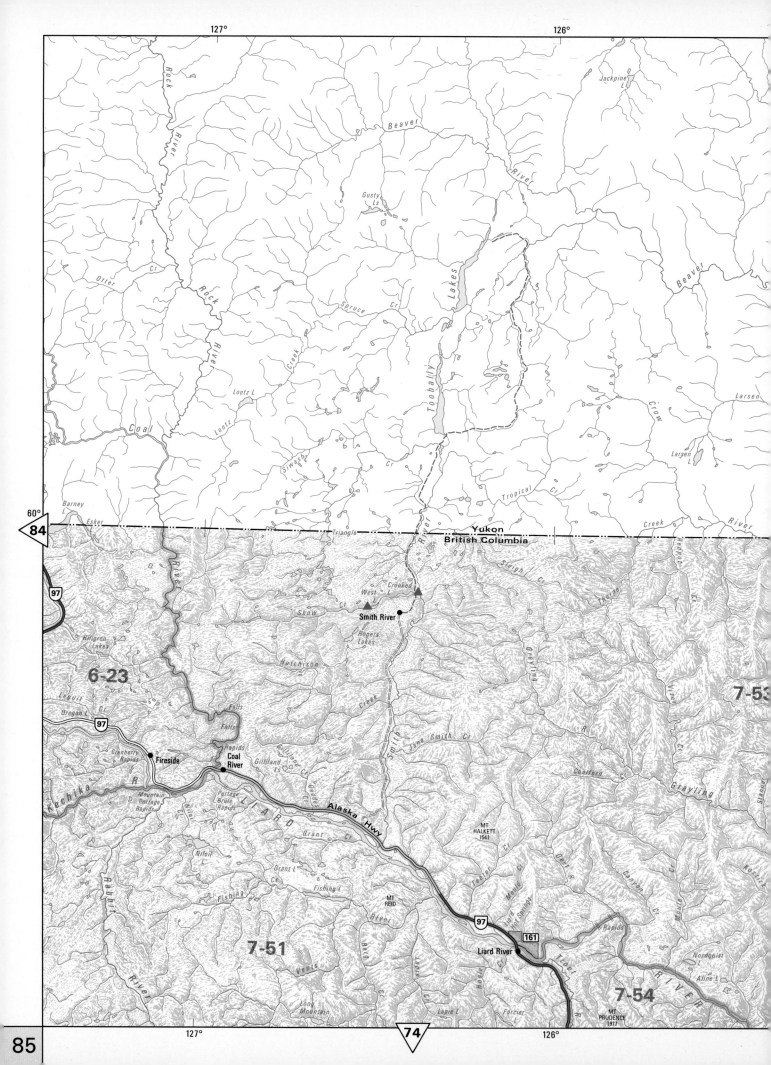

Rock River

Beaver River

Jackpine L

Gusty Ls

Otter Cr

Spruce Cr

Lakes

Larsen

Lootz L

Rock River

Toobally

Crow

Coal

Siwash Cr

Lootz

Larsen L

Barney L

Tropical Cr

60°

Esker

Triangle

Creek

River

84

Yukon
British Columbia

97

West L

Crooked L

Sleigh Cr

Hilgren Lakes

Shaw

Cr

Smith River

Thorne

6-23

Rogers Lakes

Grayling

7-53

Hutchison

Leguit

Oregon L

Cr

Falls

Creek

Smith

Jane Smith Cr

R

97

Falls

Chalford Cr

Cranberry Rapids

Fireside

Rapids
Coal River

Gillilland Ls

Gething Cr

Grayling

Kechika R

Mountain Portage Rapids

Portage Brûlé Rapids

LIARD

Alaska Hwy

MT
HALKETT
1541

Deer R

Canyon Cr

Kosick

Rabbit

Niloil Cr

Grant Cr

Tobin Cr

Mould Cr

Nifoil L

Grant L

Fishing L

MT
REID

97

Liard Hot Springs

Rapids

Nordquist L

7-51

Fishing L

River

Beth Cr

161

Liard River

Trout

Aline L

Vents

Hogie Cr

7-54

River

Long Mountain

Lapie L

Forciat L

R

MT
PRUDENCE
1977

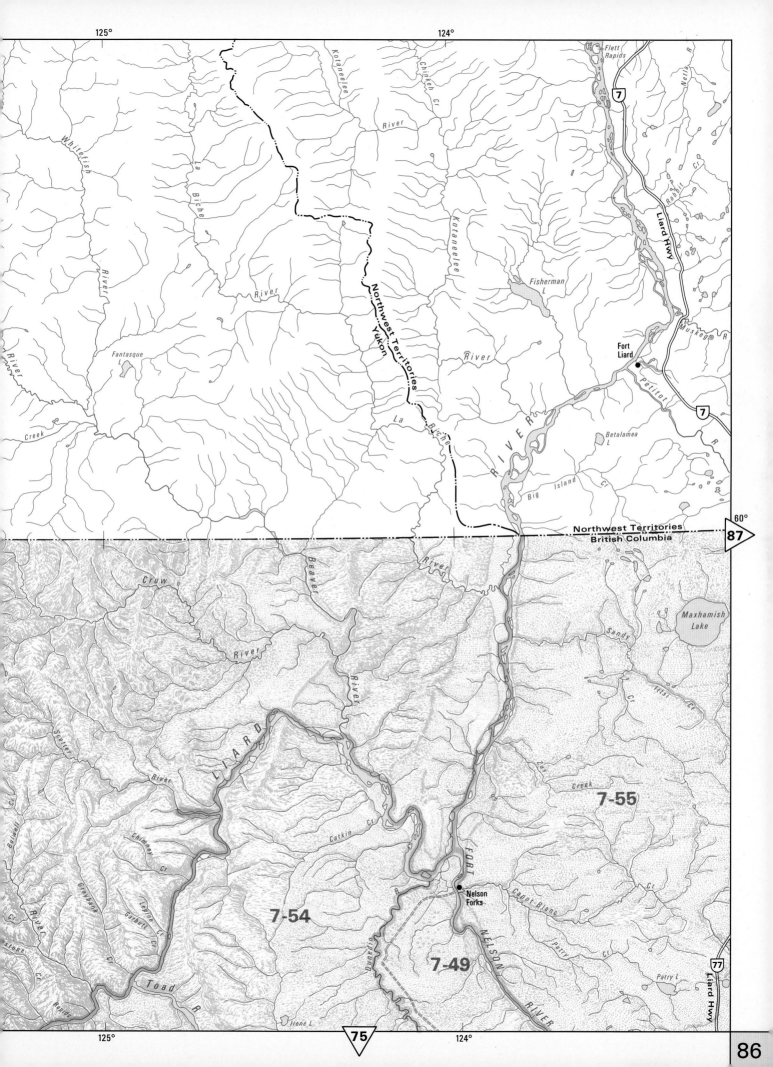

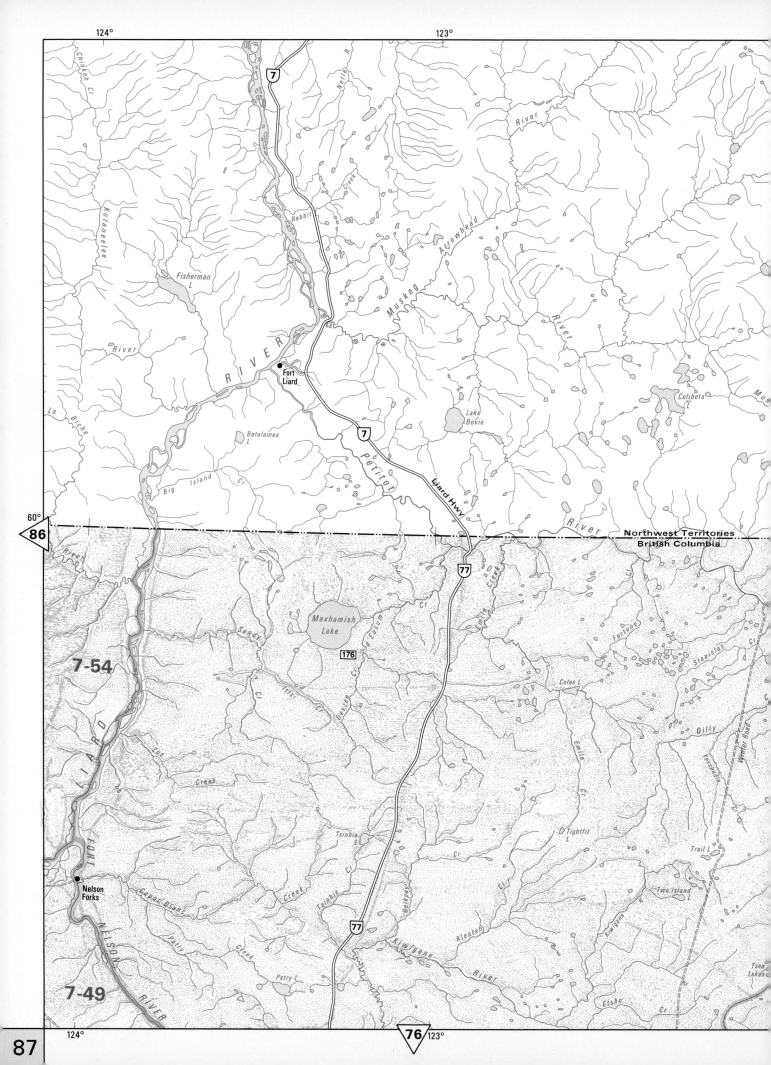

7

Chinkeh Cr

Netla R

River

Kotaneelee

Rabbit

Creek

Muskeg

Arrowhead

Fisherman L

River

River

RIVER

Fort Liard

La Biche

Betalamea L

Big Island Cr

Lake Bovie

Celibeta L

7

Petitot

Liard Hwy

Mus

River

◁ 86

Northwest Territories
British Columbia

77

River

7-54

Maxhamish Lake

Sandy

Cr

Emile Creek

Fortune

Coles L

Stanislas Cr

176

Cr of Easum

Oaszen Cr

LIARD

Tetsi Cr

Emile Cr

Dilly

Yasshadie Cr

Winter Road

Zus

Creek

Tightfit L

FORT

Tsinhia L

Cr

Trail L

Nelson Forks

Capot Blanc

Creek

Tsinhla Cr

Deltkga

Cr

Two Island L

Kiwigana R

Patry

Creek

77

Kiwigana River

Klenteh

Tsea Lakes

7-49

Patry L

NELSON

RIVER

77

Etsho Cr

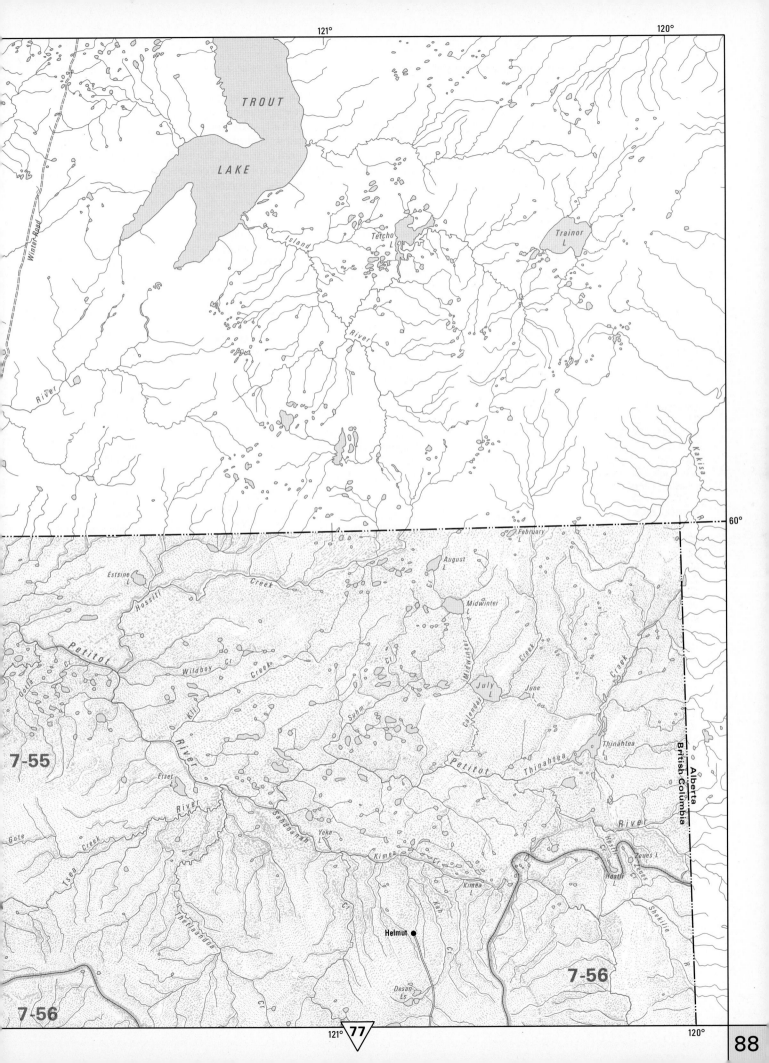

TROUT

LAKE

Winter Road

Island

Tetcho L

Trainor L

River

River

Kakisa

February L

August L

Estsine L

Creek

Midwinter L

Hassiti

Midwinter

Cr

Petitot

Cr

Wildboy Cr

Creek

Creek

Kli

Suhm

Cr

July L

June L

Calendat

7-55

River

Thinahtea

Etset

Alberta

British Columbia

Gote

Petitot

Thinahtea

River

Creek

Sandoanah

Yeka L

Hosth

Zeues L

Tsea

River

Kimea

Hostli L

Thetaandoa

Cr

Kimea Cr

Kimea L

Kah Cr

Helmut ●

7-56

7-56

Cr

Desan Ls

B.C. FOREST SERVICE RECREATION SITES

Forest recreation in B.C. involves dozens of activities, ranging from the passive enjoyment of scenery to the physically demanding challenges of mountaineering and kayaking. Approximately two million people annually take advantage of the more than one thousand recreation sites and thousands of kilometres of trails provided.

The sites are rustic and usually small without sophisticated amenities but do include basic facilities. They are located near lakes and rivers, blending in with the natural surroundings. The overall goal of the B.C. Forest Service recreation program is to provide opportunities for outdoor recreation by protecting the provincial forest recreation resource and managing its use. For more information regarding specific sites, please contact the nearest forest district office listed below.

Ministry of Forests
Box 65
ALEXIS CREEK, B.C.
V0L 1A0
394-4215

Ministry of Forests
185 Yellowhead Hwy.
Box 269
BURNS LAKE, B.C.
V0J 1E0
692-7515

Ministry of Forests
370 Dogwood St. South
CAMPBELL RIVER, B.C.
V9W 4L9
286-3282

Ministry of Forests
845 Columbia Ave.
CASTLEGAR, B.C.
V1N 1H3
356-2131

Ministry of Forests
Box 6201, RR #1
CLEARWATER, B.C.
V0E 1NO
674-2265

Ministry of Forests
1902 Theatre Road
CRANBROOK, B.C.
V1C 4H4
426-3391

Ministry of Forests
9000-17th St.
DAWSON CREEK, B.C.
V1G 4A4
784-2350

Ministry of Forests
Stikine & Commercial
Gen. Del., Hwy 37
DEASE LAKE, B.C.
V0C 1L0
771-4211

Ministry of Forests
7233 Trans-Canada Hwy.
Box 689
DUNCAN, B.C.
V9L 3Y1
746-5123

Ministry of Forests
Alaska Hwy.
RR #1, Mile 301
FORT NELSON, B.C.
V0C 1R0
774-3936

Ministry of Forests
Stones Bay Road
Box 100
FORT ST JAMES, B.C.
V0J 1P0
996-7131

Ministry of Forests
10716 - 100 Ave.
FORT ST JOHN, B.C.
V1J 1Z3
787-3301

Ministry of Forests
600 - 9th St. North
Box 1380
GOLDEN, B.C.
V0A 1H0
344-7514

Ministry of Forests
Sagamore Ave.
Box 2650
GRAND FORKS, B.C.
V0H 1H0
442-5411

Ministry of Forests
Sawmill Road
Box 190
HAGENSBORG, B.C.
V0T 1H0
982-2621

Ministry of Forests
West Hwy 62
Box 215
HAZELTON, B.C.
V0J 1Y0
842-6581

Ministry of Forests
Box 69
HORSEFLY, B.C.
V0L 1L0
620-3417

Ministry of Forests
3429 - 10th St.
Bag 2000
HOUSTON, B.C.
V0J 1Z0
845-7712

Ministry of Forests
406 - 7th Ave.
Box 189
INVERMERE, B.C.
V0A 1K0
342-4200

Ministry of Forests
1255 Dalhousie Place
KAMLOOPS, B.C.
V2C 5Z5
372-5832

Ministry of Forests
Bag 700
LILLOOET, B.C.
V0K 1V0
256-7531

Ministry of Forests
120 Mackenzie Blvd.
Bag 5000
MACKENZIE, B.C.
V0J 2C0
997-3310

Ministry of Forests
Box 40
McBRIDE, B.C.
V0J 2E0
569-2265

Ministry of Forests
2196 Quilchena Ave.
MERRITT, B.C.
V0K 2B0
378-9311

Ministry of Forests
Ridgewood Road, RR #1
NELSON, B.C.
V1L 5P4
825-4415

Ministry of Forests
Box 129
100 MILE HOUSE, B.C.
V0K 2EO
395-3812

Ministry of Forests
102 Industrial Pl.
PENTICTON, B.C.
V2A 7C9
492-8721

Ministry of Forests
4227 - 6th Ave.
PORT ALBERNI, B.C.
V9Y 4N1
724-9205

Ministry of Forests
2291 Mine Road
Box 7000
PORT McNEILL, B.C.
V0N 2R0
956-4416

Ministry of Forests
7077 Duncan St.
POWELL RIVER, B.C.
V6A 1W1
485-9831

Ministry of Forests
1600 - 3rd Ave.
Box 38,
PRINCE GEORGE, B.C.
V2L 3G6
565-6295

Ministry of Forests
125 Market Place
PRINCE RUPERT, B.C.
V8J 1B9
627-0452

Ministry of Forests
120 - 2nd Ave.
Box 39
QUEEN CHARLOTTE, B.C.
V0T 1S0
559-8447

Ministry of Forests
322 Johnston Ave.
QUESNEL, B.C.
V2J 3M5
992-4400

Ministry of Forests
1761 Big Eddy Road
Box 470
REVELSTOKE, B.C.
V0E 2S0
837-7611

Ministry of Forests
9850 South McGrath Road
Box 159
ROSEDALE, B.C.
V0X 1X0
794-3361

Ministry of Forests
Box 340
SALMON ARM, B.C.
V1E 4N5
832-7153

Ministry of Forests
3793 Alfred Ave.
2nd Floor
SMITHERS, B.C.
V0J 2NO
847-7555

Ministry of Forests
42000 Loggers Lane
Box 1970
SQUAMISH, B.C.
V0N 3G0
898-9671

Ministry of Forests
310 - 4722 Lakelse Ave.
TERRACE, B.C.
V8G 1R6
638-3290

Ministry of Forests
560 Spruce St.
Box 190
VANDERHOOF, B.C.
V0J 3A0
567-6363

MINISTRY OF ENVIRONMENT CONTACTS

REGIONAL OFFICES

Vancouver Island	2569 Kenworth Rd., Nanaimo, V9T 4P7, 758-3951
Lower Mainland	10334-152A st., Surrey, V3R 7P8, 584-8822
Thompson-Nicola	1259 Dalhousie Dr., Kamloops, V2C 5Z5, 374-9717
Kootenay	310 Ward St., Nelson, V1L 5S4, 352-2211, 354-6333
	106-5th Ave. S., Cranbrook, V1C 2G2, 489-1450
Cariboo	540 Borland St., Williams Lake, V2G 1R8, 398-4530

Skeena	Bag 5000 3726 Alfred Ave., Smithers, V0J 2N0, 847-7303
Omineca-Peace	Plaza 400, 1011 Fourth Ave., Pr. George, V2L 3H9, 565-6145
	10142-101 Ave., Fort St. John, V1J 2B3, 787-3295
Okanagan	3547 Skaha Lake Rd., Penticton, V2A 7K2, 493-8261
Victoria	Wildlife Branch, 780 Blanshard St., V8V 1X5, 387-9737

CONSERVATION OFFICER SERVICE DISTRICT OFFICES

Vancouver Island
Campbell River	101-370 S. Dogwood St., V9W 6Y7, 286-7630
Duncan	238 Government St., V9L 1A5, 746-6183
Nanaimo	2569 Kenworth Rd., V9T 4P7, 758-3951
Port Alberni	4515 Elizabeth St., V9Y 6L5, 724-9290
Port Hardy	Bag 11000, 8755 Granville, V0N 2P0, 949-6272

Lower Mainland
Chilliwack	9365 Mill St., V2P 4N3, 795-8422
Maple Ridge	20450 Dewdney Trunk Rd., V2X 3E3, 465-4011
Powell River	125-6953 Alberni St., V8A 2B8, 485-2554
Sechelt	Box 535, V0N 3G0, 885-2004
Squamish	Box 187, V0N 3G0, 892-5971
Surrey	10334-152A St., V3R 7P8, 584-8822

Thompson-Nicola
Clearwater	Box 490, V0E 1N0, 674-3722
Clinton	Box 220, V0K 1K0, 459-2341
Kamloops	1259 Dalhousie Dr., V2C 5Z5, 374-9717
Lillooet	Bag 700, V0K 1V0, 256-4636
Merritt	Bag 4400, V0K 2B0, 378-9377

Kootenay
Castlegar	2205-14th Ave., V1N 3M7, 365-8522
Cranbrook	106-5th Ave. S., V1C 2G2, 426-1450
Creston	Box 1550, V0B 1G0, 428-3220
Fernie	Bag 1000, V0B 1M0, 423-7551
Golden	Box 1313, V0A 1H0, 344-7101
Invermere	Box 2949, V0A 1K0, 342-4266
Nakusp	Box 183, V0G 1R0, 265-3522
Nelson	310 Ward St., V1L 5S4, 354-6397

Cariboo
Alexis Creek	V0L 1A0, 394-4343
Hagensborg	Box 190, V0T 1H0, 982.2626
100 Mile House	Box 187, V0K 2E0, 395-5511
Quesnel	350 Barlow St., V2J 2C1, 922-4244
Williams Lake	340 Borland St., V2G 1R8, 398-4569

Skeena
Atlin	Box 180, V0W 1A0, 651-7501
Burns Lake	Box 285, V0J 1E0, 692-7777
Dease Lake	General Delivery, V0C 1L0, 771-3566
New Hazelton	Box 309, V0J 2J0, 842-5319
Queen Charlotte City	Box 370, V0T 1S0, 559-8431
Smithers	Bag 5000, 3726 Alfred St., V0J 2N0, 847-7303
Terrace	4825 Keith Ave., V8G 1K7, 638-3279

Omineca-Peace
Chetwynd	Bag 105, 4729-51st St., V0C 1J0, 788-3611
Dawson Creek	1201-103rd Ave., V1G 4J2, 784-2304
Fort Nelson	Box 247, V0C 1R0, 774-3547
Fort St. John	10142-101st Ave., V1J 2B3, 787-3295
Prince George	1011 Fourth Ave., V2L 3H9, 565-6145
Valemount	Box 39, V0E 2Z0, 566-4398
Vanderhoof	Box 980, V0J 3A0, 567-6304

Okanagan
Penticton	3547 Skaha Lake Rd., V2A 7K2, 493-8261
Vernon	5-4320 29th St., V1T 5B8, 549-5558
Princeton	Box 1000, 151 Vermilion St., V0X 1W0, 295-6343

Mountain Goat

Cougar

WILDLIFE VIEWING

British Columbia offers many opportunites to see wildlife in a natural setting. "Just looking" can be a fascinating experience, but remember these are wild animals. Respect their need for space and avoid crowding them. Use binoculars for that really close look. Use caution, especially when viewing or photographing bears or other potentially dangerous large animals, and do not try to feed them. Wild animals that become habituated to regular handouts may lose much of their ability to fend for themselves, and subsequently suffer in the lean months when their human benefactors are no longer around. They may also lose their fear of humans, and in their trust or their belligerance, endanger both themselves and people they encounter.

Some of the viewing areas shown on the Atlas maps and listed below have no viewing facilities, interpretive aids, or developed access. Developed areas with trails, blinds, viewing towers, informative signs, etc. are most likely to be found near population centres, along highways, within wildlife reserves or sanctuaries, or parks.

AREAS	SPECIES/VIEWING DETAILS
1 ▷ ADAMS RIVER - Page 16A	Spawning sockeye salmon (largest run in North America) — major runs occur once every 4 years (1990, 1994...) in October with minor runs in the intervening year, wintering waterfowl — full interpretive facilities.
2 ▷ ARROW LAKES - Page 17C	Waterfowl viewing from Galena Bay in the north to Castlegar in the south.
3 ▷ ATNARKO RIVER - Page 23B	Bears, raptors.
4 ▷ BABINE RIVER - Page 53D	Spawning sockeye salmon in September-October.
4a ▷ BERESFORD GRASSLANDS - Page 16C	High numbers of raptors including short-eared owls, marsh hawks, red-tailed hawks. Migrating Swainsons and rough-legged hawks, migrating sandhill cranes in April and October.
5 ▷ BLACKFISH SOUND - Page 12C	Killer whale, Dahl porpoise, other marine mammals.
6 ▷ BOTANICAL BEACH - Page 3C	The deep, clear sandstone tidal pools of this area make it unique for the viewing of a variety of intertidal species. The best time being at low tide — check a tide table before you go. Also a good viewpoint for Pacific gray whales, especially during spring migration.
7 ▷ BOUNDARY BAY - Page 5C	Excellent opportunities, during migration periods, to view waterfowl (herons, ducks, grebes and sandpipers) as well as snowy and short-eared owls, eagles, hawks and shorebirds, occasional whales — visitor facilities.
8 ▷ BOUNDARY LAKE - Page 50C	Bear, moose, deer, furbearers, birds.
9 ▷ BOWRON RIVER - Page 39C	Spawning chinook salmon in September.
10 ▷ BOWRON SLOUGH - Page 39C	Access by canoe only — viewing of moose, deer, caribou, waterfowl, birds, beaver, muskrat, and river otter.
11 ▷ BRIDGE CREEK - Page 17A	Spawning rainbow trout and kokanee salmon in June-September — partial interpretive facilities.
11a ▷ BRUNSWICK POINT - Page 5C	Excellent birding all year. Overwintering swans and waterfowl, shore birds in late summer. Close to Reifel Refuge. Easy walk along dike.
12 ▷ BULKLEY RIVER / MORICETOWN FALLS - Page 45B	Spawning chinook salmon; native fishery in September. People have been catching salmon here for 5,000 years.
13 ▷ BULL MOUNTAIN - Page 9B	Big game — all species.
14 ▷ BUNSBY ISLANDS - Page 11D	Marine mammals, sea birds.
15 ▷ CATHEDRAL PARK - Page 7C	Deer, mountain goat, California bighorn sheep, golden eagle, hawks.

16	**CHAPPERON LAKE** - Page 16C	Viewing of grassland birds, raptors, swans, geese, hawks, plus sandhill cranes during April migration.
16a	**CHEAKAMUS RIVER** - Page 5A	Large numbers of bald eagles visible from the road November-February.
17	**CHILANKO MARSH** - Page 24B	Wildlife Management Area for migratory shore birds and waterfowl, osprey, bald eagle, moose, deer, coyote and furbearers. Viewing tower, trails & interpretive signs.
18	**CHILKO RIVER** - Page 25A	Spawning steelhead trout in May.
19	**CHRISTINA LAKE** - Page 8C	Deer, California bighorn sheep, bald and golden eagle, coyote, cougar, rattlesnakes.
20	**COLUMBIA LAKE PARK** - Page 18D	Wildlife Reserve — wildlife winter range.
21	**COQUIHALLA RIVER** - Page 6A	Spawning steelhead trout in June-July — partial interpretive facilities.
22	**COURTENAY RIVER ESTUARY** - Page 2A	Trumpeter swans (threatened species) - highest wintering concentration in North America, waterfowl, shore birds.
23	**CRANBERRY MARSH** - Page 40D	Wildlife Reserve — waterfowl, raptors, song birds, moose, furbearers.
24	**CRESTON** - Page 9C	Federal-Provincial Wildlife Management Area. Excellent opportunities for viewing birds (over 240 species), including Canada and snow geese, waterfowl, upland birds, as well as small mammals and deer.
25	**CROOKED RIVER** - Page 48B	Moose, furbearers, waterfowl and trumpeter swans in winter.
25a	**DOWNIE CREEK** - Page 28C	Moose, grizzly bear, woodland caribou, marten, beaver, golden eagle, otter, wolverine and a wide range of mountain birds.
26	**DUNLEVY CREEK** - Page 56B	Stone sheep, deer, Rocky Mountain elk, moose, golden eagle.
27	**EDZIZA PARK** - Page 60B	Moose, Osborne caribou, mountain goat, stone sheep, wolf, waterfowl.
28	**ELK RIVER** - Page 1B	Roosevelt elk, deer.
29	**ENGLISHMAN RIVER** - Page 2D	Spawning steelhead trout in May — partial interpretive facilities.
30	**GERRARD** - Page 17D	Spawning rainbow trout (up to 14 kilograms) in May-June — partial interpretive facilities.
31	**GOLDSTREAM RIVER** - PAGE 3D	Spawning chum salmon in October — full interpretive facilities.
31a	**GROVE BURN** - Page 38B	Moose, hares, song birds, beaver, raptors, waterfowl (nesting), squirrels and grouse.
32	**HAINES ROAD** - Page 79C	Bear, moose, woodland caribou, stone sheep — viewing from Pleasant Camp to B.C./ Yukon border.
32a	**HALFWAY RIVER** - Page 17D	Mountain goat, grizzly bear summer areas — back country with difficult access.
33	**HANNA-TINTINA** - Page 52B	Bear, sockeye salmon spawning in early August.
34	**HARRISON RIVER** - Page 6C	Bald eagle, herons, swans, waterfowl, as well as spawning salmon from October to February.
35	**HEIGHT OF THE ROCKIES** - Page 19C	Grizzly bear, black bear, cougar, wolf, coyote, moose, bighorn sheep, mountain goat, elk, deer, eagles.
35a	**HIGH BAR** - Page 14B	California bighorn sheep, spring mule deer, chukar partridge, grassland birds.

36	HILL CREEK - Page 17B	Spawning kokanee salmon in September — full interpretive facilities.
37	ILGACHUZ - Page 37C	Woodland caribou can be seen in June-July and September-November — no road access.
37a	INONOAKLIN - Page 8A	Elk, moose, white-tailed deer, mule deer.
38	JUNCTION - Page 25D	Wildlife Management Area for California bighorn sheep (largest herd in North America), deer, coyote, cougar, curlews — four-wheel drive truck or small vehicle access only.
38a	KEREMEOS - Page 7C	Mountain goats viewable from highway.
39	KHUTZEYMATEEN - Page 44C	The name means "a confined place of fish and bears" and is one of the best places in the world to observe grizzly bears as they fish for spawning salmon. Access is by boat from Prince Rupert.
40	KIKOMUN CREEK - Page 10C	Spawning kokanee salmon in September.
40a	KITCHENER - Page 9C	Moose, elk, white-tailed deer, mule deer, golden eagle, bald eagle, raven.
41	KOKANEE CREEK - Page 8B	Spawning kokanee salmon in August-September — full interpretive facilities.
41a	KOOTENAY LAKE - Page 8B	Osprey nesting, bald eagle nesting, waterfowl, great blue heron.
42	KOOTENAY NATIONAL PARK - Page 18B	Moose, Rocky Mountain elk, Rocky Mountain goat and black bear may be seen along the park highway. Coyote, wolf and grizzly bear also inhabit the park.
43	LAKELSE LAKE - Page 45C	Various species of spawning salmon in spring and fall. Trumpeter swans winter on lake. Moose, wolf, bear and cougar also in area.
44	LOWER SKEENA RIVER -Page 44D	Eagles, shore birds, raptors.
45	MANNING PARK - Page 6D	Hoary marmot and other small mammals , deer, birds, black bear.
46	MEADOW CREEK - Page 17D	Moose, bear, spawning kokanee salmon in September — full interpretive faculties.
47	MOBERLY MARSH - Page 28D	Wildlife Reserve — waterfowl.
48	MORICE LAKE - Page 45D	Spawning chinook salmon in September.
48a	MT. REVELSTOKE SUMMIT - Page 17A	Woodland caribou, black bear, blue grouse, white-tailed ptarmigan, gray jay, barred owl, northern pygmy owl, golden eagle, wide range of mountain bird species.
49	MUNCHO LAKE PARK - Page 74B	The mineral salt licks at km 760 (mile 474) and elsewhere in the park provide an excellent opportunity for focused viewing of stone sheep, caribou and moose. Black bear, the occasional grizzly, mule deer and mountain goat are also native to the park.
50	NADINA RIVER - Page 46C	Wildlife Reserve — moose winter range.
50a	NANCY GREENE - Page 8C	Ground squirrels, moose, mule deer, white-tailed deer, black bear.
51	NASS RIVER - Page 44B	Sea mammals, birds, spawning sockeye salmon in July-August.
52	NEVIS CREEK - Page 65A	Grizzly and black bear, coyote, wolf, lynx, elk, bison, caribou, mule and white-tailed deer, moose, stone sheep, furbearers, birds in a spectacular alpine setting.
52a	NICOMEN SLOUGH - Page 5D	Wintering ducks, geese, swans and eagles. November to February.
53	NIMPKISH RIVER (Woss Branch) - Page 12C	Spawning sockeye salmon in September.

NORTHEAST ROCKIES
- Page 64B

Grizzly and black bear, coyote, wolf, lynx, elk, bison, mountain goat, caribou, mule and white-tailed deer, moose, stone sheep, furbearers, birds (over 60 species) in an impressive open setting.

 100 MILE MARSH
- Page 26C

Waterfowl viewing, trails, tourist information centre.

 OSOYOOS OXBOWS
- Page 7C

Wildlife Reserve for birds and reptiles such as burrowing owl, white-headed wood-pecker, turkey vulture, California quail, bats, lizards, bull snake, rattlesnakes.

 PACIFIC RIM NATIONAL PARK
- Page 1D

Pacific gray whale, killer whale, other marine mammals, and a variety of waterfowl and shore birds. The best time to observe the migrating gray whales (as many as 17,000) is March-April.

 PEND d'OREILLE
- Page 8D

White-tailed deer, elk, yellow-bellied marmot, osprey, turkey vulture, Lazuli bunting, black bear.

 PENNASK LAKE
- Page 7A

Spawning rainbow trout in June — partial interpretive facilities.

 PINK MOUNTAIN
- Page 65D

Grizzly and black bear, coyote, wolf, lynx, bison, mule and white-tailed deer, elk, caribou, moose and an abundance of birds at North America's earliest known site of man.

 PITT-ADDINGTON MARSH
- Page 5B

Wildlife Management Area for waterfowl and other marsh species. Area has a variety of breeding song birds, waterfowl and raptors. Tundra and trumpeter swans overwinter. Small population of greater sandhill cranes breeding. Associated Ecological Reserve for bog habitat — viewing facilities and hiking trails.

  PREMIER LAKE
- Page 9B

Bighorn sheep, elk, deer, spawning rainbow trout in June — full interpretive facilities.

 RATTLESNAKE HILL
- Page 15A

Chukar partridge, rattlesnakes, wintering peregrine falcons and deer.

 REDFISH CREEK
- Page 8B

Spawning kokanee salmon in August-September — partial interpretive facilities.

 REIFEL MIGRATORY BIRD SANCTUARY
- Page 5C

This sanctuary is comprised of managed habitat and estuarine marsh where thou-sands of migratory birds stop to feed and rest or spend the entire winter. More than 230 species observed, from the plentiful Canada goose to the uncommon black-crowned night heron and the extremely rare temmink's stint.

 ROSE SPIT
- Page 43C

Deer, waterfowl, sea birds.

 RUBY CHANNEL
- Page 2B

Spawning coastal cutthroat trout in May-June.

  SALMON ARM
- Page 16B

Bird and waterfowl nesting area. Large migrations of geese and ducks in spring and fall. Of particular interest is the breeding displays of western grebes, which nest be-tween April and June.

 SEA / IONA ISLANDS
- Page 5C

Sea birds, waterfowl, shore birds, raptors.

 **SERPENTINE WILDLIFE AREA**
- Page 5D

Excellent area for viewing waterfowl and shore birds. There are dykes, trails, observa-tion towers and interpretive signs.

SETON
- Page 15A

Year-round viewing of goats, especially high in winter and spring.

  SIDNEY SPIT PARK
- Page 5C

Fallow deer, black-tailed deer.

SKEENA ISLANDS
- Page 44D

Moose viewing platform.

 SKUTZ FALLS
- Page 2D

Various species of spawning salmon in the fall, rainbow trout, steelhead trout, brown trout.

95

SOMENOS LAKE
- Page 2D

Wildlife Reserve for wintering waterfowl.

 SOUTH MORESBY
- Page 20A

South Moresby is a national park and visitors can see a wide variety of sea birds, marine and land mammals.

 SOUTH THOMPSON R.
- Page 16A

California bighorn sheep, wintering swan, geese, eagles, nesting osprey.

 SPATSIZI PLATEAU WILDERNESS PARK
- Page 62A

Spatsizi means "red goat" from those animals' habit of rolling in red oxide dust. Nearly all the mountain goats in the world live in B.C. Visitors also share the park with stone sheep, woodland caribou, moose, grizzly bear, many smaller mammals, and over 140 species of birds including gyrfalcons.

 SPENCES BRIDGE
- Page 15C

Winter and spring viewing of Rocky Mountain bighorn sheep on highway from Lytton to Spences Bridge.

 SQUAMISH ESTUARY
- Page 5A

Eagles, all types of waterfowl and shore birds.

 STAMP / SOMASS RIVERS
- Page 2C

Spawning sockeye, coho and chinook salmon in the fall — full interpretive facilities.

 STONE MOUNTAIN PARK
- Page 75C

Stone mountain sheep, caribou, moose, snowshoe hare, porcupine and many species of birds including three species of ptarmigan.

 STUMP LAKE
- Page 15D

Migrating waterfowl, sharp-tailed grouse, grassland birds including horned larks, and vesper sparrows.

 SWAN LAKE
- Page 58C

Furbearers, waterfowl, song birds.

 SWAN LAKE / CHRISTMAS HILL NATURE SANCTUARY
- Page 3D

Excellent area for birdwatching, especially in winter. There are bird blinds, interpretive facilities and wheelchair accessible trails.

  SYRINGA
- Page 8B

Rocky Mountain bighorn sheep, white-tailed deer, mule deer, elk, cougar, coyote, canyon wren.

 TAYLOR RIVER
- Page 2C

Spawning coastal cutthroat trout in May — partial interpretive facilities.

 TELKWA MOUNTAINS
- Page 45D

Woodland caribou, mountain goat.

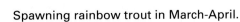 **TRANQUILLE**
- Page 15B

Wildlife Management Area for extremely active waterfowl habitat, especially during spring and fall migrations. Canada geese, whistling and trumpeter swans, song birds, great blue heron, migratory shore birds, wintering eagles, deer, California bighorn sheep.

 TUNKWA LAKE
- Page 15D

Canada geese nesting on island, spawning rainbow trout in June — partial interpretive facilities.

 VASEUX LAKE
- Page 7C

Wildlife Reserve for California bighorn sheep, waterfowl and other migratory birds.

 WEAVER LAKE
- Page 6A

Spawning rainbow trout in March-April.

WELLS GRAY PARK
- Page 27A

Grizzly and black bear, coyote, timber wolf, wolverine, furbearers, mule deer, moose, caribou, mountain goat and many species of waterfowl and upland birds.

WHITESWAN LAKE
- Page 18D

Moose, spawning rainbow trout in May-June — partial interpretive facilities.

WILMER SLOUGH
- Page 18D

Deer, Rocky Mountain elk, Rocky Mountain bighorn sheep, waterfowl, song birds.

WINDERMERE LAKE
- Page 18D

Bald eagle, spawning kokanee salmon in September-October.

WILDLIFE RESERVES

Areas, including both Crown land and private land held under lease, reserved for the protection of wildlife and fisheries habitat or to facilitate recreational use. Hunting and fishing may or may not be permitted in these areas – check the regulations.

— list shows wildlife/habitat type protected

1	**ANTLERS SADDLE** - Page 7A	Deer winter range
2	**ASHNOLA RIVER** - Page 7C	California bighorn sheep
3	**BEAVER COVE** - Page 12C	Estuary
4	**BERGENHAM** - Page 28D	Waterfowl
5	**BOTANIE CREEK** - Page 15C	California bighorn sheep, rattlesnakes
6	**BOUNDARY BAY/ MUD BAY** - Page 5C	Fisheries and aquatic birds
7	**BOUNDARY LAKE** - Page 50C	Waterfowl
8	**BULL RIVER** - Page 9B	Rocky Mountain bighorn sheep, mule deer, white-tailed deer, cougar, black bear, grouse
9	**BUMMERS FLATS** - Page 9B	Waterfowl, elk, deer
10	**BUTTERTUBS SLOUGH** - Page 2D	Freshwater marsh
11	**CHERRY CREEK** - Page 9B	Waterfowl, elk, deer, upland birds, coyote
12	**CHILCOTIN LAKE** - Page 24B	Moose, white pelican, waterfowl
13	**CHILLIWACK RIVER** - Page 6C	Access to fisheries
14	**CHURN CREEK** - Page 25D	California bighorn sheep
15	**CLUXEWE ESTUARY** - Page 11D	Coastal salt marsh
16	**COLUMBIA LAKE** - Page 18D	Wildlife winter range
17	**COLUMBIA LAKE WEST** - Page 18D	Wildlife winter range
18	**COLUMBIA RIVER FLOODPLAIN** - Page 18D	Waterfowl, furbearers, elk, deer
19	**COQUITLAM** - Page 5D	Undyked cottonwood forest
20	**COWICHAN ESTUARY** - Page 5C	Waterfowl

21	**CRANBERRY MARSH (R.W. STARRATT)** - Page 40D	Waterfowl, raptors, song birds, moose, furbearers
22	**DUCK, BARBER & WOODWARD ISLANDS** - Page 5C	Waterfowl and aquatic bird habitat
23	**DUDLEY MARSH** - Page 2D	Freshwater marsh
24	**ENGLISHMAN RIVER ESTUARY** - Page 2B	Fisheries / waterfowl
25	**FORSLUND/WATSON PROPERTY** - Page 5D	Forest birds and deer
26	**FORT ST. JOHN POTHOLES** - Page 57B	Wetlands
27	**GARNET VALLEY** - Page 7A	Deer winter range
28	**GILPIN** - Page 8C	Deer winter/spring range
29	**GREEN MOUNTAIN** - Page 2D	Vancouver Island marmot
30	**KINGCOME RIVER ESTUARY** - Page 12A	Estuary
31	**KITSUMKALUM LAKE** - Page 44B	Salmon and steelhead spawning
32	**LADNER MARSH** - Page 5C	Winter waterfowl and year 'round marsh birds
33	**LAKELSE LAKE** - Page 45C	Wetlands
34	**LAKELSE RIVER** - Page 44D	Fisheries
35	**LOCH LAMOND** - Page 15A	Canada geese
36	**LARDEAU/DUNCAN FLATS** - Page 18C	Waterfowl
37	**LAZO MARSH** - Page 2A	Freshwater marsh
38	**MARINERS ISLAND** - Page 5C	Estuary
39	**McGILLIVARY WILDLIFE AREA** - Page 5D	Riparian habitat is home to deer, bears, coyotes, beaver, muskrat and a range of wetland and forest birds

40	McQUEEN'S SLOUGH - Page 58C	Waterfowl
41	MOBERLY MARSH - Page 28D	Waterfowl
42	MOUNT ROBSON RANCH - Page 40D	Wildlife habitat
43	MULLER BAY - Page 45C	Beaver marsh
44	NADINA RIVER VALLEY - Page 46C	Moose winter range
45	NANAIMO RIVER ESTUARY - Page 2D	Estuary
46	NELSON RIVER - Page 44B	Wetlands
47	NEWGATE - Page 10C	Deer
48	OSOYOOS OXBOWS - Page 7C	Birds and reptiles
49	PEND d'OREILLE - Page 8D	White-tailed deer, marmot
50	PORPOISE BAY - Page 2B	Waterfowl, fisheries
51	PREMIER RIDGE - Page 9B	Wildlife winter range
52	RCMP FLATS - Page 18B	Migrating waterfowl, furbearers
53	REDFISH CREEK - Page 8B	Kokanee spawning
54	ROBERTS BANK - Page 5C	Aquatic bird and fish habitat
55	ROBIN WAY MARSH - Page 7B	Waterfowl
56	ROUNDTOP REFUGE - Page 27C	Waterfowl
57	SALMON ARM FORESHORE - Page 16B	Waterfowl
58	SALMON RIVER ESTUARY - Page 12D	Estuary
59	SERPENTINE WILDLIFE AREA - Page 5D	Aquatic bird and fish habitat
60	SHEEP MOUNTAIN - Page 10C	Mountain sheep winter range, deer, elk, raptors, yellow badger
61	SHORTS CREEK - Page 16C	California bighorn sheep
62	SILVERHOPE CREEK - Page 6C	Fisheries

63	SKAHA LAKE EAST - Page 7A	California bighorn sheep winter range
64	SKULL MOUNTAIN - Page 16A	Mule deer
65	SOMENOS LAKE - Page 2D	Wintering waterfowl
66	STELLAKO RIVER - Page 37A	Fisheries, sockeye salmon in September
67	STRAUSS - Page 10C	Elk, white-tailed deer
68	SWAN LAKE - Page 16D	Waterfowl
69	TAUTRI-ROSITA - Page 25A	Moose, white pelican
70	THETIS ISLAND - Page 3B	Bats
71	TOFINO - Page 1D	Estuary
72	TREPANIER CREEK - Page 7A	Mule deer winter range
73	VASEUX - Page 7C	California bighorn sheep, waterfowl, raptors
74	WALHACHIN CROSSING - Page 15B	Access to fisheries, chukar partridge, wintering golden eyes and merganzers
75	WALTER CLOUGH WILDLIFE AREA - Page 8B	Deer and birds
76	WARDS LAKE - Page 8C	Waterfowl and song birds
77	WASA SLOUGH - Page 9B	Waterfowl
78	WHITE RIVER - Page 18D	Deer, elk, sheep, mountain goat, bear, wolf, cougar
79	WIGWAM FLATS - Page 10C	Deer, elk, bear, cougar
80	WILLOW POINT - Page 2A	Fish spawning
81	WOLF CREEK - Page 9B	Deer, elk, mountain sheep

WILDLIFE MANAGEMENT AREAS

Areas designated under the Wildlife Act because of their special importance to wildlife. They are administered by the Ministry of Environment with wildlife conservation and wildlife-related uses always in the forefront, although multiple resource use may be permitted in some of them. The Wildlife Act provides for specific protection against damage to the wildlife habitat within them.

— List shows wildlife/habitat type protected

82	**CHILANKO MARSH** - Page 24B	Waterfowl, moose winter range
83	**DEWDROP-ROSSEAU CREEK** - Page 15B	Mule deer, California bighorn sheep, rattlesnakes, chukar partridge
84	**JUNCTION** - Page 25D	California bighorn sheep (largest non-migratory population in the world - 400-500 animals)
85	**PITT-ADDINGTON MARSH** - Page 5B	Waterfowl and aquatic birds (one of the last homes of breeding Sandhill Cranes in the lower mainland)
86	**SKEDANS, LIMESTONE & REEF ISLANDS** - Page 31C	Aquatic birds
87	**TRANQUILLE** - Page 15B	Migratory waterfowl and shore birds, also song birds
88	**UPPER CARIBOO RIVER** - Page 39C	Riparian habitat, moose winter range

FEDERAL MIGRATORY BIRD SANCTUARIES

Areas set out in the schedule of the Migratory Bird Sanctuary Regulations, pursuant to the Migratory Birds Convention Act, where hunting of migratory birds is prohibited, except by permit.

— List shows wildlife/habitat type protected

89	**CHRISTIE ISLET** - Page 5A	Seabird nesting
90	**ESQUIMALT LAGOON** - Page 3D	Saltwater lagoon, water birds
91	**GEORGE C. REIFEL** - Page 5C	Wintering and migration habitat for waterfowl and shore birds
92	**NECHAKO RIVER** - Page 37B	Canada geese migration habitat
93	**SHOAL HARBOUR** - Page 5C	Wintering habitat for waterfowl
94	**VASEUX LAKE** - Page 7C	Trumpeter swans
95	**VICTORIA HARBOUR** - Page 3D	Wintering habitat for water birds

NATIONAL WILDLIFE AREAS

Areas set out in the schedule of the Wildlife Area Regulations, pursuant to the Canada Wildlife Act, where hunting and fishing is prohibited except by permit.

— List shows wildlife/habitat type protected

96	**ALAKSEN** - Page 5C	Migratory birds, herons, raptors, song birds
97	**BRISCO** - Page 18A	Migratory birds of the Pacific Flyway
98	**HARROGATE** - Page 18A	Migratory birds of the Pacific Flyway
99	**MARSHALL-STEVENSON** - Page 2B	Estuarine habitat
100	**NANOOSE** - Page 2D	Resting and feeding area for migratory birds
101	**ROSEWALL CREEK** - Page 2A	Winter habitat for waterfowl and shore birds
102	**SPILLIMACHEEN** - Page 18A	Migratory birds of the Pacific Flyway
103	**VASEUX-BIGHORN** - Page 7C	Unique desert habitat
104	**WIDGEON VALLEY** - Page 5B	Migratory bird habitat
105	**WILMER MARSH** - Page 18D	Migratory birds of the Pacific Flyway

FEDERAL - PROVINCIAL WILDLIFE MANAGEMENT AREAS

— List shows wildlife protected

| 106 | CRESTON WILDLIFE MANAGEMENT AREA
- Page 9C | Waterfowl |

DEPARTMENT OF FISHERIES AND OCEANS

— List shows wildlife protected

| 107 | CHEHALIS RIVER
- Page 6C | Raptors, waterfowl, swans |

Northern Flicker

PROVINCIAL FISH HATCHERIES

Facilities which are operated by the Fish Culture Section of the Ministry of Environment to sustain freshwater fish populations in the province of British Columbia. Over 1200 B.C. lakes and streams are stocked with 12 million fish each year, including several species of trout and char as well as one species of land-locked salmon.

| 108 | FRASER VALLEY TROUT HATCHERY
- Page 5D | VISITOR FACILITIES: Large display area interpreting the provincial hatchery system, fishes' life cycle and aquatic ecosystems. Upgrade of display area in 1991 to feature new technologies, including interactive display components. Self-guided and guided tours available year-round. Open 7 days/week, but hours vary seasonally. Phone for seasonal hours and to book group tours. TELEPHONE: 852-5338 SPECIES RAISED: domestic and native rainbow trout, anadromous and coastal cutthroat and steelhead trout. |

| 109 | KOOTENAY TROUT HATCHERY
- Page 9B | VISITOR FACILITIES: A self-guided tour area includes aquaria, displays and an outdoor moat with large fish. Open 8:00 a.m. - 4:00 p.m., 7 days a week. Guided tours by appointment only. TELEPHONE: 429-3214 SPECIES RAISED: rainbow trout, brook char, westslope cutthroat trout. |

| 110 | LOON CREEK HATCHERY
- Page 15A | VISITOR FACILITIES: The general public is welcome to view the hatchery and grounds 8:30 - 3:30 p.m., 7 days a week, but tours are given by appointment only. TELEPHONE: 459-2454 SPECIES RAISED: rainbow trout and kokanee salmon. |

| 111 | SUMMERLAND TROUT HATCHERY
- Page 7A | VISITOR FACILITIES: A small self-guided tour, with views of the rearing rooms and outdoor rearing ponds. Self-guided and guided tours are available year-round. Open 7 days/week, but hours vary seasonally. Phone for seasonal hours and to book group tours. TELEPHONE: 494-0491 SPECIES RAISED: rainbow trout and brook char. |

| 112 | VANCOUVER ISLAND HATCHERY
- Page 3D | VISITOR FACILITIES: The general public is welcome to visit the hatchery at its present site by appointment between 10:30 a.m. - 3:30 p.m., 7 days/week. Please telephone hatchery staff to arrange visits. Construction of a new hatchery and visitor's centre which will be located in Duncan, across the river from the present site, are scheduled for completion in 1992. TELEPHONE: 746-1425 SPECIES RAISED: anadromous cutthroat, steelhead, brown and coastal cutthroat trout. |

BRITISH COLUMBIA PARKS

It's little wonder B.C.'s 5 National and 335 Provincial Parks are admired by people from around the world. They comprise nearly 60,000 square kilometres, more than 5 percent of B.C.'s total land area, and vary from little known beaches to vast tracts of mountains, forests and waterways.

Caves and alpine meadows, mountain peaks, virgin rain forests, extinct volcanoes, paddling and portage routes, historic towns, Pacific islands and the nation's highest waterfall are park features which make up more than half of the "representative landscapes" of B.C.

B.C. PARKS – VISITOR SERVICES CONTACTS

Visitor Services staff can provide you with specific information about visitor programs, facilities, services, and recreational opportunities within Provincial Parks.

B.C. Parks
Alice Lake Park
Box 220
BRACKENDALE, B.C.
V0H 1H0
(604) 898-3678

B.C. Parks
Cultus Lake Park
Box 10
CULTUS LAKE, B.C.
V0X 1H0
(604) 858-7161

B.C. Parks
Charlie Lake Park
SS #2, Comp. 39, Site 12
FORT ST. JOHN, B.C.
V1J 4M7
(604) 787-3407

B.C. Parks
101 West Columbia Street
KAMLOOPS, B.C.
V2C 1L4
(604) 828-4501

B.C. Parks
1265 Dalhousie Drive
KAMLOOPS, B.C.
V1L 5P6
(604) 828-4494

B.C. Parks
Kokanee Creek Park
RR #3
NELSON, B.C.
V1L 5P6
(604) 825-4421/22

B.C. Parks
1610 Indian River Drive
NORTH VANCOUVER, B.C.
V7G 1L3
(604) 929-1291

B.C. Parks
Rathtrevor Beach Park
Box 1479
PARKSVILLE, B.C.
V0R 2S5
(604) 248-3931

B.C. Parks
1011- 4th Avenue
PRINCE GEORGE, B.C.
V2L 3H9
(604) 565-6270

B.C. Parks
Box 2045
PRINCE GEORGE, B.C.
V2N 2J6
(604)565-6340

B.C. Parks
Bag 5000
SMITHERS, B .C.
V0J 2N0
(604) 847-7565

B.C. Parks
2930 Trans-Canada
Highway
RR #6
VICTORIA, B.C.
V8X 3X2
(604) 387-4363

B.C. Parks
Wasa Park
Box 118
WASA, B.C.
V0B 2K0
(604) 422-3212/13

B.C. Parks
640 Borland Street
WILLIAMS LAKE, B.C.
V2G 1R8
(604) 398-4414

NATIONAL PARKS
Canadian Parks Service
Western Region
220-4th Ave. S.E. Room 520
CALGARY, ALBERTA
T2P 3H8
(403) 292-4401

B.C. PARKS FACILITIES GUIDE

The next 6 pages list all the available facilities in B.C. Parks. The information below lists the columns in order and gives a brief description of how to read the codes.

PARK / MAP NUMBER	This number corresponds with the boxed number on the Atlas maps indicating Park location.
MAP REFERENCE	The number refers to the page in the Atlas and the letter identifies the location on that page (see Atlas map legend).
PARK	Park area is shown in hectares RA indicates recreational area.
NEAREST HIGHWAY	Indicates the route number of the highway nearest the main entry of the park.
ROAD ACCESS	The number indicates distance from nearest highway in kilometres and the letter indicates road surface P = Paved G = Gravel R = Rough NO = roads do not enter park F = Vehicle Ferry.
FEE (Y, N)	Y = fee charged for vehicle/tent overnight camping N = no fee charged.
VEHICLE / TENT CAMPSITES	A number indicates campsites available on site * = group camping.
WILDERNESS / WALK-IN	A number indicates campsites available X = camping is permitted.
PICNICKING / DAY USE	A number indicates parking spaces for cars X = facilities available.
BOAT LAUNCH / CANOEING	24R = number of boat launching ramps available C = canoeing / kayaking area.
FIREWOOD / WATER	F = firewood available on site W = certified drinking water source is available.
SANI-STATION	X = effluent dumping and water replenishment facility for Recreational Vehicles is available on site.
TOILETS / SHOWERS	F = flush toilets on site P = toilets other than flush type S = showers available.
SWIMMING	X = indicates that swimming is a principal on site activity.
FISHING	X = indicates that fresh water fishing is available on site or nearby.
HIKING / WALKING TRAILS	H = hiking trails with total lengths given in kilometres W = indicates short, generally easy trails occasionally leading to special features. Local knowledge may be required to locate starting points of many trails.

PARK / MAP NUMBER	MAP REFERENCE	Park / AREA IN HECTARES (ha)	NEAREST HIGHWAY	ROAD ACCESS	OPERATING DATES	FEE (Y, N)	VEHICLE / TENT CAMPSITES GROUP CAMPING (*)	WILDERNESS / WALK-IN CAMPSITES	PICNICKING / DAY USE (Car Spaces)	BOAT LAUNCHING RAMP (R) CANOEING / KAYAKING (C)	FIREWOOD (F) DRINKING WATER (W)	SANI-STATION	FLUSH TOILETS (F) PIT TOILETS (P) SHOWERS (S)	SWIMMING	FISHING	HIKING TRAILS (km H) WALKING TRAILS (W)
1	16A	ADAMS LAKE RA / 56 ha	1	15 PG			15							X	X	
2	10D	AKAMINA-KISHINENA RA / 10,915 ha	3	NO				X								H
3	6A	ALEXANDRA BRIDGE / 55 ha	1	P	All Year				75		W		4P			
4	5A	ALICE LAKE / 397 ha	99	1P	All Year	Y	88*		312	C	F W	X	24F 20P	X	X	7H W
5	6B	ALLISON LAKE / 23 ha	5A	P	May-Oct	Y	24		40	R	F W		8P	X	X	
6	76D	ANDY BAILEY RA / 174 ha	97	14G	May-Oct	Y	32	X	15	R C	F W		5P	X	X	
8	7A	ANTLERS BEACH / 8 ha	97	P	Apr-Oct				30	C	F W		10F 2P	X	X	W
9	7A	APEX MOUNTAIN RA / 575 ha	97	32G	All Year											H
10	5A	APODACA / 8 ha	99	NO	All Year											
11	2D	ARBUTUS GROVE / 22 ha	19	NO	All Year											
12	17C	ARROW LAKES / 93 ha	6	P	Apr-Oct				X	R				X	X	
12A	17C	ARROW LAKES (Shelter Bay)	23	P				13	X	R				X	X	
13	18B	ATHALMER BEACH / 14 ha	93	3P	Apr-Oct				82	R	W		10F	X		
14	81C	ATLIN / 271,140 ha	7	NO				X								2H
15	46A	BABINE MOUNTAINS RA / 32,400 ha	16	14G				X								60H
16	5C	BALLINGALL ISLETS / 1 ha	17	NO	All Year											
17	3D	BAMBERTON / 28 ha	1	1P	All Year	Y	50		120		F W		10F 14P	X	X	
18	39C	BARKERVILLE / 55 ha	26	10P	May-Oct	Y	168*		420		F W	X	S 16F 26P			
19	7A	BEAR CREEK / 178 ha	97	8P	Mar-Nov	Y	80		184	C	F W	X	S 22F 6P	X	X	10H
20	57B	BEATTON / 312 ha	97	13G	May-Oct	Y	37		100	R C	F W		12P	X	X	W
21	47C	BEAUMONT / 191 ha	16	P	May-Oct	Y	49*		224	R C	F W	X	6F 10P	X	X	
22	5C	BEAUMONT MARINE / 34 ha	17	NO	All Year				11	X			4P	X	X	3H W
23	8D	BEAVER CREEK / 44 ha	22A	P	Apr-Oct	Y	15		24	7R	F W		4P	X		1H
24	3B	BELLHOUSE / 2 ha	17	9P	All Year				4						X	1H W
25	26C	BIG BAR LAKE / 332 ha	97	33G	May-Oct	Y	33		90	20R C	F W		8P	X	X	4H W
26	56D	BIJOUX FALLS / 41 ha	97	P	May 15				50				6P			
27	14D	BIRKENHEAD LAKE / 3,642 ha	99	55G	Apr-Nov	Y	105	X	X	50R C	F W	X	19P	X	X	1H
28	17A	BLANKET CREEK / 316 ha	23	P	Apr-Oct	Y	64	X	185		F W		16P	X	X	1H
28A	3C	BOTANICAL BEACH / 14 ha	14	3G												H W
29	7D	BOUNDARY CREEK / 2 ha	3	P	Apr-Oct	Y	18				F W		2F 2P	X		
30	39D	BOWRON LAKE / 123,117 ha	26	18G	May-Oct	Y	25	103	60	80R C	F W		65P	X	X	14H W
31	83D	BOYA LAKE / 4,597 ha	37	P	May-Oct	Y	34	10	17	10R C	F W		10P	X	X	
31A	2A	BOYLE POINT	19	F 10P												H W
32	14C	BRANDYWINE FALLS / 148 ha	99	P	Apr-Nov	Y	15		35		F		4P	X	X	1H W
33	6C	BRIDAL VEIL FALLS / 32 ha	1	P	All Year				60		W		4F 2P			2H
34	26D	BRIDGE LAKE / 6 ha	24	50P	Apr-Oct	Y	19		X	22R C	F W		4P	X	X	
35	7A	BROMLEY ROCK / 149 ha	3	P	All Year	Y	17		30		F W		6P	X	X	
36	11C	BROOKS PENINSULA RA / 28,780 ha	19	NO												
36A	2B	BUCCANEER BAY MARINE / 1 ha	101	NO												
37	65B	BUCKINGHORSE RIVER / 55 ha	97	G	May-Oct	Y	30			C	F W		6P		X	
38	18A	BUGABOO GLACIER / 25,274 ha	95	45G	June-Oct	Y		18	30		W		4P			13H
39	25A	BULL CANYON RA / 123 ha	20	G	May-Oct	N	25		5		F W		4P		X	
40	28D	BURGESS & JAMES GADSDEN / 352 ha	1	P												
41	5C	CABBAGE ISLAND MARINE / 4 ha	17	NO	All Year			8	X				2P	X	X	
42	18D	CANAL FLATS / 6 ha	93	3P	Apr-Oct				64	34R			4P	X		
43	26D	CANIM BEACH / 6 ha	97	43G	May-Oct	Y	7	9	15		W		4P	X	X	
44	11A	CAPE SCOTT / 15,054 ha	19	60R	All Year			19					3P	X	X	40H
45	26C	CARIBOO NATURE / 98 ha	97	NO												
46	48A	CARP LAKE / 19,344 ha	97	32G	May-Oct	Y	105*	15	65	R C	F W		15P 2P	X	X	11H
47	6D	CASCADE RA / 16,680 ha	3	NO				X	50				2P			75H
48	7C	CATHEDRAL / 33,272 ha	3	25G	Apr-Oct	N	16	38	30				13P	X		85H
49	8D	CHAMPION LAKES / 1,425 ha	3B	10P	May-Oct	Y	88		180	25R C	F W	X	28F 16P	X	X	6H W
50	57B	CHARLIE LAKE / 92 ha	97	P	May-Oct	Y	58		40	10R	F W	X	14P	X	X	1H W
51	15A	CHASM / 141 ha	97	3P	June-Sept			8	X	R			2P			
52	3B	CHEMAINUS RIVER / 86 ha	1	11G	All Year									X	X	
53	6C	CHILLIWACK LAKE / 162 ha	1	47G	All Year	Y	87	13	15	R	F W		24P	X	X	H
54	6C	CHILLIWACK RIVER / 23 ha	1	11G	All Year				16				2P		X	
55	3C	CHINA BEACH / 61 ha	14	P	All Year				60				4P			1H
56	7A	CHRISTIE MEMORIAL / 3 ha	97	P					27	C	W		7F	X	X	
57	8C	CHRISTINA LAKE / 6 ha	3	P	May-Sept				220		W		10F 6P	X	X	

PARK / MAP NUMBER	MAP REFERENCE	Park / AREA IN HECTARES (ha)	NEAREST HIGHWAY	ROAD ACCESS	OPERATING DATES	FEE (Y, N)	VEHICLE / TENT CAMPSITES GROUP CAMPING (*)	WILDERNESS / WALK-IN CAMPSITES	PICNICKING / DAY USE (Car Spaces)	BOAT LAUNCHING RAMP (R) CANOEING / KAYAKING (C)	FIREWOOD (F) DRINKING WATER (W)	SANI-STATION	FLUSH TOILETS (F) PIT TOILETS (P) SHOWERS (S)	SWIMMING	FISHING	HIKING TRAILS (km H) WALKING TRAILS (W)
58	16B	CINNEMOUSUN NARROWS 158 ha	1	NO	Apr-Oct	N	28		X	C	W	X	8P	X	X	4H
59	9A	CODY CAVES 63 ha	31	13R	June-Sept				4				1P			1H
60	6B	COLDWATER RIVER 76 ha	5	P	All Year				66				4P		X	1H
61	18D	COLUMBIA LAKE 260 ha	93	NO												
62	17A	COLUMBIA VIEW 23 ha	23	P	Apr-Oct				56		W		4F			
63	7D	CONKLE LAKE 587 ha	33	16R	May-Oct	Y	24	2	24	R C	F W		8P	X	X	4H
64	13C	COPELAND ISLANDS MARINE 437 ha	101	NO	All Year									X	X	
65	6A	COQUIHALLA CANYON RA 150 ha	5	4P G					20						X	H
66	6A	COQUIHALLA RIVER RA 100 ha	5	P					34				2P	·	X	
67	6B	COQUIHALLA SUMMIT 5,750 ha	5	P					X							
68	38D	COTTONWOOD RIVER 66 ha	26	P	May 24		15		50		W		4P		X	
69	48D	CROOKED RIVER 1,016 ha	97	P	May-Oct	Y	90*		545		F W	X	28F 12P	X	X	9H W
70	10A	CROWSNEST 46 ha	3	P	May-Oct		25		107				8P			
71	6C	CULTUS LAKE 656 ha	1	16P	All Year	Y	300		716	4R C	F W	X	S 85F 30P	X	X	11H W
72	5A	CYPRESS 2,849 ha	1	10P	All Year				100		W		10P			30H
73	3D	D'ARCY ISLAND MARINE 84 ha	17	NO	All Year			6						X	X	
74	38A	DAHL LAKE 749 ha	16	17G					10	C			1P	X	X	1H
75	7A	DARKE LAKE 1,470 ha	97	16G	May-Sept	N		5		C			2P		X	
76	5D	DAVIS LAKE 192 ha	7	20G										X	X	
77	13C	DESOLATION SOUND MARINE 8,256 ha	101	NO	All Year			4			F		2P	X	X	H
78	44C	DIANA LAKE 233 ha	16	2G	May 15				180		F W		8P	X	X	2H
79	3D	DISCOVERY ISLAND MARINE 61 ha	17	NO	All Year			8						X	X	H
80	28C	DOWNIE CREEK	23	P	May-Oct	Y	21		X	1R	W		4P	X	X	
81	15A	DOWNING 100 ha	97	17P	May-Oct	Y	25	7	44		F W		6P	X	X	
82	9A	DREWRY POINT 21 ha	3A	NO	May-Sept		2	X					1P	X	X	
83	46A	DRIFTWOOD CANYON 23 ha	16	10G					15				2P			
84	3B	DRUMBEG 20 ha	1	F 12P	All Year				10				2P	X	X	H
85	18D	DRY GULCH 29 ha	93	1G	Apr-Oct	Y	25				F W		6F 8P			
86	56B	DUNLEVY RA 110 ha	29	30P	Apr-Oct				X	R			2P		X	
87	57C	EAST PINE 14 ha	97	P	May-Oct	Y	12		20	R C			4P		X	

PARK / MAP NUMBER	MAP REFERENCE	Park / AREA IN HECTARES (ha)	NEAREST HIGHWAY	ROAD ACCESS	OPERATING DATES	FEE (Y, N)	VEHICLE / TENT CAMPSITES GROUP CAMPING (*)	WILDERNESS / WALK-IN CAMPSITES	PICNICKING / DAY USE (Car Spaces)	BOAT LAUNCHING RAMP (R) CANOEING / KAYAKING (C)	FIREWOOD (F) DRINKING WATER (W)	SANI-STATION	FLUSH TOILETS (F) PIT TOILETS (P) SHOWERS (S)	SWIMMING	FISHING	HIKING TRAILS (km H) WALKING TRAILS (W)
88	12A	ECHO BAY MARINE 2 ha	19	NO	All Year										X	
89	16D	ECHO LAKE 154 ha	6	20G	Apr-Oct		5*		X				4P	X	X	
90	12D	ELK FALLS 1,087 ha	28	P	Apr-Oct	Y	121		30		F W	X	2F 26P	X	X	6H
91	19C	ELK LAKES 17,245 ha	3	125 R				20					3P		X	23H
92	10A	ELK VALLEY 81 ha	3	10G	Apr-Oct											
93	16D	ELLISON 200 ha	97	16P	Mar-Nov	Y	54		120	C	F W		18F 4P	X	X	2H
94	6A	EMORY CREEK 15 ha	1	P	Apr-Nov	Y	34		X		F W		4F 2P		X	1H
95	7A	ENEAS LAKES 1,036 ha	97	20R											X	
96	2D	ENGLISHMAN RIVER FALLS 97 ha	4	8P	All Year	Y	105		105		F W		7F 26P	X	X	3H W
97	48C	ESKERS 1,603 ha	97	NO											X	H
98	46D	ETHEL F. WILSON 29 ha	16	24G	May-Oct	N	5	5	10	R C	R W		2P	X	X	
99	44D	EXCHAMSIKS RIVER 18 ha	16	P	May-Oct	Y	18		20	R	R W		4P	X	X	
100	6C	F. H. BARBER 9 ha	1	P	All Year											
101	2A	FILLONGLEY 23 ha	19	F 4P	All Year	Y	10		X		F W		4P	X	X	2H W
102	35C	FIORDLAND RA 91,000 ha	37	NO												
104	2C	FOSSLI 53 ha	4	NO	All Year				X	C			1P	X	X	3H
105	3D	FRENCH BEACH 59 ha	14	P	All Year	Y	69		140		F W	X	16P	X	X	1H W
106	18C	FRY CREEK CANYON RA 550 ha	31	NO	May-Sept			1							X	10H
107	3B	GABRIOLA SANDS 6 ha	1	F 2P					25		W		4P	X		
108	2B	GARDEN BAY MARINE 163 ha	101	2R												
109	5B	GARIBALDI 194,904 ha	99	NO	June-Oct			196	200	C			22P		X	62H
110	17D	GERRARD (Trout Lake) 316 ha	31	P	Apr-Oct		12		25				2P	X	X	
111	1B	GIBSON MARINE 142 ha	4	NO										X	X	
112	44D	GITNADOIX RIVER RA 58,000 ha	16	NO												
113	5B	GOLDEN EARS 55,594 ha	7	10P	All Year	Y	344	X	1088	R C	F W	X	S 36F 60P	X	X	60H W
114	15C	GOLDPAN 5 ha	1	P	Apr-Dec	Y	14		24		F W		8P	X		
115	3D	GOLDSTREAM 327 ha	1	P	All Year	Y	159*		82		F W	X	S 28F 20P		X	16H W
116	2D	GORDON BAY 51 ha	18	14P	All Year	Y	130		120	R	F W	X	S 19F 16P	X	X	1H
117	26C	GREEN LAKE 347 ha	97	16P	May-Oct	Y	121*		160	R	F W	X	2F 36P	X	X	
118	8B	GROHMAN NARROWS 10 ha	3A	P	May-Sept				15				2P		X	1H W

PARK / MAP NUMBER	MAP REFERENCE	Park — AREA IN HECTARES (ha)	NEAREST HIGHWAY	ROAD ACCESS	OPERATING DATES	FEE (Y, N)	VEHICLE / TENT CAMPSITES	GROUP CAMPING (*)	WILDERNESS / WALK-IN CAMPSITES	PICNICKING / DAY USE (Car Spaces)	BOAT LAUNCHING RAMP (R) CANOEING / KAYAKING (C)	FIREWOOD (F) DRINKING WATER (W)	SANI-STATION	FLUSH TOILETS (F) PIT TOILETS (P) SHOWERS (S)	SWIMMING	FISHING	HIKING TRAILS (km H) WALKING TRAILS (W)
119	57C	GWILLIM LAKE 9,199 ha	29	P	Apr-Oct	Y	49				R C	F W		8P		X	
120	22C	HAKAI RA 122,998 ha	16	NO													
121	5A	HALKETT BAY MARINE 309 ha	99	NO					X	X				1P	X	X	
122	28A	HAMBER 24,518 ha	93	NO						10				1P		X	H
123	7D	HAYNES POINT 13 ha	97	1P	Mar-Nov	Y	36			33	R C	F W		8F 1P	X	X	
124	2A	HELLIWELL 69 ha	19	F 21P	All Year					30				4P	X	X	6H W
125	3B	HEMER 93 ha	1	7P	All Year					8				2P	X		6H W
126	16B	HERALD 79 ha	1	13P	Apr-Oct	Y	51			68	29R	F W	X	S 18P		X	2H
127	2A	HORNE LAKE CAVES 75 ha	19	16G	All Year									1P			2H
128	26A	HORSEFLY LAKE 148 ha	97	65G	May-Oct	Y	22	10		50	R	F W		6P	X	X	
128 A	84C	HYLAND RIVER 97	97	G					31								X
129	5A	INDIAN ARM MARINE 5 ha	1	NO	All Year				X	X				2P	X	X	1H
130	7C	INKANEEP 9 ha	97	P	All Year	Y	7					F W		4P			
131	6C	INTERNATIONAL RIDGE RA 1,905 ha	1	NO													10H
132	5C	ISLE-DE-LIS MARINE 5 ha	17	NO	All Year					2					X	X	1H
133	8C	JEWEL LAKE 49 ha	3	8G						6				2P	X	X	
134	9B	JIMSMITH LAKE 12 ha	3	2P	May-Sept	Y	28			58	R	F W		12P	X	X	
135	14D	JOFFRE LAKES RA 1,460 ha	99	20G					X	X							H
136	3D	JOHN DEAN 155 ha	17A	5P	All Year					20		W		2P			3H W
137	7D	JOHNSTONE CREEK 38 ha	3	P	Apr-Oct	Y	16					F W		4P			1H
137 A	15B	JUNIPER BEACH 260 ha	1	P	Apr-Oct	Y											
138	49D	KAKWA RA 127,690 ha	16	NO					X					2P		X	H
139	16D	KALAMALKA LAKE 890 ha	6	8P	Apr-Oct					85	C			7P	X	X	5H
140	6A	KAWKAWA LAKE 7 ha	3	3P						150	R	W		2P	X	X	
141	6B	KENTUCKY–ALLEYNE 144 ha	5A	3G	Apr-Oct	Y	61				C	F W		13P	X	X	5H
142	7C	KEREMEOS COLUMNS 20 ha	3A	NO													H
143	7D	KETTLE RIVER RA 179 ha	33	P	Apr-Oct	Y	49	6		25		F W	X	S 10P	X	X	2H
144	7A	KICKININEE 49 ha	97	P						102	R	W		10F 3P	X	X	
145	10C	KIKOMUN CREEK 682 ha	3	11P	Apr-Oct	Y	74			596	R	F W	X	S 24P	X	X	6H
146	6C	KILBY 3 ha	7	1P	All Year	Y			38	50	R C	F W		8F 4P	X	X	
147	60B	KINASKAN LAKE 1,800 ha	37	G	May-Oct	Y	36				R	F W		8P		X	2H
148	8D	KING GEORGE VI 162 ha	25	P	Apr-Oct	N	12		30			F W		4P			
149	57D	KISKATINAW 58 ha	97	5P	May-Oct	Y	28					F W		6P		X	
150	44B	KITSUMKALUM 40 ha	16	24G	May-Sept		20							4P	X	X	
151	45C	KLEANZA CREEK 269 ha	16	P	May-Oct	Y	11			25		F W		4P			1H
152	8B	KOKANEE CREEK 260 ha	3A	P	Apr-Oct	Y	112			380	R C	F W	X	32F 18P	X	X	4H
153	8B	KOKANEE GLACIER 32,137 ha	3A	16R	All Year	Y		5	70					8P			113 H
154	3D	KOKSILAH RIVER 210 ha	1	10G	All Year											x	x
155	18C	KOOTENAY LAKE 345 ha	31	P	May-Sept		30		10	X	R			8P	X	X	
156	64A	KWADACHA WILDERNESS 158,475 ha	97	NO					X							X	H
157	26C	LAC LA HACHE 24 ha	97	P	May-Oct	Y	83*			55	R	F W	X	18F 6P	X	X	
158	15D	LAC LE JEUNE 47 ha	1	29P	Apr-Oct	Y	144			104	R C	F W		S 24P	X	X	
159	5A	LAKE LOVELY WATER RA 1,300 ha	99	NO					X							X	H
160	45C	LAKELSE LAKE 362 ha	37	P	May-Oct	Y	156*			360	R	F W	X	S 16F 38P	X	X	3H
161	85D	LIARD RIVER HOT SPRINGS 668 ha	97	G	May-Oct	Y	53			60		W		12P	X		1H
162	2C	LITTLE QUALICUM FALLS 444 ha	4	P	All Year	Y	91			122		F W		18F 21P	X		6H W
163	9A	LOCKHART BEACH 3 ha	3A	P	Apr-Oct	Y	13			12		F W		4P	X	X	
164	15A	LOON LAKE 3 ha	97	26P	May-Oct	Y	14					F W		4P		X	
165	3C	LOSS CREEK 21 ha	14	G													H
166	13C	LOVELAND BAY 30 ha	28	20G	All Year	N	24		X		R			5P	X		
167	16D	MABEL LAKE 182 ha	6	35G	Apr-Oct	Y	81			30	R	F W		16P	X	X	
168	2C	MacMILLAN 136 ha	4	P	All Year					40				6P		X	4H W
169	6D	MANNING 65,884 ha	3	P	Apr-Nov	Y	353	70		780	R C	F W	X	34F 63P	X	X	255H W
170	13C	MANSONS LANDING MARINE 100 ha	19	F 21P					X					4P	X	X	H
171	1A	MAQUINNA 39 ha	4	NO												X	1H
172	16B	MARA 5 ha	97A	P	Apr-Oct					110	R			4F 4P	X	X	1H
173	15A	MARBLE CANYON 335 ha	12	P	Apr-Nov	Y	34	2		22	C	F W		5P	X		
174	17A	MARTHA CREEK 23 ha	23	P	Apr-Oct	Y	28			50	R			6P	X	X	
175	3D	MATHESON LAKE 162 ha	14	13P	All Year					60	C	W		2P	X	X	4H
176	87C	MAXHAMISH LAKE 520 ha	77	NO												X	

PARK / MAP NUMBER	MAP REFERENCE	Park — AREA IN HECTARES (ha)	NEAREST HIGHWAY	ROAD ACCESS	OPERATING DATES	FEE (Y, N)	VEHICLE / TENT CAMPSITES GROUP CAMPING (*)	WILDERNESS / WALK-IN CAMPSITES	PICNICKING / DAY USE (Car Spaces)	BOAT LAUNCHING RAMP (R) CANOEING / KAYAKING (C)	FIREWOOD (F) DRINKING WATER (W)	SANI-STATION	FLUSH TOILETS (F) PIT TOILETS (P) SHOWERS (S)	SWIMMING	FISHING	HIKING TRAILS (km H) WALKING TRAILS (W)
177	5C	McDONALD 14 ha	17	2P	All Year	Y	30				F		8P			
178	17D	McDONALD CREEK 468 ha	6	P	All Year	N	10		24	R	W		9P	X	X	
179	3D	MEMORY ISLAND 1 ha	1	NO	May-Sept				X				2P	X	X	
180	52B	MEZIADIN LAKE 335 ha	37	P	June-Oct	Y	42			R C			6P		X	
181	2A	MIRACLE BEACH 135 ha	19	3P	All Year	Y	185		230		F W		22F 29P	X	X	2H W
182	2A	MITLENATCH ISLAND 155 ha	19	NO	All Year				X				1P	X		1H
183	57C	MOBERLY LAKE 97 ha	29	3G	May-Oct	Y	109*		60	R C	F W	X	22P	X	X	2H W
184	17C	MONASHEE 7,513 ha	6	NO	June-Sept	Y	6	6	25				5P		X	24H
185	15D	MONCK 87 ha	5	11P	Apr-Dec	Y	71		130	R C	F W	X	16F 6P	X	X	5H
186	49C	MONKMAN 32,000 ha	29	NO				X								22H
187	5C	MONTAGUE HARBOUR MARINE 97 ha	17	F 10P	All Year	Y	30	X	26	15R C	F W		10P	X		5H
188	16C	MONTE LAKE 8 ha	97	P	Apr-Oct	Y	7		4	C	F W		4P	X	X	
189	10A	MORRISSEY 5 ha	3	P	Apr-Oct				38		W				X	
190	12D	MORTON LAKE 67 ha	19	20G	Apr-Oct	Y	24		30	6R C	F W		10P	X	X	
191	3B	MOUAT 22 ha	17	F 13P	All Year	Y	15		15		F W		6P			
192	18B	MOUNT ASSINIBOINE 39,052 ha	93	NO	All Year			75			W		24P		X	176H
193	60B	MOUNT EDZIZA 232,698 ha	37	NO				X								119H
194	10A	MOUNT FERNIE 259 ha	3	P	June-Sept	Y	38		44		F W		12F 10P			1H
195	5B	MOUNT JUDGE HOWAY 1,930 ha	7	NO	All Year											
196	5C	MOUNT MAXWELL 199 ha	17	F 15P	All Year				15				1P			1H
197	40D	MOUNT ROBSON 219,829 ha	16	P	Apr-Sept	Y	177*	80	461	R C	F W	X	S 10F 47P	X	X	62H
198	5A	MOUNT SEYMOUR 3,508 ha	1	6P	All Year			15	150		F W		4P			21H W
199	40D	MOUNT TERRY FOX 1,930 ha	16	NO												H
200	9B	MOYIE LAKE 90 ha	3	1P	Apr-Oct	Y	104		90	R C	F W	X	6F 22P	X	X	3H
201	74B	MUNCHO LAKE 88,416 ha	97	P	May-Oct	Y	29		X	R C	F W		19P		X	
202	5A	MURRIN 24 ha	99	P	All Year				40		W		4P	X	X	
203	31A	NAIKOON 72,641 ha	16	P	All Year	Y	50		92		F W		13P	X	X	14H
204	14D	NAIRN FALLS 171 ha	99	P	Apr-Oct	Y	88		24		F W	X	18P		X	2H
205	8C	NANCY GREENE 198 ha	3	P	All Year				50	C	W		4P	X	X	5H
206	8C	NANCY GREENE RA 8,086 ha	38	P	All Year											19H
207	3B	NEWCASTLE ISLAND MARINE 336 ha	1	NO	All Year	Y	18*		X		F W		13F 6P	X	X	19H
208	7A	NICKEL PLATE 105 ha	97	30G											X	H
209	6A	NICOLUM RIVER 24 ha	3	P	All Year	Y	9		10		F W		4P		X	
210	16A	NISKONLITH LAKE 238 ha	1	8G	Apr-Oct	N	30			C			8P		X	
211	9B	NORBURY LAKE 97 HA	93	16P	Apr-Oct	Y	46		110	R C	F W		18P	X	X	2H
212	27C	NORTH THOMPSON RIVER 126 ha	5	P	Apr-Oct	Y	61		78		F W	X	4F 20P		X	2H
213	13C	OCTOPUS ISLANDS MARINE 109 ha	19	NO											X	
214	7C	OKANAGAN FALLS 2 ha	97		Apr-Oct	Y	20				F W		2F 2P			
215	7A	OKANAGAN LAKE 81 ha	97	P	Mar-Nov	Y	156		70	28R C	F W	X	S 35F 3P	X	X	2H
216	7A	OKANAGAN MOUNTAIN 10,462 ha	97	NO					20				5P	X	X	24H
217	13C	OKEOVER ARM 4 ha	101	5G	All Year	N	4		X				1P		X	
218	8C	OLE JOHNSON 15 ha	3	NO					10				2P	X	X	
219	75C	115 CREEK 51 ha	97	P	May-Oct	Y	8		10		W		2P			
220	57D	ONE ISLAND LAKE 61 ha	2	30R	May-Oct	Y	30			R C	F W		8P	X	X	
221	6B	OTTER LAKE 51 ha	5A	22P	May-Oct	Y	45		25	R C	F		12P	X	X	
222	47D	PAARENS BEACH 43 ha	27	11P	May-Oct	Y	65*		100	C	F W		15P	X	X	H
223	16A	PAUL LAKE 402 ha	5	17P	Apr-Oct	Y	111	18	342	R C	F W	X	30P	X	X	7H
224	5D	PEACE ARCH 9 ha	99	P	All Year				240		W		10F			
225	46D	PENDLETON BAY 8 ha	16	25G	May-Oct	N	12		10	R	W		2P	X	X	
226	7A	PENNASK LAKE 244 ha	97	50R	June-Sept	N	20		25	C			7P		X	
227	3B	PETROGLYPH 2 ha	1	P	All Year				25							1H W
228	9A	PILOT BAY 347 ha	3A	NO	May-Sept			2	X				2P	X	X	3H
229	38D	PINNACLES 124 ha	97	8R	May				30				1P			H
230	3B	PIRATES COVE MARINE 31 ha	1	NO	All Year			12	X				6P	X	X	4H
231	3B	PLUMPER COVE MARINE 57 ha	101	NO	All Year			16	X				6P	X	X	2H
232	2B	PORPOISE BAY 61 ha	101	4P	All Year	Y	84		280		F W	X	S 16F 4P	X	X	3H
233	5A	PORTEAU COVE 50 ha	99	P	All Year	Y	44	15	100	R	F W		S 21F 1P	X	X	
234	9B	PREMIER LAKE 662 ha	95	16G	All Year	Y	41	14	X	R C	F W		14P	X	X	3H
235	13D	PRINCESS LOUISA MARINE 65 ha	101	NO	All Year			5	X		W		2P	X	X	3H
236	5C	PRINCESS MARGARET MARINE 194 ha	17	NO	All Year				20	X		W		5P	X	X	7H

PARK / MAP NUMBER	MAP REFERENCE	Park / AREA IN HECTARES (ha)	NEAREST HIGHWAY	ROAD ACCESS	OPERATING DATES	FEE (Y, N)	VEHICLE / TENT CAMPSITES GROUP CAMPING (*)	WILDERNESS / WALK-IN CAMPSITES	PICNICKING / DAY USE (Car Spaces)	BOAT LAUNCHING RAMP (R) CANOEING / KAYAKING (C)	FIREWOOD (F) DRINKING WATER (W)	SANI-STATION	FLUSH TOILETS (F) PIT TOILETS (P) SHOWERS (S)	SWIMMING	FISHING	HIKING TRAILS (km H) WALKING TRAILS (W)
237	5C	PRIOR CENTENNIAL 16 ha	17	F 6P	Apr-Nov	Y	17				F W		4P			1H
238	65B	PROPHET RIVER RA 115 ha	97	G	May-Oct	Y	36				F W		4P		X	
239	44C	PRUDHOMME LAKE 7 ha	16	P	Apr-Nov	Y	18				F W		4P		X	
240	38C	PUNTCHESAKUT LAKE 38 ha	97	32P	May-Oct				180	R C	W		10P	X	X	
241	9A	PURCELL WILDERNESS 131,523 ha	31	NO	June-Sept			6					X			171H
242	39A	PURDEN LAKE 140 ha	16	2P	May-Oct	Y	78*		150	R C	F W	X	15P	X	X	7H W
243	30B	PURE LAKE 130 ha	16	P					15				2P	X	X	
243 A	11C	RAFT COVE 670 ha	19													H
244	2B	RATHTREVOR BEACH 347 ha	19	P	All Year	Y	174	X	1116		F W	X	S 48F 38P	X	X	5H W
245	40D	REARGUARD FALLS 48 ha	16	P					10				2P		X	2H
246	13C	REBECCA SPIT MARINE 177 ha	19	F 9P	All Year				100	R	W		9P	X	X	1H
247	46B	RED BLUFF 83 ha	16	48P	May-Oct	Y	64*		22		F W		16P	X	X	1H
248	3B	ROBERTS CREEK 40 ha	101	P	All Year	Y	25		20		F W	X	6P	X		1H
249	3B	ROBERTS MEMORIAL 14 ha	1	19P					10				1P	X	X	1H
250	16A	RODERICK HAIG-BROWN 988 ha	1	5P	Apr-Oct				1500	C			6P	X		24H
251	5D	ROLLEY LAKE 115 ha	7	8P	All Year	Y	64		120	C	F W	X	S 8F 16P	X	X	6H W
251 A	13C	ROSCOE BAY MARINE 247 ha	101	NO												
252	17D	ROSEBERY 32 ha	6	P	Apr-Oct	Y	36		X		F W		6P		X	
253	2A	ROSEWALL CREEK 63 ha	19	P											X	
254	45B	ROSS LAKE 307 ha	16	P					60	R			8P	X	X	5H
255	5C	RUCKLE 486 ha	17	F 9G	All Year		70	25			F W		20P	X	X	2H
255 A	1C	RUGGED POINT MARINE 518 ha	4	NO												
256	26D	RUTH LAKE 30 ha	97	30P	April 15				14	R C			4P	X		
257	2B	SALTERY BAY 69 ha	101	P	All Year	Y	45		120		F W	X	12P	X	X	1H
258	3B	SANDWELL 12 ha	1	F 8P					X					X		
259	2A	SANDY ISLAND MARINE 33 ha	19	NO				8					2P	X	X	
260	6A	SASQUATCH 1,220 ha	7	12P	All Year	Y	159*		365	R C	F W	X	12F 24P	X	X	5H
261	15B	SAVONA 2 ha	1	P	May-Sept				30		W		4P	X		
262	12C	SCHOEN LAKE 8,170 ha	19	12R	Apr-Oct	N	10	X		C			2P	X	X	5H
263	2B	SECHELT INLETS MARINE RA 155 ha	101	NO				20	X				5P	X	X	
264	45B	SEELEY LAKE 24 ha	16	P	Apr-Oct	Y	20		20	C	F W		6P	X	X	
265	5A	SHANNON FALLS 87 ha	99	P					108				8F			1H
266	16A	SHUSWAP LAKE 124 ha	1	19P	Apr-Oct	Y	260*		409	147R C	F W	X	S 64F 15P	X	X	5H
267	16B	SHUSWAP LAKE MARINE 460 ha	1	NO	Apr-Oct	N	44	50	X	C			25P	X	X	5H
268	5C	SIDNEY SPIT MARINE 400 ha	17	NO	All Year	Y		27	X		F W		14P	X	X	3H
269	16B	SILVER BEACH 76 ha	1	65G	Apr-Oct	Y	30		40				10P	X	X	1H
270	6C	SILVER LAKE 77 ha	1	6G	All year			50					2P		X	
271	16D	SILVER STAR 8,714 ha	97	10G	All Year	N			120				8P			
272	2B	SIMSON MARINE 461 ha		NO												
273	22B	SIR ALEXANDER MACKENZIE 5 ha	20	NO	All Year				X							
274	6D	SKAGIT VALLEY RA 32,508 ha	1	35G	All Year	Y	44	35			W		22P	X	X	35H
275	15D	SKIHIST 33 ha	1	P	Apr-Dec	Y	68		33		F W	X	20F 7P			
276	2B	SKOOKUMCHUCK NARROWS 123 ha	101	P	All Year				20				5P			8H
277	2A	SMELT BAY 16 ha	19	F 25P	All Year	Y	23		35		F W		4P	X	X	
278	2B	SMUGGLER COVE MARINE 182 ha	101	P	All Year		4	X	10	R			1P	X	X	2H
279	3D	SOOKE MOUNTAIN 450 ha	14	NO	All Year											
280	3D	SOOKE POTHOLES 7 ha	14	1P	All Year				62				4P	X	X	
280 A	47C	SOWCHEA BAY RA 13 ha	27	P	May-Oct											
281	27C	SPAHATS CREEK 306 ha	5	15P	Apr-Oct	Y	20		40		F W		8P			3H
282	62A	SPATSIZI PLATEAU WILDERNESS 656,785 ha	37	25G				X					4P		X	100H
283	3D	SPECTACLE LAKE 65 ha	1	2P	All Year				60		W		2p	X	X	W
284	57C	SPENCER TUCK 4 ha	29	P	Apr-Oct				20	R	W		2P	X	X	
285	2A	SPIDER LAKE 65 ha	19	8G	All Year				60	C	W		5P	X	X	1H
286	2C	SPROAT LAKE 39 ha	4	P	All Year	Y	59		200	R	F W	X	S 8F 16P	X	X	2H
287	2B	SQUITTY BAY MARINE 13 ha	19	NO											X	
288	9A	ST. MARY'S ALPINE 9,146 ha	95A	45R				X								H
289	8D	STAGLEAP 1,133 ha	3	P	All Year				30		W		4P		X	1H
289 A	15D	STAKE-McCONNEL LAKES RA	5	P				X							X	
290	2C	STAMP FALLS 236 ha	4	14P	All Year	Y	20		30		W		6P		X	2H
291	7A	STEMWINDER 4 ha	3	P	All Year	Y	23			C	F W		6P		X	

PARK / MAP NUMBER	MAP REFERENCE	Park / AREA IN HECTARES (ha)	NEAREST HIGHWAY	ROAD ACCESS	OPERATING DATES	FEE (Y, N)	VEHICLE / TENT CAMPSITES GROUP CAMPING (*)	WILDERNESS / WALK-IN CAMPSITES	PICNICKING / DAY USE (Car Spaces)	BOAT LAUNCHING RAMP (R) CANOEING / KAYAKING (C)	FIREWOOD (F) DRINKING WATER (W)	SANI-STATION	FLUSH TOILETS (F) PIT TOILETS (P) SHOWERS (S)	SWIMMING	FISHING	HIKING TRAILS (km H) WALKING TRAILS (W)
292	61B	STIKINE RIVER RA 217,000 ha	37	NO												
293	75C	STONE MOUNTAIN 25,691 ha	97	G	May-Oct	Y	28	X	5		W		7P		X	5H
294	1B	STRATHCONA 211,973 ha	28	P	All Year	Y	161	26	37	R C	F W		54P	X	X	107 H
295	47C	STUART LAKE 315 ha	27	35R	Apr-Oct					R						
296	58C	SUDETEN 5 ha	2	P	May-Oct	Y	15		25		F W		6P			
297	57C	SUKUNKA FALLS 360 ha	97	25G	Apr-Oct											
298	5D	SUMAS MOUNTAIN 185 ha	1	4G	All Year				5							4H
299	7A	SUN-OKA BEACH 21 ha	97	P					190		W		11F 2P	X		
300	16B	SUNNYBRAE 25 ha	1	6P	Apr-Oct				56		W		4F 2P	X	X	1H
301	58C	SWAN LAKE 67 ha	2	3G	May-Oct	Y	41*		75	R C	F W		12P	X	X	H
302	8A	SYRINGA CREEK 226 ha	3	19P	Apr-Oct	Y	60		220	R C	F W	X	22F 12P	X	X	5H
303	62D	TATLATUI 105,826 ha	37	NO	May-Nov			X						X		H
304	2C	TAYLOR ARM 71 ha	4	P	All Year		*	60	15				8P	X	X	1H W
305	57B	TAYLOR LANDING 2 ha	97	P					20	R			1P	X		
305 A	13C	TEAKERNE ARM MARINE 128 ha	101	NO												
306	38D	TEN MILE LAKE 241 ha	97	P	May-Oct	Y	142*		350	R C	F W	X	10F 24P	X	X	H
307	75B	TETSA RIVER 115 ha	97	1R	May-Oct	Y	25		6		F W		4P		X	H
308	8C	TEXAS CREEK 112 ha	3	P	Apr-Oct	Y	16		X					X	X	
309	18D	THUNDER HILL 44 ha	93	P	Apr-Oct	Y	23				F W		6P			
310	13C	THURSTON BAY MARINE 389 ha	19	NO	All Year									X		
311	9B	TOP OF THE WORLD 8,791 ha	93	54R	All Year	Y		28	20				6P		X	40H
312	46B	TOPLEY 12 ha	16	40P					55		W		4P	X	X	
313	2A	TRIBUNE BAY 95 ha	19	F 10P	All Year				100		W		6P	X	X	
314	16D	TRUMAN DAGNUS LOCHEED 7 ha	97	P												
315	48A	TUDYAH LAKE 56 ha	97	P	May-Oct	Y	36*		40	R C	F W		6P	X	X	
316	36C	TWEEDSMUIR 994,246 ha	20	G	Apr-Oct	Y	38	11	63	R C	F W	X	28P	X	X	489 H
317	46A	TYHEE LAKE 33 ha	16	1P	Apr-Oct	Y	55		200	R C	F W	X	16F 18P	X	X	1H
318	8B	VALHALLA 49,800 ha	6	NO	All Year			16		C			9P	X	X	88H
319	7C	VASEUX LAKE 12 ha	97	P	All Year	Y	9		5	C	F W		4P	X	X	
320	17A	VICTOR LAKE 15 ha	1	P	Apr-Oct				45				4P			
320 A	15D	WALLOPER LAKE 55 ha	5	P					X						X	
320 B	13C	WALSH COVE MARINE 85 ha	101	NO												
321	9B	WARDNER 4 ha	3	2P	Apr-Oct				20		W		2P	X		
322	9B	WASA 144 ha	93	1P	All Year	Y	104		500	R C	F W	X	47F 20P	X	X	2H
323	27A	WELLS GRAY 529,748 ha	5	40G	Apr-Oct	Y	83	23	321	R C	F W		72P	X	X	284 H
323 A	26D	WELLS GRAY (Mahood L.)	97	86 PG		Y	34	20	40	R			8P	X	X	H
324	38B	WEST LAKE 256 ha	16	13P	May-Oct				200	R C	W		8F 10P	X	X	5H
325	3D	WEST SHAWNIGAN LAKE 9 ha	1	16P	All Year				120	C			6P	X	X	
326	3B	WHALEBOAT ISLAND MARINE 10 ha	1	NO	All Year										X	
327	48B	WHISKERS POINT 52 ha	97	P	May-Sept	Y	69*		50	R C	F W	X	6F 6P	X	X	H
328	25A	WHITE PELICAN 1,247 ha	20	NO												
329	18D	WHITESWAN LAKE 1,994 ha	93	25R	All Year	Y	56	24	15	R C	F W		21P	X	X	8H
330	5C	WINTER COVE MARINE 91 ha	17	F 6G	All Year				10				2P	X		2H
331	36A	WISTARIA 40 ha	35	66G				5	30	R			2P	X		
332	75C	WOKKPASH RA 37,800 ha	97	NO												
333	9D	YAHK 9 ha	3	P	Apr-Oct	Y	24		30		F W		4P		X	
334	16B	YARD CREEK 61 ha	1	P	Apr-Oct	Y	90		14		F W	X	2F 20P			2H

NATIONAL PARKS WITHIN OR BORDERING ON BRITISH COLUMBIA

PARK / MAP NUMBER	Park	NEAREST HIGHWAY	ROAD ACCESS	OPERATING DATES	VEHICLE / TENT CAMPSITES GROUP CAMPING (*)	WILDERNESS / WALK-IN CAMPSITES	PICNICKING / DAY USE (Car Spaces)	BOAT LAUNCHING RAMP (R) CANOEING / KAYAKING (C)	FIREWOOD (F) DRINKING WATER (W)	SANI-STATION	FLUSH TOILETS (F) PIT TOILETS (P) SHOWERS (S)	SWIMMING	FISHING	HIKING TRAILS (km H) WALKING TRAILS (W)
Page 18	BANFF	1 93	P	May-Sept	2800	X	X	R C	F W	X	S F P	X	X	H W
Page 17	GLACIER	1	P	Apr-Sept	394*	X	X		F W		S F P		X	H W
Page 41	JASPER	16 93	P	May-Nov	1900	X	X	R C	F W	X	S F P	X	X	H W
Page 78	KLUANE	7	P	June-Oct	41		X		F W		F P		X	H W
Page 18	KOOTENAY	93	P	May-Oct	450*	X	X	C	F W	X	S F P	X	X	H W
Page 17	MT. REVELSTOKE	1	P	All Year			X						X	H W
Page 1	PACIFIC RIM	4	P	All Year	175	X	X	C		X	F P	X	X	H W
Page 10	WATERTON	3	P	All Year	300	X	X	C	F W	X	S F P	X	X	H W
Page 18	YOHO	1	P	May-Oct	200	X	X		F W	X	S F P		X	H W

NOTE : For complete listing of facilities, see "Guide to Camping and Activities in National Parks" – available from Canada Parks Service Offices.

GAZETTEER

Location references in this gazetteer consist of a page number and a letter indicating position on the page, according to the diagram below.

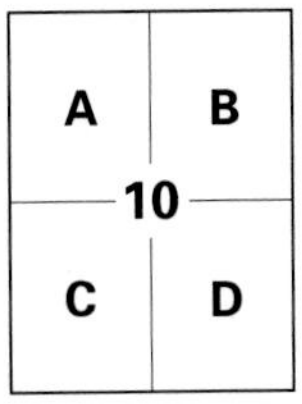

Place Names are shown in red

● Hospital

❍ Diagnostic and Treatment Centre

A

Aaltanhash In 35C
Aaltanhash R 35C
Aaron Hill 8D
● Abbotsford 5D
Abbott Cr 26A
Aberdeen L 16D
Abies Cr 53B
Abraham Cr 54B
Abuntlet L 23B
Aconitum Cr 82C
Aconitum L 82C
Actaeon Sd 11B
Active Pass 3B, 5C
Adam R 12C
Adamant Mtn 28C
Adams Cr 56B
Adams L 16A, 27D
Adams Lake 16A
Adams R 16A, 27D
Addenbroke I 22C
Adolf Cr 27B
Adoogacho Cr 62B
Adsett Cr 76D
Adsit L 71B, 72A
Advance Mtn 56A
Aeneas L 7A
Aero 31C
Aeroplane L 73A, 84C
Agamemnon Chan 2B
Agassiz 6C
Ahbau Cr 38D
Ahbau L 38D
Ahclakerho Chan 11B
Ahnuhati R 12B
Ahousat 1D
Ahwhichaolto In 11C
Aid L 28D
Aiken L 54B
Aikman Cr 56B
Ain R 30B, 32A
Ainslie Cr 6A
Ainsworth Hot Springs ... 9A
Airdrie 19B
Airline L 47A
Airplane L 81C
Airport Cr 46D
Airy Mtn 8A
Aitken Cr 66C
Aiyansh 44B
Akamina Cr 10D
Akamina Pass 10D
Akehurst L 26D
Akie Mtn 64C
Akie R 64C
Akluky Cr 65A
Akokli Cr 9A
Akokli Mtn 9A
Akolkolex R 17A
Aktaklin L 24A
Akue Cr 75D, 76C
Alan Cr 82D, 83C
Alan Reach 35A
Alans L 26D
Alastair L 44D
Albas 16B
Alberni In 2C
Albert Canyon 17A
Albert Cr 17A
Albert L 54D
Albert Pk 17A
Albert R 18D
Albert Snowfield 17B
Alberta L 15A, 26C
Alberts Hump 62B
Albion 5D
Albreda R 27B
Albright Cr 58C
Alcantara Cr 18B
Alces R 57B, 58A
Alcock L 57D, 58C
Alder Cr 28D, 44D
Alder Pk 44B
Aldergrove 5D
Aldridge Cr 19C
Alec Chief L 83C
● Alert Bay 12C
Alex Cr 16A
Alex Graham L 25A
Alexander Cr 10A
Alexander Cr 57A, 66C
Alexander In 22A, 35C
Alexandra Pass 11A
Alexandra Pk 1B
Alexandria 38D
Alexis Cr 25A
Alexis Creek 25A
Alexis Pk 48B
Aley Cr 55B, 56A
Alford Cr 48D
Alger Cr 61C
Alice Arm 52D
Alice Arm 52D
Alice Cr 38D
Alice Cr 44D
Alice L 11D
Alice Pk 44D
Aline L 74B, 85D
Alison Sd 11B
Alixon Cr 25D
Alkali Cr 25D
Alkali L 25D
Alkali L 60A
Alkali Lake 25D
Allan Cr 27B
Allan L 16A
Allard L 22D
Allen Cr 15A
Allenby 6B
Alleyne L 6B
Aleza Lake 48D
Alliford Bay 31C
Allin Cr 46D
Allison Cr 6B
Allison L 6B
Allison Pass 6D
Allison Pk 10A
Alma Cr 62C
Alma Pk 62D
Alma Russell Is 2C
Almond Cr 8C
Almond Mtn 8C
Alnus Cr 28A
Alocin Cr 16C
Alocin L 7A
Alouette L 4A, 5D
Alouette R 4A
Alpha Cr 31B, 33B, 34A
Alpha Mtn 60C
Alsek R 78D
Aluk Cr 53C
Amai Creek 11D
Ambition Mtn 60A
America Cr 9D
American Cr 52A
Ames Cr 39A
Amor de Cosmos Cr 12D
Amor L 12D
Amos Cr 26B, 39D
Amoth L 44A
Anaconda 7D
Anacortes 4C
Anahim Cr 25A
Anahim L 23B
Anahim Lake 24A
Anahim Pk 36D
Anarchist Mtn 7D
Anchor L 34D
Anderson Cr 15A
Anderson L 14D
Anderson L 27A
Anderson R 6A
Andesite Pk 45C
Andy Cr 55B, 56A
Andy Good Cr 10A
Aneko Cr 24B, 25A
Angel L 81D
Angel Pk 75C
Anger I 33D, 34A
Anglemont 16B
Angly L 47C
Angus Cr 2B
Angus Cr 9B
Angus Horne Cr 27A
Angus Horne L 27A
Angusmac Cr 48D
Ankitree Cr 23C
Ankwill Cr 54C
Anstey Arm 16B
Anstey R 16B
Ant L 48A
Anthony Cr 62C
Anthony I 20A
Anthracite Cr 62C
Antle Is 31B, 33D
Antler Cr 39C
Antoine Cr 14B
Antoine L 26A
Anudol Cr 44B
Anuk R 60C
Anvil Mtn 14A, 25C
Anyox Cr 52C
Anzac R 48B
Anzus L 37A
Apalmer Cr 16B
Ape L 23B
Apex Cr 8B
Apex Mtn 7A
Apex Mtn 28A
Apple R 12B
Appledale 8B
Applegrove 8A
Apsassin Cr 65D
Aramis Ls 63B
Arcat Cr 7A
Archer Cr 26B, 27A
Archer Cr 39C
Archie L 34D
Arctic L 49C
Argenta 18C
Argentine Mtn 28C
Argillite Cr 71D, 72C
Argonaut Cr 28C
Argonaut Mtn 28C
Aristazabal I 21B, 34D
Arlington 4D
Arlington Ls 7B
Arlington Pk 8B
Armadillo Pk 60B, 61A
● Armstrong 16D
Armstrong L 17B
Arnell Cr 75D, 76C
Arnhem Mtn 74D
Arnoup Cr 34D
Arras 58C
Arrow Cr 9C
Arrow Creek 9C
Arrow Park Cr 17C
Arrow Park L 17C
Arrow Pass 12A
Arrowhead 17A
Arrowview Heights 2C
Arthur I 33A, 43D
Arthur L 16D
Artlish R 11D, 12C
Ash Mtn 71B, 72A
Ash R 1B, 2A
● Ashcroft 15A
Asher Cr 17D
Ashlu Cr 5A, 14C
Ashlulm Cr 23C
Ashnola R 7C
Ashton Cr 16D
Ashton Creek 16D
Asitka L 54A
Asitka Pk 54A
Asitka R 54A
Askom Mtn 15C
Asp Cr 6B
Aspen Grove 6B
Asseek R 23C
Assiniboine Pass 18B
Asulkan Br 17B
Atan L 72B
Athabasca Pass 28A
Athalmer 18D
Athlone I 22A
Athlow B 30A, 32C
Atick Cr 65D
Atis Cr 39C
Atlatzi R 12B
Atli In 20A, 31C
Atlin 81C
Atlin L ... 69B, 70A, 80D, 81C
Atlin Mtn 80D, 81C
Atlin R 80D, 81C
Atluck 12C
Atluck L 12C
Atna L 35A, 45C
Atna Pk 35A
Atna R 35A, 45C
Atnarko 23B
Atnarko R 23B
Attachie 57A
Attichika Cr 62D, 63C
Attycelley Cr 63C
Atwaykellesse R 12A
Augier L 46D
August L 88D
Austerity Cr 28C
Australian 38D
Australian Cr 25B, 38D
Avalanch Pass 40A
Averil Cr 48D
Averil L 48D
Avola 27D
Avon Cr 25A
Avun L 30B, 32C
Axelgold Pk 54B
Axnegrelga Cr 52D
Aylard Cr 56B
Ayton Cr 33B, 44C
Azouzetta L 56D
Azuklotz Cr 54A
Azuklotz L 54A
Azure Cr 27A
Azure L 27A
Azure Mtn 27A

B

Babcock Cr 49B
Babcock L 39C
Babiche Hill 53A
Babine L 46B
Babine R 53D, 54C
Bachelor Cr 28C
Back L 18B
Bacon Cr 69D, 70A
Badger Cr 16A
Badger L 16A
Badman Point 71A
Baezaeko R 37D
Bain Br 17B
Baird Br 17B
Baker Cr 7D
Baker Cr 28A
Baker Cr 38C, 38D
Baker I 12A
Baker In 33B, 34A
Balaklava I 11B
Bald Mtn 25D
Bald Range Cr 16C
Balden Cr 55B, 56A, 64D, 65C
Baldface Mtn 37C
Baldonnel 57B
Baldy Cr 7D
Baldy Hughes 38A
Baldy Mtn 7D
Baldy Mtn 8B
Baldy Mtn 24A, 37C
Baldy Mtn 27C
Baldy Mtn 55C
Balfour 9A
Ball Cr 60D, 61C
Ballenas Chan 2D, 3A
Ballenas Is 2B
Balmoral 16B
Bamberton 3D
Bambrick Cr 25C
Bamfield 2C
Bamford Lagoon 11B
Bancroft Cr 1B
Banff 18B
Banks I 31B, 33D, 34A
Banks L 33D, 34A
Bannock Burn Cr 8B
Banon Cr 2D, 3B
Banshee L 16A
Banting Cr 17C
Banville 8C
Baptiste Cr 47A
Barbara L 49D, 50C
Barbour Cr 18C
Bardolph L 16D
Bardswell Group 22A
Barella Cr 26B, 27A
Barker Cr 62C
Barker Cr 65D
Barkers Cr 39C
Barkerville 39C
Barkley Sd 1D
Barkshack Cr 13D

Barnes Cr 8A, 17C
Barnes Cr 15B
Barnes L 15A
Barney L 84D, 85C
Baron I 33A, 43D
Barr Cr 1A
Barr Cr 19C
Barrett Lake 46C
Barrie Reach 35A
Barrier Pass 64C
Barrier Pk 64C
◯ Barrière 16A
Barrière R 16A, 27C
Barrington R 60A
Barton Hill 16C
Barton L 38A
Basalt L 36D
Base Camp Cr 80D, 81C
Bassett Cr 26B
Bastille Cr 39B, 40A
Bastille Mtn 40A
Bastion Bay 16B
Bat Cr 64B, 65A
Batchelor L 34A
Bate Pass 11A
Bates Cr 54D
Batnuni L 37B
Battle Br 17B
Battle Gla 78C
Battle L 12A
Bay Tree 58C
Baynes Lake 10C
Baynes Sd 2A
Bayton 2A
Beach Grove 5C
Beachcomber Bay 16D
Beady Cr 71B, 72A
Beak Cr 16C
Beale L 72B
Beale Mtn 72B
Beany Cr 56B
Bear B 13A
Bear Canyon 58A
Bear Cr 10C
Bear Cr 25C
Bear Cr 71C
Bear Creek Res 3D
Bear Flat 57A
Bear L 17D
Bear L 34D
Bear L 53B, 54A
Bear Mtn 57D, 58C
Bear R 13A
Bear R 52A
Bear R 53B, 54A
Bear River Gla 52A
Bear River Pass 52A
Bearcub Cr 47D
Beard Cr 18A
Bearpaw L 26C
Beasley 8B
Beaton 17B
Beaton Cr 17B
Beatrice Cr 8B
Beatrice L 8B
Beattie Cr 55B, 56A
Beattie Pks 56D
Beatton R 57B, 58A,
                              65D, 66A
Beatton Ranch 65D
Beatton River 66A
Beatty Cr 71C
Beauchamp Pk 75C
Beauchemin
    Chan 21B, 34D
Beaudette Cr 56D
Beaumont Cr 25D
Beauregard L 16A
Beaver Cove 12C
Beaver Cove 12C
Beaver Cr 8D
Beaver Cr 26A

Beaver Cr 65B
Beaver Creek 2C
Beaver Har 11B
Beaver In 12D
Beaver L 25A
Beaver Mines 10B
Beaver Pass .. 31B, 33D, 34A
Beaver R 17B, 28D
Beaver R 86C
Beaverdell 7B
Beaverdell Cr 7B
Beaverfoot R 18A
Beaverley 38B
Beaverley Cr 38B
Beaverlodge 50B
Beaverlodge L 50A, 58C
Beaverpond Cr 54D
Beaverskin Cr 77D
Becher B 3D
Beckman Cr 75D, 76C
Bedaux Pass 64A
Bedingfield L 26C
Bedji Cr 77D
Bednesti L 38A
Bedwell L 1B
Bedwell R 1B
Bedwell Sd 1D
Beece Cr 14A, 25C
Beechey Head 3D
Beedy Cr 25B
Beef Trail Cr 23B, 36D
Beehive Mtn 19C
Beggerlay Cr 61B, 72D
Behrman Cr 18C
Beirnes Cr 62C
Belcarra 5C
Belcourt Cr 49D, 50C
Belcourt L 49D, 50C
Belgo Cr 7B
Belize In 11B
Bell Bay Cr 44A, 52C
Bell Cr 25A
Bell I 22C
Bell L 70B, 81D
Bell-Irving R 52B, 61C
Bella Bella 22A
● Bella Coola 23A
Bella Coola R 23A
Belle Cr 63C
Belleisle Sd 12A
Bellevue 10B
Bellevue Cr 7B
Bellingham 5D
Bellos L 38D
Bells L 26A
Ben Abel Cr 18D
Ben L 25B
Bend Mtn 63A
Benhur Cr 8B
Bennison Cr 17B
Benno Mtn 51A
Benny L 26A
Benson Cr 57C
Benson Lake 11D
Benson R 11D
Bentinck Spire 22B
Bentzi L 37A
Berenden Gla 51B, 52A
Beresford 16C
Beresford B 30A
Beresford Cr 32A, 42C
Beresford I 11C
Berg Cr 74A, 85C
Bergeland Cr 35B
Berman L 38A
Bernadet Cr 57A, 66C
Bernard Cr 9A
Bernard Cr 56A
Bernhardt Cr 36C
Berry Cr 71B, 72A
Bertha L 11B

Besa R 64B, 65A
Bessborough 57D
Bessette Cr 16D
Betty Wendle Cr 39D
Bevan 2A
Bevel Cr 55B
Bevel Mtn 55B
Bews Cr 17A
Biddy Cr 25A
Bidwell Cr 24D
Bidwell Ls 24D
Big Arrow Cr 66D
Big B 33B, 43D
Big Bar Cr 14B
Big Bar Creek 14B
Big Bar L 15A, 26C
Big Bay 13C
Big Bay 44C
Big Beaver Cr 76D
Big Bend Arm 37A
Big Bend Cr 37A
Big Cr 14A, 25C
Big Creek 25C
Big Eddy Cr 17A
Big Falls Cr 34A, 44C
Big Falls L 33B, 34A, 44C
Big Goat Cr 7B
Big Kettle Fumarole 54A
Big L 26A
Big L 26C
Big Lake Ranch 26A
Big Loon L 46B
Big Sheep Cr 8C
Big Silver Cr 6A
Big Timothy Mtn 26B
Big Valley Cr 39C
Big White Mtn 7B
Bighorn Cr 10C
Bighorn R 80C
Bighorn Mtn 74C
Bigmouth Cr 28C
Bigsby In 20A
Bill Miner Cr 26B
Billings Bay 2B
Billygoat Cr 14D
Bilou Cr 64A
Bilou Pk 64A
Bingay Cr 19C
Bingley Pk 41C
Binta L 36B
Birch Bay 5D
Birch Cr 28C
Birch Cr 57A
Birch Island 27C
Birch L 26D
Birch Mtn 80D, 81C
Birches L 73A
Bird Hill 53B, 54A
Bird L 37A
Birdflat Cr 53B, 54A
Birk Cr 16A, 27C
Birken 14D
Birkenhead L 14D
Birkenhead R 14D
Birley Cr 66A
Bird Cr 34B, 44D
Bishop B 34B
Bishop Bluffs 37D
Bishop L 26C
Bishop R 13B
Bissett Cr 57C
Bissette Cr 57D, 58C
Bisson L 17C
Bitter Cr 52A
Bivouac Cr 46B
Black Angus Cr 84C
Black Cr 2A
Black Cr 66A
Black Creek 2A
Black Diamond 19B
Black Fox Cr 61B
Black L 2C

Black Martin Cr 40C
Black Mtn 80D, 81C
Black Night Mtn 7B
Black Pines 16A
Blackbear Cr 26A
Blackberry Cr 45C
Blackcome Pk 14D
Blackfish Sd 12C
Blackfly Cr 71B
Blackfly L 71B
Blackfoot Cr 18D
Blackfox Mtn 72B
Blackhawk L 49B, 50A
Blackhorn Mtn 24C
Blackjack Mtn 55C
Blackman Cr 28A
Blackpine L 54B
Blackpool 27C
Blackstock Cr 53C
Blacktail Cr 9D
Blackwater Cr 30B, 32C
Blackwater Cr 55D, 56C
Blackwater L 28D
Blackwater Mtn 28D
Blackwater Pk 53A
Blackwell L 16C
Blaeberry 28D
Blaeberry R 29C
Blaine 5D
Blair Cr 16C
Blair Cr 65D
Blair I 22C
Blairmore 10B
Blais Cr 27C
Blakeburn 6B
Blakeney Cr 3C
Blanchard Cr 64C
Blanchard R 79C
Blanchet L 36A
Blanchet R 36B
Blanket Cr 17A
Blazed Cr 9C
Bleasdell Cr 19C
Blewett 8B
Bligh I 1A
Bliss Landing 13C
Blizzard Ls 75C
Bloedel 12D
Blomley Cr 16A
Bloom Cr 9D
Bloomfield L 35C
Blowhole Bay 1A
Blubber Bay 2A
Blue Canyon Cr 37C
Blue Cr 14B
Blue Earth L 15C
Blue Grave Cr 56B
Blue Joe Cr 9C
Blue Joint Mtn 8A
Blue L 7C
Blue L 55C
Blue Lead Cr 26B, 27A,
                              39D, 40C
Blue R 27B
Blue R 82D, 83C, 83D
Blue River 27B
Blue Sheep Cr 73A
Blue Sheep L 73A
Blue Springs 16D
Blueberry Cr 8D
Blueberry Mountain 58D
Blueberry R 66C
Bluejoint Cr 8A
Bluewater Cr 28D
Bluey L 6B
Bluff Cr 74C
Bluff Hill 64C
Bluff L 24C

Blunden B 11A
Blunden I 1D
Blunt Cr 45B, 46A
Blunt Mtn 45B
Blurton Cr 16B
Blustry Mtn 15C
Boat Basin 1A
Boat Cr 65B
Bob Quinn L 60D, 61C
Bobb Cr 14B
Bobbie Burns Cr ... 17B, 18A
Bobbie Burns Mtn 16D
Bobtail Cr 26C
Bobtail Mtn 38A
Bodega Hill 3B, 5C
Bodel Cr 60A
Boise Cr 5B
Boitano L 25D
Boivin Cr 10A, 19C
Bold Point 13C
Bolean Cr 16C
Bolean L 16C
Bolton Cr 45C
Bonanza 58C
Bonanza Cr 17D
Bonanza Cr 52C
Bonanza L 12C
Bonanza L 12C
Bonaparte L 15B
Bonaparte R .. 15A, 15B, 26D
Bond Sd 12B
Bone Cr 27C
Bone Cr 35D, 36C
Bone Mtn 49B
Bones B 12C
Bones Bay 12C
Bongard Cr 16D
Bonilla I 31B, 33C
Bonnatie Cr 38A
Bonneau Cr 16D
Bonners Ferry 9C
Bonnington L 48A
Bonwick I 12A
Booker Lagoon 12A
Boomerang L 11B, 12A
Bootleg Mtn 9A
Borel L 37A
Borgeson L 6B
Boring Ranch 65D
Borrett Cr 76C
Bosk L 26B
Boss Cr 26B
Boss Mtn 26B
Boston Bar 6A
Boston Bar Cr 6A
Boswell 9A
Boswell In 11B, 22D
Botanie Cr 15C
Botanie L 15C
Botanie Mtn 15C
Botany In 31C
Bottle Cr 26A
Bottleneck Cr 36C
Boucher Cr 54C
Boucher L 57C
Bouchie L 38D
Bouchie Lake 38D
Boughey B 12D
Bougie Cr 65B
Boulder Cr 45B
Boulder Pass 54B
Bouldery Cr 26B
Bouleau Cr 16C
Bouleau L 16C
Bouleau Mtn 16C
Boundary B 4A, 5D
Boundary Bay 5C
Boundary Cr 7D
Boundary Cr 9C
Boundary Cr 58A
Boundary L 9C
Boundary L 58A

109

Bounding Cr 39B
Bourgeaux Cr 60B, 61A
Bourne Cr 28C
Bowen I 3B, 5A
Bowen Island 5A
Bower Cr 63B
Bowers L 26D
Bowes Cr 38B
Bowman L 11B
Bowron L 39C
Bowron R 38B, 39A,
39C, 48D
Bowser 2A
Bowser L 52B
Bowser R 52A
Bowsprit Mtn 62C
Boya Cr 73B
Boya L 83D
Boyd Cr 17B
Boyd L 26C
Boydell L 11B
Boyds 8C
Boyer Cr 7B
Boyer Cr 70A, 81C
Boyer L 15B
Brackendale 5A
Braden Cr 3C
Braden R 22B
Bradley Cr 26D
Bradley Lagoon 11B
Brady Ranch 65D
Braeside 47D
Bragg Creek 19A
Braid Cr 74D
Bralorne 14B
Bramham I 11B
Brandon Pk 63B
Brandt Cr 77A
Brash Cr 16D
Brassey Cr 57D
Brazion Cr 56D
Breadner Group 22C
Breccia Pk 62B, 63A
Brem R 13C
Brem River 13C
Bremner Cr 5B
Bremner Cr 17D
Brenda 7A
Brenot Cr 56B
Brentwood Bay 3D
Brew Bay 2B
Brew Cr 13A
Brewer Cr 18D
Brewery Cr 60A
Brewster L 12D
Brexton 14B
Briar Ridge 58C
Bridal Falls 6C
Bridesville 7D
Bridge Cr 26C
Bridge Creek 26D
Bridge L 26D
Bridge R 14A, 14B
Briggs In 22A
Brim R 35A
Brimstone Cr 86C
Brink L 11A
Brisco 18A
Britannia Beach 5A
Brittain R 13D
Brittanny Cr 24D
Brittanny L 24D
Britton Cr 6B
Broadview 16B
Broadview L 40A
Brocket 10B
Broken Cr 7A
Broken Group 1D
Bromley Cr 6B
Bronlund Pk 63A
Bronson Cr 51A, 60C
Brookmere 6B

Brooks B 11C
Brooks Pen 11D
Brothers L 62D
Brothers Pks 62D
Broughton Str 11D, 12C
Brousseau L 15B
Brown Cr 15B, 26D
Brown Cr 25A
Brown L 33B, 34A, 44C
Brown Pass 33A, 43D
Brownie Mtn 73D, 74C
Browning
Entrance 31B, 33C
Browning In 11C
Browning Pass 1D
Brownlee L 80C
Browns R 2A
Browntop Mtn 39C
Bruce Cr 18C
Bruce Cr 62A
Brucejack L 51B, 52A
Bruer Cr 16D
Bruin Cr 55A
Brûlé 41C
Brule Cr 10A
Brundige In 43D
Brunson L 25B
Brunswick 5A
Brunt Cr 51A
Bryan Arm 36D
Bryant Cr 24A
Bryce Cr 28B
Bryden L 16A
Brydon Cr 60A
Bubbles Cr 66C
Buchan In 33D, 34A
Buchanan Cr 39B, 40A
Buck Chan 30D, 32C
Buck Cr 7B
Buck Cr 11D
Buck Cr 46C
Buckhorn L 38B
Buckhorn Ls 24D
Buckinghorse Cr 62A
Buckinghorse L 62C
Buckinghorse R 65A
Buckley Bay 2A
Bucklin Cr 5B
Buckskin L 25B
Buckworth Cr 9C
Buffalo Cr 26C
Buffalo Creek 26C
Buffalo L 26C
Buffalo Lake 58D
Bugaboo Cr 18A
Bugle L 48C
Buhl Cr 9B
Buick Cr 66C
Bulkley L 46D
Bulkley L 60B
Bulkley R 45B, 46C
Bull Cr 7A
Bull Cr 66A
Bull Cr 71B, 72A
Bull Cr 81C
Bull Har 11A
Bull Harbour 11A
Bull R 10A, 19C
Bull River 9B
Bulldog Cr 27B, 40D
Bullhead Mtn 56B
Bullmoose Cr 49A
Bullmoose Mtn 49A
Bullock Chan 22A
Bullock L 26C
Bulman Cr 7B, 16D
Bulson Cr 1D
Bulwell Cr 86C
Bunch Grass Hill 8A
Buntzen L 4A, 5A
Burden L 55D, 56C
Burden Pk 48B

Burdick Cr 45A
Burgess Cr 25B
Burke Chan 22B
Burlington 4D
Burman L 1B
Burman R 1B
Burmis 10B
●Burnaby 5C
Burnaby I 20A
Burned L 48D
Burnie L 45D
Burnie R 45C
Burns L 46D
●Burns Lake 46D
Burnstead Cr 47D, 48C
Burnt Bridge Cr 23B
Burnt R 48B, 57C
Burrage Cr 60D, 61C
Burrard In 4A, 5C
Burton 17C
Burton Cr 8A
Burton Cr 44A
Buse L 16C
Bush Arm 28D
Bush Cr 2D, 3B
Bush Cr 16A
Bush R 28D
Buster L 26B
Butchart L 3D
Bute In 13C
Butedale L 34D
Buth Cr 48A
Butsih Cr 82C
Butte L 71B, 72A
Butterfield Cr 46B
Butterfield L 46D
Buttle L 1B
Buxton Cr 26A
Byman Cr 46C
Byron Cr 46A

C

Caamaño Pass 43D
Caamaño Sd 34C
Cab Cr 56B
Cabin Cr 10C
Cabin L 77A
Cache Cr 15A
Cache Cr 57A
Cache Cr 71B, 72A
Cache Creek 15A
Cadboro Bay 3D
Cadomin 41D
Cadorna Cr 19C
Cadorna L 19C
Cadwallader Cr 14B
Caen Mtn 75C
Cahill Cr 7A
Cahill L 8B
Cahilty Cr 16A
Cahilty L 16A
Cain Cr 16C
Caine Cr 48D
Cairie L 11B
Cairn Needle 6A
Cairn L 11B
Cake Hill 72D
Calamity B 33D, 34C
Calder Cr 10C
Cale Cr 38B
Caledonia Mtn 41C
Calendar Cr 88D
Calf Cr 84C
Calgary 19B
Call In 12D
Callaghan Cr 14C
Callaghan L 14C
Callahan L 25B
Callazon Cr 56D
Callbreath Cr 60A

Calling L 15D
Callison L 72B
Calm Chan 13C
Calnan Cr 64D, 65C
Calvert I 22C
Cambie 16B
Camborne 17B
Cambria Icefield 52C
Camel Mtn 24C
Cameo L 7A, 16C
Cameron Cr 9C
Cameron Cr 39D
Cameron Cr 65D
Cameron L 2C, 3A
Cameron Lake 2C
Cameron R 2C, 3A
Cameron R 56B
Camp Artaban 5A
Camp Cr 27B, 40D
Camp Island L 71C
Campania I 34D
Campania Sd 34D
Campbell Cr 9A
Campbell Cr 16C
Campbell I 22A
Campbell Icefield .. 28D, 29C
Campbell Island 22A
Campbell L 1B, 12D
Campbell L 16C
Campbell Pk 74B
●Campbell River 13C
Campbellton 13C
Camper Cr 3C
Campion Cr 40D
Campobasso Mtn 75C
Camsell L 47C
Canal Flats 18D
Candle Cr 27C
Cane Cr 8A
Canford 15D
Canim L 26D
Canim Lake 26D
Canim R 26D
Canimred Cr 26D
Canoe 16B
Canoe Cr 25D
Canoe R 40D
Canoe Reach 27B
Canoona L 35C
Cantin Cr 38D
Canuck Cr 9D
Canvas Cr 27B
Canyon 9C
Canyon City 44B
Canyon Cr 17B, 18A
Canyon Cr 45B, 46A
Canyon Cr 51B
Canyon Cr 51C
Canyon Cr 71B, 72A
Canyon Cr 85D
Canyon L 53A
Cape Ball 31A, 32D
Cape Ball R 31A, 32B
Cape Beale 2C
Cape Calvert 22C
Cape Caution 11A
Cape
Chroustcheff ... 31C, 32D
Cape Cook 11C
Cape George 31B, 33A
Cape Horn Cr 17C
Cape James 11A
Cape Knox 32A, 42C
Cape Mudge 13C
Cape Palmerston 11C
Cape Parkins 11C
Cape Russell 11A
Cape Scott 11A, 11C
Cape St. James 20D
Cape Sutil 11A
Capilano L 4A, 5A
Capilano R 4A, 5A

Capot-Blanc Cr 86D, 87C
Captain Cove 33B, 34A
Captain Cr 49C
Captain Harry L 36D
Captain L 83D
Caput Mtn 26B
Carabine Cr 15B
Carbon Cr 56D
Carbon L 56D
Carbon Pk 56B
Carcajou Cr 63B
Carcajou Pass 40D
Carcross 80A
Cardiff Mtn 24D
Cardtable Mtn 14A
Carey Cr 56B
Cargill Cr 49C
Cariboo Cr 72D
Cariboo L 39C
Cariboo Mtn 39C
Cariboo R 26A, 39C, 39D
Caribou Cr 8B, 72A
Caribou Mtn 23B
Caribou Mtn 39B
Carina L 55A
Carlick Cr 82C
Carlin 16B
Carmanah Cr 2C, 3C
Carmanah Mtn 2C
Carmi 7B
Carmi Cr 7B
Carnes Cr 17A
Carney Cr 18C
Carney L 52C
Carnlick Cr 37C
Caroline L 22D
Caron Cr 57C
Carp L 48A
Carpenter B 20B
Carpenter Cr 8B, 17D
Carpenter L 14B
Carrier L 47D, 48C
Carrigan Cr 53C
Carrolls Landing 17C
Carrs 16D
Carruthers Cr 54B
Carruthers Pass 54A
Carry Cr 6B
Carter L 35C
Carter Pass 12A
Cartmel L 61B
Cartmel Mtn 61B
Cartwright Sd 30D, 32C
Cascade 8C
Cascade B 4B, 6A
Cascade Cr 17D
Cascade In 22B
Casino 8D
●Cassiar 72A
Cassiar R 73C
Cassidy 2D
Castle Cr 6D
Castle Cr 39D, 40C
Castle Junction 18B
Castle Mtn 59D
Castle Rock 25B
●Castlegar 8D
Castor Cr 18A
Catala I 1C
Cataract L 2C
Cate Cr 10C
Catfish Cr 39B
Cathcart I 11B, 22D
Catkin Cr 86C
Causqua Cr 45B
Cautley Cr 66B
Caven Cr 9D
Caverhill L 26D
Cawston 7C
Caycuse 2D
Caycuse R 2C, 3A
Cayenne Cr 27D

Cayley 19D
Cayoosh Cr 14D
Cayuse Cr 8A
Cayuse Cr 11D
Cecil Cr 45C
Cecil L 57B
Cecil Lake 57B
Cecilia Cr 40A, 50C
Cecilia L 40A
Cedar 2D
Cedar Cr 26A
Cedar R 44B
Cedarvale 45A
Ceepeecee 1A
Celista 16B
Celista Cr 16B
Central Saanich 3D
Centre Cr 6C
Centre Pk 54C
Centurion R 57C
Cerberus Mtn 23D
Cerulean L 18B
Cervus Cr 1B
Cesford Cr 46D
Chaatl 30D
Chaatl I 30D, 32C
Chaba Pk 28B
Chakluk Mtn 70A
Chalco Mtn 40A
Chalco R 40A
Chalford Cr 85D
Chamberlain Mtn 49A
Chambers Cr 44A
Chamiss Bay 11D
Champion Cr 6B
Champion Ls 8D
Chancellor Chan 12D
Chantslar L 24A
Chapea Cr 62D
Chapman L 46A
Chapmans 6A
Chappelle Cr 62D
Chapperon Cr 16C
Chapperon L 16C
Chapple In 34D
Charcoal Cr 16C
Charles Cr 12A
Charleson Cr 38C
Charlie Chief Cr 83D
Charlie Cole Cr 82C
Charlie L 57B
Charlie Lake 57B
Charlotte L 23B
Chartrand Cr 15D
Chartrand L 15B
Chase 16A
Chase Cr 2D
Chase Cr 16A
Chase Mtn 55A
Chase R 3B
Chase River 2D
Chasm 15A
Chasm Cr 15A
Chasm Cr 77D
Chatfield I 22A
Chatham Sd 33A, 43D
Chatsquot Cr 35D
Chatsquot Mtn 35D
Chatter Cr 28D
Chauncey C 19C
Chaunigan L 24D
Cheakamus Cr 5A, 14C
Cheakamus Mtn ... 5B, 14D
Cheakamus R 5A, 14C
Cheam Pk 4B, 6C
Cheam View 6C
Checleset B 11D
Chedakuz Arm 37A
Chedakuz Cr 37C
Chee Mtn 73B
Cheekye R 5A
Cheeny Cr 60B, 61A

Cheewhat L 2C, 3C
Chehalis Cr 4B
Chehalis Cr 81D
Chehalis L 5B
Chehalis R 4B, 6C
Chehischic Cr 38A
Chelaslie Arm 36B
Chelaslie R 36A, 36B
Chemainus 2D
Chemainus R 2D, 3B
Cherry Cr 15D
Cherry Cr 17C
Cherry Creek 2C
Cherry Creek 15B
Cherry Point 58A
Cherryville 17C
Cheshi Cr 24D
Cheslatta L 36B
Cheslatta R 36B
Chesterfield Cr 64A
Chesterfield L 64A
Chetarpe 1D
Chettleburgh Cr 62C
Chettleburgh Pk 62C
Chetwynd 57C
Cheves Cr 75D, 76C
Chezko R 36C
Chiaz Cr 39C
Chic Chic L 22C
Chichouyenily Cr ... 56C
Chicken Cr 65A
Chief L 48C
Chief Louis Arm 36B
Chief Louis L 36B
Chief Mathews B ... 35A
Chikoida Mtn 70B
Chilako R 37B, 38A
Chilanko Forks 24B
Chilanko R 24A
Chilcotin L 24B
Chilcotin R 24A, 24B, 25A, 25D, 37C
Chilkat L 79D
Chilkat R 79D
Chilko L 13B, 24D
Chilko Mtn 13B
Chilko R 24D, 25A
Chilkoot L 79D
Chilkoot Pass 80C
Chilkoot R 79D
Chilliwack 6C
Chilliwack L 6C
Chilliwack R 4B, 6C
Chimdemash Cr 45C
Chimney Cr 25B
Chimney Cr 86C
Chimney L 26C
China Butte 7B
China Cr 2C, 3A
China Cr 7B
China Creek 2C
China Creek 8D
China L 14B, 25D
China Nose Mtn 46C
Chinaman L 56B
Chinchaga Ls 66D
Chinchaga R 66D
Chinohchey Cr 48C
Chinook Cove 16A
Chinukundl Cr 30D, 32D
Chipesia Cr 76D
Chipmunk Pk 62D
Chischa Pk 75C
Chischa R 75C, 76C
Chisel Cr 28A
Chisholm L 45D
Chismaina L 71A
Chismore Cr 61C
Chisolm Pk 63B
Chist Cr 45C
Chita Cr 14A
Chlotapecta Cr 75D, 76C

Choate Cr 26A
Choelquoit L 24D
Choquette Gla 60C
Chowade R 56A, 65C
Chowika Cr 64C
Chowika Mtn 64C
Chris L 26D
Christensen Cr 24A
Christian Valley 7B
Christie R 30B, 32A
Christina Falls 56A
Christina L 8C
Christina Lake 8C
Christmas Cr 71A, 82C
Chu Chua Cr 16A, 27C
Chuatse Cr 76B
Chub L 26C
Chubb L 38D
Chuchi L 47A
Chuchinka Cr 48D
Chuckwalla R 22D
Chudelatsa L 55A
Chuius Mtn 47A
Chukachida L 62B, 63A
Chukachida R 62B, 63A
Chum L 16A
Chuniar L 37B
Church House 13C
Church Pk 4B, 6C
Churchill Cr 75C
Churchill Pk 75C
Churn Cr 25D
Chutanli L 37A
Chute Cr 1B
Chute L 7A
Chutine L 59B
Chutine R 59B
Chuunk Mtn 69B, 70A
Chuwanten Cr 6D
Chuwanten Mtn 6D
Chuwhels Mtn 15D
Chuyazega Cr 48B
Cicero Cr 16A
Cinema 38D
Circle L 38A, 48C
Circlet L 1B
Circum L 47D
Cirque L 28D
Citroen Pk 74D
Clabon Cr 17A
Clachnacudainn
   Snowfield 17A
Clairmont 50B
Clallam Bay 3C
Clanwilliam 17A
Clapp Cr 3D
Clapperton Cr 15D
Clark L 7B
Clarke L 76B
Classy Cr 71D
Clatse L 22A
Claud Elliott L 12C
Clauminchil L 48C
Claw Mtn 62B, 63A
Clayhurst 58A
Clayoquot 1D
Clayoquot Arm 1D
Clayoquot R 1D
Clayoquot Sd 1C
Clayton Falls Cr 23A
Clear Cr 44B
Clear Cr 47D
Clear L 13C
Clear R 12A
Clearbrook 5D
Cleardale 58B
Clearwater 27C
Clearwater L 24A
Clearwater L 27A
Clearwater R . 27A, 27C, 40C
Clearwater R 56C
Clemenceau Icefield 28A

Clemina Cr 27B
Clemretta 46C
Clendenning Cr 13D
Cleswunkut L 38A
Clifford B 21B
Clifford Cr 53C
Clinchintampan Cr 24B
Cline River 29A
Clint Cr 18C
Clinton 15A
Clinton Cr 15A
Clio Chan 12C
Clipper 5D
Clisbako R 24B, 25A, 37D, 38C
Clo-oose 2C
Clore R 45C
Cloudmaker Mtn 64A
Cloutier Pk 80D
Cloverdale 5D
Clowhom L 5A
Clowhom R 5A
Cluculz Cr 37B, 38A
Cluculz L 37B
Clusko R 24B
Clute Cr 9A, 18C
Cluxewe R 11D
Clyak R 22D
Clyde Cr 39B, 40A
Coal Cr 10A
Coal Cr 45A
Coal Cr 57D, 58C
Coal Cr 65B
Coal Harbour 11D
Coal I 3D, 5C
Coal R 84D, 85C
Coal River 85C
Coalgoat Cr 17C
Coalmont 6B
Coates R 30B, 32C
Cobb L .. 37B, 38A, 47D, 48C
Cochin L 24D
Cochran Cr 18D
Cochrane 19A
Cochrane Cr 8A
Cocoa Crater 60B
Coconino Cr 81D
Coffee Crater 60B, 61A
Coffeepot Mtn 48D
Cogburn Cr 6A
Coglistiko R 37D
Cokato 10A
Colbourne Cr 48B
Cold Fish L 61B
Cold Fish Lake Camp 61B
Coldscaur L 26D
Coldstream 16D
Coldstream Cr 16D
Coldstream Cr 57C
Coldwater Cr 44D
Coldwater R 6B, 15D
Colebank Cr 38D
Coleman 10B
Coleman Cr 2C
Coles L 35B
Coles L 87D
Colin Cr 19C
Colin Cr 55B, 56A
Colledge Cr 64D, 65C
Colledge L 64D, 65C
Colleen Cr 9D
Colleymount 46D
Collie Cr 29C
Collingwood Chan 3B, 5A
Collins Cr 55A
Collins L 45D
Colonel Cr 40D
Colonial Cr 11D
Colt Cr 56B
Columbia Gardens 8D
Columbia Icefield ... 28B
Columbia L 18D

Columbia R 18A
Columbia Reach 28C
Colwell Cr 24C
Colwood 3D
Comaplix Mtn 17B
Comb Pk 54A
Combatant Mtn 23D
Comet Mtn 35D
Commerce Cr 10D
Commotion Cr 57C
Community L 16A
Como L 80D, 81C
Comox 2A
Comox L 2A
Compass Cr 23A
Compton Cr 12D
Compton Gla 13B
Compton Mtn 13B
Compton Néve 13B
Concrete 4D
Cone Hill 25C
Cone Mtn 60A
Confederation Gla 12B
Conical Pk 63D
Conkle L 7D
Connel Cr 14B
Connor Ls 19C
Conroy Cr 66A
Consolation Cr ... 80D, 81C
Constable Pk 75C
Conuna R 1A
Convey 4D
Conway Cr 9A
Cony Cr 8A
Cook L 72A
Cooke Cr 16B
Cool Cr 7C
Coolridge Mtn ... 60B, 61A
Coombs 2D
Cooper Cr 25A, 25C
Cooper Creek 18C
Cooper L 9C
Cooper Reach 12B
Copeland 9C
Copeland Cr 17A
Copley L 37A
Coplin Cr 57A
Copper B 31C, 32D
Copper Cr 6D
Copper Cr 31C, 32D
Copper Creek 15B
Copper I 69B, 80D, 81C
Copper Mtn 7D
Copper Mtn 8B
Copper River 45C
Coppercrown Mtn 18C
Copperstain Cr 17B
Coquihalla Mtn 6B
Coquihalla R 6A
Coquitlam 5D
Coquitlam L 4A, 5B
Coquitlam Mtn 4A, 5B
Coquitlam R ... 4A, 5B, 5D
Coral Mtn 18A
Corbin 10A
Corbin Cr 10A
Corbin Pk 17B
Corbold Cr 5B
Cordero Chan 12D
Cordova Bay 3D
Corkscrew Cr 24A
Corkscrew Cr 37B
Cormier Cr 83D
Cormorant Chan 12C
Corn Cr 9C
Corning Cr 16A
Cornwall Cr 15A
Cornwall In 34D
Corona Pk 45C
Corral Cr 6B
Corrigan Cr 2C, 3A
Corsica L 26D

Cortes Bay 13C
Cortez I 13C
Cortiana Cr 8A
Corya Cr 45B
Cosens Cr 16D
Cossack L 26A
Coste I 34B
Costello Pk 12B
Cotsworth L 37D
Cotsworth L 38C
Cotter Cr 1B
Cottonwood 38D
Cottonwood R 38D
Cottonwood R 71B, 72A,
                       82D, 83C
Cougar Cr 8B
Cougar L 34D
Couldrey Cr 10C
Coulee Cr 57D
Coulter Cr 51B, 52A
Coupeville 4C
Coursier L 17A
Courtenay 2A
Courtney L 6B
Courvoisier Cr 77A
Cous Cr 2C
Cousins Cr 52B
Cousins In 22A
Coutlee 15D
Cow Cr 56B
Cow Ls 72C
Cowart Cr 55B, 56A
Cowichan B 3D
Cowichan Bay 5C
Cowichan L 2D, 3A
Cowichan R 2D, 3D
Cowie Cr 57C
Cowley 10B
Cox I 11A, 11C
Coyote Cr 9B, 18D
Coyote Cr 61A
Crab L 35A
Cracroft 12C
Crag Cr 23A, 36C
Cragg Cr 3D
Craig Cr 17D
Craig Cr 51A
Craig R 60C
Craigellachie 16B
Cranberry Cr 17A
Cranberry Junction 53C
Cranberry Mtn 17A
Cranberry R 53C
Cranberry Rapids .. 84D, 85C
● Cranbrook 9B
Cranswick L 64D, 65C
Craster L 16D
Crater L 80C
Crater Mtn 7C
Crawfish L 1A
Crawford Bay 9A
Crawford Cr 9A
Crawford Cr 17A
Crazy Cr 17A
Crazy Cr 24C
Crease I 12C
Crehan Cr 64B, 65A
Creighton Cr 16D
Creighton Valley 16D
Crescent Bay 8B
Crescent Beach 5C
Crescent In 31C
Crescent L 39C
Crescent Mtn 62A
Crescent Spur 39B
Crescent Valley 8B
● Creston 9C
Creston B 8B
Creston Mtn 8C
Criccieth Mtn 64A
Cridge Pass 34D

Cridland Cr 76B
Cripple L 47B
Criss Cr 15B
Cristina Cr 60C
Crocker Cr 48B, 48C
Crofton 5C
Cronin Cr 46A
Crooked L 16D
Crooked L 26B
Crooked L 85C
Crooked R 48B
Cross Cr 16B
Cross R 18B
Crow Cr 46D
Crow R 86C
Crown Mtn 1B
Crowned Cr 1B
Crowsnest 10A
Crowsnest Pass 10A
Croydon Cr 54B
Croydon Station 40C
Cruikshank R 2A
Cruiser L 26B
Crusty Cr 75A
Cry L 72B
Crystal Butte 7B
Crystal L 26D
Cuisson Cr 25B
Cuisson L 25B
Cullite Cr 3C
Culliton Cr 5A
Cullivan Cr 61B
Cullon Cr 53C
Cultus Cr 9C
Cultus L 4B, 6C
Cultus Lake 6C
○ Cumberland 2A
Cummings Cr 10A
Cummings Cr 45D
Cummins Cr 28A
Cumsack Cr 13A
Cumsack Mtn 13A
Cumshewa 31C
Cumshewa In 31C
Cunningham Cr 39C
Cunningham I 22A
Cunningham L 15A, 26C
Cunningham L 47C
Cup Cr 81C
Cup L 7B
Cupola Cr 28D
Cupola Mtn 28D
Curlew 8C
Currie Cr 17C
Currier Cr 62C
Curve L 55D
Curwen Cr 17C
Curzon 9D
Cushing Cr 39B, 40A
Cushing Cr 62B, 63A
Cusson Cr 17C
Cut Thumb Cr 56C
Cutbank Cr 54B, 63D
Cutbank L 50A, 58C
Cutfoot Cr 53A, 62C
Cutoff Cr 37A
Cutoff Cr 63B
Cyclops Pk 64B
Cypre R 1D
Cypress B 1D
Cypress Cr 65C

D

D'Arcy 14D
D'Arcy I 3D
d'Easum Cr 87C
Daer Cr 18B
Dagaichess Cr 60B
Dagger L 15B
Dago Cr 8A

Dahl Cr 38A
Dahl Cr 44D
Dahl Cr 66B
Dahl L 38A
Dahlaks Cr 35A
Dainard Cr 18A
Dainard Cr 28A
Dairy Cr 15B
Dairy Ls 15D
Dais Gla 13A, 24C
Daisy L 5A, 14C
Dak R 52D
Dala R 35A
Dale Cr 7B
Dale L 38D
Dall L 73C
Dall R 73A
Dallery Cr 22D
Dalton Cr 72B
Damdochax Cr 53A
Damdochax L 53A
Damfino Cr 7B
Damshilgwit Cr 53A
Damshilgwit L 53A
Dana In 31C
Daniels Cr 65B
Daniels R 13D
Darb Cr 54B
Darb L 54B
Darber Cr 65D
Darby Chan 22D
Darby L 48C
Dardanelles L 16C
Darfield 27C
Dark Mtn 72D
Darke Cr 7A
Darke L 7A
Darlington Cr 16A, 27C
Darrell Bay 5A
Darrington 4D
Darsmith Cr 60C
Darwin Sd 20A, 31C
Dash Cr 3A
Dash Cr 14B
Dashwood 2A
Dasque Cr 44D
Dastaiga Cr 56C
Datcin Cr 77B
Date Cr 45A, 53C
Datlamen Cr 30B, 32C
Dave Henry Cr 40D
David L 35C
Davidson Cr 30B, 32A
Davidson Cr 37C
Davie Cr 73A
Davie L 48D
Davie R 12C
Davies Cr 45C
Davis Cr 37D, 38C
Davis L 6B
Davis L 56B
Davis R 55A, 64C
Dawson Cr 28A
Dawson Cr 57D, 58C
● Dawson Creek 58C
Dawson In 30D, 32C
Dawson R 62A
Day L 46C
Dayeezcha Mtn 36B
Dazo Cr 77C
De Winton 19B
Deacon L 38D
Dead Dog Cr 75D
Deadhorse Cr 57A, 66C
Deadman L 15B
Deadman R 15B
Deadwood L 73A
Deadwood R 73A
Dean Chan 22B, 35D, 36C
Dean Cove 5C
Dean Cr 36C
Dean R 23B, 24A, 36D

Dear Mtn 6B
Dease Cr 71B, 72C
Dease L 71D, 72C
Dease Lake 72C
Dease R 71B, 72A, 83D
DeBeck Cr 5B
Deception Cone 64C
Deception Cr 26B, 26D
Deception Mtn 26B
Dechamps Cr 13B
Decker Cr 46D
Decker L 46D
Dede Cr 66D
Dee L 16D
Deeker Cr 60A
Deena Cr 30D, 32D
Deep Bay 2A
Deep Canoe Cr 53C
Deep Cove 5C
Deep Cr 16D
Deep Cr 46C
Deep Creek 16D
Deep Har 12A
Deer I 11B
Deer L 16D
Deer L 34D
Deer Park 8A
Deer Pass 13C
Deer R 85D
Deerhorn Cr 26A
Deerhorn Hill 36B
Deescius Mtn 46B
Dehacho Cr 77C
DeHorsey I 33B, 44C
Deka Cr 26D
Deka L 26D
Dekontha L 65B
Del Cr 64C
Delano Cr 75C
Delkluz L 55A, 64C
Delkpay Cr 87C
Della Falls 1B
Della L 1B
Delphine Cr 18C
Delta 5C
Delta Cr 63C
Delta Pk 61D
Deltaic Cr 52B
Delure Cr 71B, 72A
Delusion Pk 24C
Demers Cr 27C
Demers Ls 8B
Demming 5D
Dempsey L 26C
Denain Cr 14A
Denetiah Cr 73D, 74C
Denetiah L 73D, 74C
Denison Cr 53D
Denkman Cr 64D, 65C
Denman I 2A
Denman Island 2A
Dennis Pk 62D, 63C
Denny I 22A
Denys Cr 45D
Departure Bay 2D
Depot Cr 6C
Deroche 5D
Derrick Cr 53C
Des Cr 48A
Desan Ls 77B, 88D
Deserters Cr 38D
Deserters Group 11B
Deserters Pk 64C
Desolation Sd 13C
Destilida L 48B
Destlay L 47B
Deszen Cr 87C
Detiaten Cr 60B, 71D, 72C
Detna Cr 36D
Detna L 36D
Detni Cr 54B
Deuce Cr 45A

Devastation Chan 34B
Devereux Cr 12B
Devereux Pk 75C
Devil Cr 60D, 61C
Devil L 60D, 61C
Devils Paw 69B
Devils Pk 70A
Devils Thumb 59D
Devoe Cr 26B, 39D
Devon L 33D, 34A
Dewar Cr 9A
Dewar L 26A
Dewar Pk 62D
Dewdney 5D
Dewdney Cr 6A
Dewdney I 34C
Dewdney Pk 4B, 5D
Dezadeash 79A
Diagonal Mtn 62D
Diana I 2C
Dick Booth Cr 11B
Dick Cr 51A
Dick Cr 79C
Dickebusch Cr 57C
Dickson L 4B, 5D
Didene Cr 61D
Dieppe Mtn 74D
Digby I 33B, 43D, 44C
Dillabough L 26A
Dilly Cr 87D
Dimsdale 50B
Dimsdale L 49D, 50C
Dina L 56C
Dinan B 30B, 32C
Diorite Cr 9B
Dipper L 9B
Dirst Cr 59B
Dirty Cr 56B
Discovery Cr 55C
Discovery I 3D
Discovery Pass 12D
Disella L 70B
Diskangieq Cr 44B
Diver L 1B
Diver L 54D
Diver Pk 54D
Divergence Pk 28A
Diversion Res 3D
Divide L 52A
Dixie L ... 69B, 70A, 80D, 81C
Dixon Cr 16A
Dixon Entrance 32A, 42D
Dixon L 16A
Doan Cr 75D, 76C
Dobbin B 12A
Dobbin L 16C
Docken Cr 49B
Docs Cr 48C
Doctor Cr 18D
Dodd Cr 38A
Dodd L 2B, 13D
Dodjatin Cr 60A
Doe Cr 57D, 58C
Doe River 58A
Doebay Village 5D
Dog Cr 8A
Dog Cr 25D
Dog Cr 47D
Dog Creek 25D
Doig R 57B, 58A, 66D
Dokdaon Cr 60A
Dokie Cr 57C
Dolly Varden Cr 18B
Dolphin I 31B, 33D
Dome Cr 39B
Dome Creek 39C
Dome Mtn 46A
Dome Mtn 72D
Dominion Cr 27B
Dominion Cr 39A
Dominion L 48D
Dominion Mtn 8B

Dominion Mtn 59D
Don Pen 22A
Donahue Cr 52C
Donald Cr 28D
Donald Landing 46D
Donald Station 28D
Donelly Cr 14C
Donner L 1B
Donnie Cr 65B
Dooley Cr 10A
Doos Cr 23C
Dooza L 84C
Doran Cr 13A
Doreen L 16D
Doreen L 26B
Doré R 39D, 40C
Doris L 22D
Doris L 46A
Doriston 2B
Dorman L 37A
Dorothy Cr 23D
Dorothy Gla 23D
Dortatelle Cr 54B
Dortatelle Pk 54B
Dottay Cr 65B
Douglas 5D
Douglas 69C
Douglas Chan 34B
Douglas Cr 5B
Douglas Cr 44B
Douglas In 30D
Douglas L 16C
Douglas Lake 16C
Douse Cr 53C
Dove Cr 2A
Dowager I 22A
Dowling Cr 56D
Downie Cr 28C
Downie L 17A, 28C
Downie Pk 28C
Downton Cr 14D
Downton Cr 24A, 37C
Downton L 14A
Doyle I 11B
Dragon L 38D
Dragon L 44B, 52D
Dragon Mtn 38D
Drake I 11D
Draney In 22D
Dream Cr 54D
Dresser Cr 56B
Drewry L 1B
Drift L 53B, 54A
Driftpile Cr 63B, 74D
Driftwood Cr 18A
Driftwood Cr 45B, 46A
Driftwood L 11B
Driftwood R ... 53B, 54A, 54C
Drimmie Cr 17A
Drinkwater Cr 1B
Driscoll Cr 39A
Drury In 11B
Dry Gulch 18D
Dry L 6B
Dryas Pk 64A
Drybrough Pk 62D, 63C
Drymeat L 65B
Ducette Cr 56C
Ducette Pk 56C
Duck Cr 9C
Duck L 9C
Duckfoot L 24D
Duckling Cr 54D
Duckling L 26D
Duckworth L 25B
Dudgeon Cr 27D
Dudido R 71C
Dudidontu R 71A
Dudley Cone 13C
Duff L 79D
Dufferin I 22A
Duffey L 14D

Duffield Cr 64B, 65A
Dugan L 26A
Dum L 26D, 27C
Dumbell L 24C
Dunbar Cr 18A
● Duncan 2D
Duncan Bay 13C
Duncan I 11B
Duncan L 17D, 18C
Duncan L 62D, 63C
Duncan R 17B
Dundas I 43D
Dunedin R 75A, 75B, 86D
Dungate Cr 46C
Dungeness 4C
Dunira I 33A, 43D
Dunlevy Cr 56B
Dunlevy L 56B
Dunn Cr 18C
Dunn L 27C
Dunsapie L 16A
Dunsmuir 2A
Dunster 40C
Durand Cr 15B
Durham Cr 60D, 61C
Durieu 5D
Durkin Cr 75D, 76C
Dust Cr 54D
Dutch Cr 18C, 18D
Duteau Cr 16D
Duti R 62C

E
Eagan L 26D
Eagle Bay 16B
Eagle Cr 8A
Eagle Cr 26A, 26D
Eagle Cr 46D
Eagle Creek 26D
Eagle L 24D
Eagle L 26A
Eagle R 16B
Eagle R 72B, 72D
Eaglehead L 72D
Eaglenest Cr 61B
Eaglet L 48D
Eakin L 26D
Ealue L 61A
Ear L 35D
Earl Grey Pass 18C
Earle Cr 2B
Earle L 26D
Earls Cove 2B
East Anderson R 6A
East Arrow Park 17C
East Barrière L 16A
East Barrière R 16A, 27A
East Cache Cr 57A
East Cr 18A
East In 33D, 34A
East Kelowna 7B
East Kispiox R 53C
East Pine 57C
East Port 9C
East Redonda I 13C
East Sd 5C
East Seebach Cr 48D
East Sooke 3D
East Sound 5C
East Thurlow I 12D
East Tutshi R 80C
East Twin Cr 17A
East Twin Cr 39B, 40A
East Wellington 2D
East White R 19C
Easter L 1A
Eastman Cr 60B, 61A
Echo Bay 12A
Echo Cr 18C
Echo I 4B, 6A

Echo L 16D
Echo L 16D
Echo Pk 54B
Echoes L 9B
Eclipse Nrs 12A
Ecoole 2C
Ecstall L 34B
Ecstall R 33B, 34A,
                      34B, 44C
Ed Asp Cr 71B, 72A
Ed Asp L 71B, 72A
Ed Bird Cr 63D
Ed Bird L 64C
Eddontenajon 61A
Eddontenajon L 61A
Eddy 40C
Eddy Cr 40C
Eden I 12A
Eden L 30B, 32A
Edgar L 80D
Edgegrain Cr 50C
Edgewater 18B
Edgewood 8A
Edinburgh Mtn 2D, 3C
Edison 4C
Edith L 15D
Edmond Cr 13B
Edmund L 26C
Edney Cr 26A
Edney L 26A
Edozadelly Mtn 62B
Edwards Cr 16A
Edwards L 26D
Edwards Ls 10C
Edye Pass 33A, 43D
Effingham I 2C
Effingham In 2C
Effingham R 2C
Egeria Mtn 31B, 33B, 34A
Egeria Reach 35C
Egmont 2B
Egnell Cr 71C
Egnell Ls 84C
Ehaheezetle Mtn 61A
Ehatisaht 1A
Eholt Cr 8C
Eight Mile Cr 57B, 58A
Eight Mile Cr 75A
Eightythree Cr 26C
Eightythree L 26C
Ejas L 26D, 27C
Eklund Cr 55D
Ekwan Cr 77D
Ekwan L 77D
Elaho R 14C
Elbow Cr 65D
Elbow L 26B
Elbow Mtn 51A
Elcho Har 22B
Elder Cr 10D
Eldred R 13D
Eleven Mile Cr 56D
Elfin Cove 68D
Eliguk L 36D
Eliza Dome 1C
Elizabeth L 22D
Elk Bay 12D
Elk Cr 18D
Elk Pass 19C
Elk R 1B
Elk R 10A, 19C
○ Elkford 19C
Elkhorn Mtn 1B
Elkin Cr 24D
Elkin L 24D
Elko 10C
Ella Cr 62C
Ella Frye Cr 27A, 40C
Elleh Cr 77C
Elleh L 77C
Ellen L 1A
Ellen L 7A, 16C

Ellerslie L 22A
Elliot Cr 13A
Elliot L 47A
Elliot Res 3D
Elliott Cr 45D
Ellis B 11B
Ellis R 7A
Ellis L 13C
Ellison 7B
Ellison L 16D
Elmsworth 50B
Elsie L 2A
Elwin L 46C
Elwyn Cr 60B
Embree Cr 64D, 65C
Emerslund Cr 56A
Emerslund Ls 56A
Emile Cr 87D
Emily L 22A
Emory Cr 6A
Empress Mtn 3D
Encampment Cr 28A
End L 55A
Endako 47C
Endako R 46D
● Enderby 16D
Endless Cr 53B
Eneas Cr 7A
Engen 47D
Engineer Mtn 80D
Englefield B 30D
English B 4A, 5C
English L 26D
Englishman Cr 9D
Englishman R 2D, 3A
Enright Cr 76C
Ensign Cr 29C
Enterprise 26C
Enterprise Cr 8B
Entiako L 36D
Entiako R 36D
Entrance 41B
Eon Mtn 18B
Equesis Cr 16D
Eric Cr 1B
Erickson Cr 10A
Erickson L 38A
Erie 8D
Erie Cr 8D
Erie L 8D
Erie Mtn 8D
Erlandsen Cr 44D
Errington 2D
Escalante R 1A
Eskai Cr 77C
Esker L 38A
Esker L 84D, 85C
Eskona Mtn 73A
Esling Cr 8C
Esperanza 1A
Esperanza In 1C
Esperon Cr 16C
Espinosa In 1A, 9D
Esquimalt 3D
Ess L 63B
Estella Cr 64C
Estella Ls 64C
Estero Basin 13C
Estevan Group 34C
Estevan Pt 1A
Estevan Sd 34D
Estsine L 88C
Etane Cr 75B, 76A
Etcho Cr 76B
Etschitka Cr 54B
Etset L 88C
Etsho Cr 87D
Etthithun L 66B
Etthithun R 66B, 77D
Euchiniko Cr 37D
Euchiniko Ls 37D
Euchiniko R 37B

Euchu Reach 36D
Eugene L 26D
Eulatazella L 37B, 38A
Eureka 10C
Eureka River 58B
Europa Reach 35A
Eutsuk L 35B, 36A
Eva L 11B
Evans Cr 8B
Evans In 22A
Evans L 8B
Eve R 12C
Eveline L 38D
Everett Cr 39A
Everson 5D
Evie L 76A
Evindsen Cr 52D
Ewart Cr 7C
Ewart L 1A
Ewe Mtn 74B
Ewin Cr 10A, 19C
Exchamsiks R 44D
Excursion Inlet 68D
Exeter 26C
Exshaw 19A
Exstew R 44D
Extension 2D

F
Face L 15D
Factor Ross Cr 55A
Fadear Cr 16A
Fair Harbour 11D
Fairfax In 30D
Fairless Cr 25D
Fairmont Hot Springs ... 18D
Fairview 7C
Fairweather Mtn 67B
Fairy Cr 3C
Fairy L 64B, 65A
Faith Cr 8A
Falaise Mtn 75C
Falcon Gla 13B
Falcon Mtn 13B
Falk Cr 76C
Falkland 16C
Fall Cr 16D
Fall R 54D
Falling Cr 56D
Falls Cr 27A
Falls R 14A
Falls R 35A
False Ears 11D
False L 80C
Fang Cr 17A
Fang Pk 23D
Fanny Bay 2A
Fantali L 80C
Far Cr 36D
Farmington 57D
Farnham Cr 18C
Farrant I 34B
Farrell Cr 56B
Farrell Creek 58A
Farwell Cr 25D
Faulkner Cr 72D
Fauquier 8A
Favels Cr 57C
Fawn Cr 26D
Fawn L 26D
Fawnie Cr 36D
Fawnie Cr 37C
Feak Cr 44D
Fearless Cr 49B
Feather L 30B, 32D
February Cr 53B, 54A
February L 88D
Federal Ranch 56B
Felker L 26C
Fellers Heights 57D

113

Fennell Cr 8B
Fennell R 27C
Fenton L 36A
Fenwick Cr 18D
Ferebee R 79D
Ferguson 17B
Ferguson Cr 17B
Fern L 64A
Fern Pk 64A
Ferndale 5D
● Fernie 10A
Ferrer Pt 1C
Ferris Gla 67B, 68A
Ferriston Cr 54B
Ferry Cr 72D
Fiddes Cr 65C
Fiddler Cr 45A
Fife Cr 17C
Fife Sd 12A
Fiftynine Cr 15A
Fiftyone Cr 15A
Fiftyseven Cr 15A
File Cr 27A
Filer Cr 13D
Filer Gla 13B
Fin I 34D
Findlay Cr 9A, 18C, 18D
Findlay L 46C
Finger L 37B
Finger Mtn 12A
Finlay R 62D, 63B, 63C
Finlayson Arm 3D
Finlayson Chan 22A, 35C
Finlayson I 43D
Finn Cr 27D
Fintry 16C
Fir Cr 10A
Fire Cr 5B
Fire Cr 25C
Fire Cr 77D
Fire L 5B
Fireside 84D
Firesteel R 62D, 63C
First Nrs 23C
Firth Cr 48B
Firth L 48B
Firvale 23A
Fiset L 26D
Fish Cr 52B
Fish Hawk L 16D
Fish Hawk Ls 7B
Fish L 17D
Fish L 72C
Fish L 81C
Fishem L 13B, 14A
Fisher Chan 22A
Fisher Cr 56D
Fisher L 48D
Fisherman B 11A
Fisherman R 11A
Fishing Cr 84D, 85C
Fishing L 84D, 85C
Fishing Ls 63A
Fishpot L 37D
Fishtrap Cr 16A
Fissure Cr 28C
Fitch Cr 17B
Fitz Hugh Sd 22C
Fitzsimmons Cr 14C
Fitzstubbs Cr 17D
Fizzle Mtn 51A, 60C
Flack Cr 75D, 76C
Flameau Cr 63D
Flamingo In 20A
Flat Cr 17B
Flat Cr 72D
Flat L 48C
Flat R 52D
Flat Top Mtn 63A
Flatbed Cr 49B
Flathead 10A
Flathead 10D

Flathead R 10C, 10D
Flatrock Cr 57B, 58A
Fleet Cr 39B, 40A
Fleet Pk 63D
Fleet R 3C
Flemer R 79D
Fleming I 2C
Fleming L 46B
Fletcher L 25C
Fleurbaix Cr 27A
Flint Cr 45A
Float Cr 18A
Floe Cr 18B
Floe L 18B
Flood Cr 55A, 64C
Flood Gla 60C
Flood L 60C
Floods 6A
Florence Cr 30B, 32D
Florence L 13C
Florence Pen 22A
Florencia B 1D
Flores I 1B
Flourmill Cr 27A
Flume Cr 50C
Fly Cr 39A
Flyfish L 16D
Foch L 34B
Foch Lagoon 34B
Focus Mtn 70A
Foerster Cr 54A
Foghorn Cr 27C
Foghorn Mtn 27C
Foisey Cr 10A
Foley Cr 6C
Fontaine Cr 39C
Fontas 77C
Fontas R 66B, 77C, 77D
Fontoniko Cr 49C
Foot L 63D
Forbes Chan 13C
Forbes L 26C
Forcier L 74B, 85D
Ford Pass 61B
Fording 19C
Fording Mtn 10A
Fording Mtn 19C
Fording River Pass 19C
Foresight Mtn 35D
Forest Grove 26D
Foreward Pk 36C
Forgetmenot Cr 39B, 40A
Forres Mtn 63D
Forret Ker Cr 60D
Forster Cr 18C
Forsyth Cr 19C
Fort Babine 54C
Fort Casey 4C
Fort Cr 53B
Fort Fraser 47C
Fort Langley 5D
Fort Liard 87A
Fort Mtn 53B
● Fort Nelson 76B
Fort Nelson R 75B, 76B, 76D, 86D, 87D
Fort Rupert 11B
● Fort St. James 47D
● Fort St. John 57B
Fort Steele 9A
Fortine 10C
Fortress L 28A
Fortress Mtn 28B
Fortune Chan 1D
Fortune Cr 87D
Fortynine Cr 8B
Forward In 11C
Foster Cr 27B
Foster Cr 53A
Foster L 50A
Foster Pk 18B
Foster Pk 53A

Fosthall 17C
Fosthall Cr 17C
Foul B 33D
Four Ls 22B
Four Mile Cr 75A
Four Mile L 81D
Four Mile R 72B
Four Mile Rapids 84C
Fourth of July Cr ... 80D, 81C
Fowler Cr 60C
Fox Cr 57B, 66C
Fox Cr 57D
Fox L 63B
Fox Pass 63B
Fox Pk 63B
Fox R 63B
Foxy Cr 46D
Framstead Cr 49D
Frances Cr 18A
Francis L 38B
François Cr 36B, 46D
François Lake 46D
Frank Cr 39C
Frank Cr 55A
Frank Mackie Gla .. 51B, 52A
Frank Ward Cr 16C
Franklin Arm 13B
Franklin Camp 2C
Franklin Cr 8A
Franklin Gla 12B, 23D
Franklin R 2C, 3A
Franklin R 12B
Fraser 80C
Fraser Cr 18A
Fraser L 12A
Fraser L 47C
○ Fraser Lake 47C
Fraser R 4A, 4B, 5D, 6A, 14B, 15C, 25B, 25D, 28A, 38B, 39A, 39B, 40C, 40D, 48D
Fraser Reach 34D
Fred Wright L 52D
Freda Cr 2B
Freda L 13D
Freda L 33D, 34A
Freddie L 75C
Frederick Arm 13C
Frederick I 30A, 32A
Frederick Sd. 12A
Fredrikson Cr 63C
Fredrikson L 63C
Freil L 2B
Frembd L 6B
French Bar Cr 14B
French Cr 2D, 3A
French Cr 28C
French L 26D
French Pk 53D, 54C
French Pks 27B
French R 83D
Frenchman Cr 22B
Frenchy Cr 6B
Freshwater Bay 12C
Friday Harbor 4C
Friday L 46A, 54C
Friendly L 26D
Fries Cr 55D
Frisby Cr 17A
Frog R ... 62B, 63A, 73D, 74C
Frontier Cr 23D
Frontier Mtn 24C
Frosty Mtn 6D
Froth Cr 27B
Fruitvale 8D
Fry Cr 18C
Frye Cr 38D
Frypan Cr 54D
Frypan Pk 54C
Fulford Harbour 5C
Fulmore L 12D
Fulton L 46A

Fulton R 46A
Fumar Cr 54A
Funter 69C
Furry Cr 5A
Fusilier Pk 75C

G

Gable Cr 8A
Gable Mtn 7B
Gable Mtn 35D, 36C
Gable Mtn 49C
Gabriola 2D
Gabriola I 2D, 3B
Gaffney Cr 55D
Gagnon Cr 48A, 56D
Gain Cr 3C
Gainer Cr 17B
Galbraith Cr 9B
Gale L 36A
Galena 17C
Galena B 17C
Galena Bay 17A
Galene Cr 6D
Galiano 5C
Galiano I 3B, 5C
Gallic L 83D
Galloping Mtn 8A
Galloway 10A
Gambier Har 5A
Gambier I 3B, 5A
Gamble L 34B
Gammer Cr 75D, 76C
Gamsby R 35D
Gang Ranch 25D
○ Ganges 5C
Gannett L 27D
Ganokwa Cr 45B
Garbutt Cr 86C
Garden Bay 2B
Gardner Canal 35A
Gardom L 16D
Garibaldi 14C
Garibaldi Heights 5A
Garibaldi L 5A
Garnett Cr 4B
Garvin Cr 38B
Gaspard Cr 25D
Gaspard L 25D
Gataga Mtn 73D, 74C
Gataga R 73D, 74C, 74D
Gatcho L 36D
Gates Cr 17C
Gates R 14D
Gathto Cr 64A, 75D, 76C
Gautier Pk 64A
Gauvreau Cr 55B, 56A
Gauvreau Pk 55B, 56A
Gavin L 26A
Gay L 25C
Gaylard Cr 56B
Geddes Cr 84D, 85C
Geen Ls 7B
Geesdale Cr 65C
Geese Cr 62B, 63A
Geikie Cr 28A
Gellatly 7A
Gem Hill 8C
Gem Pass 54D
Gemini Ls 73B, 84D
Genelle 8D
Genevieve L 38D
Genier Ls 16A
George Cr 38B
George Pass 12A
Georgetown Mills 43D
Georgie L 11B
Georgie R 52C
Geremi Cr 38D
Germaine L 48C
German L 58B

Germansen L 55C
Germansen Landing 55C
Germansen R 55C
Gerow Cr 46D
Gething Cr 56D
Getzuni L 36B
Ghita Cr 40D
Ghitezli L 36A
Ghost Cr 30B, 32C
Ghost L 39D
Gibbons Cr 26A
Gibsons 5A
Gidegingla L 47B
Giegerich Cr 17B
Giegerich Pk 63C
Gil I 34D
Gil Pk 62C
Gilbert Gla 13B
Gilford I 12A
Gillies B 2B
Gillies Bay 2B
Gilliland Cr 85C
Gilliland Ls 84D, 85C
Gillis Cr 9A, 18C
Gillis Cr 55C
Gilnockie Cr 9D
Gilpin 8C
Gilttoyees Cr 34B
Gilttoyees In 34B
Ginmiltkun Cr 53C
Gisborne L 15B
Giscome 48D
Gitnadoix R 44D
Glacial Mtn 72D
Glacier 6C
Glacier Cr 18C
Glacier Cr 80D, 81C
Glacier L 5B
Glade 8B
Gladhsheim Pk 8B
Gladstone Cr 8A
Gladys L 81D
Gladys R 81D
Glatheli L 36A
Gleason Cr 49C
Glen Eden 5A
Glen Vowell 45C
Glenannan 47C
Glendale Cr 12D
Glendale L 12D
Gleneden 16B
Glenlyd Cr 54B
Glenogle Cr 29C
Glenora 60A
Glenrosa 7A
Glimpse L 16C
Glossy Mtn 15C
Gloucester Cr 8A
Gloyazikut Cr 46B
Glundebery Cr 71A
Gnat Cr 72C
Gnawed Mtn 15D
Goat Cr 23B
Goat Cr 26B, 27A
Goat Cr 44B
Goat Har 34B
Goat I 13D
Goat L 13D
Goat L 80C
Goat Pk 7B
Goat Pk 28D
Goat R 9A, 9C
Goat R 8A
Goatcanyon Cr 8B, 17D
Goathead Cr 53D
Goathorn Cr 45D, 46C
Goatskin Cr 8A
Goering Cr 25A
Goguka Cr 76D
Gold Bridge 14B
Gold Cr 9D
Gold L 1B, 12D

Gold Mtn 9D
Gold R 1B
Gold R 4A, 5B
Gold R 28C
Gold River 1B
Golden 18A
Golden Gate Nrs 80D
Golden Hinde 1B
Golden Mtn 80D
Goldeneye L 63D
Goldstream 3D
Goldstream L 3D
Goldstream R 28C
Goldway Pk 54B
Goletas Chan 11C
Good Hope L ...72B, 83D
Good Hope Mtn 13B
Goodfare 50A
Goodfellow Cr 28D
Goodlow 58A
Goodrich Cr 57C
Goodrich L 36A
Goodrich Pk 48B, 56D
Goodwin Cr 81D
Goose B 22D
Goose Bay 22D
Goose Group 22C
Goose L 16D
Goosly L 46C
Gopher Cr 18C
Gopherhole Cr 55A
Gordendale 58D
Gordon Chan 11B
Gordon Cr 15D, 16B
Gordon Cr 57C
Gordon Head 3D
Gordon Horne Pk 27C
Gordon L 47D, 48C
Gordon R 2D, 3C
Gore I 1A
Gorge Cr 15B
Gorman Cr 17B
Gorrie Cr 64D, 65C
Goschen I 31B, 33A
Gosling I 22C
Gosnell Cr 45D
Gotchen L 26B
Gote Cr 88C
Gott Cr 14D
Gott Pk 14D
Government Cr 38B
Gowan Cr 5B
Gowgaia B 20A
Gracey Cr 51B, 52A
Graham Cr 50A
Graham Cr 80D
Graham I 30B, 32A,
                32C, 42D
Graham In 80D, 81C
Graham R 56A, 56B
Graham Reach 35C
Grain Cr 26A, 39C
Gramophe Cr 45B
Granby R 8A
Grand Cache 40B
Grand Forks 8C
Grand Mtn 17B
Grand Pacific Gla ..67B, 68A
Grand Prairie 50B
Grand Rapids 47A
Grandview Bench 16D
Granger Cr 65A
Granisle 46B
Granite 8B
Granite Bay 13C
Granite Cr 6B
Granite Cr 55C
Granite Knob 8B
Granite L 71A
Granite Mtn 6B
Granite Mtn 25B
Granite Pk 13A

Grant B 11C
Grant Brook 40D
Grant Cr 7A
Grant Cr 14A
Grant Cr 84D, 85D
Grant L 84D, 85C
Grant Pk 48B
Granthams Landing 5A
Grasmere 10C
Grass Cr 9C
Grass Cr 60B, 61A
Grassham L 47C
Grassy Cr 65B
Grassy Mtn 9A
Grassy Mtn 65B
Grassy Plains 46D
Grave Cr 10A
Grave L 10A
Grave Mtn 63D
Gravel Cr 26A
Gravell Cr 14D
Graveyard Cr 57C
Graveyard L 73B, 74A
Gray B 32D
Gray Cr 2B
Gray Cr 12D
Gray Creek 9A
Graybank Cr 86C
Grayling Cr 56B
Grayling L 48A
Grayling R 85D
Great Beaver L 47D, 48C
Great Central 2C
Great Central L 2A
Great Gla 60C
Great Snow Mtn 64B
Greata Cr 7A
Greaves I 11B
Greely 17A
Greely Cr 17A
Green Cove 2C
Green Cr 2D, 3A
Green Cr 65B
Green In 35C
Green L 14C
Green L 26C
Green Lagoon 35C
Greenbank 4C
Greenbush L 17A
Greendrop L 6C
Greenstone Cr ...1B, 12D
Greenstone Mtn 15D
Greenville 44B
Greenwood 7D
Greer Cr 37A
Gregg Cr 38A
Grenville Chan 33B, 34A
Grewatch Cr 65D
Grey Eagle L 8B
Grey Pk 64A
Grey Wolf Mtn 8B
Greyback Mtn 7B
Gribbell I 34B
Grice B 1D
Griffin Pass 22A, 35C
Griffith Cr 62A
Grilse Cr 1B, 12D
Grinder Cr 25D
Grindrod 16D
Griz Cr 18C
Grizzly Bear Cr 39A
Grizzly Cr 8A
Grizzly Cr 17B, 28D
Grizzly Ls 27C
Grizzly Mtn 27C
Grohman Cr 8B
Grossman Pk 62C
Ground Birch Cr 56B
Groundbirch 57D
Groundhog Cr 25C
Groundhog Mtn 62C
Groundhog Pass 62C

Grouse Cr 7B
Grouse Cr 27B
Grouse Cr 39C
Grovedale 50B
Guess Cr 46A
Guichon Cr 15D
Guilbault Cr 55B, 56A
Guise B 11A, 11C
Guish Cr 53A
Gulatch L 26C
Gullwing Cr 46D
Gun Cr 14A
Gun L 14A
Gun L 71A
Gunanoot L 53D, 54C
Gundahoo R 73B, 74A
Gundy 58C
Gundy Cr 65D
Gunn L 50A
Gunnell Cr 77A
Gunniza L 48D
Gurd I 31B, 33A
Gurney Cr 5B
Gustafsen L 26C
Gustavus 68D
Gutah Cr 66A, 66B, 77C
Gwillem Ls 8B
Gwillim L 49A, 57C
Gwillim R 57C
Gwunya Cr 52D
Gyllenspetz Cr 23B

H

Haan Cr 52D
Hackett R 71C
Hackney Hills 56B
Haddo L 16D
Hadow Cr 17B
Haffner Cr 18B
Hagan Arm 46B
Hagensborg 23A
Haggard Cr 16A
Haggen Cr 39A
Haggen L 16A
Haha Cr 9B
Haha Cr 54D
Hahas L 9B
Haida 42D
Haig 6A
Haig Br 10D
Haina 30D
Haines 68B
Haines Cr 25C
Haines L 25C
Hakai Pass 22C
Halcourt 50B
Halden Cr 76C
Hale Mtn 80C
Halfmoon Bay 2B
Halfmoon L 39A
Halfmoon L 72A
Halfway R 17D
Halfway R 56B, 64D,
                65C, 65D
Halfway Ranch 56B
Hall 8B
Hall Cr 7B
Hall Cr 8B
Hall Cr 9C
Hall L 9A
Hall L 81D
Haller Cr 9D
Hallett L 37A
Halobia Cr 55C
Hambrook Cr 49B
Hamill Cr 18C
Hamill Gla 18C
Hamilton Bay 59C
Hamling Cr 17D
Hamling Ls 17D

Hammer L 15B
Hammett Cr 48A
Hanawald Cr 53D, 54C
Hanceville 25C
Hancock R 30B, 32B
Handy Cr 2C
Haney 5D
Haney L 47C
Hanington Cr 49D, 50C
Hankin Cr 71B, 72A
Hankin L 45B
Hankin L 71B, 72A
Hankin Pk 60D
Hankins Cr 40C
Hanna Cr 52B
Hannah L 6A, 15C
Hansard L 48D
Hansen B 11A, 11C
Hanson I 12C
Hanson L 47C
Happy Cr 62C
Happy L 62C
Harbledown I 12C
Harbour Cr 27D
Hard Cr 72A
Hard L 72D
Hardscrabble Cr 45A
Hardwicke I 12D
Hardwicke Island 12D
Hardy B 11B
Hardy I 2B
Hardy In 22D
Hare L 84D
Harmac 2D
Harmer Cr 10A
Harmon L 6B, 15D
Haro Strait 3D
Harold Cr 39D
Harold Price Cr ...45B, 46A
Harper Cr 16A, 27C
Harper L 16A
Harper Reed Cr 71C
Harris Cr 2D, 3C
Harrison Hot Springs 6C
Harrison L 4B, 6A
Harrison Mills 6C
Harrison R 4B, 6A
Harrogate 18A
Harrop 8B
Harrymel Cr 51B, 52A
Hart L 26A
Hartell 19D
Hartley Cr 10A
Hartwig L 26D
Hartz Cr 71D
Harvey Cr 10C
Harvey L 83D
Harveys Cr 39C
Harvie Heights 18B
Harwood I 2A
Haslam Cr 2D, 3B
Haslam L 2B
Hasler Cr 56D
Hastings Arm 52C
Hat Cr 15A
Hat Mtn 13C
Hatchau L 71C
Hatchery Cr 45C
Hatdudatehl L 47A
Hathaway Cr 11C
Hathaway L 26D
Hatin L 71C
Hatzic L 4B
Hatzig 5D
Haul L 46A, 54C
Hautêre Cr 46B
Haven L 35D, 36C
Hawk Cr 18B
Hawkesbury I 34B
Hawkins Cr 9D
Hawkins L 26D
Hawkley Cr 26B

Hawks Cr 25B
Haworth L 64A
Hay R 77D
Hayes Cr 6B, 7A
Hayes Pk 81D
Haynes L 7B
Hayward Cr 44C
Hayward L 33B, 34A, 44C
Hazel Cr 9C
Hazelmere 50A
Hazelton 45B
Hazelton Cr 45A
Hazelton Pk 45A, 53D
Head B 1A
Headquarters 2A
Headstone Cr 65C
Headwall Cr 13B
Heakamie Gla 13A
Health B 12A
Health Bay 12A
Healy Cr 17D
Heard I 11B
Heart Cr 8A
Heart Pks 71C
Heather L 31C, 32D
Heather L 56C
Heber R 1B
Hecate I 22C
Hecate Str 20B, 21A,
                31A, 33C, 34C
Heck Cr 66B
Heckman Cr 17C
Heckman Pass 23B
Hedges Pk 63B
Hedley 7A
Hedley Cr 7A
Hedrick Cr 49D
Hedrick L 49D
Heffley Cr 16A
Heffley Creek 16A
Heffley L 16A
Hela Pk 8B
Helen L 82C
Helena L 26C
Helene L 47C
Helicopter Cr 66B
Hellroar Cr 27B
Hellroarer Cr 7B
Hellroaring Cr 9A
Hellroaring Cr 39B
Hells Gate 6A
Helmcken Falls 27C
Helmcken In 34D
Helmcken L 34D
Helmer L 15D
Helmut 88D
Help L 28D
Helveker Cr 60A
Hemlock 6A
Hemp Cr 27C
Hen Ingram L 26B
Henderson Cr 7D
Henderson Cr 58C
Henderson L 2C
Hendon R 79D
Hendrix Cr 26B
Hendrix L 26B
Hendrix Lake 26B
Henkel Cr 46D
Henning L 47D
Henretta Cr 19C
Henri L 25A
Henrietta Cr 47C
Henry Cr 75C
Henry House 41C
Henry I 31B, 33A, 43D
Henshaw Cr 1B
Hequiat Pen 1A
Herchmer Pass 55B
Herd Dome 45D
Hereron L 7B, 16D
Hernando I 2A, 13C

Herrick Cr 49C
Herring Cr 48D
Hesquiat 1A
Hesquiat Har 1A
Hesquiat L 1A
Hetty Pk 80C
Hevenor In 33D
Hevenor Lagoon ...33D, 34A
Hewer Cr 64B, 65A
Heydon L 12D
Hibbard L 11B
Hibben I 30D
Hickethier Ranch 56B
Hicks L 4B, 6A
Hidden Cr 8D
Hidden L 16D
Hidden Valley Cr 73A
Hiding Cr 50A
Hiellen R 31A, 32B, 43C
Higgins L 26D
Higgins Pass 21B
High Cr 2B
High River 19D
High Tuya L 71B, 72A
Highhat Cr 57C
Highland Valley 15D
Highrise Cr 56D
Hihium Cr 15A
Hihium L 15B
Hilary L 53D, 54C
Hilda L 39D
Hilda Pk 8A
Hill Cr 17B
Hill L 38D
Hillcrest Mines 10B
Hillgren Ls 84D, 85C
Hilliers 2D
Hillis Cr 13C
Hills 17D
Hinton 41B
Hinton Trail 50B
Hippa I 30A, 32C
Hird Ls 8B
Hiren Cr 17A
Hirsch Cr 45C
Hirshfeld Cr 81D
Hisnit In 1A
Hitchcock Cr 80D, 81C
Hiuhihill Cr 16A
Hiusta Meadow 71D
Hixon 38B
Hixon Cr 38B
Hizaca Cr 73B, 74A
Hizaza Hill 84C
Hkusam Mtn 12D
Hluey Ls 71D, 72C
Hobiton L 2C
Hoboe Cr 69B
Hobson Arm 26A
Hobson Cr 27A, 40C
Hobson L 26B, 27A, 40C
Hockey Cr 66A
Hodder Cr 61C
Hoder Cr 8B
Hoeya Sd 12B
Hoffard Cr 76B
Hogem Pass 54D
Hogg Cr 9B
Hogsback L 37B
Hohoae I 11D
Holberg 11C
Holberg In 11D
Hold Cr 12A
Hold Cr 17B, 28D
Holder Cr 48A
Holdich Cr 17A, 28C
Hole in Wall Mtn 60C
Holliday Cr 40C
Holman Cr 66C
Holman L 37A, 38A
Holmes Cr 46D
Holmes L 17C

Holmes R 40A
Holte Cr 24A
Holtry Cr 24A
Holy Cross L 37A
Holy Cross Mtn 37A, 39B
Homan L 80C
Homan R 80C
Homathko Pk 24C
Homathko R .. 13A, 24C, 24D
Homathko Snowfield 13A
Homer Cr 5B
Homfray Chan 13C
Homfray Cr 13C
Hominka R 49A
Honakta Cr 69B, 70A
Honna R 30D, 32D
Hooch L 24A
Hoodoo Cr 12B, 23D
Hoodoo Gla 60C
Hoodoo L 7B
Hoodoo Ls 48C
Hoodoo Mtn 60C
Hook Cr 49A
Hook Cr 82D
Hook L 49A
Hooker Icefield 49A
Hoole Cr 74B, 85D
Hoonah 68D
Hoop B 11B
Hoopatatkwa L 15B
Hoover L 15B
● Hope 6A
Hope Cr 17D
Hope I 11A
Hope Mtn 6A
Horetzky Cr 35A
Horn Cr 49C
Horn Cr .55B, 56A, 64D, 65C
Horn L 24C
Horn Pk 54B
Hornby I 2A
Hornby Island 2A
Horne Cr 27D
Horne L 2C, 3A
Horneline Cr 73B, 74A
Hornet Cr 6A
Hornway Cr 54B
Horse Cr 18A
Horse L 26D
Horse Range Cr 65B
Horsefeed Cr 70B
Horsefly 26A
Horsefly L 26B
Horsefly R 26A, 26B
Horseranch L 83D
Horseshoe Bay 5A
Horseshoe Cr 56B
Horseshoe L 2B
Horseshoe L 9B
Horsethief Cr 18C
Horsey Cr 40C
Horsfall I 22A
Hoskins Cr 27D
Hoskyn Chan 13C
Hosmer 10A
Hospital Cr 29C
Hospital Cr 48D
Hossitl Cr 88C
Hostli Cr 88D
Hostli L 88D
Hot L 72B, 83D
Hotel Cr 72C
Hotfish L 26D
Hotham Sd 2B
Hotlesklwa L 62C
Hotnarko L 23B
Hotnarko R 23B
Hotsprings Cove 1A
Hottah L 73C
Hoult Cr 45C
Hound Cr 17C

House Mtn 13A
○ Houston 46C
Houston Cr 17B
Houston Pass 3B, 5C
Houston R 1A
Houston Stewart Chan . 20B
Houston
  Tommy Cr 45D, 46C
Hovel B 13A
Howard Cr 27B
Howarth Cr 6B
Howe B 20B
Howe Cr 8A
Howe Sd 3B, 5A
Howell Cr 10C
Howser 18C
Howser Cr 18C
Howson Cr 45D
Hoy L 62D
Huaskin L 11B, 12A
Huble Cr 49C
Huckey Cr 39C
Hudson Bay Mtn 45B
Hudson Bay Pass 43D
○ Hudson's Hope 57A
Hugh Allan Cr 28A
Hugh Cr 34B
Huguenot Cr 50C
Hulcross Cr 56D
Humamilt L 16B
Humbug Cr 39B
Hume Cr 17B
Humphrey L 54D
Hunaechin Cr 13D
Hunakwa L 16B
Hungary Cr 39A
Hunger L 10C
Hungry Cr 9A
Hungry Valley Cr 25C
Hunter Chan 22A
Hunter Cr 7C
Hunter Cr 45C
Hunter I 22C
Hunter Ls 66A
Hunter Mtn 75C
Huntingdon 5D
Hunts Inlet 43D
Hurley R 14A
Hurricane Cr 70B, 81D
Hurst I 11B
Hustan L 12C
Hutchinson Cr 8A
Hutchison Cr 84D, 85C
Hutsigola L 81D
Hutton In 20A
Huxley I 20A
Hyas L 16A
Hydaburg 42B
Hyde Cr 39C
Hyde Creek 11D
Hyder 52C
Hydraulic Cr 7B
Hydraulic L 7B
Hyland Cr 60A
Hyland L 71A, 82C
Hyland Post 62A
Hyland R 84C
Hyman Cr 47D
Hythe 58D

I

Ian L 30B, 32A
Ice Cr 8B
Ice Mtn 49C
Ice R 18A
Icefall Brook 28D
Icewall Cr 13A
Ickna Cr 23A
Iconoclast Mtn 28D
Idabel L 7B

Idaho Pk 80D, 81C
Ideal L 7B, 16D
Idol Cr 39B, 40A
Ignatieff Cr 55B, 56A
Ikesumka L 22B
Iknouk R 44A
Illal Cr 6B
Illecillewaet R 17A
Illiance R 52D
Iltasyuko L 36C
Iltasyuko R 36C, 36D
Iltcoola Cr 7A
Impa L 65A
Imperial Cr 49A
Imperial Eagle Chan 2C
Incomappleux R 17B
Indata L 47A, 55C
Index L 16C
Indian Arm 4A, 5A
Indian Cr 57B
Indian Cr 80D, 81C
Indian I 11B
Indian L 39A
Indian L 80D, 81C
Indian Pk 18B
Indian R 5A
Indianpoint Cr 39A
Indianpoint L 39C
Ingenika Arm 64C
Ingenika Cone 64C
Ingenika Crag 64C
Ingenika R 63C, 63D
Ingraham B 30A, 32A
Ingram Cr 7D, 16C
Inhini R 51A
Ink L 1B
Inkaneep 7C
Inkaneep Cr 7D
Inkikuh Cr 15C
Inklin R 70B
Inland L 2B
Inlet Cr 18D
Inner Basin 1A
Inonoaklin Cr 8A, 17C
Inonoaklin Mtn 8A, 17C
Insect Cr 45A
Inskip Chan 30D
Inspector Pk 73A
Intata Reach 36B
Intersection Mtn 40A
Intlpam Cr 15C
● Invermere 18D
Inzana Cr 47A
Inzana L 47A
Inziana R 23C
Ioco 5C
Ione 8D
Ipec L 64A
Ireland Cr 16D
Irene L 75A, 86C
Irish Cr 16D
Irishman Cr 9D
Iron Cr 1B
Iron Cr 10A
Iron Mtn 15D
Ironside Cr 53C
Ironside Mtn 30B, 32C
Iroquois Cr 28A
Iroquois L 48A
Irvines Landing 2B
Isaac L 39D
Isaac R 39C
Isadore Cr 48B
Isaiah Cr 26B, 39D
Ishkheenickh R 44B
Isintok Cr 7A
Iskloo Cr 39D
Iskut 61A
Iskut Mtn 51A, 60C
Iskut R 51A, 60B, 60C,
              60D, 61A, 61C
Islaht L 16C

Islam Cr 53B, 54A
Island L 10A
Island L 16D
Island L 26C
Island L .60B, 61A, 71D, 72C
Island Mtn 39C
Isle Pierre 38A
Isola Cr 64C
Isolation Mtn 60A
Isolillock Pk 6C
Italia L 26D
Italy Cr 8C
Itautso L 26C
Itcha L 37C
Itcha Mtn 37C
Ithaca Gla 64B
Ittsi Cr 86D, 87C
Iverson Cr 82D, 83C
Ivor Cr 27A
Ivor Cr 64C

J

Jack Cr 7A
Jack Frost L 26D
Jack Lee Cr 62B, 63A
Jack of Clubs Cr 39C
Jack of Clubs L 39C
Jack Pine Pass 40B
Jack Stone Cr 73D, 74C
Jack Wilson Cr 60C
Jackfish Cr 55C
Jackfish Cr 76D
Jackfish L 57C
Jackknife Cr 76D
Jacklah R 1B
Jackpine Cr 49B
Jackpine L 7A
Jackpine L 26A
Jackson B 12D
Jackson Pass 22A
Jacobie Cr 26A
Jacobsen Gla 23B
Jacques L 26A
Jade L 28A, 41C
Jade L 52D
Jaffray 10A
Jakes Corner 80B
Jalun R 32A, 42D
James I 3D, 5C
James L 7B
Jamieson Cr 15B, 16A
Jane Smith Cr 85D
Janet Cr 23B
Jarvis Cr 49D, 50C
Jarvis Ls 49D, 50C
Jasper 41C
Jayam 2D
Jean Marie Cr 47A
Jedney Cr 65D
Jeffrey Cr 28A
Jekill R 51A
Jellicoe Cr 62D
Jenkins Cr 62C
Jennings Ls 82D, 83C
Jennings R 82C
Jenny In 22B
Jensen Cr 63C
Jensen Pk 63C
Jerky Cr 25B, 38D
Jerry Cr 38B
Jervis In 2B, 13D
Jesmond 15A
Jesmond Cr 15A
Jesse Cr 34B
Jesse L 34B
Jesson Cr 64D, 65C
Jeune Landing 11D
Jewakwa Gla 13A
Jewakwa R 13A
Jewel L 8C

116

Jezebel Cr 57C
Jim Brown Cr 13D
Jim Cr 26D
Jim Kelly Cr 6B
Jim L 26D
Jim L 84C
Jim May Cr 55A
Jim Smith L 9B
Joan L 7B
Joanne Cr 48C
Joanne L 48C
Jobin Cr 23D
Jock Cr 62D, 63C
Joe Irwin L 72A
Joe Poole Cr 63B
Joe Rich Cr 7B
Joe Ross L 15B
Joes L 25D
Joffre Cr 14D
Joffre Cr 19C
Johanson Cr 54A
Johanson L 54B
Johiah L 74C
John Bennett Cr 56D
John Boyd Cr 38D
John Brown Cr 45B
John Cr 16A
John Cr 17D
John Hart L 12D
John L 26C
Johnny L 36D
Johns Cr 7C
Johns Cr 22D
Johnsen Cr 56D
Johnson Chan 22A
Johnson Cr 16A
Johnson Cr 56D
Johnson Gla 60C
Johnson L 16A
Johnson R 60C
Johnsons Crossing 80B
Johnsons Landing 18C
Johnston Canyon 18B
Johnston Cr 8A
Johnston Cr 22D
Johnston L 34B
Johnstone Str 12C
Jones L 26A
Jones L 80D, 81B
Jones Pk 56B
Joniah L 73D
Joplin Cr 75C
Jordan R 3C
Jordan R 17A
Jorgensen Cr 24B
Joseph Cr 9B
Joseph Cr 27C
Josephine Cr 71B, 72A
Joss Mtn 17A
Juan de Fuca Strait 3D
Juan Perez Sd 20A
Jubilee Mtn 7B
Jubilee Mtn 12B
Julian Cr 72B
Julienne Cr 65D
Juliet Cr 6B
July Cr 8C
July L 88D
July Mtn 6B
Jumble Mtn 36C
Jumbo Cr 18C
Jumbo Mtn 18C
Jump Across Cr 23A
Jump L 2D, 3A
Jumping Cr 17D
Junction Cr 14B
June Cr 7A
June L 88D
Juneau 69C
Juniper Cr 7C
Juniper Cr 45B
Juniper Heights 16A

Junker L 23B
Junkers Cr 62B, 63A
Juskatla 30B
Juskatla In 30B, 32C
Justice Cr 56A
Justine L 47C

K

Kachook Cr 82C
Kadah L 62B, 63A
Kadeen Cr 44D
Kagan B 30D, 32D
Kah Cr 88D
Kah L 77B
Kaha Cr 71A
Kahan Cr 71A, 82C
Kahntah 77D
Kahntah R 66B, 77D
Kahta Cr 65B
Kaien I 33B, 43D, 44C
Kain Cr 18A
Kains L 11B
Kaiput Cr 12C
Kaiput L 12C
Kaisun 30D
Kakawis 1D
Kake 59C
Kaketsa Mtn 71C
Kakiddi Cr 60B
Kakiddi L 60B, 61A
Kakuchuya Cr 71C
Kakwa L 40A, 50C
Kakwa Pass 40A
Kakweiken R 12B
Kalahin Mtn 51A
Kalamalka 16D
Kalamalka L 16D
Kalder Cr 47B
Kaleden 7A
Kalone Pk 23A, 36C
Kamloops 16A
Kamloops L 16A
Kamma Cr 9A
Kanaka 15C
Kananaskis 19A
Kane Cr 17D
Kane L 6B, 15D
Kangaroo Cr 39C
Kanish B 12D
Kano In 30D, 32C
Kaouk R 11D, 12C
Kapella R 35D
Kapoose Cr 1C
Kappan Cr 23B
Kappan L 23B
Karlukwees 12C
Kashutl In 11D
Kasidaya Cr 80C
Kasiks R 44D
Kaska Cr 84C
Kaslo 9A
Kaslo Cr 9D
Kaslo R 8B, 17D
Kastberg Cr 54A
Katah Cr 66A
Katakose Cr 65A
Kataleen Cr 77D
Kate Cr 17C
Kate L 17C
Kateen R 44A
Kates Needle 59D
Katete R 63A
Katharine Cr 63A
Katina Cr 70B
Kaufmann L 18A
Kaustua Cr 70B
Kauwinch R 11D
Kawdy Cr 71A
Kaykay L 48C
Kaza L 54A

Kaza Pk 54B
Kazchek L 47A
Keap Cr 45C
Keary L 14B
Keats Island 5A
Kec Cr 47D
Kechika R 63B, 73B, 73D, 74A, 74C, 84C, 85C
Kedahda L 71A
Kedahda R 71A
Kedleston 16D
Keecha L 33D, 34C
Keefer L 17C
Keen Cr 8B
Keene Cr 17D
Kehlechoa R 61B, 72D
Keily Cr 64B, 65A
Keith L 26C
Keith R 11C
Keithley Cr 39C
Keithley Creek 39C
Kellie Cr 17B
Kellington L 26D
Kellogg Cr 38A
Kelly Cr 15A
Kelly L 15A
Kelly L 50A
Kelly Lake 15A
Kelly Lake 50A
Kelly R 7D
Kelowna 7B
Kelowna Cr 7B, 16D
Kelsall L 79C
Kelsall R 79D
Kelsey Bay 12D
Kelskiist Cr 44A, 52C
Kemano 35A
Kemano B 35A
Kemano R 35A
Kemess Cr 62D, 63C
Ken L 83D
Kenai Cr 66A, 77C
Kendell 5D
Kennedy I 33B, 34A, 44C
Kennedy L 1D
Kennedy R 1D
Kenneth Cr 39A
Kennicott L 71C
Kenny Cr 54D
Keno L 26A
Kent 6C
Kentucky L 6B
Keogh R 11D
Keremeos 7C
Keremeos Cr 7C
Kerouard Is 20D
Kerry L 48B
Kersley 38C
Kersley Cr 38D
Ketchikan 51C
Ketchum L 71C
Kettle In 21B, 34D
Kettle R 7B, 7D, 8C, 17C
Kettle Valley 7D
Kewquodie Cr 11D
Keystone Mtn 8D
Khartoum L 2B
Khtada L 44D
Khtada R 44D
Khutze In 35C
Khutze R 35C
Khutzeymateen In 44A
Khutzeymateen R 44C
Khyex R 33B, 44C
Kiakho L 9B
Kianuko Cr 9A
Kibbee L 39C
Kicking Horse Pass 29C
Kicking Horse R 18A
Kid Cr 9C
Kidney L 23B
Kidprice L 35B

Kilbella B 22D
Kilbella R 22D
Kildala Arm 35A
Kildala R 35A
Kildidt Lagoon 22C
Kildidt Sd 22C
Kildonan 2C
Kilkerran 58C
Killam Cr 39B
Killarney L 71B, 72A
Killdog Cr 26B
Kilmarnock Cr 19C
Kilpala R 11D
Kilpoola L 7C
Kiltik Cove 22C
Kiltuish In 35A
Kiltuish R 35C
Kimball Cr 39D
Kimberley 9B
Kimea Cr 88D
Kimea L 88D
Kimpton Cr 18D
Kimsquit In 35D
Kimsquit R 35D
Kinaskan L 60B, 61A
Kinbasket L 28A, 40D
Kinbasket R 28A
Kincolith 44A
Kincolith R 44A
King Cr 51B
King I 22B
King Pk 75C
King Salmon Cr 70A
King Salmon L 70B
Kingcome 12A
Kingcome In 12A
Kingcome Inlet 12A
Kingcome R 12B
Kingfisher 16D
Kingfisher Cr 16B
Kingkown In .. 31B, 33D, 34A
Kingsgate 9C
Kingsvale 6B
Kinnear L 5B
Kinney L 40D
Kinskuch L 52D
Kinskuch Pk 52D
Kinskuch R 52D
Kinuseo Cr 49A
Kinuseo Falls 49A
Kirby Cr 3D
Kirbyville Cr 27D
Kirk Cr 60A
Kirkpatrick Cr 65B
Kirkup Cr 17A
Kisgegas Pk 53D
Kishinena Cr 10D
Kiskatinaw R 49B, 50A, 57D, 58C
Kiskosh In 34B
Kispiox 53D
Kispiox Mtn 53C
Kispiox R 53C
Kistakok L 62C
Kitamaat Village 45C
Kitasu B 21B
Kitchener 9C
Kitchener Crag 62D
Kitchener L 62D
Kitchi Cr 39B, 49D
Kiteen R 44B, 52D
Kitimat 45C
Kitimat Arm 34B
Kitimat R 45C
Kitkatla 31B
Kitkatla Chan 31B, 33B
Kitkiata In 34B
Kitkiata L 34B
Kitlangas Cr 53A
Kitlope L 35C
Kitlope R 35D
Kitnayakwa R 45C

Kitsault L 52D
Kitsault R 52D
Kitseguecla 45A
Kitseguecla Mtn 45A
Kitseguecla R 45A
Kitsumkalum L 44B
Kitsumkalum R 44B
Kitsuns Cr 45A
Kitwancool 45A
Kitwancool Cr 45A
Kitwanga 45A
Kitwanga L 45A, 53C
Kitwanga R 45A
Kitza Cr 84C
Kitza L 84C
Kiwa Cr 40C
Kiwigana R 87D
Klahowya L 62C
Klaklakama Ls 12C
Klakring Cr 54B
Klanawa R 2C, 3A
Klappan R 61A, 61D
Klaskino In 11D
Klaskish In 11C
Klaskish R 11D
Klastline R 60B, 61A
Klattasine Gla 13A
Klawdetelle Cr 47A
Klawli L 47A, 55C
Klawli R 47A, 55C
Klaytahnkut L 46B
Kleanza Cr 45C
Kledo Cr 75B, 76A
Kleena Kleene 24C
Kleeptes Cr 1A
Klehini R 79C
Kleindale 2B
Klekane In 35C
Klekane R 34D
Klenteh Cr 87D
Klesilkwa R 6C
Kli Cr 88C
Klicho Cr 77A
Klinaklini Gla 12B, 23D
Klinaklini L 23D
Klinaklini R 12B, 23D, 24C
Klingzut Mtn 65A
Klinkit Cr 82C
Klinkit L 82C
Klite Cr 13D
Klitsa Mtn 2C
Kliweguh Cr 62A
Kliyul Cr 54B
Kliyul L 25C
Klo Cr 7B
Klo Cr 46C
Kloakut L 25C
Kloch L 47A
Klonas L 22D
Klootchlimmis Cr 11D
Klowee L 76D
Klowkut Pk 54D
Kloye Cr 84C
Klua Cr 65B, 76D
Klua Ls 76D
Kluachesi Cr 64B, 65A, 75D, 76C
Kluachesi L 64B, 65A, 75D, 76C
Kluachon L 60B, 61A
Kluakaz Cr 61D
Kluatantan R 62C
Kluayaz Cr 62C
Kluayetz Cr 62C
Kluea L 61A
Kluk Cr 47C
Klukshu 79A
Klukwan 79D
Kluskoil L 37D
Kluskus Ls 37C
Knapp Cr 37A
Knapp L 37A

Entry	Ref
Knappen Cr	8A
Knewstubb L	37A
Knight Cr	47D
Knight In	12B
Knob Hill	11A
Knoll Cr	24A
Knot Ls	23D
Knouff Cr	16A
Knouff L	16A
Knox L	25B
Knutsford	16C
Knutson Cr	27A
Kobes Cr	56B
Koch Cr	8A
Kodak Cataract Rapids	63A
Koeye L	22D
Koeye R	22D
Kohasganko Cr	36D
Kokanee Cr	8B
Kokanee L	8B
Kokish	12C
Kokish R	12C
Koksilah	2D
Koksilah R	2D, 3D
Koller Cr	65C
Komie Cr	76B
Komie L	77A
Konigus Cr	61D
Konni L	24D
Konthil Cr	61A
Konthill Cr	60B
Kookipi Cr	6A
Kooryet L	33D
Kootenay Bay	9A
Kootenay Crossing	18B
Kootenay In	30D
Kootenay L	9A, 18C
Kootenay R	8B, 9B, 18B, 18D
Koprino Har	11C
Koshin R	71A
Kostal L	27A
Koster Cr	25D
Kostering Cr	15A
Kostick Cr	85D
Kotcho L	77A
Kotcho R	77A, 77B
Kotsine R	54C
Kotsinta Cr	53A
Kowatua Cr	70D
Kowesas R	35C
Kravac Cr	64B, 65A
Krestova	8B
Kruger Cr	39C
Kruger L	39C
Ksedin Cr	44B
Ksemamaith Cr	44B
Kshadin Cr	52D
Kshwan R	52C
Kubicek Pass	62C
Kuldo Cr	53C
Kuldo Mtn	53C
Kulee Cr	23C
Kumdis Cr	30B, 32B
Kumdis Slough	30B, 32B
Kumealon Cr	33B, 34A
Kunga I	31C
Kunghit I	20B
Kunishma Cr	60A
Kunlin L	1B
Kunnum Cr	12C
Kuper I	3B
Kusawa R	79D
Kushya R	37C
Kuskanax Cr	17D
Kuskonook	9C
Kutcho Cr	73C
Kuthai L	69B, 70A
Kuttat Cr	9A
Kuyakuz L	37C
Kuyakuz Mtn	37C
Kuzkwa R	47A
Kwadacha Gla	64A
Kwadacha Mtn	63B
Kwadacha R	63B
Kwakshua Chan	22C
Kwanika Cr	55C
Kwashona Cr	69B, 70A
Kwatna In	22B
Kwatna R	22B
Kwatsi B	12A
Kwikoit Cr	16B
Kwinageese L	52B
Kwinageese R	52B
Kwinamass Pk	44A
Kwinamass R	44A
Kwinamuck L	44B, 52D
Kwinatah R	52D
Kwoiek Cr	15C
Kwoiek Needle	15C
Kwoiek Pk	15C
Kwokullie L	77B
Kwotlenemo L	15C
Kwun Cr	45B
Kxngeal L	33B, 34A
Kye B	2A
Kyklo Cr	77C
Kynoch In	35C
Kyoquot Chan	1C, 11D
Kyuquot	11D
Kyuquot Sd	11D

L

Entry	Ref
L. Magog	18B
L. McArthur	18A
L. O'Hara	18A
La Conner	4C
La Forme Cr	17A
La France Cr	9A
La Glace	58D
LaBiche R	86D, 87C
Labouchere Chan	11B, 22B
Labour Day L	2D, 3A
Lac des Roches	26D
Lac la Hache	26C
Lac la Hache	26C
Lac Le Jeune	15D
Lac Le Jeune	15D
Lachine Cr	18B
Lacoma Cr	7A
Ladner	5C
Lady Douglas I	22A
Lady King L	16C
Lady Laurier L	55B, 64D, 65C
Ladybird Cr	8B
Ladybird Mtn	8B
Ladysmith	2D
Lafferty Cr	55B
Lagoon In	31C
LaGuarde Cr	57B, 58A
Laib Cr	9A
Laidlaw	6C
Laidlaw L	81C
Laidman L	37C
Laird L	6B
Lake Cowichan	2D
Lake Cr	17D
Lake Eileen	18D
Lake Enid	18D
Lake Errock	5D
Lake Louise	29D
Lake Lovely Water	5A
Lake Mtn	22A
Lake of the Hanging Glacier	18C
Lake of the Mountains	11A
Lake of the Trees	26C
Lake Revelstoke	17A, 28C
Lakelse L	45C
Lakelse Lake	45C
Lakelse R	44D
Lakeview Cr	7C
Lakeview Mtn	7C
Lama Pass	22A
Lamarque Pass	73D
Lamb Cr	9D
Lambert Chan	2A
Lambert Cr	16D
Lambly Cr	7A, 16C
Lambly L	7A
Lamming Mills	40A
Lamprey Cr	45D, 46C
Lanberis Gla	64A
Landslide Cr	38C
Lanes Cr	15B, 16A
Lanezi L	39D
Lang Bay	2B
Lang Cr	2B
Lang Cr	28D
Lang L	26D
Langara I	32A, 42C
Langdale	5A
Langford	3D
● Langley	5D
Lantzville	2D
Lanz I	11C
Lapan L	12D
Lapie Cr	85D
Lapie L	74B, 85D
LaPierre Cr	38B
Lapierre Cr	55B, 56A
Lapp Cr	66B
LaPrise Cr	66A
Larchwood L	9B
Lard Cr	35C
Lardeau	18C
Lardeau Cr	17B
Lardeau R	17D
Laredo In	34D
Laredo Sd	21B
Larman Cr	75D
Larson Cr	13C
LaSalle Cr	39B
Lasca Cr	8B
Laskeek B	31C
Laslui L	62A
Lasqueti	2B
Lasquiti I	2B, 3A
Lassie L	7B
Lassiter B	11B
Lastman L	13B, 24D
Latelle Cr	12D
Latewhos Cr	17C
Lattice Cr	50A
Laundry Cr	18C
Laurel	5D
Laurie	8C
Laurier Pass	64D, 65C
Lava Fork	51B
Lava L	44B
Lavender Pk	52D
Laventie Cr	35B
Lavigure L	16C
Lavington	16D
Law Cr	18C
Lawery Pass	62D
Lawless Cr	6B
Lawnhill	31A
Lawrence	5D
Lawson L	80C
Lawyers Cr	62B
Lay Cr	54B
Lazaroff L	38D
Lazo	2A
Lazy L	9B
Leach Cr	10A
Leach L	9C
Leader L	1B
Lean-to Cr	45C
Lean-to Mtn	45C
Lebahdo	8B
LeBourdais L	39C
Leckie B	22C
Leckie Cr	14A
Ledge Cr	17C
Lee Creek	16A
Lee L	11B
Leech R	3D
Legate Cr	45A
Leguil Cr	84D, 85C
Lehman Cr	24A
Leigh Cr	38A
Leighton L	15D
Leiner R	1A
Lejac	47C
LeMare L	11C
Lemieux Cr	27C
Lemieux Cr	80C
Lemon Cr	8B
LeMoray Cr	56D
Lempriere Cr	27B
Lens Cr	3C
Leo Cr	46B
Leo L	83D
Leon Cr	14B
Leonora L	11B
Lepine Cr	86C
Leslie Cr	10C
Lessard Cr	23B
Lessard L	23B, 36D
Lesser Fish L	26D
Letain Cr	72D
Letain L	72D
Leverson L	33B, 44C
Lew Cr	17D
Lewis Chan	13C
Lewis Pass	34D
Lexau Ranch	56B
Liard R	74B, 84C, 84D, 85C, 86C, 87C
Liard River	85D
Liberty Cr	28C
Lichen Cr	77A
Lichen Mtn	16B
Lick Pk	28A
Lickskillet Cr	26B, 27A
Lightning Cr	6D
Lightning Cr	38D
Lightning Pk	8A
Lignite Cr	30B, 32A
Lihou I	30D
Likely	26A
Lilie L	24A
Lillian L	1A
Lillian L	18D
● Lillooet	15A
Lillooet Gla	13B
Lillooet L	14D
Lillooet R	5B, 14C, 14D
Lily L	36D
Lily L	37A
Lily Pad L	26C
Limestone Pk	72A
Limonite Cr	45C
Limpoke Cr	60A
Lina I	30D, 32D
Lindell Beach	5D
Lindeman L	80C
Lindmark Cr	17A
Lindquist Cr	16A
Lindquist L	35B
Line Cr	10A
Line L	81D
Lingfield Cr	24D
Link L	7A
Link L	22B
Linklater Cr	10C
Lion Cr	46A, 54C
Lions Bay	5A
Liri Mtn	75C
Lister	9C
Little Beaver Cr	76D
Little Beaverdam Cr	66D
Little Big Bar L	15A, 26C
Little Blue R	83D
Little Bobtail L	38A
Little Boulder Cr	56D
Little Bridge Cr	26C
Little Buffalo R	77D
Little Cedar R	44B
Little Charlotte L	23B
Little Cloudmaker Mtn	64A
Little Dease Cr	71D
Little Dease L	71D, 72C
Little Eagle R	72C
Little Fort	27C
Little Hay R	77D
Little Hixon Cr	38B
Little Horse L	26C
Little Iskut R	60B
Little Iskut R	61A
Little Klappan R	61B
Little L	26A
Little Momich L	16B
Little Moyie R	9C
Little Paw Cr	52D
Little Prairie Cr	49D
Little R	39C
Little Rancheria R	82D, 83C
Little River	2A
Little Salmon R	79D
Little Sand Cr	10A
Little Sheep Cr	8D
Little Shuswap L	16A
Little Slocan Ls	8B
Little Slocan R	8B
Little Swift R	39C
Little Tahltan R	71C
Little Toba R	13D
Little Tuya R	71D
Little Wedeene R	44D
Little White L	15A
Little White Mtn	7B
Little Whitesail L	35B
Littlefield Cr	39A
Livingstone Cr	57D
Liz Cr	61C
Lizard Cr	10A
Lizette L	35C
Lizzie Cr	14D
Lizzie L	14D
Lladnar Cr	10A
Llangorse L	81D
Llangorse Mtn	81D
Llewellyn Gla	69B, 70A
Llewellyn In	69B, 70A
Llgitiyuz Mtn	36B
Lloyd George Gla	64A
Lloyd George Icefield	64A
Loadstone Mtn	6B
Loakin Cr	16A
Loch Drinkie	16C
Loch Katrine	7B
Loch Lomond	15A, 26C
Lockhard Gordon Cr	22D
Lockhart Cr	9A
Lodge Mtn	9D
Lodgepole Cr	10C
Lodi L	38B
Log Cr	15C
Logan Cr	3C
○ Logan Lake	15D
Logjam Cr	82C
Lois L	2B
Lois R	2B
Loki Cr	9A
Lombard Pk	64A
London Mtn	14C
Lone Butte	26C
Lone Cabin Cr	14B, 25D
Lone Goat Cr	14A
Lone Mtn	6D
Lone Pk	9B
Lone Prairie	57C
Lone Valley Cr	14B

Lonesome L 23B
Lonesome Mtn 62C
Long Cr 39D
Long Harbour 5C
Long I 4B, 6A
Long In 30D, 32D
Long John Cr 38C
Long L 11B
Long L 24A
Long L 52A
Long Mountain
    Cr 73B, 74A
Long Mountain
    L 73B, 74A, 84D, 85C
Long Mtn 74A
Longbeach 8B
Longbow L 26D
Longview 19D
Longworth 39A
Lookout Mtn 7A
Lookout Pk 4B, 6A
Loomis 7C
Loomis L 24B, 25A
Loon Cr 15A
Loon L 10C
Loon L 15A
Loon Lake 15A
Looncry L 73A
Loop Br 17B
Loos 39B
Loose L 12A
Lopez 4C
Lord Mayor Pk 75C
Lord R 14A
Lorna L 14A
Lornager Cr 65C
Lorne Cr 45A
Lorne L 6B
Loss Cr 3C
Lossy Cr 16B
Lost Cabin Cr 55B, 56A
Lost Cr 8D
Lost Cr 18B
Lost Dog Cr 9B
Lost Mtn 8D
Lost Shoe Cr 1D
Lost Valley Cr 14D
Lostway Cr 39C
Lottie L 39C
Loudon Chan 1D
Loughborough In 12D
Louis Cr 16A
Louis Creek 16A
Louis L 16A
Louis Lee Cr 28C
Louise I 31C
Louise Nrs 31C
Loup Cr 2D, 3C
Louscoone In 20A
Lovola Cr 9A
Low Fog Cr 78D
Lowe Cr 19C
Lowe L 34B
Lower Belle L 62B, 63A
Lower Blue L 49D
Lower Elk L 19C
Lower L 26C
Lower Nicola 15D
Lower Post 84C
Lowrie B 11A
Lowry L 2A
Lowry L 80C
Lucas L 37A
Luck Mtn 24B
Ludwig Cr 63A, 74C
Lue Cr 74B
Luke Cr 9B
Lull Cr 12B
Lulu I 4A, 5C
Lumby 16D
Lumby Junction 16D
Lumme L 32B, 43C

Lummi 5D
Lunar Cr 62B
Lunch L 24D
Lund 13C
Lundbreck 10B
Luno Cr 45B
Lupin Ls 15B, 26D
Lupin Ridge 64A
Lussier R 9B, 18D
Lutz Cr 83D
Luxana B 20B
Luxor Cr 18B
Lyell Cr 28D
Lyell I 20A, 31C
Lyell Icefield 28D
Lymburn 58C
Lynch Cr 8C
Lyne Cr 25B
Lynx Cr 26B
Lynx Cr 57A
Lynx Mtn 40D
Lyon Cr 45B
Lys Cr 27A
● Lytton 15C

M

Mab L 15D
Mabel L 16D
Mabel Lake 16D
Macaulay Cr 18B
MacDonald Cr 75A
Machete Cr 26D
Machete L 26D
Machmell R 23C
Macjack R 11C
Mackay R 26B
● Mackenzie 56C
Mackenzie Cr 17D
Mackenzie Cr 39B
Mackenzie L 12A
Mackie Cr 56B
Mackin Cr 25B
Macktush Cr 2C
Macleod Cr 39B
Mad R 27D
Madden Cr 17D
Madden L 25B
Madeira Park 2B
Madeline L 33B, 34A
Madely Cr 52B
Maeford L 39D
Magar Cr 44D
Maggie L 1D
Magna Bay 16B
Mahatta R 11D
Mahatta River 11D
Mahood Falls 26D
Mahood L 26D, 27C
Mahood R 27C
Maiden Cr 15A
Main L 13C
Mainguy L 24D
Maitland I 34B
Majerus Falls 27A
Major Hart R 73A
Majuba L 36D
Maka Cr 6B
Makinson 17C
Malachite Cr 18A
Malakwa 16B
Malaput L 36D
Malaspina Pen 2A, 13C
Malaspina Pk 1A
Malaspina Str 2B
Malcolm I 11D
Maligne L 28A
Malkope In 11D
Mallandaine Cr 9A
Malloch Cr 62C
Malloch Pk 62C

Malloy Cr 18A
Mamin R 30B, 32C
Mamit L 15D
Mamquam L 5A
Mamquam Mtn 5A
Mamquam R 5A
Mann Cr 26D, 27C
Manning Park 6D
Mansfield Cr 71D
Manson Creek 55C
Manson Ls 55D
Manson Pass 2A
Manson R 55C, 55D
Mansons Landing 13C
Manteau Cr 27B
Mantle Gla 13A
Many Bear Cr 45C
Mapes 37B
Maple Bay 5C
Maple Falls 5D
● Maple Ridge 5D
Maquilla Cr 12C
Mara 16B
Mara Cr 16B
Mara L 16B
Marble Cr 23C
Marble Dome 81D
Marble I 30D, 32C
Marble R 11D
Marchant Taylors Pks ... 75C
Marcus Pass . 33B, 43D, 44C
Margaret L 1B
Margaret L 47D, 48C
Margie L 17C
Margison Cr 75C
Marguerite 25B
Maria Cr 71B, 72A
Maria L 71B, 72A
Marian L 30B, 32A
Marie L 47C
Marietta 5D
Marina I 13C
Marion L 11B, 12A
Marion L 65C
Mark Cr 9B
Marktosis 1D
Marl Cr 28D
Marl L 10C
Marmot L 38C
Marmot Mtn 6D
Marmot R 52C
Maroon Cr 44B
Maroon Mtn 45A
Marron Valley 7A
Mars Cr 17A, 28C
Mars I 12A
Marsh Adams Cr 17B
Marsh L 8D
Marsh Lake 80A
Marshall Cr 14B
Marten Cr 10A
Marten Cr 39D
Martin Cr 29C
Martin Cr 57C, 66A
Martin L 24C
Marvin Cr 38D
Mary Cr 38D
Marysville 9B
Mason Cr 65D
Mason L 65B
Masset 42D
Masset In 30B, 32D
Masset Sd 30B, 32B
Massive 18B
Mat Cr 17D
Matchlee B 1B
Matchlee Mtn 1B
Matetlo Cr 54B
Mather Cr 9B
Mathers Cr 31C
Mathers L 31C
Mathieson Chan ... 22A, 35C

Matilpi 12C
Matsatu Cr 71C
Matsiu Cr 12B
Matsqui 5D
Matterhorn Pk 23A
Matthew Cr 9B
Matthew R 39D
Matulka Cr 73B, 74A
Matzehtzel Mtn 46D
Maud Cr 39C
Maud L 39C
Maude l 30D, 32D
Maunsell B 12A
Maurelle I 13C
Maurice Cr 57C
Maurier Cr 8B
Maury L 26D, 27C
Maxan Cr 46D
Maxan L 46D
Maxhamish L 86D, 87C
Maxwell Cr 24B
May L 13C
Mayer L 30B, 32D
Mayer R 31A, 32D
Mayfield L 84C
Mayne 5C
Mayne I 3B, 5C
Mayo Cr 44B
Mayson L 15B
Maze L 26C
McAllister Cr 56D
McArthur Cr 18A
● McBride 40C
McBride Cr 1B
McBride L 45D
McBride R 61B, 72D
McCannel L 13D
McCauley I 31B, 33D, 34A
McClair Cr 62B, 63A
McClinchy Cr 24A
McClinchy L 23B
McClinton B 30B, 32C
McColloch 7B
McConachie Cr 76B
McConachie Pk 62C
McConnell Cr 63C
McConnell Gla 64A
McConnell L 15D
McConnell Ls 63C
McConnell Pass 63A
McCook R 63B
McCool Cr 10A
McCreight L 12D
McCullagh Cr 49D
McCully Cr 53C
McCurdy Cr 1A
McCusker Cr 64D
McDame 72B
McDame Cr 72B
McDermid Cr 10A
McDermott Cr 25C
McDonald L 47A
McDonald L 80D, 81C
McDonell L 45B
McDougal Cr 17B
McDougall Falls 27A
McDougall L 27A
McDougall R 48A
McEvoy Cr 10A
McEwan L 48D
McEwen Cr 25D
McFarland Cr 38C
McFarlane Cr 8A
McGavin Cr 70A
McGillivray 10A
McGillivray Cr 14D
McGillivray Cr 16A
McGillivray L 16A
McGraw Cr 63D
McGraw Pk 63D
McGregor 49C
McGregor R .. 39B, 49C, 49D

McIntire L 48A
McIntosh Cr 39D
McIntosh Ls 26A
McIntyre B 32B, 43C
McKale R 39B, 40A
McKay Cr 2D, 3A
McKay Cr 15A
McKay Cr 45C
McKay Reach 34D
McKearney Ranch 56B
McKee Cr 80D, 81C
McKelvey L 47A
McKelvie Cr 1A
McKendrick Cr 46A
McKian Cr 17D
McKinley Cr 81C
McKinley L 26B
McKinney Cr 7D
McKinnon Lagoon 11B
McKnab L 47C
McKusky Cr 26B
McLean Ranch 56B
McLeary L 39D
McLeese Lake 25C
McLennan R 40D
McLeod L 15D
McLeod L 48A
McLeod Lake 48A
McLeod R 48A
McLure 16A
McMicking I .. 33B, 43D. 44C
McMillan Cr 38C
McMurdo 18A
McMurdo Cr 17B
McMurray 4D
McNab Cr 5A
McNab Creek 5A
McNab L 84C
McNair Cr 5A
McNaughton Cr 82C
McNaughton Group 22C
McNeil Cr 9B
McNeil L 6B
McNeil R 33B, 44C
McNomee Cr 16B, 27D
McNulty Cr 7A
McParlon Cr 14A
McPhail Cr 6B
McPherson L 22A, 35C
McQuarrie L 46C
McTavish L 84C
McWater L 57D, 58C
Meachen 9A
Meachen Cr 9A
Meade Cr 2D, 3A
Meadow Cr 15D
Meadow Cr 17D
Meadow Cr 27D
Meadow Creek 18C
Meadow L 15A, 26C
Meadows 8D
Meager Cr 14C
Meaoulie L 77A
Meares I 1D
Meason Cr 25D
Medana Cr 65B
Medicine Cr 15A
Meehaz Mtn 71A
Meek L 72B
Meers Cr 12B
Megatushon Cr 71C
Megin R 1B
Mehatl Cr 14D
Meikle Cr 49A
Melanistic Pk 62D
Melbern Gla .. 67B, 68A, 78D
Meldrum Cr 25B
Meldrum Creek 25B
Meldrum L 25B
Mellersh Cr 13A
Mellin Cr 16C
Mellin L 16C

Melville I 33A, 43D
Memekay R 12D
Memory L 1B
Menard Cr 63C
Menhinick Cr 17B
Mercer L 32C
Mercers Pk 75C
Mereworth Sd 11B
● Merritt 15D
Merston Cr 38C
Merton Cr 48C
Merton L 48C
Merville 2A
Mesachie Lake 2D
Mesilinka R 54B, 55A
Mess Cr 60A, 60B
Mess L 60B
Meszah Pk 71C
Metah Mtn 71A
Metchosin 3D
Metlahdoa Cr 77A
Metlakatla 43D
Metlatulin Mtn 70D
Metsantan L 62B
Metsantan Pass 62B
Meyers Pass 22A
Meziadin L 52B
Meziadin Junction ... 52B
Mica Cr 28C
Mica Creek 28C
Mica Pk 55A
Michel 10A
Michel Cr 10A
Michel Cr 36B
Michel L 36A
Michel Pk 36A
Michelle Cr 37D, 38C
Midas Cr 62B, 63A
Midas L 62B, 63A
Middle Cr 71C
Middle Fork Cr 65B
Middle Kootenay Pass .. 10D
Middle L 24C
Middle Memekay R ... 12D
Middle R 47A
Middle River 47A
Midge Cr 9A
Midsummer I 12C
Miduski Cr 76A
Midway 7D
Midwinter Cr 88D
Midwinter L 88D
Miette Hotsprings ... 41D
Milbanke Sd 21B
Milburn L 38D
Milburn Pk 48B
Miledge Cr 27B
Milk Cr 45D
Milk R 39D
Mill Bay 5C
Mill Bay 44A
Mill Cr 5A
Mill Cr 45A
Millar Chan 1B
Millarville 19B
Miller Cr 14C
Miller L 16C
Millet Cr 65C
Milligan Cr 66D
Milliken Cr 64B, 65A
Milnes Landing 3D
Milo Cr 76C
Milo L 76C
Milton R 22D
Mimenuh Mtn 15C
Minaker R 65B
Minaret Cr 53B
Minaty Bay 5A
Mincho L 71D
Miner L 24C
Mineral Cr 18C
Miners Cr 45C

Minerva L 33B, 44C
Minette B 35A, 45C
Ministik Cr 49B, 50A
Mink Cr 12B
Mink Cr 62A
Mink L 36C
Minnie L 6B, 15D
Minstrel Island 12C
Minton Cr 25C
Miocene 26A
Mirror Lake 9A
Mischinsinlika Cr 48B
Misinchinka R 48B
Misko Cr 18A
Missezula L 6B
Missezula Mtn 6B
Missinka R 49C
Mission 5D
Mission Cr 7B, 16D
Mission Cr 9C
Mission L 7B, 16D
Missioner Cr 25B
Missusjay Cr 60A
Mistanae Cr 65D
Mistanusk Cr 50C
Mit L 38D
Mitchell B 12C
Mitchell Bay 12C
Mitchell L 39D
Mitchell R 18B
Mitchell R 39D
Mitla Cr 1B
Mitlenatch I 2A
Mitre Cr 17B
Mitre Mtn 52A
Mizzen Cr 37C
Moakwa Cr 12D
Moat L 1B
Mobbs Cr 17D
Moberly L 57C
Moberly Lake 57C
Moberly R 56D, 57A
Moccasin Cr 54B
Moffat Cr 16D
Moffat Cr 26A
Moffat Ls 26B
Moffatt L 84C
Moh Cr 13C
Moha 14B
Mohawk Cr 17B
Mohun L 12D
Moira L 27C
Moketas I 11D
Molen Cr 27A
Mollice L 36B
Mollimarn L 15B
Molson Cr 28A
Molybdenite Cr 26B
Momich L 16B, 27D
Momich R 16B, 27D
Monarch Mtn 23D
Monashee Cr 17C
Monashee Pass 17C
Monckton In 34C
Monias L 57A
Monitor Cr 17D
Monkman Cr 49A
Monkman L 49C
Monkman Pass 49C
Monkton Cr 39C
Monmouth Mtn 13B
Monroe L 9B
Mons L 25C
Montague Chan 5A
Montague Cr 12C
Montana L 26D
Montase L 54A
Monte Cr 16C
Monte Creek 16C
Monte L 16C
Monte Lake 16C
Monticola L 26D

Montney 57B
Montrose 8D
Montrose Cr 13D
Moodie Cr 73B
Moody Cr 8C
Moon L 80C
Moonbeam Cr 27B
Moonlight Cr 58A
Moonlit Cr 53C
Moore B 12A
Moore Chan 30D
Moore Cr 15D
Moore Is 21B, 34D
Moore L 34B
Moore Pk 15A
Moose Cr 18A
Moose Cr 61B, 72D
Moose Cr 81C
Moose Heights 38D
Moose L 26D
Moose L 40D
Moose L 49A
Moose L 74B
Moose Lick Cr 65D
Moose Ls 72C
Moose Pass 40D
Moose Pond 84C
Moose R 40D
Moosecall L 56D
Moosehorn Cr 62B, 63A
Moosehorn Cr 62B, 63A
Moosevale Cr 63C
Moosmoos Cr 55C
Mooto L 22A, 35C
Mooyah B 1A
Mooyah R 1A
Morchuea Cr 60B, 61A
Morchuea L 61A, 71D, 72C
More Cr 60D, 61C
Moresby Camp 30D
Moresby I 3D, 5C
Moresby I 20A, 30D, 31C
Morfee Ls 48A, 56C
Morice L 35B, 45D
Morice R 45D, 46C
Moricetown 45B
Morkill R 39D, 40A
Morley 19A
Morley L 81D
Morrell Cr 8C
Morrisey L 16A
Morrison L 46A
Morrissey Cr 10A
Morte L 13C
Moses In 22D
Moses L 38C
Moskow Cr 18D
Mosley Cr 13A, 24C
Mosque Mtn 53B
Mosque R 53B
Mosquito L 30D
Moss Cr 77A
Moss Mtn 62C
Mossvale L 48C
Motase L 53B
Motase Pk 53B, 54A
Mouat B 2B
Moul Cr 27C
Mould Cr 85D
Moule Cr 85D
Mt. Abbl 49A
Mt. Abbot 17D
Mt. Abel 18C
Mt. Abruzzi 19C
Mt. Adrian 1B
Mt. Aida 75C
Mt. Aitken 48B
Mt. Albert Dease ... 62C
Mt. Alcock 63B
Mt. Alex Graham ... 25A
Mt. Alexander 47A
Mt. Alger 61C

Mt. Anderson 52A
Mt. Armour 78C
Mt. Armstrong 19C
Mt. Armstrong 80C
Mt. Arrowsmith 2C, 3A
Mt. Arthur Meighen . 40D
Mt. Arthurs 8A
Mt. Ashmun 79D
Mt. Assiniboine 18B
Mt. Averil 48D
Mt. Aylesworth 78C
Mt. Bagot 69A, 80C
Mt. Bairnes 62C
Mt. Baker 6C
Mt. Baker 9B
Mt. Baldy Hughes .. 38A
Mt. Balourdet 63B
Mt. Barham 80D, 81C
Mt. Barker 39C
Mt. Barnard 67B, 68A
Mt. Barr 56B
Mt. Barrington 60A
Mt. Barton 49C
Mt. Basnett 63B
Mt. Bates 47C
Mt. Bayard 51B, 52A
Mt. Beals 47C
Mt. Beauregard ... 48D
Mt. Becker 49D
Mt. Bedaux 64A
Mt. Beelzebub 23D
Mt. Begbie 17A
Mt. Begbie 30B
Mt. Bell 23D
Mt. Bell-Irving 52B
Mt. Benedict 12A
Mt. Bennett 49A
Mt. Bennett 63B
Mt. Benson 2D, 3A
Mt. Berendon 51B, 52A
Mt. Berkeley 12D
Mt. Bertha 64D, 65C
Mt. Bess 40B
Mt. Bigfoot 76D
Mt. Bigger 79C
Mt. Bisson 55D
Mt. Blaine 51B
Mt. Blair 73C
Mt. Blake 12B
Mt. Blanchard 64C
Mt. Blanchet 46B
Mt. Blane 35D
Mt. Blanshard 4A, 5B
Mt. Bleasdell 19C
Mt. Blenheim 2C
Mt. Bodine 54D
Mt. Bolom 35B
Mt. Bonney 17B
Mt. Boofus 81D
Mt. Bower 63B
Mt. Bowman 15A
Mt. Bracey 48B
Mt. Brandes 11C
Mt. Breakenridge .. 6A
Mt. Brent 7A
Mt. Brenton 2D, 3B
Mt. Brew 15C
Mt. Brewer 18C
Mt. Brewster 56A
Mt. Brock 61B
Mt. Brown 28A
Mt. Brundage 70C
Mt. Buchanan 40A
Mt. Bud 47C
Mt. Bulman 16C
Mt. Burden 56A
Mt. Burkett 59D
Mt. Burnett 9C
Mt. Buxton 22C
Mt. Byng 11D
Mt. Cain 12C
Mt. Callaghan 14C

Mt. Cambridge 13D
Mt. Cameron 80D, 81C
Mt. Canning 69A
Mt. Cardin 34D
Mt. Carl 31C
Mt. Carlyle 8B
Mt. Carnarvon 29C
Mt. Caro Marion .. 22B
Mt. Carruthers ... 54A
Mt. Carter 80D, 81C
Mt. Cartier 17A
Mt. Casey 9D
Mt. Chapleau 33B, 34A, 44C
Mt. Chapman 28C
Mt. Chapperon ... 16C
Mt. Charlie Cole .. 82C
Mt. Cheadle 27B
Mt. Chief Davie ... 63B
Mt. Churchill 2B, 13D
Mt. Circe 64B
Mt. Clive 80C
Mt. Cochrane 8A
Mt. Colley 46C
Mt. Colonel Foster . 1B
Mt. Columbia 28B
Mt. Connaught ... 16D
Mt. Connell 9D
Mt. Conover 60A
Mt. Cooper 17D
Mt. Cornelia 24C
Mt. Cote 51A
Mt. Coulahan 71B, 72A
Mt. Coutlee 33B, 34A, 44C
Mount Cr 38C
Mt. Crawford 9A
Mt. Creswell 23A
Mt. Cridge 12B
Mt. Crocker 48B
Mt. Crompton 75C
Mt. Cronin 45B, 46A
Mt. Crosby 64A
Mt. Crum 49A
Mt. Crysdale 56C
Mt. Cummings 28A
Mount Currie 14D
Mt. Cushing 62B, 63A
Mt. D'Arcy 22A
Mt. Daer 18B
Mt. Dalgleish 13B
Mt. Dalton 72B
Mt. Davidson 37C
Mt. Davies 45C
Mt. Dawson 17B
Mt. DeCosmos ... 2D, 3A
Mt. Del 64C
Mt. Dent 37D
Mt. Denver 8B
Mt. Derby 12C
Mt. Dewdney 6D
Mt. Dick 51A
Mt. Dickie 52C
Mt. Dimsdale 39B, 49D
Mt. Disraeli 52A
Mt. Donnaker ... 60A
Mt. Dopp 64B, 65A
Mt. Downton 24A, 37C
Mt. Drew 2B
Mt. Drewry 9A
Mt. Dubose 35A
Mt. Dudzic 49A
Mt. Duff 78C
Mt. Dunn 51B
Mt. Dyer 12B
Mt. Earle 84C
Mt. Edziza 60B, 61A
Mt. Elise 8B
Mt. Elphinstone . 3B, 5A
Mt. Elsie 54B
Mt. Elwin 33B, 34A
Mt. Espinosa ... 1A
Mt. Evans 9A

Mt. Everard 12B
Mt. Evindsen 52C
Mt. Fagervik 6A
Mt. Faith 8A
Mt. Farnham 18C
Mt. Farrow 13B
Mt. Fawcett 51A
Mt. Ferguson 55A
Mt. Fergusson 14B
Mt. Fernie 10A
Mt. Ferroux 7B
Mt. Filberg 1B
Mt. Filer 13B
Mt. Findlay 18C
Mt. Finlay 63B
Mt. Fisher 9B
Mt. Forde 67B, 68A
Mt. Forrest 62D, 63C
Mt. Forsyth 19C
Mt. Foster 79D
Mt. Fosthall 17C
Mt. Fougner 23A
Mt. Frank Roy 56D
Mt. Fraser 28A, 41C
Mt. Frederic 12B
Mt. Fremont
  Morse 69D, 70C
Mt. Freshfield 28D, 29C
Mt. Gallatin 60C
Mt. Garbitt 56D
Mt. Gardiner 13C
Mt. Garibaldi 5A
Mt. Garland 45A
Mt. Geddes 23D
Mt. Geodfrey 62C
Mt. George 38B
Mt. Germansen 55C
Mt. Geryon 23D
Mt. Gething 56B
Mt. Gil 34D
Mt. Gilbert 8B
Mt. Gilliland 48B, 56D
Mt. Gladstone 8C
Mt. Gladstone 52A
Mt. Glenora 60A
Mt. Goddard 13B
Mt. Gomm 75C
Mt. Goodsir 18A
Mt. Gordon 29C
Mt. Gordon 60A
Mt. Gordon 62C
Mt. Gordonia 62D, 63A
Mt. Gorman 50C
Mt. Gottfriedsen 7A
Mt. Grahame 55A
Mt. Graves 62B, 63A
Mt. Greene 56A
Mt. Greer 37A
Mt. Grenville 13A
Mt. Griffin 17A
Mt. Grohman 8B
Mt. Guanton 52C
Mt. Guichon 15D
Mt. Gunanoot 61D
Mt. Gunnell 75B, 76A
Mt. Guyet 39C
Mt. Halkett 85D
Mt. Halvorson 39D
Mt. Hamill 18C
Mt. Hamilton 15D
Mt. Hammell 39B
Mt. Haney 69B, 70A
Mt. Hanington 50C
Mt. Hannah 2C
Mt. Hansen 11C
Mt. Harkin 18B
Mt. Harris 68A
Mt. Haskin 72B, 83D
Mt. Hawkins 12D
Mt. Haworth 63B
Mt. Hay 67B
Mt. Hazel 82C

Mt. Headman 70A
Mt. Hebert 78C
Mt. Hedrick 49D
Mt. Heger 26D
Mt. Heimdal 8B
Mt. Heinze 8D
Mt. Helen 64D, 65C
Mt. Helveker 60A
Mt. Henderson 45C
Mt. Hendrix 26B
Mt. Henning 6B
Mt. Henri 55A
Mt. Henry 12B
Mt. Hentig 75C
Mt. Hewett 62D
Mt. Hickman 60C
Mt. Hickson 24C
Mt. Hills 12B
Mt. Hoadly 44B
Mt. Hobson 37A
Mt. Hogue 27A
Mt. Holben 64A
Mt. Holmes 40A
Mt. Hooker 2D, 3A
Mt. Hooker 9A
Mt. Hooper 2C, 3A
Mt. Horetzky 53D, 54C
Mt. Hosmer 10A
Mt. Hoy 62D
Mt. Hulcross 56D
Mt. Huntingdon 44A
Mt. Irish 63B
Mt. Irvine 9A
Mt. Irving 34D
Mt. Isola 64C
Mt. Jackson 62C
Mt. Jacobsen 23B
Mt. James Turner 14D
Mt. Jancowski 52A
Mt. Jane 22A
Mt. Jardine 17D
Mt. Jefferson
  Coolidge 51B, 52A
Mt. Jette 78C
Mt. Jobe 40A
Mt. Joffre 19C
Mt. John Jay 51B, 52A
Mt. Johnny 51A
Mt. Johnson 52A
Mt. Johnston 21B
Mt. Jones 13C
Mt. Jorgensen 62D, 63C
Mt. Josefina 63B
Mt. Joseph 9B
Mt. Josephine 71B, 72A
Mt. Judge Howay 4B, 5B
Mt. Kappan 23B
Mt. Kaslo 9A
Mt. Katharine 62B, 63A
Mt. Kathleen 7A
Mt. Kelly 8D
Mt. Kennedy 12B
Mt. Kenney 44D
Mt. Kenny 64D, 65C
Mt. Keyes 22A
Mt. Kimmel 27B
Mt. King Albert 18B
Mt. King Edward 28B
Mt. King George 18D
Mt. Kinney 48B
Mt. Kitchener 59B
Mt. Klappan 61D
Mt. Knudsen 49D
Mt. Kobau 7C
Mt. Kruger 39C
Mt. Lady
  Laurier 56A, 64D, 65C
Mt. Laidlaw 62C
Mt. Lang 12B
Mt. Lanning 80C
Mt. Lasca 8B
Mt. Laurier 64D, 65C

Mt. Laussedat 28D, 29C
Mt. Lawson 80C
Mt. Lay 54B
Mt. Le Hudette 56D
Mt. Learmonth 21B, 34D
Mt. Lempriere 27B
Mt. Leonard 80D, 81C
Mt. Leslie 16A
Mt. Lester Jones 70A
Mt. Lewis Cass 51A
Mt. Light 44D
Mt. Lloyd George 64A
Mt. Lodge 67B
Mt. Loki 9A
Mt. Lolo 16A
Mt. Longstaff 40D
Mt. Lorenz 47C
Mt. Loring 45D
Mt. Lowe 12B
Mt. Ludington 56A
Mt. Lyall 19C
Mt. Lyell 28D
Mt. Mabel 17A
Mt. Machray 40D
Mt. MacKenzie King 40C
Mt. Mackenzie 23B
Mt. Mackie 8D
Mt. MacKinnon 47B, 48A
Mt. Madely 52B
Mt. Madge 51B, 52A
Mt. Mansfield 79C
Mt. Manville 69B, 70A
Mt. Mara 16B
Mt. Marconi 19C
Mt. Marion 17D
Mt. Mark 74D
Mt. Marvin 23B
Mt. Mary Henry 75C
Mt. Mathison 12A
Mt. McAllister 56D
Mt. McArthur 29C
Mt. McCallum 69B, 70A
Mt. McClennan 27C
Mt. McClure 14A
Mt. McCook 63B
Mt. McCrae 63B
Mt. McCullagh 49D
Mt. McCusker 64D, 65C
Mt. McDame 72A, 83C
Mt. McDonnell 79C
Mt. McEvoy 62C
Mt. McGavin 71B, 72A
Mt. McGregor 9A
Mt. McGuire 4B, 6C
Mt. McInnes 15D
Mt. McKay 9A
Mt. McLearn 74B
Mt. McLeod 14A
Mt. McLeod 71D, 72C
Mt. McMaster 70A, 81C
Mt. McNamara 62B, 63A
Mt. McNeil 43D, 44C
Mt. McQuillan 2C, 3A
Mt. Medgeley 9C
Mt. Meehaus 71D, 72C
Mt. Melvin 63D
Mt. Merrick 49A
Mt. Michell 39D
Mt. Middleton 51B
Mt. Milburn 38D
Mt. Milligan 47B
Mt. Milton 27B
Mt. Minto 80D, 81C
Mt. Mobley 16B
Mt. Moloch 17A, 28C
Mt. Monckton 84C
Mt. Monkley 44A
Mt. Moodie 55B
Mt. Moore 7B
Mt. Moriarty 2D, 3A
Mt. Morice 46C
Mt. Morris 44D

Mt. Morrison 33B, 44C
Mt. Morse 33B, 43D, 44C
Mt. Mortella 35A
Mt. Mowat 40D
Mt. Muir 3D
Mt. Mummery 29C
Mt. Munday 13A, 24C
Mt. Murray 17D
Mt. Murray 39C
Mt. Musclow 35D
Mt. Myhon 49A
Mt. Nagle 28A
Mt. Nation 47A
Mt. Neal 14D
Mt. Needham 30D, 32D
Mt. Nelson 18C
Mt. Nemaia 24D
Mt. Neptune 8C
Mt. Nesselrode 69B
Mt. New 74C
Mt. Nicola 15D
Mt. Niord 8B, 17D
Mt. Nivelle 19C
Mt. O'Keefe 70A
Mt. O'Leary 8A
Mt. Oakes 62C
Mt. Oates 28A
Mt. Odin 17C
Mt. Ogden 54D
Mt. Ogden 69D, 70C
Mt. Ogilvie 69B
Mt. Olson 9D
Mt. Osmington 12D
Mt. Outram 6D
Mt. Ovington 49D
Mt. Ozzard 1D
Mt. Palmer 24B
Mt. Palsson 49A
Mt. Pambrun 18C
Mt. Parry 34D
Mt. Parton 79C
Mt. Patcha 53D, 54A
Mt. Patterson 29C
Mt. Patterson 80C
Mt. Pattullo 52D
Mt. Paul 63B
Mt. Pauline 40A
Mt. Pearce 28D
Mt. Peck 19C
Mt. Pender 34D
Mt. Pendleton 72B
Mt. Penelope 64D
Mt. Pereleshin 60C
Mt. Perseus 26B
Mt. Pierce 4B, 6C
Mt. Pike 6B
Mt. Pitt 5B
Mt. Poelzer 60B
Mt. Poletica 69A
Mt. Pondosy 36C
Mt. Pool 17B
Mt. Pootlass 23A
Mt. Pope 47D
Mt. Pope 53C
Mt. Pounder 51A
Mt. Pratt 59D
Mt. Preston 36C
Mt. Prideaux 12B
Mt. Priestley 44B
Mt. Prince 47D
Mt. Prinsep 79D
Mt. Procter 10A
Mt. Prudence 74B, 85D
Mt. Ptolemy 10A
Mt. Puggins 57D
Mt. Quanstrom 40C
Mt. Queen Bess 13A, 24C
Mt. Queen Mary 18D
Mt. Quincy Adams 67B
Mt. Raleigh 13B
Mt. Ratcliff....................23B
Mt. Rath 71B, 72A

Mt. Ratz 59B
Mt. Read 12B
Mt. Reesor 49A
Mt. Reid 85C
Mt. Remo 44D
Mt. Renshaw 40A
Mt. Reynolds 48B
Mt. Richard Bennett 40C
Mt. Rider 39B
Mt. Ritchie 52B
Mt. Robb 64D, 65C
Mt. Robert 57C
Mt. Robinson 11B
Mt. Robson 40D
Mount Robson 40D
Mt. Rodell 12B
Mt. Roderick Dhu 8C
Mt. Rodney 13A
Mt. Rogers 28D
Mt. Rognaas 62D, 63C
Mt. Ronayne 14D
Mt. Roosevelt 74D
Mt. Root 67B
Mt. Ross 55A, 64C
Mt. Rothenberg 74B
Mt. Rowgeen 60A
Mt. Russel 63D
Mt. Ruth 40A, 50C
Mt. Rykert 9C
Mt. Sandin 84D
Mt. Sanford 81D
Mt. Sarah 22A
Mt. Saugstad 23A
Mt. Scriven 12D
Mt. Seaton 45B
Mt. Sedgwick 5A
Mt. Selwyn 55D, 56C
Mt. Sepulchre 75C
Mt. Severeid 49C
Mt. Seymour 4A, 5A
Mt. Shawcross 75C
Mt. Sheba 14A
Mt. Sheffield 64A
Mt. Shields 8C
Mt. Sidney Williams 46B
Mt. Sinclair 18D
Mt. Sir Alexander 39B,
                40A, 50C
Mt. Sir Douglas 19A
Mt. Sir Francis Drake 13A
Mt. Sir Richard 5B, 14D
Mt. Sir Sandford 28C
Mt. Sir Wilfrid Laurier ... 40C
Mt. Skinner 24D
Mt. Skowill 61D
Mt. Skuyhil 53A
Mt. Slocomb 63B
Mt. Smallpiece 81D
Mt. Smith 13A
Mt. Smythe 64A
Mt. Snowdon 81D
Mt. Sparling 69B, 70A
Mt. Spieker 49A
Mt. Spranger 39D
Mt. Sproat 17A
Mt. St. George 75C
Mt. St. Magnus 75C
Mt. St. Mary 9A
Mt. St. Mary 61B, 72D
Mt. St. Paul 75A
Mt. St. Thomas 8C
Mt. Stalin 75C
Mt. Stearns 65C
Mt. Stephen 29C
Mt. Stephens 12A
Mt. Stephens 52B
Mt. Stephenson 56B
Mt. Stevenson 39C
Mt. Stockdale 18C
Mt. Stoeckl 51B
Mt. Strong 69D, 70C
Mt. Suden 44D

Mt. Suprenant 49A, 57C
Mt. Swannell 37A
Mt. Sweeney 35B
Mt. Sylvester 47B, 55D
Mt. Sylvia 75C
Mt. Talbot 60C
Mt. Tanner 8A
Mt. Tantalus 5A
Mt. Tatlow 24D
Mt. Taylor 10A
Mt. Tegart 18D
Mt. Tellot 24C
Mt. Temple 18A, 29C
Mt. Templeman 17B
Mt. Terraze 62C
Mt. Terry Fox 40D
Mt. Thoen 53D, 54C
Mt. Thor 17C
Mt. Thule 62C
Mt. Thurston 4B, 6C
Mt. Thynne 6B
Mt. Tiedemann 24C
Mt. Tinniswood 13D
Mt. Tinsdale 39C
Mt. Toby 18C
Mt. Tod 16A
Mt. Todd 2D, 3D
Mt. Tom 14A, 25C
Mt. Tom 54D
Mt. Tomlinson 53D
Mt. Tommy Jack 53A
Mt. Trimble 64D, 65C
Mt. Truax 14B
Mt. Trygve 62D
Mt. Tsaydizkun 64C
Mt. Turner 67B, 68A
Mt. Tuxford 19C
Mt. Tyrrell 18C
Mt. Ulysses 64B
Mt. Umbach 62C
Mt. Upshur 51B, 52A
Mt. Urquhard 6A
Mt. Valpy 44D
Mt. Van Wagenen 80C
Mt. Vaux 18A
Mt. Vedder 4B, 5D
Mt. Vernon 4D
Mt. Vingolf 17D
Mt. Vreeland 49C
Mt. Waddington 24C
Mt. Wade 78C
Mt. Wadman 75C
Mt. Wakefield 12B
Mt. Walbran 2D, 3C
Mt. Walker 23B
Mt. Ward 63A
Mt. Wardle 18B
Mt. Warne 44B
Mt. Warner 14A
Mt. Warren 26A
Mt. Watson 12B
Mt. Watson 67B
Mt. Weart 14D
Mt. Weber 53C
Mt. Wendt 49A
Mt. West 56D
Mt. Whipple 51A
Mt. White-Fraser ... 51B, 52A
Mt. Whymper 2D, 3A
Mt. Wiley 39C
Mt. Will 61B
Mt. William Brown 44D
Mt. Willibert 51B, 52A
Mt. Winston 73D, 74C
Mt. Withrow 65C
Mt. Wooliever 65C
Mt. Yakatchie 65B
Mt. Young 12B
Mt. Yuen 64A
Mountain Cr 28D
Mountain Cr 56D
Mountain Point 42A

Mountain Portage
   Rapids 84D, 85C
Mouse Cr 44C
Mouse Mtn 38D
Mow Cr 15B
Mowchilla L 60B, 61A
Mowdade L 60B, 61A
Mowhokam Cr 15C
Mowich L 15B
Moxley Cr 39A
Moyeha R 1B
Moyez Cr 62B
Moyie 9D
Moyie L 9D
Moyie R 9B, 9D
Moyie Springs 9C
Muchalat In 1A
Muchalat R 1A
Muckaboo Cr 52B, 61D
Mud B 4A, 5C
Mud Bay 2A
Mud Cr 14B
Mud Cr 27C
Mud Gla 60C
Mud L 27B
Mud River 38A
Muddy Cr 33B, 34A
Mugaha Cr 56C
Muinok Mtn 49D, 50C
Muir Cr 3D
Muller Cr 49D
Mulvaney Cr 62B, 63A
Mulvehill Cr 17A
Mulvey Ls 8B
Mumm Pk 40D
Muncho Cr 74B
Muncho L 74B
Muncho Lake 72B
Munro Cr 55D
Munro L 47B, 55D
Murch L 48C
Murchison I 20A
Murder Cr 53C
Murphy Cr 8D
Murray Cr 15C
Murray Cr 39C
Murray Cr 47C
Murray L 6B
Murray L 37A
Murray R 49A, 57C
Murtle L 27A
Murtle R 27A
Muscovite Ls 55D
Musgrave Cr 16D
Muskeg L 49B, 57D
Muskeg R 48C
Muskeg River 41A
Muskwa 64B
Muskwa R 64B, 65A,
               75D, 76A, 76C
Mussel In 35C
Mussel R 35C
Mussell Pk 59B
Mustela Cr 84C
Myers Cr 7D
Mylor Pen 44A
Myoff Cr 16B
Myra Cr 1B
Myrtle Point 2B

N

Nabesche R 56A
Nadahini Cr 79C
Naden Har 30B, 32A, 42D
Naden R 30B, 32A
Nadila Cr 14A, 25C
Nadina L 35B, 36A
Nadina Mtn 45D, 46C
Nadina R 35B, 46C
Nadsilnich L 38B

Nagle Cr 27B
Nahatlatch L 6A, 15C
Nahatlatch Needle .. 6A, 15C
Nahatlatch R 5B, 15C
Nahlin Mtn 70B
Nahlin R 71A
Nahlouza Cr 36D
Nahlouza L 36D
Nahmint 2C
Nahmint L 2C
Nahmint R 2C
Nahounli L 47D
Nahun 16C
Nahwitti L 11A
Nahwitti R 11A
Naka Cr 12C
Nakina L 70B
Nakina R 36A
Nakina R 70A, 70B
Nakinilerak L 46B
Nakonake R 69B, 70A
● Nakusp 17D
Nakusp Cr 17D
Nalachaga Mtn 71C
Nalau I 22C
Nalbeelah Cr 45C
Nalmet L 8B
Naltesby L 38A
Namu 22C
Namu L 22C
● Nanaimo 2D
Nanaimo Ls 2D, 3A
Nanaimo R 2D, 3A
Nancut 47C
Nancy Cr 66D
Nancy L 84C
Nangeese R 53C
Nanika L 35B
Nanika Mtn 45D
Nanika R 35B, 45D
Nanitsch L 54A
Nankai Pk 54D
Nanna L 47C
Nanoose Bay 2D
Nanoose Cr 2D, 3A
Nanoose Har 2D, 3A
Nanton 19D
Naramata 7A
Naramata Cr 7B
Narboe Cr 10A
Narcosli Cr 25B, 38D
Narcosli Creek 38D
Narraway R 49D, 50C
Narrow L 39A
Narrowgut Cr 1C, 11D
Narrows Cr 9A
Narrows In 2B
Nascall L 22B
Nascall R 22B, 35D
Nash Cr 16C
Nasoga Gulf 44A
Nasparti In 11D
Nass B 44A
Nass Camp 44B
Nass R 52B, 53A, 61D
Nasswald Pk 18B
Naswhito Cr 16C
Nata Cr 46A
Natadesleen L 60B, 61A
Nataga Cr 79D
Natal 10A
Natalkuz L 37A
Nataniko Cr 37B, 38A
Nation Ls 47A
Nation Pk 61B
Nation R 47B, 48A,
                54D, 55D, 56C
Natlan Cr 45B, 53D
Natlan Pk 53D
Natowite L 46B
Natsy L 25B
Natuza Cr 36D

Natuza L 36D
Naumulten Mtn 8A
Naver Cr 38B
Navy Chan 3B, 5C
Navy Cr 28D
Naysash In 11B, 22D
Nazcha Cr 71A
Nazko 38C
Nazko Falls 25A
Nazko L 25A
Nazko R 25A, 37D, 38C
Nechako R 37A, 38A,
               47D, 48C
Neck L 38D
Necleetsconnay R 23A
Necoslie R 47D
Neds Cr 16C
Neechanz R 23C
Needa L 26D
Needham Cr 56A
Needles 8A
Neekas In 22A
Negro Cr 9B
Nehatl Cr 5B
Nekite R 22D
Nelles Pk 69B, 70A
Nels Bight 11A
● Nelson 8B
Nelson Cr 52B
Nelson Forks 86D
Nelson I 2B
Nelson Kenny Cr 38D
Nelson Kenny L 38D
Nelson L 69B, 80D
Nelson R 44B
Nelway 8D
Nemaia Cr 24D
Nemaiah Valley 24D
Nemo Cr 8B
Nenahmail Lagoon 11B
Nep Pk 54A
Nepah Lagoon 12A
Nepean Sd 34C
Nepopekum Cr 6D
Neroutsos In 11D
Nesabut Pks 46B
Nesakwatch Cr 6C
Nesook B 1A
Ness L 38A, 48C
Nesoook B 1A
Ness L 38A, 48C
Ness, ... -
Netalzul Mtn 45B, 46A
Netson Cr 73B, 74A
Netson L 73B, 74A
Nettie Cr 10D
Nettle I 2C
Nevada Mtn 8D
Nevertouch L 7B
Neveu L 16C
Nevin Cr 40C
Nevis Cr 64B, 65A
New Aiyansh 44B
New Clew 31C
● New Denver 17D
New Hazelton 45B
New L 9B
New Moon L 62B, 63A
● New Westminster 5A
Newcastle Cr 12D
Newcombe Har 33D, 34A
Newcombe In 30D
Newcombe L 35B
Newcombe Pk 30D
Newgate 10C
Newton 5C
Newton Cr 6B
Next Cr 9C
Neyasri L 37C
Nez L 46D
Niagara Cr 26B, 39D
Niagara Mtn 70A
Nicholl L 48C
Nicholls Cr 28C

Nichols Cr 14A
Nicholson 18A
Nichyeskwa Cr 53D, 54C
Nicklen Cr 16D
Nicklen L 16D
Nickoll Pass 12A
Nicoamen R 15C
Nicola 15D
Nicola L 15D
Nicola R 15C, 16C
Nicolum Cr 6A
Nielsp Cr 47C
Nig Cr 66C
Nigei I 11B
Nikwikwaia Cr 16A
Nile Cr 2A, 3A
Nilkitkwa L 46A, 54C
Nilkitkwa R 53D, 54C
Niloil Cr 85C
Niloil L 84D, 85C
Nimbus Mtn 45C
Nimbus Mtn 70B
Nimmo B 12A
Nimpkish 12C
Nimpkish Heights 11D
Nimpkish L 11D, 12C
Nimpkish R 12C
Nimpo L 24A
Nimpo Lake 24A
Nina Cr 55C
Nina L 55C
Nine Mile Cr 45B
Nine Mile Cr 60A
Nine Mile Narrows 8B
93 Mile House 26C
Ningunsaw R 60D, 61C
Nipple Mtn 7B
Nisconlith Cr 16A
Nisconlith L 16A
Niska Ls 52D
Nissen Bight 11A
Nitaga Cr 38D
Niteal Cr 77C
Nithi Mtn 37A, 47C
Nithi R 37A
Nitinat 2D
Nitinat L 2C, 3C
Nitinat R 2C, 3A
Niven Pk 62D, 63C
Niven R 62D, 63C
Nixon Cr 2D, 3A
Nizi Cr 72B
Noaxe Cr 14B
Noble Mtn 33D, 34A
Nodales Chan 12D
Noeick R 23A
Noel Cr 14B
Noel Pk 59B
Nogan Cr 77C
Noisy Cr 17A
Noke Cr 9B
Nolaka Cr 39C
Nomans L 38D
Nomash R 1A, 12C
Nome Cr 82D
Nome L 82D
Nonda Cr 74B
Nooksack 5D
Noomst Cr 23A
Nooseseck R 22B, 23A
Noosgulch R 23A
Nooskulla Cr 36C
Nooskulla Pk 36C
Nootka 1A
Nootka I 1A, 1C
Nootka Sd 1A
Nootum R 22D
Noralee 46C
Norbury Ls 9B
Nordegg 29B
Nordquist L 85D
Nordschow Cr 23B

Norgate Cr 1A
Norge Cr 9D
Norman Cr 38A
Norman Wood Cr 28C
Norns Cr 8B
Norrie L 57D
Norrish Cr 4B, 5D
North Aitken Cr 66C
North Anzac R 48B
North Arm 26B, 39D
North Barrière L 16A, 27C
North Bend 6A
North Bentinck Arm 23A
North Blue R 27B
North Bonaparte 26D
North Broughton I 12A
North Burnt R 48B
North Cache Cr 57A
North Cr 14C
North Cr 71B, 72A
North Fork Pass 10A
North Galbraith Cr 10A
North Galiano 5C
North Hill 37D
North Horseshoe Gla 23D
North Klinaklini R 23D
North Kootenay Pass 10A
North Kwadacha R 64A
North Moyie R 9B
North Pass 11A, 22C
North Pender I 3D, 5C
North Pine 57B
North
   Seaskinnish Cr ... 44B, 52D
North Star Cr 39D
North Star Hill 9B
North Star Mtn 9C
North Tetsa R 75C
North Thompson R 16A,
                                  27B, 27C
● North Vancouver 5A
North White R 19C
Northeast Arm 17A
Northport 8D
Northwest Arm 46B
Nostetuko R 13B, 24D
Notch Hill 16B
Notch Pk 54B
Notchtop Pk 53B
Notsah Cr 65B
Nowish In 22A
Nowitka Mtn 9A
Noyse Cr 3C
Nuaitch Cr 15D
Nuchatlitz 1A
Nuchatlitz In 1C
Nude Cr 24C
Nugent Sd 11B
Nukko L 48C
Nukko Lake 48C
Nulki L 37B
Numas I 11B
Nuntzun L 38C
Nusash Cr 22B, 23A
Nusatsum R 23A
Nustlo Cr 84C
Nuthinaw Mtn 71A
Nutli L 36A
Nuttlude L 60B
Nyland L 38D

O

O'Connor L 11D
O'Connor R 79C
O'Donnel R 69B, 70A,
                                  80D, 81C
O'Dwyer Cr 53A
O'Ne-el Cr 46B
Oak Bay 3D
Oak Beck Cr 22B

Oak Harbor 4C
Oasis 8D
Obed 41B
Oblique Cr 82D
Obo L 62B, 63A, 73D, 74C
Obo R 63A
Obole Cr 75B, 76A
Observatory In 44A
Ocean Falls 22B
Ocean Grove 2A
Ocean Park 5C
Ochre Cr 18A
Ocock L 47D
Ocock R 47D
Octopus Cr 8A
Odayin Cr 75B, 76A
Odin Cr 17C
Oetata Cr 57D, 58C
Og L 18B
Ogden 14B
Ogden Chan .. 31B, 33B, 34A
Ogden Cr 54D
Ogilvie Cr 60D, 61C
Ogston L 47C
Oie L 26A
Okanagan Centre 16D
Okanagan Falls 7A
Okanagan L 7A, 16D
Okanagan Landing 16D
Okanagan Mission 7B
Okanagan Mtn 7A
Okanagan R 7C
Oke Cr 9D
Okeover In 2A, 13C
Okisollo Chan 13C
Okotoks 19B
Oksa Cr 60A
Oktwansh R 1A
Olalla 7C
Olalla Cr 7C
Olatine Cr 51A
Old Baldy 30B, 32C
Old Baldy Mtn 9B
Old Fort Mtn 46A
Old Fort Nelson 76B
Old Friend Mtn 48B
Old Glory Mtn 8C
Old Wives Mtn 50A
Olh Cr 52C
● Oliver 7C
Oliver Cr 27D
Oliver Cr 45A
Olivia Cr 10A
Olivine Cr 6B
Olivine Mtn 6B
Olsson Cr 48D
Omega Hill 50C
Omega Mtn 30A
Omineca Arm 55B
Omineca R 54A, 54D, 55C
Ominicetla Cr 54B
One Ace Mtn 83D
One Eye L 24C
One Island L 49B, 50A,
                                  57D, 58C
One L 25A
● 100 Mile House 26C
103 Mile L 26C
108 Mile L 26C
111 Mile Cr 26C
130 Mile L 26C
150 Mile House 26A
Onerka L 53D, 54C
Onion Cr 49B
Onion Cr 76B
Onion L 49D
Onyx Cr 16B
Oona L 47C
Oona River 43D
Ootischenia 8D
Ootla Cr 88C
Ootsa L 36A

Ootsa Lake 36B
Ootsanee L 36B
Open Bight 22D
Operator Mtn 62C
Opitsat 1D
Oppy Cr 36C
Oppy L 36C
Orcas 4C
Oregon Jack Cr 15C
Oregon L 84D, 85C
Orford B 13C
Orford R 13C
Orient 8C
Orion Cr 54B
Ormond Cr 47C
Ormond L 47C
Oroville 7D
Ortona Mtn 75C
Osborn R 57B, 58A, 66D
Oscar L 38B
Oscar Pass 22A
Oscar Pk 44B
Osgood Cr 13D
Oshinow L 1B
Osilinka R 54B, 55A
Oso 4D
Osoyoos 7D
Osoyoos L 7D
Ospika Arm 55B
Ospika R 55B, 64D
Osprey L 7A
Oswald B 34C
Otard Cr 30A, 32A
Otelsas Cr 74B
Otsi Cr 62C
Ottarasko Mtn 24C
Ottawa Cr 17D
Otter Chan 34D
Otter Cr 6B
Otter Cr 27D
Otter Cr 49C
Otter Cr 80D, 81C
Otter L 6B
Otter L 16D
Otter L 49C
Otter Pass 33D, 34C
Otter Point 3D
Ottertail R 18A
Otun R 30B, 32B, 42D
Ououkinsh In 11D
Ououkinsh R 11D
Outaanetdey L 77A
Outlet Cr 17C
Oval B 31B, 43D
Oval Bay 33A
Ovington Cr 49D
Ovis Cr 27A
Oweegee Cr 52A
Oweegee L 52A
Owen Bay 13C
Owen L 46C
Owens Pk 59B
Owikeno L 22D, 23C
Owl Cr 14D
Owl Cr 61C
Owlet Cr 61C
Owossitsa L 1A, 1C
Owyacumish Cr 35A
Oyama 16D
Oyama L 16D
Oyster B 2A
Oyster R 1B
Oyster River 2A

P

Pablo Cr 25B
Pachena B 2C
Pachena Pt 2C
Pacific Cr 28A
Pacific L 49C

Pacific Ocean 1C, 20C,
                            30A, 42C
Pack L 11B
Pack R 48A
Packhorse Pk 10C
Packsaddle Cr 40D
Paddy Cr 73D, 74C
Paddy L 70B
Paddy Pk 8B, 17D
Pagoda Pk 24C
Paint Pot Cr 56B
Paldi 2D
Palliser Pass 18B
Palliser R 18D, 19C
Palmer Cr 24A
Palmer Cr 28C
Palmer L 25A
Palmer L 80D, 81C
Pan Cr 37C
Panorama 18C
Panorama Cr 62C
Panorama Mtn 62C
Pantage Cr 38C
Pantage L 38C
Papoose L 39A
Paradise Cr 14A
Paradise L 7A
Paradise Pk 69B, 70A
Paradise Point 16B
Parallel Cr 82D, 83C
Pardonet Cr 56A
Pardonet Hill 56A
Park Cr 17A, 28C
Park Mtn 17C
Park Rill 7C
Park Siding 8D
Parkdale 5A
Parker Cr 76D
Parker L 26A
Parkers Cr 9A
Parkland 57D
Parksville 2D
Parminter Cr 26A
Parrott Cr 46C
Parrott Ls 46C
Parry Pass 32A, 42C
Parsnip R 48B, 49C
Parsnip Reach 48A, 56C
Parson 18A
Parsons Cr 2C, 3A
Parting Ls 26C
Parton R 79C
Partridge Cr 82C
Partridge L 80C
Partridge R 79D
Pasayten R 6D
Pashleth Cr 23C
Pashleth Gla 23C
Paska L 15D
Pass Cr 8C
Passby Cr 45B
Passmore 8B
Pasulko L 15C
Pat Cr 27D
Patcha Cr 53B, 54A
Paterson 8D
Paterson L 12D
Patmore Cr 59D
Patricia B 3D, 5C
Patricia L 26D
Patry Cr 86D, 87C
Patry L .. 75B, 76A, 86D, 87C
Patterson L 24C
Pattinson L 7A, 16C
Pattinson Pk 55B, 56A
Paul Cr 7C
Paul Cr 16A
Paul L 16A
Paul R 64A
Paula Cr 46B
Pavilion 15A
Pavilion Cr 15A

Pavilion L 15A
Paw Cr 52D
Payne Cr 17D
Peace R 57A, 58A
Peace Reach 55B, 56A
Peachland 7A
Peachland L 7A
Peacock Cr 46C
Pearl L 1B
Pearse Canal 43B, 44A
Pearse I 43B, 44A
Pearson Pk 49D
Peason Cr 7B
Peavine Cr 9B
Peavine Cr 58C
Pebble Cr 14A
Peck Cr 56D
Peculiar L 48C
Peel I 11B
Peel In 30D
Peeve Cr 6D
Peffer Cr 66A
Pefferle L 7A, 16C
Peggy Pk 54A
Pekisko 19D
Pelican 68C
Pelican L 37D, 38C
Pelly Cr 63D
Pelly L 63D
Pelly Pk 63D
○ Pemberton 14C
Pemberton B 34C
Pemberton I 16A
Pement L 16A
Pend Oreille R 8D
Pendant Cr 59C
Pendant Gla 59B
Pender Har 2B
Pender Island 5C
Pendleton B 46D
Pendrell Sd 13C
Penfold Cr 39D
Pennask Cr 7A
Pennask L 7A, 16C
Pennask Mtn. 7A
Pennie L 15B
Penny 39A
Penrose I 22D
Penteuch Pass 35B
● Penticton 7A
Penticton Cr 7B
Pentreath Cr 75D, 76C
Peridotite Cr 14B
Perkins Pk 24C
Perpendicular Mtn 12A
Perry B 3D
Perry Cr 9B
Perry Cr 17C
Perry Cr 49A
Perry R 1A
Perry R 16B
Perrys 8B
Perseverance Mtn 40A
Pesh Cr 77B
Pesika Cr 64C
Pesika Mtn 64C
Peter Aleck Cr 46C
Peter Cr 8C
Peter Hope L 16C
Peters Cr 39C
Peters L 17C
Petersburg 59D
Peterson Cr 16A
Peteyaz Pk 53B, 54A
Petitot R 88C, 88D
Petrel Chan 33D, 34A
Petrie Cr 64B, 65A
Phacops Mtn 60A
Phair Cr 14D
Phelix Cr 14D
Pheno Mtn 60C
Phililloo L 26C

Philip Cr 47B, 48A
Philip Ls 47B, 48A
Phillips Arm 12D
Phillips Cr 1B
Phillips Cr 10C
Phillips L 12D
Phillips L 16A
Phillips R 13C
Phoenix 8C
Pickell Cr 66C
Pickle L 84C
Pierre Cr 46D
Piers I 3D, 5C
Pike L 69B, 70A
Pike R 69B, 70A, 80D, 81C
Pillar L 16C
Pillar Pk 45C
Pillman Cr 69B, 70A
Pilot Cr 62D, 63C
Piltz Pk 25C
Pimainus Cr 15C
Pimainus Ls 15D
Pimpernel Cr 45D, 46C
Pimpernel Mtn 45D, 46C
Pinantan L 16A
Pinantan Lake 16A
Pinaus L 16C
Pincher Creek 10B
Pinchi 47C
Pinchi L 47D
Pinchi Mtn 47C
Pincut Cr 46D
Pincut L 46D
Pinder Pk 12D
Pine Cr 45B
Pine Cr 80D, 81C
Pine R 56D
Pine Valley 56D
Pinecone Cr 5B
Pinecone L 5B
Pinenut Cr 53D
Pinetree L 72A
Pingel Cr 57B
Pingston Cr 17C
Pingston L 17A
Pink Mountain 65D
Pink Mtn 65D
Pinkerton Pk 39A
Pinnacle Cr 18A
Piper R 22D, 23C
Pipestem In 2C
Pisima Mtn 16B
Pitka Cr 47C
Pitka Mtn 47C
Pitman R 62A, 73C
Pitoney Cr 38B
Pitoney L 38B
Pitt I 33D, 34A
Pitt L 4A, 5B
Pitt Meadows 5D
Pitt R 4A, 5B
Pitts Cr 18B
Pivot Mtn 30A, 32A, 42C
Pivot Pk 63D
Place L 26C
Placer Cr 6D
Plaid L 9A
Plant Cr 17C
Plate Cr 82D
Plate L 82D, 83C
Plateau Cr 80D, 81C
Plateau L 16C
Pleasant Camp 79C
Plug Cr 75C
Plughat Mtn 55C
Plumper Sd 3D, 5C
Pocahontas 41C
Pocketknife Cr 65A
Point Cr 56C
Point No Pt 3C
Point Roberts 5C
Poison Cove Cr 35C

Poison Cr 12D
Poison Cr 53A
Poison Mtn 53A
Polaris Cr 54B
Polebridge 10D
Police Cr 64C
Polley L 26A
Pomeroy Cr 39C
Pondosy L 35D, 36C
Pool Cr 17B
Pooley Cr 72B
Pooley I 22A, 35C
Poorman L 72B, 83D
Poplar Cr 17D
Poplar Cr 46C
Poplar Creek 17D
Poplar L 48C
Poquette L 39C
Porcher I 31B, 33B,
                   34A, 43D, 44C
Porcher In 31B, 33B, 34A
Porcher Pen 31B, 33A
Porcupine Cr 8D
Porcupine Cr 18A
Porcupine Cr 25D
Porcupine Cr 79D
Porcupine Gla 60C
Porcupine L 71B, 72A
Porcupine R 60C
Pork Cr 18C
Porky Cr 62C
Porphyry Cr 45B
Port Alberni 2C
Port Albion 1D
Port Alice 11D
Port Alworth 68D
Port Angeles 3D
Port Chilkoot 68B
Port Clements 30B
Port Coquitlam 5D
Port Douglas 5B
Port Edward 44C
Port Eliza 1C
Port Elizabeth 12A
Port Essington 44C
Port Hardy 11B
Port Harvey 12C
Port McNeill 11D
Port Mellon 5A
Port Moody 5D
Port Neville 12D
Port of Roosville 10C
Port Renfrew 2C
Port San Juan 3C
Port Simpson 43D
Port Simpson 43D, 44C
Port Stanley 4C
Port Stephens 33D, 34A
Port Townsend 4C
Portage Brûlé
    Rapids 84D, 85C
Portage Cr 56B
Portage L 49C
Portage Mtn 56D
Porteau 5A
Porter Cr 39C
Porthill 9C
Portland
    Canal 43B, 44A, 52C
Portland I 3D, 5C
Portland In 43B, 44A
Porto Rico 8B
Postern Mtn 28A, 41C
Postill L 7B, 16D
Pothole Cr 6B
Potlatch Cr 28A
Pouce Coupe 58C
Pouce Coupé R 58C
Pouce Cr 76D
Pounder Cr 51A
Poutang Cr 55B, 56A
Powder Cr 9A

Powder L 16A
Powell Cr 14A
Powell L 2B, 13D
Powell Pk 35A
Powell R 13D
Powell River 2A
Powers Cr 7A
Powles Cr 34D
Prairie 4D
Prairie L 71A
Prairie Mtn 63B
Prattle Cr 28D
Premier L 9B
Prescott I 33A, 43D
Prespatou Cr 66C
Pressy L 26D
Prevost I 3B, 5C
Price Cr 1B
Price I 21B
Primrose R 79D
Prince George 38B
Prince of Wales Reach 2B
Prince Rupert 44C
Prince Rupert Har ...33B,
                      43D, 44C
Princess Gla 23D
Princess Louisa In 13D
Princess Royal Chan 35C
Princess Royal I 21B, 34D
Princess Royal Reach ...13D
Principe Chan 33D, 34A
Princeton 6B
Principe Chan 33D, 34A
Pritchard 16A
Procter 9A
Procter L 10D
Progress 57D
Projectile Mtn 24C
Prophet R 64B, 65A, 76D
Prophet River 76D
Prospect Cr 15C
Prospect Lake 3D
Prospector Cr 55A
Prospector Cr 55A
Proulx L 81C
Prudential Mtn 62C
Prudhomme L 33B, 44C
Pryce Chan 13C
Pt. Grey 3B, 5C
Ptarmigan Cr 27B
Ptarmigan Cr 39B
Ptomaine Cr 40A
Pub Cr 8A
Puder Cr 64B
Puder Cr 65A
Pugh Cr 11A
Pukaist Cr 15C
Pukeashun Mtn 16B
Pulopit Pk 63A
Pulpit L 62B
Pulpit L 63A
Pulpit Pk 62B
Punch Bowl 6D
Punchaw 38A
Punchaw L 38A
Pundata Cr 39C
Punkutlaenkut Cr 24A
Punkutlaenkut L 24A
Puntataenkut Cr 38C
Puntataenkut L 38C
Puntchesakut L 38C
Punti L 24B
Puntledge 2A
Puntledge R 2A
Puntzi Cr 24A, 24B
Puntzi L 24B
Purden L 39A
Purvis L 46B
Putnam Cr 16D
Pye L 12D
Pyne L 34D

Pyper L 24B
Pyramid Bluff 62C
Pyramid Cr 27B
Pyramid Cr 72A
Pyramid Mtn 9A
Pyramid Mtn 72A
Pys Cr 57C

Q

Quaal R 34B
Quadra I 13C
Qualcho L 36D
Qualicum B 2A, 3A
Qualicum Beach 2B
Qualicum R 2A, 3A
Quarrie Cr 19C
Quarry B 2B
Quartcha Cr 22A
Quartz Cr 28D
Quartz Cr 39B
Quartz Cr 71B, 72A
Quartzite Cr 54D
Quartzrock Cr 72B
Quash Cr 60B, 61A
Quatam R 13C
Quathiaski Cove 13C
Quatlena R 22B
Quatse L 11D
Quatse R 11D
Quatsino 11D
Quatsino Sd 11C
Quattoon In 44C
Queen Bess Gla 13A
Queen Charlotte 30D
Queen Charlotte
    Chan 3B, 5A
Queen Charlotte Is 30A
Queen Charlotte
    Sd 11A, 21D
Queen Charlotte Str 11B
Queen Mary Cr 18D
Queens Bay 9A
Queens Reach 13D
Queens Sd 22C
Queest Cr 16B
Quenada Cr 54C
Quentin L 64A
Quenville Cr 15D
Quesnel 38D
Quesnel L ...26B, 27A, 39D
Quesnel R 26A, 38D
Quilchena 15D
Quilchena Cr 6B, 7A,
                        15D, 16C
Quill Cr 45A
Quiltanton L 15D
Quinn Cr 10A
Quinn L 26C
Quinsam L 1B
Quinsam R 1B
Quintette Mtn 49B

R

Rabbit Cr 10C
Rabbit R 73B, 74A, 84D, 85C
Race Rocks 3D
Racine Cr 80C
Racine L 80C
Racing R 75C
Racoon Cr 13D
Radium Hot Springs 18D
Radnor 19A
Radnor Cr 81C
Raffuse Cr 5A
Raft Cove 11C
Raft Mtn 27C
Raft R 27C
Raging R 11D

Rail Cr 26C
Rail L 26C
Railroad Cr 17C
Rainbow Cr 12A
Rainbow Cr 27D
Rainbow L 33B, 44C
Rainbow L 36D
Rainbow Ls 73C
Rainbow R 74C
Raleigh Cr 13B
Raleigh Gla 13B
Raley Cr 44D
Ralph R 1B
Ram Cr 75A
Ramage 16A
Ramillies Chan 5A
Ramose Cr 13B
Rampalo Cr 8A
Rampart Cr 6B
Ramsay Arm 13C
Ramsay I 20A
Ramsey I 25A
Ramsey Cr 36C
Ramsey Pk 36C
Ranch Cr 17D
Ranger Cr 62C
Rankine Is 20B
Rapid Cr 17D
Rapid R 72B
Rapid Roy Cr 81D
Rapids of the Drowned . 74B
Raspberry Cr 60B
Raspberry Cr 75B, 76A
Rat L 7A, 16C
Rat L 49B, 50A
Ratchford Cr 16B, 27D
Raush Gla 27A, 40C
Raush R 27A, 40C
Raven L 25B
Raven Mtn 51A, 60C
Ravenal Cr 55A, 64C
Ravenal Pk 63D
Rawlings L 16D
Rayfield R 15B, 26D
Raymond Pass 22A
Raymond Pk 79D
Raza I 13C
Raza Pass 13C
Razor Cr 24C
Razorback Mtn 24C
Read I 13C
Read Island 13C
Reco Mtn 8B
Reco Mtn 17D
Red Bluff L 34A
Red Canyon Cr 45A
Red Cr 7A
Red Cr 54A
Red Cr 57A
Red Crag 62D
Red Deer Cr 49D, 50C
Red L 15B
Red Pass 40D
Red R 73A, 84C
Red Ridge Pk 75C
Red Rock 38B
Red Rock Cr 38B
Red Rock L 38B
Redburn Cr 29C
Redding Cr 9A
Redfern Cr 26B
Redfern L 64B, 65A
Redfern Mtn 64B, 65A
Redfern Rapids 36D
Redfish Cr 82C
Redfish L 36C
Redonda Bay 13C
Redpot Cr 85D
Redrocky Cr 48D
Redrocky L 48D
Redslide Mtn 35B
Redstone 25A

Redtop Cr 46C
Redwater Cr 37D, 38C
Redwater L 37D
Redwillow R 49B, 50A
Reef I 31C
Reef Icefield 40D
Rees Cr 2A
Reflector L 27C
Refuge Cove 13C
Refuge L 60B, 61A
Reg Christie Cr 27D
Reid B 12A
Reid L 38A, 48C
Reid Lake 38A
Reienecker Cr 16B
Reimer Cr 64B, 65A
Reiseter Cr 45B, 46A
Reiswig 16D
Reiter Cr 17C
Relay Cr 14A
Relay Mtn 14A
Reliance Mtn 13A, 24C
Remac 8D
Remote Cr 23D
Remote Mtn 23D
Renata 8A
Rendell Cr 7B
Renfrew Cr 3C
Rennell Sd 30B, 32C
Renner L 25B
Rennison I 34D
Reno Mtn 8D
Renolds Cr 48B
Republic 7D
Resplendent Cr 40D
Resplendent Mtn 40D
Retreat Pass 12A
Return Chan 22A
● Revelstoke 17A
Rexford 10C
Rey Cr 15D
René L 57C
Rhone 7D
Rice Brook 28B
Rich Cr 37C
Richards Chan 11B
Richards Cr 64B, 65A
Richardson 4C
Richardson I 31C
Richfield Cr 46C
Richie Cr 27C
● Richmond 5C
Richmond Centre 5C
Richmond L 9A
Riddle Cr 7A
Ridgeway Cr 9D
Ridgeway L 63A
Ring Cr 5A
Ring Reid Cr 66B
Riondel 9A
Rioulx Cr 17C
Rioux L 26D
Ripley L 22A
Ripon I 22D
Ripple Mtn 8D
Ripple Pass 11B
Riske Cr 25D
Riske Creek 25D
Ritchie Cr 52B
Ritchie L 78D
Rithet Cr 3D
River Bight 34D
River Jordan 3C
River L 66A
River Ls 15A
Rivers In 22D
Rivers Inlet 22D
Rivers L 26C
Rivers Pk 36C
Riverside Mtn 19C
R N Mtn 61C
Roan Horse Cr 65B

Roaring Cr 39C
Roaring R 26B, 39D
Robbins Cr 16C
Robert Arm 22D
Roberts Creek 5A
Roberts L 12D
Roberts Pk 39D
Robertson Cr 15A
Robertson Cr 65D
Robinson Cr 7A
Robinson Cr 48A
Robson 8B
Robson Bight 12C
Robson Cr 35D
Robson Pass 40D
Robson R 40D
Roche Cr 10D
Roche Harbor 4C
Roche L 16C
Rochester Cr 61D
Rock Bay 13C
Rock Cr 7D
Rock Creek 7D
Rock L 18B
Rockbluff L 9B
Rocky Pk 63B
Roderick I 22A, 35C
Roderick L 22A
Rododendron Cr 75A
Roe Lake 26D
Roger L 26D
Rogers Cr 14D
Rogers Ls 85C
Rogers Pass 28D
Rolla 58C
Rolla Cr 57D, 58C
Rollie Cr 39C
Ronning Cr 11C
Roosville 10C
Rory Cr 18C
Rosario 5C
Roscoe In 22A
Roscoe L 15D
Rose In 20B
Rose L 26A
Rose Pass 9A
Rose Prairie 57B
Rose Spit 32B, 43C
Rosebery 17D
Rosedale 6C
Roseland Cr 57B
Rosella Cr 83D
Rosen L 10A
Rosewall Cr 2A
Rosita L 25A
Ross Cr 16B
Ross Cr 24B, 25A
Ross Cr 71D, 72C
Ross L 25B
Ross Moore L 15D
Ross R 62A
Ross Spur 8D
Rossé L 24D
● Rossland 8D
Rostrum Pk 28D
Rothwell Pk 79D
Rottacker Cr 47A, 55C
Rough B 11D
Rough Cr 3C
Round L 16D
Round L 26D
Round Mtn 60B, 61A
Round Prairie 19C
Rowland Cr 12C
Roy L 32A
Royal Oak 3D
Royal Roads 3D
Royston 2A
Rubi Cr 6A
Ruby Cr 4B
Ruby Cr 80D, 81C
Ruby Creek 6A

Ruby L 2B
Rubyred Cr 64C
Rubyrock Cr 46D
Rubyrock L 47C
Ruddock Cr 27D
Ruddy Cr 56B
Rudolf B 21B
Rugged Mtn 1A, 12C
Rugged Mtn 60A
Rumble Beach 11D
Rupert Cr 80D
Rupert In 11D
Ruric Cr 38D
Rush Cr 2D, 3A
Rush L 16C
Ruskin 5D
Russel Cr 63D
Russell Cr 9C
Russian Cr 39C
Ruth Cr 26B
Ruth L 26D
Ruth L 70B
Rutherford Cr 14C
Ryan R 14C
Rycroft 58D
Rykerts 9C

S

● Saanich 3D
Saanich In 3D, 5C
Saar Cr 5D
Sabina L 36B
Sabine Chan 2B
Sable Cr 17B
Sachs Cr 31C, 32D
Saddle Mtn 60C
Sadie Cr 2D, 3A
Safety Cove 22C
Sagar L 22A
Sage Cr 10D
Sahcho Cr 77B
Sahdoanah Cr 77B, 88C
Saiya Cr 54A
Saiya L 54A
Sakeniche R 46B
Sakinaw L 2B
Sakumtha Pass 36C
Sakumtha R 36C
Saladamis Cr 52B
Salahagen Cr 35D, 36C
Salal Cr 14A
Salient Cr 35D, 36C
Salix Cr 53B, 54A
Salloomt R 23A
Sally Cr 8A
Sallysout Cr 53A
Salmo 8D
Salmo R 8D
Salmon Arm 12A
Salmon Arm 16B
● Salmon Arm 16B
Salmon Chan 12A
Salmon Gla 52A
Salmon In 2B, 5A
Salmon L 16C
Salmon L 47B, 48A
Salmon R 1B, 12D
Salmon R 16C
Salmon R ... 47B, 48A, 48C
Salmon R 52C
Salmon Valley 48D
Saloon L 71C
Salt Cr 57D
Salt Lagoon 31B, 33B,
                          34A, 43D
Salter L 33D, 34A
Saltery Bay 2B
Saltspring I 3B, 5C
Sam Green Cr 53C

Samatosum Mtn 16A
Sambo Cr 84C
Samotua R 70D
San Jose R 26A
San Josef 11C
San Josef R 11A
San Joseph B 11C
San Juan R 2D, 3C, 3D
Sanabar Cr 62A
Sanca 9A
Sanca Cr 9A
Sand Cr 8C
Sand Cr 10A
Sand L 10A
Sand L 44B
Sandell L 22D
Sandell R 22D
Sandford I 2C
Sandifer Pk 35B
Sandilands ! 30D, 32D
Sandner Cr 8C
Sandon 8B
Sandpile Cr 73A
Sandpile Ls 73A
Sandspit 31C
Sandwich 2A
Sandy Cr 86D, 87C
Sandy L 39D
Sandy Point 16B
Sangan R 31A, 32B
Sangrida Pk 8A
Sangster I 2B
Sansixmor Cr 53C
Sanskisoot Cr 52B
Sansum Nrs 3B, 5C
Sanyam Cr 52B
Sapeye L 24C
Sarah I 22A, 35C
Saratoga Beach 2A
Sardine Cr 38D
Sardis 6C
Sarita 2C
Sarita L 2C
Sarita R 2C
Sartine I 11C
Saskatoon Cr 57D
Saskum L 27C
Saskum Mtn 16A, 27C
Sass Cr 65B
Satah Mtn 24A
Satellite Chan 3D, 5C
Satsalla R 12B
Saturna 5C
Saturna I 5C
Saunders Cr 63A
Saunier Cr 7B
Savary I 2A
Savary Island 2A
Savio Mtn 75C
Savona 15B
Saw Cr 39A
Sawmill Cr 6A
Sawyer Cr 9A
Saxon Cr 50C
Saxton Cr 48C
Saxton L 38A, 48C
Sayward 2D
Scaffold Cr 75A
Scallon Cr 25C
Scallon Cr 45D
Scallop Mtn 54A
Scar Cr 13A
Scarcity Mtn 63B
Scarp Mtn 28A
Scatter R 86C
Schaft Cr 60B
Schoen Cr 12C
Schoen L 12C
Schooler Cr 56B
Schulbuckhand Cr 45C
Schwarzenberg Lagoon 11B
Scimitar Cr 24C

Scimitar Gla 24C
Scoop L 73B
Scot Cr 15B
Scotch Cr 16B
Scotch Creek 16B
Scotia R 44C
Scott Chan 11A, 11C
Scott Cr 52A
Scott Cr 55D, 56C
Scott L 57D
Scottie Cr 15A
Scovil Cr 48A
Screw Cr 82C
Scrip Cr 27D
Scud Gla 60C
Scud R 60C
Scudamore Cr 14D
Scum L 25C
Scuzzy Cr 6A
Scuzzy Mtn 6A
Sea I 4A, 5C
Sea Lion Pk 36C
Sea Otter Cove 11C
Sea Otter Group 11A
Seabird L 12D
Seaford 13C
Seaforth Chan 22A
Seal In 30B, 32C
Seaside Park 5A
Seaskinnish Cr 44B
Sebalhall Cr 1A
● Sechelt 2B
Sechelt Cr 5A
Sechelt In 2B
Sechelt Pen 2B
Second Nrs 23C
Secret Cove 2B
Section Mtn 80D, 81C
Security In 30D
Secus Mtn 49D, 50C
Sedan Cr 45A
Sedgwick B 20A
Sediesh Cr 53D
Sedro Woolley 4D
Seebe 19A
Seeds Cr 65A, 76C
Seel L 35B
Seguthooth Cr 71A
Sekiu 3C
Selish Mtn 6B, 15D
Seller Cr 26A, 39C
Seltat Cr 79C
Seltat Pk 79D
Selwyn Cr 55D, 56C
Selwyn In 31C
Senio Mtn 75C
Sentinel Mtn 80D, 81C
Sentinel Pk 49A
Sentry Mtn 28D
Septimus Cr 57B
Serac Cr 18B
Serb Cr 45B
Serpentine Cr 27B
Serreted Pik 63C
Seshal Cr 13D
Seton L 14B
Seton Portage 14B
Settea Cr 72D
Seven Mile Corner 58D
Seven Mile Cr 56D
Seven Sisters 45A
70 Mile House 26C
Severide Cr 17C
Sewall 30B
Sewell In 31C
Sewell Inlet 31C
Sexsmith 58D
Seymour Arm 16B
Seymour Arm 16B
Seymour Cr 28C
Seymour In 11B, 12A
Seymour L 4A, 5A

Seymour L 45B
Seymour Nrs 12D
Seymour R 4A, 5A
Seymour R 12A, 23C
Seymour R 16B, 27D
Shadwell Pass 11A
Shag Cr 37C
Shakan Cr 15C
Shakatah Cr 71A
Shaker Cr 80D, 81C
Shaker L 80D, 81C
Shakes Cr 60A
Shalalth 14B
Shames Cr 44D
Shana Cr 70A
Shandalope Cr 53A
Shangweshi Cr 56D
Shanley L 47D
Shannon Bay 30B
Shannon Cr 17D
Shannon L 12D
Shanoss Cr 52B
Sharktooth Mtn 73C
Sharpe L 15B, 26D
Shaslomal Cr 53A
Shass Mtn 47C
Shatford Cr 7A
Shaw Cr 2D, 3A
Shaw Cr 9C
Shaw Cr 84D, 85C
Shawatum 6D
Shawl B 12A
Shawnigan Lake 5C
Shazah Cr 69B, 70A
Shea L 6B
Shearer Dale 58A
Shedin Cr 53D
Sheemahant R 23C
Sheep Cr 8D
Sheep Cr 72B
Sheep L 8C
Sheep Pass 35C
Shegisic Cr 53D
Shegunia R 45B, 53D
Shekilie R 77B, 88D
Sheladamus Cr 53A
Shelagyote Pk 53D
Shelagyote R 53D, 54C
Shell Cr 25B
Shelley 38B
Shelley L 15B
Shelter B 11B
Shelter Bay 17C
Shelter In 1A
Shelter Point 2A
Shelton L 2D, 3A
Shenismike Cr 53D
Shepherd Cr 1B
Shepp Cr 10C
Sheppard Pk 59B
Sheraton Cr 46D
Sheridan Cr 25B
Sheridan L 26D
Sheslay R 70D
Shields I 30B, 32C
Shiko L 26A
Shilahou Cr 53A
Shingle Cr 7A
Shingle Creek 7A
Shinish Cr 7A
Shirley 3D
Shoal L 55D
Shonektaw Cr 71A, 82C
Shoreacres 8B
Shoreholme 17C
Shorts Cr 16C
Shotgun Cr 37A
Shotnana L 10C
Shovel Cr 47C
Shovel Cr 55A
Shovelnose Mtn 6B
Showel Cr 47C

Shrimpton Cr 6B
Shroud Mtn 44D
Shulaps Cr 14B
Shumal R 44B
Shumway L 16C
Shush Cr 76B
Shushartie Mtn 11A
Shushartie R 11A
Shuswap 18D
Shuswap Cr 18D
Shuswap Falls 16D
Shuswap L 16B
Shuswap R 16D, 17C
Shutty Bench 18C
Sialun Cr 32A, 42C
Sibley Cr 27D
Sicamous 16B
Sicamous Cr 16B
Sicily L 26D
Sicily Mtn 75C
Sicintine R 53A
Sidenius Cr 64D, 65C
Sidina Mtn 53D
Sidney 5C
Sidney Cr 46B
Sidney I 3D, 5C
Sifton Pass 63B
Sigutlat Cr 36D
Sigutlat L 36C
Sihun Cr 1B
Sikanni Chief 65D
Sikanni Chief R 64D, 65B,
                      65C, 77C
Silence L 27C
Silent L 25B
Silica 8D
Silt Cr 18D
Silt L 79D
Silver Cr 16D
Silver Cr 54C
Silver Creek 6A
Silver Creek 16D
Silver L 6C
Silver Ls 66A
Silver Mtn 17D
Silver Salmon R 70A
Silver Star Mtn 16D
Silver Valley 58B
Silverado Cr 1A
Silverhope Cr 6C
Silverthrone Mtn 23D
Silvertip Cr 17B
Silvertip Mtn 6C
Silverton 8B
Silverton Cr 8B
Simem Cr 7A
Similk Beach 4C
Similkameen R 6D, 7C
Simma Cr 51A
Simma Mtn 51A
Simmons L 12D
Simmons L 72A
Simonds Group 22C
Simoom Sound 12A
Simpson Cr 69B, 70A
Simpson L 34B
Simpson L 69B, 70A
Simpson Pass 18B
Simpson Pk 82C
Simpson R 18B
Simpson Ranch 56B
Sims Cr 13D
Sinawa Eddy Mtn 70B
Sinclair Mills 49C
Sinkut L 37B
Sinkut Mtn 37B
Sinkut R 37B
Sinmax Cr 16A
Sinta Cr 46B, 54D
Sinwa Cr 70A
Sinwa Mtn 69B, 70A

Siphon Cr 57B, 58A
Sirdar 9C
Siska Cr 15C
Sitchiada Mtn 54A
Sitkum Cr 8B
Sitkum Cr 17C
Sitkum L 17C
Sitlika Cr 54D
Sittakanay Gla 70C
Sittakanay Mtn 69D, 70C
Sittakanay R 69D, 70C
Siwash B 12D
Siwash Cr 6A
Siwash Cr 6B
Siwash L 7A
Siwash Mtn 8B
Siwash Rock Mtn 16C
Siwhe Cr 15C
Siwhe Mtn 15C
Six Mile Cr 56C
Six Mile Point 16B
Sixtyone Cr 15A
Skaat Har 20A
Skady Mtn 62A
Skagit R 6D
Skagway 80C
Skagway R 80C
Skaha L 7A
Skaist Mtn 6D
Skaist R 6D
Skedans 31C
Skeena R 44D, 45A,
                      53B, 53C
Skelhorne Cr 62C
Skelton L 25B
Skelu B 30B, 32C
Skidegate 30D
Skidegate Chan 30D,
                      32C, 32D
Skidegate In 30D, 32D
Skidegate L 31C, 32D
Skidegate Mission 31C
Skihist Mtn 15C
Skim L 2B
Skimikin L 16B
Skincuttle In 20A
Skins Cr 36B
Skmana L 16A
Skonun R 30B, 32B
Skookum Cr 5A
Skookum L 15B
Skookumchuck 9B
Skookumchuck Cr 9B, 18D
Skookumchuck Mtn 9A
Skowill Cr 52B, 61D
Skowootum Cr 16A
Skowquiltz R 22B, 35D
Skuhun Cr 15D
Skull Cr 15B, 16A
Skundale L 30B, 32C
Skunk L 55D
Skwawka R 13D
Skwim L 13D
Slamgeesh R 53A
Slate Cr 71B, 72A
Slave Cr 77C
Sleigh Cr 85D
Slender L 48C
Slesse Cr 6C
Slesse Mtn 4B, 6C
Sliammon 2A
Sliammon L 2A
Slick Cr 15B
Slim Cr 14A
Slim Cr 39A
Slim L 39A
Slim R 12B
Slingsby Chan 11B
Slocan 8B
Slocan L 8B, 17D
Slocan Park 8B
Slocan R 8B

Slok Cr 15A
Sloko L 69B, 70A
Sloko R 69B, 70A
Slollicum Pk 4B, 6A
Sloquet Cr 5B
Slousiska Cr 22B
Slowmaldo Cr 53A
Slowmaldo Mtn 53A, 62C
Smaby Cr 35D
Small Cr 40D
Smanit Cr 13D
Smart R 82C
Smelter Ls 6B
Smith Cr 7A
Smith Cr 37A
Smith I 33B, 43D, 44C
Smith In 11B, 22D
Smith R 85C
Smith River 85C
Smith Sd 11A
● Smithers 46A
Smithers Landing 46A
Smitley R 23A
Smoke Cr 27B
Smoke Mtn 35B
Smokehouse Cr 11B,
                      12A, 23C
Smyth Cone 12B
Smyth Cr 17C
Snake Cr 75A
Snake L 36A
Snake R 76B
Snake River 76B
Snaking R 38C
Snass Cr 6D
Snass Mtn 6D
Snehumption Cr 7C
Snippaker Cr 51B
Snippaker Mtn 51B, 60D
Snohoosh L 15B
Snow Cr 8B
Snow Dome 28B
Snow Pk 71D, 72C
Snowball Cr 8C
Snowbank Cr 61C
Snowcap Cr 5B
Snowcap L 5B
Snowdon Cr 81D
Snowdrift Cr 72D
Snowfall Cr 77D
Snowshoe Cr 39B
Snowside Mtn 23A
Snowtop Mtn 69A
Snowtop Pk 64C
Snowy Mtn 7C
Snyder Cr 66C
Soards Cr 27B
Sob L 37B, 38A
Sock L 27C
Soda Cr 25B
Soda Creek 25B
Soda L 26C
Sointula 11D
Soles Cr 18A
Solitary L 73A
Solo Cr 54B
Solsqua 16B
Sombrio Pt 3C
Sombrio R 3C
Somerville I 43B, 44A
Songhees Cr 11B
Sonora I 13C
Soo R 14C
Sooke 3D
Sooke Basin 3D
Sooke In 3D
Sooke L 3D
Sooke R 3D
Sorcerer Cr 28C
Sorcerer Mtn 28C
Sorrento 16B
South Anahim Cr 25A

South Barrière L 16A
South Bentinck Arm 23A
South Canoe 16B
South Cr 14C
South Cr 36C
South Cranberry Cr 17A
South Fosthall Cr 17C
South French Bar Cr 14B
South Gataga R ... 63B, 74D
South Germansen R 55C
South Hawks Cr 25B
South Hazelton 45B
South Kootenay Pass ... 10D
South Nanaimo R 2D, 3A
South Pass 11A
South Pass Pk 53B, 62D,
                      63C
South Pender 5C
South Pender I 5C
South Redwillow R 49B, 50A
South Riske Cr 25D
South Salmo R 8D
South Shekilie R 77B
South Slocan 8B
South Thompson R 16A
South Unuk R 51B, 52A
Southbank 46D
Southgate R 13A
Sovereign Cr 39C
Sovereign Mtn 39C
Sowaqua Cr 6B
Sowchea Cr 47C
Sowsap Cr 16D
Spa Cr 16D
Spa L 16D
Spacwaniko Cr 49C
Spahats Cr 27C
Spahomin Cr 16C
Spahomin L 16C
Spaist Mtn 15D
Spallumcheen L 16D
Spanish Cr 26A
Spanish Cr 26B, 27A
Spanish L 16D
Spanish L 26A
Spanish Mtn 26A
Spapilem Cr 16A
Sparkling Cr 33B, 34A
● Sparwood 10A
Spatsizi R 61D, 62A
Spatsum 15C
Spawning L 54B
Specs Ls 16D
Spectacle Ls 39C
Spectre Pk 63B
Spectrum Cr 17C
Specularite L 46D
Spence Cr 31A, 32B
Spences Bridge 15C
Spey Cr 38B
Sphaler Cr 60C
Sphinx Cr 72A
Sphinx Mtn 9A
Sphinx Mtn 72A
Spicer I 31B, 33D
Spider I 22C
Spike Mtn 72A
Spiked Pk 62B, 63A
Spiller Chan 22A
Spiller In 22A
Spillimacheen 18A
Spillimacheen R 17B, 18A
Spillman Cr 16A
Spinel Cr 63A
Spinel L 63A
Spirit River 58D
Spittal Cr 40D
Spius Cr 6B, 15D
Splinter Hill 24D
Split Cr 7B
Split Cr 29C
Split Pk 18B

Split Top Mtn 74C
Spokin L 26A
Sprague Cr 16A
Spring Cr 83D
Spring House 25D
Spring L 26C
Spring Mtn 38B
Springer Cr 8B
Sproat L 2C
Sproat Lake 2C
Sproule Cr 8B
Spruce Cr 14D
Spruce Cr 39A
Spruce Cr 80D, 81C
Spruce Hill 62A
Spruce L 14A
Spuzzum 6A
Spuzzum Cr 6A
Squalicum L 2C
Squally Chan 34D
● Squamish 5A
Squamish R 5A, 14C
Square L 36B
Squaw Cr 10A
Squaw Fish L 36B
Squaw Mtn 49B, 50A
Squawk L 26A
Squiness L 36D
Squingula R 53B, 54A
Squirrel Cove 13C
St. Annes Cr 8A
St. Eugene Mission 9B
St. George Cr 38A
St. Ives 16B
St. John Cr 57B
St. Julien Cr 27A
St. Leon Cr 17D
St. Mary L 9A
St. Mary R 9A, 9B
St. Thomas B 35B, 36A
St. Thomas R 36A
Stafford L 12B
Stafford R 12B
Stagleap Cr 8D
Stagnant Gla 64A
Stagoo Cr 44A
Stakawus Cr 13D
Staki B 20A
Stalk Ls 62D
Stalk Pk 62C
Stamp R 2A
Standard Cr 28C
Stanislas Cr 87D
Stanley 39C
Stanley Cr 79C
Stanley Pk 18B
Stanner Cr 85D
Stanolind Cr 76A
Stanwood 4D
Star Cr 17C
Star Cr 44B
Star L 27C
Starbird Gla 18C
Stark Cr 18C
Starlike L 26A
Starr Cr 45D
Starvation Cr 10D
State Cr 7B
Statlu Cr 4B, 5B
Staubert L 17B
Stave Falls 5D
Stave L 4B, 5B
Stave R 5B
Stawamus R 5A
Steamboat Cr 75B, 76A
Steamboat Mtn 75B, 76A
Steamer Pass 43B, 44A
Steele Cr 12C
Steele L 48C
Steep Canyon Cr 53C
Steeple Mtn 9C
Steeprock Cr 50A

Steffens Cr 15D
Stein Mtn 15C
Stein R 15C
Stelkuz Cr 63D
Stelkuz L 63D
Stella L 12D
Stenstrom Cr 45A
Stephen L 39A
Stephen Pk 53A
Stephens I 33A, 43D
Stephens Pass 2B
Stephney Cr 17B
Stepp L 35B, 45D
Sterling Cr 44B
Stern Cr 47C
Stern L 47C
Steven Cr 7A
Stevens Cr 17B
Stevens Ls 16C
Stevens Ls 27C
Stevenson 5C
Steward Cr 45C
Stewardson In 1A
Stewardson Inlet 1A
● Stewart 52C
Stewart Cr 57C
Stikelan Cr 24D
Stikine R 51A, 60A, 60C,
          61B, 62A, 62C, 71D, 72C
Stillwater 2B
Stirling Cr 7B
Stirling I 22C
Stitt Cr 28C
Stobart Cr 25D
Stockdale Cr 18C
Stocke Cr 5B
Stoddart Cr 18D
Stoddart Cr 57A
Stone Cr 38B
Stone Cr 57C
Stone Mtn 75A
Stonehouse Cr 79C
Stoner 38D
Stony Cr 37B
Stony L 39A
Stony L 49B
Stopper Is 1D
Storie Cr 57D
Stork Cr 19C
Storm Cr 10C
Storm Hill 7D
Storm Mtn 18B
Stormking Cr 27A
Stovel Pk 80D
Stoyoma Cr 6A
Stoyoma Mtn 6A, 15C
Strachan B 11B
Straight Pass Cr 63A
Strait Cr 27A
Strait L 26C
Strait L 27B
Strait of Georgia . 2A, 3B, 5C
Stranby R 11A
Strange I 1A
Stranger L 26B, 27A
Strata Cr 60A
Strata Mtn 60A
Strathnaver 38D
Stratton Cr 27C
Streak L 16D
Strohn Cr 52B
Strutell Cr 8A, 17C
Stryen Cr 15C
Stryker 10C
Stuart Chan 2D, 3B
Stuart Island 13C
Stuart L 47C
Stuart R 47D, 48C
Stuhini Cr 69D
Stuie 23B
Stukemapten L 16B, 27D
Stum L 25A

Stump L 15D
Stupendous Mtn 23B
Sturdee R 62D, 63C
Styx Gla 13B
Success Cr 23D
Succour L 63B
Sucha Cr 37D
Sucha L 37D
Suck Cr 18C
Sucker Cr 24A
Sucker Cr 26A
Sucker L 16C
Sucker L 24A
Sucker L 26C
Sucwoa R 1A
Sue Chan 34B
Suey L 26B
Sugar Cr 17C
Sugar L 17C
Sugarbowl Mtn 39A
Sugarcane 26A
Sugarloaf Mtn 15D
Suhm Cr 88C
Suka Cr 6A
Sukunka R 49A, 57C
Sullivan Hill 9B
Sullivan L 16A
Sullivan R 28C
Sulphur Cr 10A
Sulphur Cr 74B
Sulphurets Cr 51B, 52A
Sulphurous L 26D
Sumallo R 6C
Sumas Mtn 4B, 5D
Sumas R 4B, 5D
Summer L 9B
● Summerland 7A
Summers Cr 6B
Summit Cr 9C
Summit Cr 39C
Summit L 17D
Summit L 48D
Summit L 75C
Summit L 80C
Summit Lake 48D
Summit Pass 73C
Summit Pass 75C
Summit Pk 17D
Sumquolt Cr 23C
Sunday Cr 6D
Sunday In 20A
Sunday Pk 80D
Sundberg L 39C
Sunderland Chan 12D
Sundown Cr 9D
Sundown Cr 57D
Sunnybrae 16B
Sunrise Cr 9D
Sunrise Valley 57D
Sunset Cr 27D
Sunset Cr 57D
Sunset Mtn 8B
Sunset Prairie 57D
Sunsets Cr 45D
Sunshine L 84C
Superb Mtn 13A
Surel L 35B
Surf In 34D
Surge Narrows 13C
Surgeon Mtn 79D
Surprise 81C
Surprise Cr 18B
Surprise Cr 52B
Surprise L 80D, 81C
● Surrey 5C
Surrey L 15D
Survey B 31B, 33D, 34A
Survey Cr 30B, 32D
Survey Mtn 3D
Surveyors Cr 52B
Susan I 22A
Susap Cr 7C

Suschona Cr 47B
Suset L 46C
Susie Cr 60A
Suskwa Pass 45B, 46A,
                  53D, 54C
Suskwa R 45B, 46A, 54C
Sussex L 15D
Sustut L 54A
Sustut Pk 54A
Sustut R 53B, 54A, 63C
Sutherland Cr 8C
Sutherland R 47C
Sutil Chan 13C
Sutlahine R 70D
Sutlej Chan 12A
Sutslem Cr 35D
Sutton Cr 2D, 3A
Sutton R 52C
Suzanne L 10C
Suzannie L 25B
Swakum Mtn 15D
Swallop Cr 23A, 36C
Swalwell L 16D
Swamp L 48C
Swan Cr 28C
Swan L 16D
Swan L 52D
Swan L 58C
Swan L 82C
Swannell R 54B
Swanson Cr 37A
Swanson I 12C
Swanson R 69A, 80C
Swartz Bay 5C
Swede Cr 37B
Swede Cr 38B
Sweden Cr 38A
Sweeney L 35B
Sweetin R 53C
Sweetwater 57D
Swehaw Cr 8C
Swift Cr 8D
Swift Cr 40D
Swift L 82C
Swift R 39C
Swift R 81D, 82C
Swift River 82A
Swindle I 22A
Sydnew In 1A
Sydney R 1A
Sylvester Cr 47B
Sylvester Pk 72B
Symond Cr 18A
Syncline Mtn 10A
Syringa Cr 8A

T

T Mtn 59D
Table Cr 56B
Table Hill 31B, 33D, 34A
Table Mtn 62C
Table Mtn 80D, 81C
Table R 48B
Tabletop Cr 62D, 63C
Tabor Cr 38B
Tabor L 38B
Tacheeda Ls 48B
Tacheeda Mtn 48B
Tachick L 37B
Tachie R 47A
Tachilta L 71B
Tachintelachick Cr 38A
Tackek Cr 46B
Taft Cr 52B
Tagai L 37B, 38A
Tagetochlain L 35B, 36A,
                  45D, 48C
Taghum 8B
Taginchil L 48C
Tagish 80A

Tagish L 80D
Tahaetkun Mtn 16C
Taharti L 25A
Tahini R 79D
Tahla L 6B
Tahlo Cr 54C
Tahltan 71D
Tahltan L 60A, 71C
Tahltan R 60A, 71C
● Tahsis 1A
Tahsis In 1A
Tahsis Mtn 1A
Tahsis R 1A
Tahsish In 11D
Tahsish R 11D
Tahtsa L 35B
Tahtsa Reach 35B, 36A
Tahtsedle Cr 61D
Tahultzu L 37A
Tahumming Gla 13B
Tahumming Mtn 13B
Tahuntesko L 36C
Tahyesco R 23A, 36C
Taiataeszi Cr 36D
Taite Cr 8A
Taiya In 79D
Taiya R 79D
Takatoot L 47A
Takhini R 79D
Takia R 36C
Takla L 46B, 54D
Takla Landing 54D
Taku Arm 80C
Taku R 69D, 70C
Takush R 11B
Takysie L 36B
Takysie Lake 36B
Talaha B 80D, 81C
Talbot Cr 1B
Talchako Gla 23D
Talchako Mtn 23B
Talchako R 23B
Taleomey Gla 23C
Taleomey R 23A
Tally Cr 53A
Taltapin L 47C
Taltapin Mtn 47C
Talunkwan I 31C
Tam O'Shanter Cr 9A
Tamarack L 9B
Tamihi Cr 6C
Tan Mtn 30B, 32C
Tanah Cr 71A
Tandzie Cr 74B
Tangier R 17A, 28C
Tangle Cr 18B
Tangle Pk 18D
Tanglefoot Cr 9B
Tanilkul L 25A
Tanswanket Cr 36D
Tanu I 31C
Tanya Ls 36D
Tanzilla Butte 72C
Tanzilla R 71D, 72C
Taper Mtn 64C
Tappen 16B
Tarnezell Cr 47A
Tarnezell L 47A
Tarrys 8B
Tartu In 30B, 32C
Taseco R 14A
Taseko Ls 14A, 25C
Taseko R 24D, 25C
Taslincheko Cr 47B
Tasse L 26A
Tasu 30D
Tasu Sd 30D
Tata Creek 9B
Tatalaska L 36B, 46D
Tatalrose 46D
Tatchu Cr 1C

Tate Cr 57D, 58C
Tatelkuz L 37C
Tatelkuz Mtn 37C
Tatin L 47C
Tatisno Cr 84C
Tatisno Mtn 84C
Tatla Hill 24C
Tatla L 24C
Tatla Lake 24C
Tatla Lake Cr 24B
Tatlatui L 62D, 63C
Tatlatui Pk 62D
Tatlayoko 24D
Tatlayoko L 24D
Tatley Cr 18D
Tatogga L 60D, 61A
Tatsadah L 47D
Tatsamenie L 70D
Tatsatua Cr 70D
Tatshenshini R 78D, 79C
Tatsho Cr 71D, 72C
Tatsho Mtn 71D, 72C
Tatsutnai Cr 47C
Tatton 26C
Tatuk L 37B
Tatzille Cr 84C
Taurus 7D
Tautri Cr 25A
Tautri L 25A
Tavistock Gla 13B
Tavistock Mtn 13B
Taweel L 26D, 27C
Taweh Cr 60B
Tawina L 69B, 70A
Tay Cr 48D
Taylor 57B
Taylor Cr 14B
Taylor L 26C
Taylor Pk 62C
Taylor R 1D
Taylor R 52B, 61D
Taynton Cr 18C
Taysen Cr 70B
Tchaikazan R 13B
Tchentlo L 47A
Tchentsut Mtn 47A
Tchesinkut Cr 46D
Tchesinkut L 46D
Tchesinkut Lake 46D
Tchitin R 52D
Tea Cr 18C
Teakerne Arm 13C
Teapot L 38B
Teapot Mtn 48D
Teaquahan Mtn 13A
Teaquahan R 13A
Tedideech Cr 71A
Tedideech L 71A
Teditua Cr 70B
Teepee Cr 9D
Teepee Cr 80C
Teeta Cr 11D
Teeter Cr 85D
Teetzel Cr 9C
Teh Cr 82C
Tehran Pk 75C
Teigen Cr 61C
Teigen L 60D, 61D
Teklo Cr 77D
Telegraph Cove 12C
Telegraph Cr 23B
Telegraph Cr 80D, 81C
Telegraph Creek 60A
Telegraph
   Pass 33B, 34A, 44C
Telford Cr 10A
Telkwa 46A
Telkwa Pass 46B
Telkwa R 45D, 46C
Tellot Cr 24C
Tellot Gla 13A, 24C
Temapho L 24B

Temple Cr 65B
Templeton R 18A
Ten Mile Cr 56D
Ten Mile L 38D
Tenaka Cr 75D, 76C
Tenakini Cr 54B
Tenas Cr 14D
Tenas Cr 45D
Tenas L 23B
Tenderfoot Cr 17D
Tennent L 1B
Tenquille Cr 14C
Tentsi Cr 75C
Tepee Cr 49B
Tepee Cr 65B
Tepee Mtn 75B, 76A
Teresa I 80D, 81C
Terminus Mtn 73B, 74A
Terrace 45C
Terrace Cr 16C
Terrace Mtn 16C
Terraced Pk 7B
Terrahina Cr 81D
Terry Cr 38B
Tescla Cr 65B
Teseko Mtn 14A
Tesla L 36C
Teslin 81B
Teslin R 71A, 81D
Tetachuck L 36D
Tetachuck R 36B
Tete Hill 25C
Tetsa Pk 75C
Tetsa R 75C, 76C
Tête Angela Cr 25C
Tête Cr 40C
Tête Jaune Cache 40D
Thabah Mtn 48B, 56D
Thalia L 6B
Thane 69C
Thane Cr 54B
Thatue Mtn 61A
Thautil R 45D
The Bookworm 5A
The Elbow 65D
The Jaws 35A
The Knob 60C
The Lions 4A
The Monarch 18B
The Nipple 6A
The Old Settler 6A
The Pillar 62D, 63C
The Pinnacles 17C
The Red Pillar 1B
The Steeples 9B
The Thumb 54A
The Wart 6B
Thelwood Cr 1B
Thenatlodi Mtn 72C
Theodosia R 13C
Thetis I 2D, 3B
Thetlaandoa Cr 77A, 88C
Thibert Cr 71B, 72A
Thinahtea Cr 88D
Thinahtea L 88D
Third Nrs 23C
Thirty Mile Cr 81D
Thirty Mile L 71D, 72C
Thomas Cr 45C
Thomas Cr 60D, 61C
Thomas Pk 62D, 63C
Thompson Cr 46C
Thompson Pass 28B
Thompson R 15C

Thompson Sd 12B
Thompson Sound 12B
Thone Cr 7B
Thor Cr 17C
Thorald Cr 18D
Thormanby Is 2B, 3A
Thornbrough Chan ... 3B, 5A
Thorne L 63C
Thornhill 45C
Thorpe Cr 85D
Thorsen Cr 23A
Thorwald Cr 22B
Three Brothers Mtn 6D
Three Forks Cr 72B
3 Mile Cr 26A
Three Mile L 15A
Three Valley 17A
Through Cr 74C
Thrums 8B
Thudaka Cr 62B, 63A
Thule Cr 62C
Thulme R 44C
Thunder Cr 49B, 50A
Thunder Mtn 23A
Thunder Mtn 24B
Thunder R 27B
Thurlow 12D
Thurston Bay 13C
Thutade Cr 62D
Thutade L 62D, 63C
Thuya Cr 26D, 27C
Thynne L 6B
Tibble Cr 38C
Tie L 9B
Tiedeman Gla 13A, 24C
Tighe Cr 27A
Tightfit L 87D
Tildesley Cr 46B
Till L 25B
Tiltzarone L 38C
Timberwolf Cr 77D
Timothy Cr 26C
Timothy L 26C
Tin Cup L 26C
Tingle Cr 4B, 5B
Tingley Cr 25B
Tingley L 25B
Tinmusket Cr 25D
Tinsdale Cr 39C
Tintina Cr 52B
Tintlhohtan L 26D
Tipella Cr 5B
Tipperary L 18D
Tisdall L 26B
Titetown L 37D
Tlakwa Mtn 11D
Tlatlos Cr 12C
Tlell 30A
Tlell R 30B, 32D
Tlools Cr 1B
Tlupana In 1A
Tlupana R 1A
Toad Hot Springs 75A
Toad Mtn 8B
Toad R 74D, 75A, 86C
Toad River 73A
Toba Gla 13B
Toba In 13C
Toba Pk 13B
Toba R 13D
Tobacco Cr 15B
Tobe L 26D
Tobin L 55B
Toboggan Cr 45B
Toby Cr 18C
Toby Creek 18C
Toby Gla 18C
Tochcha L 46B
Todagin Cr 61A
Todagin L 61A
Todd Cr 52A

Todd Cr 81C
Todoggone Pk 62B, 63A
● Tofino 1D
Tofino Cr 1D
Tofino In 1D
Tokumm Cr 18A
Tolmie Chan 35C
Tom Browne L 12D
Tom Cr 54D
Tom Mackay L 51B, 52A
Tomias L 55A
Tomias Mtn 62A
Tomlinson Cr 53D
Tommy Cr 14B
Tommy Jack Cr 53A
Tommy L 6B, 15D
Tommy Ls 66A
Tomslake 58C
Tonasket 7D
Toneko L 39A
Tonquin Cr 41C
Tonquin Hill 41C
Tony Cr 56C
Toodoggone L 62B, 63A
Toodoggone R 62B, 63A
Tooga Cr 77B
Tooga L 77B
Toon L 44C
Toon R 44C
Tootsee L 82D, 83C
Tootsee R 82D, 83C
Toozaza Cr 82D, 83C
Topaze Har 12D
Topknot L 11C
Topley 46C
Topley Landing 46B
Toquart B 1D
Toquart R 1D
Tornado Mtn 10A, 19C
Tornado Pass 10A, 19C
Torpid Cr 75A
Torpy R 39A, 49C
Torrens R 50C
Torres Chan 80D, 81C
Tortoise L 26D
Tosh Cr 14A
Tower Cr 9A
Tower L 57B
Tower Mtn 75C
Towkuh Cr 39C
Towler Cr 38D
Town Cr 17B
Townsend Cr 38C
Townsend Cr 65D
Townsley Cr 64B, 65A
Townsoitoi Cr 77D
Towydkin L 25C
● Trail 8D
Trail Cr 62C
Trail Creek 10D
Trail L 87D
Tranquil Cr 1D
Tranquille 15B
Tranquille L 15B
Tranquille R 15B
Trap Mtn 3D
Trapline Cr 45C
Trapp L 16C
Trapper Cr 57C
Trapper L 70D
Trapping Cr 38B
Trapping L 38B
Treat Cr 2B
Treble Mtn 52C
Tregillus Cr 39C
Trego 10C
Tremblay Cr 57D
Trembleur L 47A
Tremor Mtn 14D
Trent R 2A
Trepanier 7A
Tretheway Cr 5B

Trevor Chan 2C
Trevor L 11B
Trépanier Cr 7A
Trépanier Cr 84C
Trial Is 3D
Triangle I 11C
Triangle L 84D, 85A
Tribune Chan 12A
Trident Mtn 28C
Trident Pk 64D
Trimble Cr 65C
Trimble L 64D, 65C
Trincomali Chan 3B, 5C
Trinity B 12A
Trinity Cr 16D
Trinity Valley 16D
Trio L 26A
Triple L 53B, 54A
Triplex Mtn 23D
Triumph Cr 59B
Triumph Gla 59B
Troitsa Cr 35B
Troitsa L 35B
Troitsa Pk 35B, 36A
Trophy Mtn 27C
Trout Cr 7A
Trout Cr 45B
Trout L 17D
Trout L 81D
Trout Lake 17D
Trout Mtn 17D
Trout R 74B, 85D
Troutline Cr 72A
Troy Cr 8C
Truax Cr 14B
Truncate Cr 64C
Truncate Mtn 64C
Trutch Cr 65B
Trutch I 33D, 34C
Trygve L 62D
Tsable I 2A
Tsable R 2A
Tsacha L 37C
Tsachehdza Cr 76C
Tsah Cr 47D
Tsai Cr 45D
Tsalit Mtn 45D, 46C
Tsar Cr 28C
Tsartus I 2C
Tsawwassen 5C
Tsayakwacha L 36D
Tsaybahe Cr 60B, 61A
Tsaybahe Pass 61A
Tsaydaychuz Pk 36C
Tsaydiz Cr 63D
Tsayta L 54D
Tsaytis Mtn 35D
Tsaytis R 35C
Tsaytut B 53B, 54A
Tsazia Mtn 60B, 61A
Tschick L 36D
Tsea Ls 87D
Tsea R 88C
Tseax R 44C
Tsedeka Cr 48A, 56C
Tsenaglode L 71D, 72C
Tsenglode Mtn 61B
Tseta Cr 70B
Tsetia Cr 61B
Tsetogamus Cr 61A
Tsetzi L 37C
Tsezakwa Cr 46A, 54C
Tsia Cr 84D
Tsia L 84C
Tsibass Lagoon 11B
Tsichgass L 46C
Tsikhini Cr 60A
Tsikwustum Cr 27D
Tsikwustum L 27D
Tsilbekuz L 37C

Tsilcoh R 47D
Tsimeh Cr 76B
Tsimeh Ls 76B
Tsimpsean
  Pen 33B, 43D, 44A
Tsimtack L 34B
Tsinhia Cr 87C
Tsinhia L 87C
Tsinitla Cr 84C
Tsintsunko Cr 15B
Tsintsunko L 15B
Tsirku Gla 68A, 79C
Tsirku R 79D
Tsitika R 12C
Tsitsutl Mtn 46B
Tsitsutl Pk 36D
Tsoloss Cr 24D
Tsolum R 2A
Tsoo Cr 75B, 76A
Tsuh Cr 7A
Tsuh L 25C
Tsuius Cr 17C
Tsuius Mtn 17A
Tsulquate R 11B
Tsuniah L 24D
Tsus Cr 39A
Tsusiat L 2C
Tuaton L 62C
Tuaton Pk 62C
Tubbs L 26C
Tucha Cr 63D
Tucha L 63D
Tucho L 73C
Tucho R 73C
Tuchodi Ls 75C
Tuchodi R 64A, 75C, 76C
Tuck In 33B, 43D, 44C
Tuck L 2C, 3A
Tudyah L 48A
Tuff Pk 62B
Tugulnuit L 7C
Tugwell Cr 3D
Tuktakamin Mtn 16C
Tuktsayda Mtn 60B, 61A
Tulameen 6B
Tulameen Mtn 6B
Tulameen R 6B, 6D
Tulip Cr 8A
Tullin Mtn 24D
Tulsequah Gla 69B, 70A
Tulsequah L 69B, 70A
Tulsequah R 69B, 70A
○ Tumbler Ridge 49B
Tumeka Cr 61D
Tumeka L 61D
Tumtum L 27D
Tumuch L 39A
Tumult Gla 12B
Tunjony L 70D
Tunkwa L 15D
Tupper 58C
Tupper Cr 57D
Tupper R 58C
Turn Cr 81D
Turnagain L 72D
Turnagain R 72D, 73A
Turner Cr 39C
Turner L 23B
Turner Pk 30D, 32D
Turner Valley 19B
Turning Mtn 49A
Turnoff Cr 65C
Turnour I 12C
Turret I 1D
Turtle L 80D
Tusulko R 23B
Tutachi L 63D
Tutesheta Cr 71C
Tutiai Mtn 37C
Tutizika R 54B
Tutizzi L 54B
Tutshi L 80C

Tutshi R 80C
Tutsingale Mtn 71B
Tutu Cr 56C
Tuwartz L 34A
Tuwasus Cr 5B
Tuya L 72A
Tuya R .. 71B, 71D, 72A, 72C
Tuzcha L 13B, 14A, 25C
Tuzo Cr 7B
Twaal Cr 15C
Twain Cr 46D
Twan Cr 25B
Tweedsmuir Gla 78C
Tweedsmuir Pk 36A
Twelve Mile Cr 18A
Twenty Mile Cr 55C
Twidwell Cr 49A
Twig Cr 16C
Twin Bays 9A
Twin Butte 10D
Twin Cr 39B
Twin Cr 55C
Twin Gla 60C
Twin Is 2A, 13C
Twin Island L 73A
Twin L 9D
Twin Ls 7C
Twin Ls 50A
Twin One Cr 14D
Twin Two Cr 14D
Twist Cr 24C
Twist L 24C
Two Bit Cr 65C
Two Cr 49A
Two Fish Cr 72D
Two Island L 87C
Two L 25A
Two Lake Cr 53B, 54A
Two Mile Rapids 84C
Two Rivers 57B
Two Sisters Mtn 39C
Twobit Cr 8A
Tyaughton Cr 14B
Tyaughton L 14B
Tyee L 25B
Tyee L 45B
Tzahny L 62C
Tzahy Mtn 62C
Tzazati L 25A
Tzeetsaytsul Pk 23A
Tzenzaicut L 25B, 38D
Tzeo R 23C
Tzoonie R 2B

U

Ucluelet 1D
Ucona R 1B
Uduk L 36B
Udy Cr 38C
Ulkatcho 36D
Umbach Cr 66C
Umiti Cr 38D
Uncha Cr 36B
Uncha L 36B
Uncha Mtn 36B, 46D
Union Bay 2A
Union Cr 81C
Union I 1C, 11D
Union In 43D, 44A
Union L 43D, 44C
Union Mtn 80D, 81C
Unna L 39C
Unuk Finger 51B
Unuk Finger Mtn 52A
Unuk R .. 51B, 52A, 60D, 61C
Upana L 1A
Upana R 1B
Upper Arrow L 17C
Upper Belle L 62B, 63A
Upper Blue L 49D

Upper Campbell L 1B
Upper Elk L 19C
Upper Fraser 49C
Upper Habour L 27D
Upper L 26C
Upper Liard 83D
Upper Loon L 15B
Upper Quinsam L 1B
Upright Cr 40D
Upright Mtn 40D
Upset Cr 66C
Ure Cr 14D
Urquhart Cr 6A
Ursula Chan 34B
Ursula Cr 56A
Ursus Cr 1B
Useless Cr 31B, 33A, 43D
Usk 45C
Uslika L 55A
Ussa L 26A
Utahn Cr 76B
Uztlius Cr 6A

V

Vachon Cr 27A
Valanciennes R 28D
Valdes I 3B, 5C
Valemont Mtn 74C
○ Valemount 40D
Valentine Mtn 3D
Valhalla Centre 58D
Valhalla Mtn 60A
Valleau Cr 47A, 55C
Vallee Cr 46C
Valley Cr 8A
Vallican 8B
Vama Vama Cr 38B
Van Horne Br 17B
Van In 30D, 32C
Van Zandt 5D
Vananda 2A
Vance Cr 16D
● Vancouver 5C
Vancouver I 1B, 2C,
  3A, 3C, 11D
Vancouver R 2B
● Vanderhoof 47D
Vansittart I 11B
Vanstone Cr 17C
Vanwyk Cr 17A
Vargas I 1D
Varrick Cr 64B, 65A,
  75D, 76C
Vaseux Cr 7D
Vaseux L 7C
Vavenby 27C
Vedan Cr 25D
Vedan L 24D
Vedder Crossing 6C
Vega Cr 55A
Venables L 15C
Ventego Cr 28D
Ventego L 28D
Vents R 73B, 74A,
  84D, 85C
Verdant Cr 18B
Vermilion Crossing 18B
Vermilion R 18B
Vermillion Pass 18B
Vermont Cr 18A
Vern Ritchie Gla 78C
Verney Pass 34B
● Vernon 16D
Vernon Cr 7B, 16D
Vernon Hill 16D
Vernon L 1A, 12C
Verrett R 60D
Vert L 25D
Vertical Mtn 9B
Vevey Cr 8B

Vic L 14A
Vickers Cr 5B
● Victoria 3D
Victoria Cr 38D
Victoria L 11D
Victoria L 70B
Victoria Pk 12D
Vidette 15B
View L 1B
View Royal 3D
Vignal Pk 64A
Vigue Cr 17C
Vile Cr 53A
Village I 12C
Vincent L 83D
Viner Sd 12A
Vines L 72B
Viola L 11B
Violin L 8D
Virago Sd 32A, 42D
Vizer Cr 85D
Vlem Cr 16D
Voght Cr 6B
Volcano L 1B
Vowell Cr 18A
Vuich Cr 6B

W

Waddington Chan 13C
Waddington Gla 13A
Waddington Har 13A
Wadin Cr 84C
Wagner Ranch 56B
Wahkash Cr 12B
Wahla L 36C
Wahleach Cr 4B, 6C
Wahleach L 6C
Wahpeeto Cr 12A
Wahshihlas B 12B
Wahthinli Mtn 64A
Waiparous 19A
Waitabit Cr 28D, 29C
Waitabit L 29C
Wakeman R 12A, 23C
Wakeman Sd 12A
Walbran Cr 2C, 3C
Walbran I 22D
Wales Cr 25C
Wales I 43B, 44A
Walhachin 15B
Walker Cr 39B
Walker Cr 73A
Walker Group 11B
Walker L 22A
Walkum B 11B, 22D
Walkus L 23C
Wall Cr 7C
Wall Cr 16D
Wall L 10D
Wallensteen L 16D
Waller B 33D, 34A
Waller Cr 33D, 34A
Wallop Mtn 39B
Walt L 2B
Waneta 8D
Wann R 69A, 80D
Wannock R 22D
Wanokana Cr 11D
Wansa Cr 38B
Wap Cr 17A
Wap L 17A
Wapiti 50B
Wapiti L 49D
Wapiti Pass 49D
Wapiti R 49B, 50A
Wapoose L 36B
Wapumun L 40A, 50C
War L 48A
Ward Cr 9D
Ward Cr 14B

Wardner 9B
Ware 63B
Warfield 8D
Wargen Ls 66A
Warm Beach 4D
Warm Cr 80C
Warn B 1D
Warneford R 63B
Warner Pk 63B
Warren Cr 18A
Warren L 16A
Warsaw Mtn 28A
Wasa 9B
Wasa L 9B
Wash Cr 62C
Washwash R 23C
Wasi Cr 55A
Wasi L 55A
Wasko Ls 26B
Waskulay Cr 65A
Wasley L 16C
Wasp Cr 14C
Watch L 26D
Watching Cr 15B
Watchman Mtn 26B
Waterlily L 47D
Waterloo Mtn 2D, 3D
Waterton Park 10D
Watson B 22A, 35C
Watson Bar Cr 14B
Watson I 12A
Watson L 26C
Watson Lake 83B
Watson Lake Airport 83B
Watson Pk 48B
Watt Cr 39C
Watta Cr 1B
Wauconda 7D
Waump Cr 12A
Wavey L 26D
Wawa L 24A
Weare L 34B
Weasel Cr 56A
Weaver Cr 9B
Weaver L 6A
Weaver Pk 49D
Webber L 47D, 48C
Webberly L 47B
Weber Cr 53C
Webster Cr 25B
Webster L 22A
Wedeene Mtn 44C
Wedeene R 44D
Wedge Cr 14C
Wedge Mtn 14D
Wedge Pk 55B, 56A
Wee Sandy Cr 8B, 17D
Wee Sandy L 8B, 17D
Weedon Cr 48A
Weedon L 48C
Weeks L 3D
Weewanie Cr 34B
Weir Mtn 81D
Weissener Cr 63B
Welch Pk 4B, 6C
Wellington 2D
Wells 39C
Wells Cove 20A
Wells Gray Pk 36A
Wells Pass 12A
Wembley 50B
Wendle Cr 39A
Wendy Cr 66A
Wendy L 66A
Weneez 47D
Wenger Cr 64B, 65A
Wentworth Cr 38C
Wentworth L 15B
Werner B 20A
Wesach Cr 44B
West Arm 8B
West Cache Cr 57A

West Churn Cr 14B, 25D
West Conroy Cr 66A
West Fork 51A
West Grenville Gla 13A
West Gutah Cr 66A
West Kettle R 7B
West Kiskatinaw R 49B, 57D, 58C
West Klua Cr 76B
West Kwanika Cr 54D
West L 2B
West L 85C
West Landing 54D
West Milligan Cr 66D
West Nabesche R 56A
West Nadila Cr 25C
West Redonda I 13C
West Road (Blackwater) R 37C, 37D, 38C
West Sound 5C
West Taylor R 52B
West Thurlow I 12D
West Toad R 74D
West Torpy R 49C
West Twin Cr 17A
West Twin Cr 39B
West Vancouver 5A
West Yahk R 9D
Westbank 7A
Westbridge 7D
Westfall Cr 17B
Westham I 3B, 5C
Westman Cr 26C
Westmere L 7A
Weston Cr 55D, 56C
Westside 7A
Westwick L 25D
Westwold 16C
Weyman Cr 16C
Whale Chan 34D
Whalen L 34D
Whaletown 13C
Whatshan L 8A, 17C
Whatshan Pk 17C
Whatshan R 17C
Wheaton Cr 72D
Wheeler Cr 10A
Whelakis Lagoon 11B
Whidbey Reach 35A
Whiffle L 26A
Whip Cr 17C
Whipsaw Cr 6D
Whirlpool Pass 28A
Whiskey Cr 25B
Whistle Cr 7A
Whistler 14C
Whistler Basin 54B
Whitburn 58D
White Boar L 9A
White Cr 9A
White Cr 44D
White Eye L 36B
White Grouse Mtn 9A
White L 16B
White L 26C

White Lake 16B
White Man Mtn 18B
White Man Pass 18B
White Pass 80C
White Pass 80C
White R 12D
White R 18D, 19C
White R 52D
● White Rock 5D
White Spruce Cr 77B
Whitecap Cr 14B
Whitecape Gla 12B
Whitecone Pk 35D
Whitecrow Mtn 28A
Whitefish L 47C
Whitehorse 80A
Whiteman 16D
Whiteman Cr 16C
Whitemantle Gla 13A
Whitemantle Mtn 13A
Whitepine Cr 28D
Whiterocks Mtn 7A, 16C
Whiterose Mtn 28D
Whitesaddle Mtn 24C
Whitesail L 35B, 36A
Whitesail Reach 36A
Whitesand L 24D
Whiteshield Mtn 40D
Whiteswan L 18D
Whitetail Cr 18B
Whitetail L 18D
Whitetop Mtn 24A, 37C
Whitewood Cr 16A
Whiting Cr 35B
Whitting R 70D
Whitton Cr 23B
Whitworth Pk 6C
Whudzi Mtn 63A
Whyac 2C
Wichcika Cr 48D
Wickaninnish B 1D
Wicked L 55B, 56A
Wicked R 55B, 56A
Widgeon Cr 4A
Widgeon L 4A, 5B
Widgeon L 23B
Wiggins Cr 26A
Wigwam B 12A
Wigwam R 10C
Wild Horse R 9B
Wildboy Cr 88C
Wildcat Cr 29C
Wilde L 57D
Wilder Cr 57A
Wilderness Mtn 23D
Wildfire Cr 52B
Wildmare Cr 57C
Wildwood Heights 2A
Wilfred Cr 2A
Wilkie Cr 17D
Wilkinson Cr 7B
Willan Cr 25C
Willan L 25C
William L 11A
Williams Cr 45C

Williams L 25B
● Williams Lake 25B
Williams Lake R 25B
Willie Jack Cr 71A
Willis Cr 6B
Willis L 16B
Willison B 69B
Willison Gla 69A
Williston L 48A, 55B, 56B, 56C, 64C
Willoughby Cr 52D
Willow Cr 54A
Willow Point 8B
Willow R 38B, 39C, 48D
Willow River 48D
Willow Valley 57D
Willowbrook 57D
Willowy Cr 47B
Wilma L 16D
Wilms Cr 69B, 70A
Wilson Cr 1A
Wilson Cr 17D
Wilson Cr 80D, 81C
Wilson L 17D
Wilson L 26D
Wilson Landing 7A
Wiminasik L 53A
Windermere 18D
Windermere Cr 18D
Windermere L 18D
Windfall Cr 7D
Windfall Cr 27B
Windfall Cr 49A
Windham 59A
Windrem Cr 57C
Windsor Cr 33B, 44C
Windsor L 2B, 13D
Windsor L 48C
Windy Camp Cr 81C
Windy Cr 26D
Windy Cr 28C
Windy Cr 57C
Winfield 16D
Winfield Cr 45D
Wingdam 39C
Winlaw 8B
Winnifred Cr 8A
Winslow Cr 5B
Winter Cr 60A
Winter Har 11C
Winter Harbour 11C
Winter In 43B, 44A
Winters Cr 7C
Wistaria 36A
Witch L 47A
Witches Br 15D
Witness Cr 18D
Woden Cr 8A
Woden Pk 8B
Wokas L 1B
Woking 58D
Wokkpash Cr 75C
Wokkpash L 75C

Wolf Cr 9B
Wolf L 2A
Wolf R 1B
Wolfe Cr 6B
Wolfe L 12C
Wollaston L 16D
Wolverine L 26A, 39C
Wolverine L 73C
Wolverine R 39B
Wolverine R 49A
Wonowon 66C
Wood Arm 28A
Wood L 16D
Wood R 28A
Woodall Cr 49C
Woodfibre 5A
Woodham 5C
Woodhus Cr 1B
Woodjam Cr 26A
Woods L 16C
Woods Lagoon 11B
Woods Landing 16B
Woodsdale 16D
Woodyadilinka Cr 48B
Woolsey Cr 17A
Word Cr 25D
Work Chan 33B, 43D, 44C
Wormwold Cr 39C
Worry Cr 62A
Worsley 58B
Woss L 12C
Woss L 12C
Wragge Cr 17D
Wrede Cr 63D
Wriggle Cr 60A
Wright 26C
Wright Cr 48D
Wright In 33D, 34A
Wright Pass 21B
Wright Pks 69D, 70C
Wright Sd 34B
Wuho Cr 9B
Wutak L 36A
Wutlus L 38C
Wyclees Lagoon 11B
Wye Cr 3C
Wyndham L 33D, 34A
Wynndel 9C

Y
Yaak 9D
Yaculta 13C
Yahk 9D
Yahk Mtn 9D
Yahk R 9D
Yakoun L 30D, 32D
Yakoun R 30B, 32D
Yalakom R 14B
Yale 6A
Yale Cr 6A
Yalta Pk 75C
Yankee Flats 16D
Yanks Pk 39C

Yard Cr 16B
Yardley L 38B
Yash Cr 74B
Yatzutzin L 47B
Yaza Cr 53A, 62C
Yedhe Cr 74D
Yedhe Ls 74D
Yedhe Mtn 75C
Yehiniko Cr 60A
Yehiniko L 60A
Yeka L 88C
Yeko L 9C
Yellow Cr 28A
Yellow L 7A
Yellowhead L 41C
Yellowhead Pass 41C
Yellowjacket Cr 40D
Yeo I 22A
Yeo L 22A
Yeoward Cr 17C
Yesshadle Cr 87D
Yeth Cr 70B
Yimpakluk L 37D, 38C
Ymir 8D
Ymir Cr 8D
Ymir Mtn 8B
Yohetta Cr 13B
Yohetta L 13B
Yookwa Cr 12C
Yorston L 25B
Youbou 2D
Young Cr 23B
Young L 15B
Young R 22D
Youngs Cr 48C
Yoyo 77A
Yuen L 54A
Yule L 35C
Yuquot 1A
Yuzkli Cr 39C

Z

Zagoddetchino Mtn 60A
Zakwaski Mtn 15C
Zamora 7D
Zancudo L 70B
Zayas I 43D
Zeballos 12C
Zeballos In 1A
Zeballos L 12C
Zeballos R 1A, 12C
Zechtoo Mtn 61A
Zelkwas Cr 38A
Zenazie Cr 81D
Zenzaco Cr 25C
Zeues Cr 88D
Zeues L 88D
Zohini Cr 69B, 70A
Zuciarte Chan 1A
Zus Cr 86D, 87C
Zymagotitz R 44D
Zymoetz R 45A, 45C